DC SPORTS

SPORT, CULTURE & SOCIETY

DAVID K. WIGGINS, SERIES EDITOR

DC SPORTS

The Nation's Capital at Play

Edited by Chris Elzey
and David K. Wiggins

FAYETTEVILLE
THE UNIVERSITY OF ARKANSAS PRESS
2015

*To Edwin Bancroft Henderson: teacher, civil rights
activist, and historian of the African American
athlete who represented the very best of Washington, DC*

Contents

Series Editor's Preface

Sport is an extraordinarily important phenomenon that pervades the lives of many people and has enormous impact on society in an assortment of different ways. At its most fundamental level, sport has the power to bring people great joy and satisfy their competitive urges while at once allowing them to form bonds and a sense of community with others from diverse backgrounds and interests and various walks of life. Sport also makes clear, especially at the highest levels of competition, the lengths that people will go to achieve victory as well as how closely connected it is to business, education, politics, economics, religion, law, family, and other societal institutions. Sport is, moreover, partly about identity development and how individuals and groups, irrespective of race, gender, ethnicity, or socioeconomic class, have sought to elevate their status and realize material success and social mobility.

Sport, Culture, and Society seeks to promote a greater understanding of the aforementioned issues and many others. Recognizing sport's powerful influence and ability to change people's lives in significant and important ways, the series focuses on topics ranging from urbanization and community development to biographies and intercollegiate athletics. It includes both monographs and anthologies that are characterized by excellent scholarship, accessible to a wide audience, and interesting and thoughtful in design and interpretations. Singular features of the series are authors and editors representing a variety of disciplinary areas and who adopt different methodological approaches. The series also includes works by individuals at various stages of their careers, both sport studies scholars of outstanding talent just beginning to make their mark on the field and more experienced scholars of sport with established reputations.

DC Sports: The Nation's Capital at Play makes clear how important sport has been in one of the most famous and powerful cities in the world. The first of several books in the series to be published on sport in major American cities, the anthology is edited by Chris Elzey and myself and includes seventeen essays written by noted historians and sport studies scholars. Included are essays ranging from an analysis of the Howard-Lincoln Thanksgiving Day football games of the 1920s and a history of the Marine Corps Marathon to a chronicling of the Ted-Williams-led Washington Senators of 1969 and an assessment of the Washington Bullets NBA Championship in 1978. Not unexpectedly, race is a central theme in the book. As a southern city in style, manners, and temperament, Washington, DC, organized itself along a color line. For much of the first half of the twentieth century, sports were segregated at all levels of competition, with black and white athletes unable to participate with or against one another because of the color of their skin. The book is, however, also about fandom, local pride, identity, gender, and community building in a city where politics often seemed far more important and meaningful than athletic accomplishments and participation in sport.

David K. Wiggins

Acknowledgments

One of the first decisions we made in the process of creating this book was to assemble a list of contributors who would write interesting, meaningful, and important articles on the history of sport in Washington, DC. Ultimately, the strength of the collection is a result of the insights, analysis, and eloquence of those contributors. Their work made our responsibilities as editors much easier and more satisfying. For that, we are truly grateful.

Accompanying each chapter in the collection is a photograph. Many were found with the assistance of Mark Greek, Derek Gray, and Faye Hawkins of the Washingtoniana Division at the Martin Luther King Jr. Library in Washington, DC. They were generous in sharing their knowledge of the Washington Star Collection and helping us locate several pictures. Archivists Clifford Muse and Tewodros "Teddy" Abebe in the Archives Division of the Moorland-Spingarn Research Center located an image of a halftime celebration of the 1922 Howard-Lincoln football game. That picture is included in the book. Archivist JoEllen ElBashir, also from the Moorland-Spingarn Research Center, provided leads to other images. Preston Williams and George Solomon proved invaluable in finding a picture of Shirley Povich.

The staff at the University of Arkansas Press provided excellent editorial assistance and advice. Without them, this book would not have been possible. Julie Watkins, Tyler Lail, and Deena Owens were our go-to people and answered all questions. Brian King and David Scott Cunningham oversaw the final production of the book and greatly enhanced it. Mike Bieker gave us his unwavering support from start to finish. His confidence in our abilities helped inspire us to complete this book. Deborah Upton did a marvelous job copyediting the manuscript, and we are very much appreciative of her efforts and expertise.

The idea for the book was first embraced by Larry Malley. He encouraged us to think about questions we would have never considered and steered us in a direction that not only broadened the scope of the book, but also made it more meaningful. Like many scholars of sport down through the years, it was our great fortune to have benefited from his knowledge and expertise. No doubt, we, and the book, are better for it.

Lastly, we would be remiss if we did not acknowledge the patience, honesty, thoughtfulness, and understanding of our wives. Throughout every stage of the project, Karen Elzey and Brenda Wiggins served as important sounding boards, lent us encouragement, and offered invaluable assessment of our work. It is difficult to imagine the book being completed if not for them.

Introduction

In early fall 1971, the unfathomable occurred: Washington, DC, lost big-league baseball. The national pastime had been a constant fixture in the city almost ever since the Washington Monument was completed in 1884. Generations of Washingtonians had lived their lives against this backdrop of baseball certainty. But now, speedier than a Walter Johnson fastball, it was gone. The city felt less whole, as if a cherished keepsake had gone missing.

The owner of Washington's former team, the expansion Senators, was Robert E. Short, a multimillionaire with slicked-back hair, a weak chin, and enough business ventures to keep a small army of CPAs busy round the clock. A native Minnesotan who previously owned the Minneapolis/Los Angeles Lakers of the National Basketball Association (NBA)—he had transferred the Lakers to California in 1960—Short had taken control of the Senators in late 1968. At the time of the sale, he was also the Democratic National Committee treasurer. After the end of the 1971 season, he shifted the Senators to Texas. He claimed that the nation's capital had not adequately supported his franchise.[1]

Unlike in 1960 when the District was given an expansion team to replace the departed original Senators (the expansion team would play its first season in 1961), Washington in 1971 received no such substitute franchise. And it stayed that way, even though Washingtonians had been told repeatedly that they would get a new team. Understandably, people grew cynical. Shortly after moving away from Washington in 1977, sportswriter Joan Ryan, reflecting on her years covering sports in the nation's capital, wrote: "I miss Washington's baseball team. Not the deposed Senators, mind you. No, I'm missing that mythical, wonderful-but-only-on-paper, promised-but-stalled-on-delivery, congressionally investigated Washington baseball team that has a banner flying high over RFK Stadium in my imagination." It would not be until 2005 that the District got another franchise. That year, the Washington Nationals (formerly the Montreal Expos) played their inaugural season.[2]

For a city routinely thrust into the national spotlight, Washington has had a strange history of being ignored by big-time professional sports. In addition to Major League Baseball's thirty-four-year hiatus, the city was without an NBA franchise from 1951 to 1973, and it was not until 1974 that it acquired a National Hockey League (NHL) team—meaning that between 1971 and 1973 the only professional sports franchise in town was the football Redskins. That such an important city as Washington had just one team is surprising, especially since it was the then-seventh-most-populated metropolitan area in the country. More surprising, of the ten largest cities, seven had teams in each of the four major professional sports leagues, while the other two—Pittsburgh and St. Louis—had clubs in three.[3]

What was it about Washington? Why did sports moguls regularly shun it and place teams in other cities instead? In baseball's case, Congress may have had something to do with it. Before 1971, lawmakers often weighed in on matters relating to baseball in the District of Columbia, all but ensuring that a team remained in the city. (In July 1958, after word circulated that Senators owner Calvin Griffith was trying to move the club out of Washington, South Dakota senator Karl Mundt said: "Having baseball as our national sport without a franchise in the Nation's Capital would be a good deal like having a football season without a team at Notre Dame. It would be like having boxing in America without Sugar Ray Robinson.") But after the expansion Senators left in 1971—the original Senators had moved to Minnesota in October 1960—politicians seemed less willing to intervene in the affairs of baseball in DC. It was as if the powers-that-be in the federal capital did not want the national pastime around.[4]

Maybe it was a consequence of the times. After the Senators bolted in 1971, Congress had much graver issues to consider: Vietnam, the energy crisis, Watergate, skyrocketing inflation, and high unemployment. Not helping matters were baseball's executives, who cared little about the plight of Washington baseball fans. As the years slipped by, a baseball-less DC became the new normal.[5]

It could also be argued that Washington itself helped keep baseball away. During much of the 1980s and 1990s, the District was the poster city for nearly all that could go wrong with urban America. Crime and drugs were pervasive. Local government was riddled with graft and dysfunction. City finances were in shambles. Neighborhoods were dangerous. Violence was so common that Washington was dubbed "the murder capital of America."[6]

By the first decade of the twenty-first century, however, the city was being revitalized. Blighted areas were cleaned up. Crime decreased. Shiny new condos stretched skyward. High-end retailers opened stores. People began moving back into the city, thus reversing the exodus to the Maryland

and Virginia suburbs that was initiated by middle-class whites in the 1950s and 1960s and continued by their black counterparts in the decades that followed.[7]

Such change was not uncommon. Since its founding in 1790, Washington has been a city in flux. But its period of greatest transformation may have come during the twentieth century when the District, once a largely inconsequential, sleepy hamlet, grew to become one of the most significant capitals in the world. Fueling that change was the newfound economic and military might of a post–WWII United States and its ever-expanding role on the global stage.[8]

At the same time, Washington developed into a booming metropolis. The number of people living in the greater Washington area swelled from 968,000 in 1940 to 2.91 million in 1970—a three-fold increase. The expansion of the federal workforce after World War II contributed to the growth. Moreover, as the size of government ballooned, professionals whose occupations were loosely connected to politics, such as newspapermen and women and lobbyists and policy wonks and attorneys, joined the legions of federal workers in the nation's capital. The result was that Washington became a predominantly white-collar city.[9]

Issues of race were glaring. The arrival of tens of thousands of African Americans between 1920 and 1940 aggravated already tense race relations. Located just below the Mason-Dixon Line, Washington had been a slave-holding city until 1862. But the subjugation of black citizens would persist, and for many decades after the Civil War, Washingtonians sorted out social rank and opportunity according to one's skin color. As a result, African Americans were refused entry to white eateries, hotels, amusement parks, swimming pools, and theaters. Discriminatory housing covenants limited black residents' access to neighborhoods. White and black children attended different schools. The best jobs were reserved for whites. In July 1919, a race riot tore through the city, killing at least nine people and injuring dozens more. Almost thirty years later, racial discrimination remained just as virulent—a point underscored by the National Committee on Segregation in the Nation's Capital in its 1948 report, *Segregation in Washington*. That same year, the *Negro Digest* rated Washington one of "America's 10 Worst Cities for Negroes."[10]

Sport reflected such bigotry. Playgrounds, swimming pools, parks, golf courses, sports teams, and high school athletics—all were segregated. Before 1947, black boxers and track and field athletes were forbidden from taking part in competitions sponsored by the District branch of the Amateur Athletic Union (AAU). In 1937, the visiting Syracuse University football squad was forced to withdraw its top running back, Wilmeth Sidat-Singh, an African American, from a game against the University of Maryland because Maryland officials threatened to cancel the contest if he played. According to *Segregation in Washington*, the yearly marbles tournament for local youths prohibited the mixing of white and black contestants.[11]

Perhaps more insulting for black residents was being told which sporting events they could and could not watch. From 1941 to 1948, Michael Uline, owner of the Uline Arena, the city's first large-scale sports venue, refused to allow African Americans to attend basketball games and ice shows at his arena but let them watch cruder spectacles like boxing and wrestling—events Uline judged to be more attune with African American "sensibilities." Edwin B. Henderson, a local African American sports leader, writer, and champion of civil rights, called Uline's arena "the Palace of Bigotry." In the 1940s, Henderson spearheaded a boycott of the arena. Feeling the financial pinch, Uline ended the exclusionary practice in early 1948.[12]

Though Washington was mostly integrated by the mid-1950s, racial discrimination in sports remained very much alive. The Senators, for instance, did not ink their first African American player until 1957—a full decade after Jackie Robinson broke the color barrier in baseball. For their part, the Redskins held out until 1962 before a black player—actually it was three players—donned the Burgundy and Gold and played a game. Bobby Mitchell, John Nisby, and Leroy Jackson hold that distinction. Rather than swim in the same pools with African Americans, many white residents during the 1950s and 1960s joined private clubs that had whites-only pools. In 1987, Doug Williams made history when he became the first African American to start as quarterback for the Redskins. Later that season, he propelled Washington to victory in Super Bowl XXII, and was named MVP—a first for a black quarterback. In the years that ensued, Williams—as well as other black athletes, coaches, referees, and sports administrators in the Washington area—continued to feel the sharp sting of racial prejudice.[13]

And yet sport could sometimes transcend difference. Since the early 1970s, the act of supporting the Redskins, by far the city's most popular team, has remained an emotional and psychological experience shared by Washingtonians of all backgrounds. Indeed, to be a Redskins fan is to be a true Washingtonian. In large part, such self-identification resulted from the massive influx of people who settled in the Washington region after WWII. As journalist Christopher Lydon wrote in the *New York Times* in 1974, "In a city of transients . . . the Redskins are a 'hometown' rallying point, a cherished common denominator for a peculiar body of fans."[14]

Modern Washington is a metropolis with multiple personalities. It is a tourist destination, brimming with museums and bleach-white marble memorials and guidebook lodestones like the US Capitol and the White House. It is a jumble of neighborhoods, suburbs, and exurbs. Its mental space radiates outward from the District of Columbia and extends into Virginia and Maryland, well beyond the Beltway, creating a schizophrenic hodgepodge of local, state, and federal jurisdictions. Washington is an affluent city, but it also has pockets of poverty. It is a place where people come to hold rallies and have their voices heard. It is a city of official-looking men in blue suits and ties. It has an edgy side. Yet it can evince extraordinary sophistication. It is a city whose summers fill up with bright-eyed college interns. It is the seat of the American government. And it is a metropolis with a distinct international flair. Tens of thousands of immigrants from countries around the globe reside in greater Washington. Foreign embassies and consulates abound.

But what of sport? Is Washington a city distinguished by a passion for it? Many say no. The obsession with the Redskins notwithstanding, the belief is that Washingtonians are fickle and unfaithful fans. Why this is so has been the subject of much discussion. Writing in the *Washington Post Magazine* in 1994, journalist Tom McNichol attributed DC's blasé attitude to what makes the city go round. "The big game in Washington has always been politics," McNichol observed, "and even sports in the city has a polit-ical edge. Washington fans know as much about the NFL salary cap and baseball's antitrust exemption as they do about quarterback ratings and batting averages." Howard Bryant of *ESPN The Magazine* suggested in an October 2012 article that the reasons why Washingtonians are not exactly gung-ho sports supporters are because DC's transient population and its changing demographics undercut efforts of local "teams to build a loyal constituency" and because Washington sports franchises are synonymous with failure.[15]

These indictments have been leveled against Washington for years. Some have refuted the accusations. Shirley Povich, for example, the venerable sports journalist for the *Washington Post*, was quoted in Tom McNichol's 1994 *Washington Post Magazine* piece as saying, "Washington's been stuck with a terrible slander. The city's reputation is that it couldn't keep its base-ball team, but it's untrue. Measured against the performance of its teams, Washington rated in the upper middle class of cities." Howard Bryant, in his October 2012 *ESPN The Magazine* article, concluded that given the Nationals' sensational 2012 season, the Messiah-like reception bestowed upon Redskins quarterback Robert Griffin III, and the wild optimism generated by the city's other youthful athletic heroes, Washington was finally shedding its timeworn reputation as a sports graveyard. Borrowing FDR's presidential campaign motto from 1932, the cover of the *ESPN The Magazine* issue containing Bryant's piece captured the headiness: "Washington, D.C. Happy Days Are Here Again!"[16]

The fact is that sport has been an essential part of the city's character almost ever since the late nineteenth century. Washingtonians participated in sport and watched it. They wrote about it and built stadiums and arenas where teams could play. Vast sums of money were invested in franchises, and residents by and large supported those clubs. At times sport united disparate parts of the city, while on other occasions it intensified divisions. Every now and then, Congress and the Supreme Court stepped in to settle sport's most contentious issues. Many renowned athletes and sports officials came from Washington—a fact that residents proudly embraced and helped define who they were.[17]

The essays in this collection illustrate these points—and more. They show the ways in which Washington served as both a trendsetter and focal point for cycling; college and professional football; golf; high school, college, and professional basketball; sportswriting; professional hockey; and distance running. They examine the involvement of American presidents, members of Congress, and local officials in affairs of amateur, intercollegiate, and professional sports. The intersection of gender, women's sports, and the coverage by the press is explored, as is the post–WWII jurisdictional battle over the integration of Washington's playgrounds. The interplay between race and sport is the central theme of many chapters.

No edited anthology is wholly comprehensive. This one does not claim to be any different—and for good reason. There are so many fascinating stories about Washington sports that additional volumes could easily be written. For instance, the history of American presidents tossing out the first pitch on Opening Day would make for an interesting chapter, as would the biography of Norvel Lee, a Howard University alumnus who won the light heavyweight boxing title at the 1952 Olympic Games in Helsinki. There is also the story of Washington's Spingarn High School and its pipeline to athletic stardom. Basketball's Elgin Baylor and Dave Bing, among other notable athletes, attended Spingarn. Essays on the famous African American gymnast Dominique Dawes, who is a native of Silver Spring, Maryland, and the University of Maryland's women's basketball team that won the NCAA title in 2006 could also be included.

Think of this collection, then, as a volume of stories about the history of sport in Washington, DC. The ultimate aim of the anthology is to have people—sports fans or otherwise—realize that Washington is more than just a government town. It is also a city in which sport occupies an equally important place. In many ways, to understand Washington is to understand its sport history. And the essays contained herein can help anyone interested in learning more about the nation's capital do just that.

1

The Extraordinary History of Cycling and Bike Racing in Washington, DC

John Bloom

On April 15, 1984, Matt Eaton rode his racing bicycle around the national Ellipse for one hour, two minutes, and fifty-three seconds to win the six-teenth annual National Capital Open. The race, the pro-am senior 50-K, was the featured event of the day, and drew 2,000 spectators to watch a tightly packed group of cyclists elbow one another while racing around the oval like Roman chariot drivers. In a less publicized race on the card that day, Justin Gilbert of Metro Delivery won the first annual Golden Wheel two-kilometer race. Unlike Eaton, Gilbert was not on the pro-am circuit, but instead was a bicycle messenger whose profession was delivering parcels on two wheels around the city of Washington, DC. He won his race that day against other bicycle messengers who plied their trade on the asphalt of the nation's capital. Perhaps unbeknown to many of those present on that spring day, they were witnessing an event that echoed a century-long his-tory of bicycles in the nation's capital. Like the National Capital Open, this history is connected to both a larger national and international story about cycling, and to a local story of cycling and cycling culture in the District.[1]

In the early twenty-first century, it is not uncommon to find bicycle races in the District and its surrounding regions. From DC Velo, a local cycling team affiliated with the United States Cycling Federation, to moun-tain biking competitions in suburban Virginia and Maryland, cycling is a vibrant competitive and recreational sport in the capital city's metropolitan area. Within the city and throughout its surrounding regions, cyclists can find hundreds of miles of bike lanes and trails. In the early decades of the twenty-first century, people wandering the streets of Washington can even instantly rent a bike from a self-service kiosk operated by a company called Capital Bikeshare.

Since its formation, however, bicycle riding has been a sport that Washingtonians have experienced from a wide variety of perspectives. For some, cycling has been a sport of pricey equipment and exclusive, even segregated, clubs. For others, it has been part of a gritty livelihood earned on the city's pavement, delivering packages through dense downtown traffic to lobbyists and political workers. Ironically, a sport that could be highly exclusive and male dominated could simultaneously be a source of freedom, mobility, and even triumph for women, minorities, and working people.

If a bicycle were a living organism, and not a machine created by humans, one might justifiably suspect that a conflict between elite and democratic cultures was part of its DNA. A British company, Reynolds and May, developed the first prototype of a bicycle in 1869.[2] Reynolds and May's invention was the first to be actually powered by a rider pushing on pedals—the iconic high-wheeled models known as the "ordinary." Expensive, dangerous, and difficult to ride, this model was ridden primarily by the wealthy sporting leisure classes of the Gilded Age. They understood it as a "manly" activity not open to female participation. In Washington, as in other municipalities, male riders organized themselves into clubs, the first being the Capital Bicycle Club in 1879.[3] Yet organizations like the Capital Club did not define cycling in the District for long. In fact, in Washington by the end of the nineteenth century, the bicycle became many things in addition to a leisure pastime for the elite: It was a source of emancipatory mobility for women, a mode of transportation that was faster and more affordable than the horse, and a source of exciting entertainment in the form of races that were among the most popular sporting events of their era. This was especially true in the last decades of the nineteenth century and first decades of the twentieth when Washington became a hub of a nationwide bicycle "craze."

Americans saw their first bicycle, a more refined version of the Reynolds and May prototype, in the 1870s at such venues as the 1876 Centennial Exposition in Philadelphia.[4] It was not long before businesses in the United States began to manufacture and sell them to the public, and by the early 1880s, bicycle enthusiasts had begun to organize themselves into clubs and to publish journals devoted to their pastime.[5] A *Washington Post* article from 1882 claimed that the first bicycle was introduced to the District in 1878, and reported that there were 175 riders in the city who owned their own bicycles. Costing between $60 and $100, a bicycle was far too expensive for an ordinary worker to afford, and, according to the *Post*, "has prevented [bicycles] from being more generally used."[6]

Despite a rather limited number of people who could pay to participate in the sport, Washington, DC, provided a promising landscape for cyclists. Since the high-wheeled, early models called ordinaries proved to be treacherous vehicles on bumpy roads, cyclists were attracted to areas with smoothly paved surfaces. According to the *Post*, the District contained a bounty of these. "Old bicycle riders assert that no city in this country, or perhaps in the world, presents such a field for bicycle practice as does Washington," the article gushed. "With forty-five miles of concreted streets and over two hundred miles of level gravel roads on the outskirts of the city, the bycicle [*sic*] rider may be said to be in his paradise, and with such advantages the riders here compare very creditably in point of speed with any in this country."[7]

The description of the District as a bicycle rider's "paradise" reflected the language used by members of the city's first organization of riders, the Capital Bicycle Club. In November 1883, a committee from the club penned an article about cycling in the city for the *Wheelman* (a publication later known as *Outing*). The essay used the phrase "bicycler's paradise" that headlined the *Post* article published two years earlier. Like the *Post* article, and like many other articles published in the *Wheelman*, it cited "broad, asphalt paved streets" in a city whose beauty "even a Parisian visitor will not deny." According to the piece, the favorable conditions offered by Washington provided the perfect backdrop for the establishment of the club in the shadows of the Capitol rotunda on a frigid day in January 1879.[8]

Indeed, the popularity of the bicycle in DC, and in the United States more generally, grew rapidly over the decades of the 1880s and 1890s. By the end of the century, it was no longer a sport enjoyed exclusively by an affluent upper-middle-class male population. As early as the late 1880s, the increase in national production of bicycles had dropped prices to a degree, while used bikes increasingly became more available. Perhaps most significantly, redesigned bicycles made riding more accessible to a general population. The most important redesign, which came in the mid-1880s, was the creation and production of the "safety bicycle," the early prototype of the contemporary bike with evenly sized wheels and a free-wheel mechanism linked to the pedals by a chain. Together with the introduction of the pneumatic tire, which replaced the bulky and bumpier solid rubber tire, the popularity of bike riding boomed between 1889 and 1895.[9]

The 1883 article in the *Wheelman*, however, provides a window into the earliest years of bicycle riding in the District. It reflected a bicycle subculture centered upon associations of white, affluent, and middle-class men engaged in expressions of manliness and masculinity, sensibilities fairly typical of middle-class sporting cultures of the late nineteenth century. Club members would typically gather for well-organized "runs" around the city and into the countryside on a regular basis. In their clubhouse—located in the LeDroit Building on the southwest corner of Eighth and F Streets, NW— Capital members would store their bikes, make repairs, take them apart, and rebuild them just for recreation. The space served as a locus for spontaneous social gatherings where "many a watermelon has been cut" and "many a cider jug has come in full and gone out empty."[10] Members would also play music and engage in debates over the merits of various bicycle components. When the weather outside prohibited riding, they would invent bicycle competitions appropriate to an indoor space. For example, they regularly engaged in "stand still" matches in which riders would mount their high-wheeled ordinaries and attempt to stay balanced for as long as possible (the record was two hours and twenty-two minutes).[11]

Members of the club came from a variety of elite and middle-class occupations. Some held prominent positions in the federal government. Leland Howard, one of the committee members who authored the *Wheelman* article, was a prominent government entomologist who, in 1894, became the director of the federal Bureau of Entomology. His work established him as a leader in the creation of strong government support for agricultural pest control.[12] Yet despite the social prominence individual members of such clubs enjoyed, many citizens of the District were concerned about these new machines and the dangerous potential for accidents with them, day or night. According to the authors of the article, which doubled as a self-promotion piece, complaints about dangerous bicycle riding were entirely unfounded and based only upon "prejudice" from those wishing to exploit their "inherent right to grumble and oppose the silent innovation."[13]

Nevertheless, in a sign of members' social prominence, the Capital Bicycle Club had a friend in District commissioner Major Thomas P. Morgan. After imploring the club to establish rules of the road that might assure a public concerned about safety, Morgan expressed his general support for the organization and its activities. According to the *Wheelman* article, he stated, "I approve of bicycling. My duties as chief of police enable me to see a great deal in which the young men of Washington are concerned, and as a result of my observation I shall do all in my power to encourage honest, manly exercise promoting the physical health of participants, and tending to keep them out of bar-rooms and other questionable resorts."[14]

Like other sports emerging in the late nineteenth century, cycling negotiated a fine line between manly self-control and masculine physicality. The quote attributed to Morgan, in which he positions cycling in contrast to "bar-rooms and other questionable resorts," suggests that cycling clubs labored to establish themselves as consistent with Victorian ideals of emotional restraint. On their regular Wednesday and Sunday runs, members of the Capital Bicycle Club displayed this restraint to the public. The white-capped and blue-uniformed riders were renown for their disciplined organization and intricate drills on the city's celebrated paved streets. Club members were careful to comply with Morgan's expectations, passing a resolution that stated: "Any member becoming intoxicated on a club run, or who shall be under the influence of liquor while wearing the club uniform shall be expelled."[15] According to the *Wheelman* article, "It has always been a matter of surprise to clubs and wheelmen from abroad that the order and discipline maintained in the Capital Club, mounted or un-mounted, whether at home or abroad, while together *as a club*, are worthy of a well-regulated military company."[16] In 1884, members brought this discipline into their lives outside of the club, agreeing to wear their bicycle breeches to work with their business suits at least three days a week.[17]

Yet such controlled displays of riding prowess were clearly not entirely satisfying to members, many of whom looked forward to escaping the city and venturing into the nearby countryside of Virginia and Maryland. The authors of *The Wheelmen* article wrote:

> There is an exhilaration in a coast down a stony hill, in a source of danger on every side, which makes even a timid rider feel that he has more thoroughly *lived* in an hour of such riding than a week of bowling over asphalt. It is this feeling which takes Capital men miles away from home upon every opportunity, and which has caused a thorough exploration of the neighboring counties of "My Maryland" and the "Old Dominion."[18]

Other club members enjoyed various forms of "trick riding." In a stunt that would impress any contemporary BMX cycler, Herbert S. Owen rode a fifty-four-inch ordinary down the steps of the United States Capitol.[19] Capital Club member Rex Smith later performed the same feat.[20]

Although members used their clubs to exhibit masculine physical prowess tempered by disciplined manly restraint, many also used their clubs as relaxed homosocial spaces in which men could cast aside notions of Victorian decorum. In a *Washington Post* article headlined "None Like the Queers," one exclusive club in the District called the Queer Wheelmen was celebrated as being "favorites among cyclists" for wearing "unique costumes." At a citywide bicycle parade, members dressed as clowns and wore "cornucopia" caps and white shoes. Such distinctive *ensembles* earned the Queer

Rex Smith of the Capital Bicycle Club, tagged by *Outing* magazine as "the best fancy rider in the United States," takes a 54-inch ordinary bike down the steps of the United States Senate building in 1884. Capital Bicycle Club Collection (#57). Series 1, Box 1. Washingtoniana Collection, Martin Luther King Jr. Library, Washington, DC.

Wheelmen a prize for best appearance. "Every man had a zobo instrument," the *Post* wrote, "and they made the night hideous with weird music."[21]

Even the relatively staid Capital Bicycle Club created its own carnivalesque ritual. In a parody of Frederick Arthur Bridgeman's orientalist painting, *Procession of the Sacred Bull Anubis*, displayed at Washington's Corcoran Gallery, Capital members in the winter of 1887 created their own Procession of the Sacred Cat. Dressing in vaguely Middle Eastern costumes, with some members looking like women, they mounted a stuffed cat's head on the handlebars of an ordinary and had their portraits taken.[22]

As early as 1880, the Capital Club also began to sponsor annual races. While such competitions occasionally involved riders from out of town, the early cycling scene in Washington was relatively isolated from the activities of clubs in other cities, such as New York and Philadelphia. Local racers preferred to stay in the area around the Capital. The Capital Club's first series of annual races took place on June 29, 1880, on an asphalt track at Iowa Circle. The club reported that 5,000 people attended the races.[23] Such events were clearly popular, and they would become even more so as the sport grew in popularity over the next decade.

In 1890, *Outing* magazine, by now one of the leading sports publications in the country, once more lauded Washington as a city with both a vibrant sporting scene and an active cycling culture.[24] In a profile entitled "Athletics in Washington," Herbert Janvrin Browne commended the District's paved roads, thus echoing the praise that first appeared in the *Post* and the *Wheelman* almost a decade earlier. "The roads that lead to Washington will in the future be as certain in their quality as the roads that led to Rome," wrote Browne. "This is a paradise for lovers of healthy recreation in the open air. Through the smooth streets glide thousands of bicycles and tricycles."[25]

Browne's article mostly described the various athletic clubs that called Washington home, particularly those that began as cycling clubs. In the article, he celebrated the affluence and social prominence of club members and the opulence of their clubhouses. Indeed, his article had a clearly elitist tone. For example, he praised the largest club of the time, the Georgetown-based Columbia Athletic Club (CAC) for rescuing Analostan Island—once occupied by Senator James M. Mason, who served as a Confederate diplomat in Britain—from "disrepute" after it had become a "resort of negro roughs and gamblers."[26] After quoting Article II of the club's constitution—"to encourage all manly sports, promote physical culture and for social purposes"—Browne described in detail the luxurious accommodations of the club, which included basement bowling alleys, a swimming pool, a Turkish bath, reception rooms, a library, as well as locker rooms with bath facilities, dressing rooms, and almost 300 lockers. Upstairs, the clubhouse featured a fifty-by-ninety-foot gymnasium, a twenty-lap-to-the-mile running track, fencing rooms, and boxing halls.[27]

Browne not only celebrated the athletic clubs in the vanguard of bicycle culture in the city, he associated cycling itself with a utopian vision of what the bicycle as a piece of technology could bring to society. He wrote, "The day is within coming distance when bicycles will be as numerous and cheap as sewing machines, and as universally used in America as skates on winter canals in Holland. When that day comes the health of America will improve, the death rate will drop a notch, and several medical colleges will nail up their doors."[28] While still connoting the idea that the pastime of the elite would lift up the masses, the sentiment that Browne expressed here also contained a utopian vision that the bicycle might become a democratizing force, one that could bring swift transportation to the masses who would have otherwise had a hard time purchasing and caring for a horse. Seeing this democratic spirit reflected in the cycling scene of Washington, Browne noted that there was a "Ladies' Bicycle Club organized to encourage the timid fair in attempting the innovation of riding wheels." Browne wrote that Washington even possessed "probably the only colored bicycle club in the United States, if not the world."[29]

Actually, by the late 1890s, there were several local clubs that African American cyclists had organized, and by making bicycle mobility more accessible to all, the safety bicycle had offered women a newfound freedom of mobility. Browne's tone of surprise in reporting of African American and female involvement, however, reflected the exclusivity and sense of entitlement that held sway over the culture of white male cyclists. In the 1883 *Wheelman* article, for example, the authors revealed a white supremacist orientation when they described the joys of runs to the Cabin John Bridge by recalling, "quiet breakfast parties, with luscious spring-chicken (the genuine article), and flaky 'flour doin's,'—of snowy whiteness by contrast with the kindly black face of the 'old aunty' who rules the 'cook-house.'"[30]

Such commentary certainly showed that club members were not particularly reluctant to disseminate the harmful stereotypes commonly directed toward African Americans during the Jim Crow era. However, the city's black bicyclists were much more directly affected by discrimination reflected in the application of cycling statutes and safety laws. In the 1883 *Wheelman* article, the authors recalled that many cyclists in the city reacted with fear when police arrested and fined an African American rider $20 for colliding with and injuring a pedestrian. Many of these same riders were relieved,

however, after one of their own avoided any encounter with the law following a similar incident. In fact, the victim and rider "became great friends."
The Capital Club authors noted that the local press provided positive coverage of riding, "even suppressing accounts of accidents."[31]

In 1895, the *Washington Post* reported an arrest of Ebenezer Williams,
a "colored bicycle professor," and William Sedwick, "a colored grocer,"
for violating an 1881 ordinance that required cyclists to walk their bikes
after dark if it was not outfitted with a lamp. Rather than simply being
asked to dismount, they were instead placed in the Georgetown jail. The
article made light of the incident, which took place after members of a local
African American cycling club were caught returning home in the dark after
a road race had gone later than expected. After Williams and Sedwick were
arrested, the rest of the group scattered, some returning later with lanterns.
"They were all pretty badly scared," the article concluded. "Safe to say, they
won't try to ride through Georgetown again without lights."[32]

Browne was correct to predict that the bicycle would become more
popular among a general population, but as African Americans entered
the sport, they did not find themselves particularly welcomed. Meanwhile,
the nation's leading organization of cyclists, called the League of American
Wheelmen (LAW), was debating whether the organization should be exclusively white. After rejecting proposals to exclude black members at national
conventions in 1892 and 1893, the organization limited membership in
1894 to "any amateur (white) wheelman of good character, 18 years of age
or older."[33]

Perhaps LAW was reacting to an increasing national presence of African
American cyclists involved in the sport. Certainly by the mid-1890s, cycling
had become very popular among African Americans in Washington. By
1895, the *Washington Post* estimated that there were between 400 and 500
black bicycle riders in the city. In the early 1890s, clubs like the Capital
City Bicycle Club competed quite successfully in races in nearby cities like
Richmond.[34] By 1900, the all-black Cross-Country Club organized a set of
races to celebrate that year's Fourth of July.[35] Facing discrimination by police
and other riders in the District, and the color line within LAW nationally,
African American riders in DC moved to form their own national organization. In September 1895, Samuel E. Lacy, a notary public from Northwest
DC, began to work with black bicyclists in the District and in other cities
to form a separate, all–African American, national cyclist organization. At
the center of the movement in Washington were two core African American
bicycling clubs: the Ideal Club, and the Capital League Wheelmen. In 1895
the *Washington Post* praised the formation of an all-black organization of

riders, arguing that even if only a fraction of the total African American population of cyclists in the city joined, they would outnumber the seventy-three LAW members who resided in the District.[36]

Despite the color line, the local chapter of LAW debated whether or not to allow African American riders to participate in their annual parade in July 1896. Some member organizations threatened to boycott if the parade was integrated. In the end, the group passed a resolution allowing black riders to participate "since it was seen that no action preventing them could be taken."[37] Clearly not feeling embraced by the local chapter of LAW, Lacy led a group of African American cyclists to form the District League of Colored Wheelmen in August 1896. More than a collection of cycling enthusiasts, the organization explicitly stated that its mission was to battle discrimination by both white riders and the police. The league's members also promised to organize a "mammoth colored bicycle parade" that would include "nearly every colored wheelman and wheelwoman in the city" dressed in "fancy costume for an exhibition ride through the streets."[38]

The exclusivity of bicycle club culture became challenged in another arena as the sport boomed in the late nineteenth century: racing. As was true in many other competitive sports, the ethic of amateurism governed participation in bicycle racing during its early years in the 1880s. While lauded for creating a pure and wholesome playing field untainted by worldly contaminations, amateurism operated in fact to restrict participation in sports only to those wealthy enough to have excessive leisure time. By the end of the 1890s, however, professional racing had developed into a popular and profitable spectator sport as racing grounds became connected more with commercial amusements than private clubs.

What is more, the local racing scene provided opportunities for cyclists not affiliated with a club to emerge as local heroes, overshadowing the influence of clubs upon the sport. In 1893, L. C. Wahl, a recent transplant from Minnesota who worked in the Government Printing Office, established a twenty-four-hour cycling record on Conduit Road. The sports gossip columnist in the *Washington Post*, however, noted that he received very little "encouragement" during his race from members of local bicycle clubs. "The fact that Wahl has not been given much of an indorsement [sic] should not cut any figure in his being given full credit for his performance. In fact, the public generally will likely think more of the plucky young man for his determination in going through the trial without the influences of a large gathering of riders to cheer him on."[39]

Although amateur clubs like the Capital Bicycle Club or Georgetown's Columbia Athletic Club organized races by the early 1880s, there were professional riders who nevertheless participated in many of these races. The 1883 Capital Club races at Athletic Park included professional riders from England and the United States.[40] Even the early races in Washington rapidly became popular. Articles about cycling in the *Washington Post* received billing on par with those about baseball. The Athletic Park grounds constructed for the 1883 contests contained a grandstand and field stands with seating for 5,000. Undercutting its own principles, the Capital Club paid out a total of $500 in prize money and medals to winners of races.[41]

The Columbia Athletic Club first promoted its races on their Analostan Island quarter-mile track. Later, the Columbia Club held races at Columbia Field, near the intersection of Seventeenth and C Streets, Northwest.[42] Unlike those at the Capital Club, Columbia members attempted to remain entirely amateur. Browne's October 1890 article in *Outing* praised Columbia as setting an example for other clubs in the city with regard to the amateur ideal. Browne wrote somewhat hopefully, "One word can be said of not only the Columbia Club, but of all the athletic associations of Washington: No taint of professionalism has ever appeared in any form or in the slightest degree. Amateur athletism [*sic*] in the District of Columbia is imbued with the fairest spirit of honorable emulation."[43] In addition to races on the track, cycling enthusiasts participated in long distance road races. Columbia Club member W. T. Robertson, for example, took part in an 1892 relay from Washington to Pittsburgh. In cooperation with other clubs, they hoped to complete their 290-mile ride in twenty-two hours.[44]

In fact, from an early stage, racers and clubs struggled with one another over the issue of professionalism and corruption in racing. In July 1886, an up-and-coming racer named W. E. Crist requested that the Capital Bicycle Club manage a race called the Flint Challenge Cup. The club, however, refused. Later that summer, during an executive board meeting, members charged that Crist had not only received payment for riding in the Flint Challenge race, he had taken money specifically to alter the results. A resolution before the club's board charged that Crist and another racer named Howell Stewart had agreed that "neither of them shall win," but would "permit another contestant to win the race."[45]

As safety bicycles became increasingly popular in the 1890s, riding generally became more widespread and less tied to local clubs. By the early 1890s, sports pages began to report increasingly of "safety races" featuring riders who guided their vehicles on pneumatic tires.[46] Moreover, safety bicycles, cheaper and easier to ride than ordinaries, allowed a greater percentage of the population to take up cycling, eventually outstripping the capacity of club membership. The *Washington Post* reported in 1894 that there were between 8,000 and 10,000 cyclists in the nation's capital, but fewer than 500 belonged to any sort of riding club. Even fewer counted themselves as members of LAW.[47]

During the early years of the 1890s, bicycle racing had begun to produce stars in Washington who had been successful in both local and regional races. Crist, now riding for the Columbia Bicycle Club, earned more than 100 racing trophies by 1890, and was featured on collectable tobacco cards. His tandem partner and fellow club member, Philip S. Brown, competed nationally in distance races.[48] By the end of the 1890s, some of DC's top cyclists began to turn professional. They were well known to a small set of bicycling enthusiasts and to a general population that had come to enjoy bicycle racing as an exciting spectator sport. Lacking an adequate racing venue in Washington, local cycling club members clamored for a track worthy of hosting large races on a national circuit. By the early 1890s, local entrepreneurs began to see a market for such an attraction.

George Wagner, a member of a Philadelphia family that had made its fortune in the butchering business, was one of the first to make an attempt at funding professional racing in Washington. He had already made money in sports, starting major league baseball franchises in Philadelphia and Washington, and selling each for a substantial profit. Known to pinch pennies, Wagner was interested in exploiting the popularity of bicycle racing for profit, and he had none of the pretenses that the bicycle club memberships so uninhibitedly expressed. By 1893, the Wagner family had already promoted professional racing by creating the National Cycling Association (NCA). His initial idea was to create a pro circuit in which racers would compete on tracks laid down in baseball stadiums. Wagner devised bylaws, racing rules, and schedules for the NCA, but baseball team owners in major cities like Baltimore and Cleveland opted out of participating. In addition, the country's top amateur racers affiliated with LAW had decided not to participate in the professional circuit out of fear of being expelled from the organization. Eventually, even Wagner backed out, essentially acknowledging the primacy of amateur racing.[49]

Demand for a quality track in DC continued into the middle of the decade, however. In February 1896, in an article in which it proclaimed cycling as the "National Sport of America," the *Washington Post* reported the "need of a cycle track." "For years the cycling fraternity of this city have been clamoring for a good track for their race meets," the article stated. "But thus far they have failed to construct an oval."[50]

In 1896, a group of investors led by affluent Toronto lawyer Jacob P. Clark created the International Athletic Park and Amusement Company with the intention of developing a sports and entertainment complex within the city's limits. Located in a suburban neighborhood east of the Georgetown Reservoir near Canal Road, the International Athletic Park (IAP), Clark envisioned, would enhance land values in the Palisades of the Potomac housing development, a nearby residential area that he had spearheaded through his creation of the Palisades of the Potomac Land Improvement Company. In fact, the park would be located three miles from downtown along the proposed, but not completed, Washington and Great Falls Electric Railway Company line, a company over which Clark also presided.[51]

By the spring of 1896, an oval track, one-third of a mile around, had been completed, as had a 30-by-208-foot grandstand for high-paying customers on one side and an open 25-by-100-foot bleacher opposite the grandstand. The price of admission was between twenty-five and seventy-five cents; a box cost six dollars. Clark's operation of IAP did not begin smoothly, however. First, because his rail line did not yet extend to the Palisades area, it was difficult for spectators to get to the track. Second, he often sparred with LAW and the city over issues of professionalism and public morality. During the 1896 season, for example, LAW put severe restrictions upon riders accepting any money, even for endorsements. This, along with the organization's scheduling demands, forced Clark to move his inaugural race on LAW's circuit from May to October. Clark also attempted to build a clientele by purchasing a liquor license to allow International Park to operate a bar in the clubhouse, and by sponsoring spectacles like a mock jousting contest. The jousting contest ended in chaos with the entertainers engaging in a real-life fistfight, and Clark refusing to pay them their $1,500 fee. Meanwhile, local church leaders and the Women's Christian Temperance Union protested against the sale of alcohol. In the end, the renewal of Clark's liquor license was denied.[52]

Nevertheless, IAP became a central location for many races in the late 1890s and early 1900s. After an expansion of the grandstands, 5,000 fans attended the national circuit races held in the fall of 1897. Yet LAW also hampered the ability of IAP managers to make money by refusing to allow them to hold races on dates when sanctioned meets were being held in nearby cities. Although the park hosted fifty-four races between May and September of 1897, few drew large crowds or had high-profile riders participating in races.[53]

While the managers of IAP were open to hosting drinking, jousting, and a wide variety of bicycle races, they did not allow female bicycle racers to compete. With the advent of the safety bicycle by the middle of the 1890s, riding had become quite popular among women.[54] This was particularly true in the District. In a column for the *Christian Advocate*, Professor J. W. Chickering, himself a bicycle enthusiast who claimed to be in his sixties and to have logged 10,000 miles on a bike, noted that "in the nation's capital city, the paradise of bicyclers, with its hundreds of miles of clean, wide, concreted streets, are seen thousands, old and young, boys and girls, men, women and children, thoroughly enjoying their wheels." Chickering commented that he had seen numerous boys who were misusing their riding privileges by engaging in stunts and trick riding. About girls, however, he observed, "It is a matter of satisfaction that the writer has never seen a girl or woman thus abusing the art."[55] Officially, LAW and IAP management felt that allowing women to race would only bring controversy and bad publicity. Thus women were forbidden from racing.[56] Given the fact that the IAP was willing to serve liquor at its venue, however, its management did not always avert controversy. It is more likely that racing promoters envisioned their clientele to be men seeking to be entertained by male competition.

Nevertheless, the local press did represent the bicycle as constituting an opportunity for mobility and freedom for women. In a retrospective article in 1927 on the history of sports in the District, part of a fiftieth anniversary issue, the *Washington Post* wrote that the paper had reported 150 female cyclists in 1888. According to the *Post*, "The advent of the safety opened a new field of sport to woman, a sport that could be enjoyed by the two sexes together, and thus it exerted a most tremendous social influence. With it came the 'new woman,' who cast off hampering traditions, reforming her wearing apparel, adopting bloomers and the 'rainy-daisy' skirt, and finally stood forth unfettered and emancipated."[57]

But many other press accounts, which focused mostly upon racing, tended to be about male riders. As the turn of the century approached, successful racers in Washington began to achieve more fame as athletic stars. Edward E. Clapp, Fred Sims, Harry Ward, E. C. Yeatman, and C. E. Gause were some of the more recognized elite racers in the early 1890s. The most famous in the first years after the opening of IAP, however, was Fred Schade. Even before the International Athletic Park opened, Schade had developed a reputation as one of the fastest amateur riders in the United States, challenging Sims as one of the two fastest in the District. Initially riding a safety that weighed fifty-two pounds, Schade would follow bicycle clubs as they traveled to meet locations. After club members, hoping to embarrass him, goaded Schade into entering a race as a youth in 1893, Schade ended up almost winning. This impressive performance became a local legend and propelled him into a racing career. He eventually rode collegiately for both Columbia University and Georgetown University. In May 1896, he proved himself to be the top cyclist in a meet against Georgetown. The following spring, he returned the favor, this time helping shut out Columbia in a five-mile race he won while representing Georgetown. By the summer of 1896, Schade had established himself as Sims's main rival. The two dueled throughout the summer in mile-long sprints at various locations, including the oval at International Athletic Park.[58]

Throughout the summer of 1896, Schade raced in Washington and throughout the South. He lost early races to Sims, but defeated him in their last race, then moved on to win races in Anderson, South Carolina, and Charlotte. Schade continued his local racing schedule upon returning to Washington in early August. On August 21, 1896, Schade performed a one-mile time trial at IAP faster than anyone else ever had in Washington. His time of two minutes and two and one quarter seconds shattered George S. Ball's previous mark by almost four seconds.[59] At that year's season finale, the *New York Times* reported that "the sky was cloudy, the track fast, and the attendance large." Schade once again was the victor, winning both of his heats in the one-mile open race.[60] By the end of the season, the *Washington Post* declared Schade the city champion, having won ten races. Schade had also come in second three times, and never finished in third. Finishing in second place on the city tables, Sims won three races, came in second nine times, and earned third place in three other races.[61]

The most spectacular racing event of the nineteenth century, however, came at the end of 1896 in Washington's Convention Hall. The event was a six-day bicycle race, one of the most popular events in the professional bicycle-racing world at the turn of the twentieth century. Six-day races involved riders competing to cover as many miles as possible over a period of six days. Races often took place during the winter months inside indoor arenas such as New York's Madison Square Garden, and spectators would come and go during the event. Racers would typically ride twenty hours per day, resting only for brief periods on cots. They would also pause for occasional small meals that usually included vast quantities of coffee. Races usually required that all contestants complete a minimum of 1,350 miles to receive any prize money.[62] The "Flying Dutchman," Frank Waller, won the 1896 Convention Hall event, finishing one and a half laps in front of Harry Maddox. Eight thousand spectators were on hand to watch the finish.[63]

The success of such a professional event caught the attention of racing promoters in the Washington area. Ross Klosterman, a lawyer from Baltimore, envisioned building a new track in Northeast Washington, closer to an established streetcar line than International Athletic Park, where he could promote national circuit professional races that were part of the

NCA. Ultimately, Klosterman was able to get a permit to build cycling's Washington Coliseum on the square bounded by Fourteenth and Fifteenth Streets, and Fourth and Fifth Streets, Northeast. The venue was ready by the racing season of 1901. It contained lights for night racing, and could seat 5,000 people with additional standing room. The racing oval was only one-sixth of a mile around, only half the size of the IAP oval, but the stadium was also half the distance by streetcar from where most Washington residents lived at the time.[64]

Although bad weather and power failures canceled important races, the Coliseum drew thousands of fans in 1901, often selling out for big races. Three thousand attended several races to see Marshall "Major" Taylor, perhaps the most famous African American professional athlete at the time, compete at the Coliseum that season. Fans were also treated to motorcycle races that were sponsored by the NCA, and bicycle races that followed a motorcycle pace bike. However, over the next two years, bad weather and continual breakdowns of the pace motorbikes made it difficult to develop a steady fan base, and racing promoters began to withdraw their support for professional bicycle racing. As a city with a relatively small and transient population, Washington also had a difficult time competing with cities in the northeast—Philadelphia, New York, and Boston, for instance—that had become the hub of bicycle racing. Even NCA began to disintegrate, with professional racers returning to LAW.[65]

The end of racing at the Washington Coliseum marked the end of an era for bicycle racing in Washington. Even as races continued at IAP and other venues, sports such as baseball, boxing, and horse racing grew in popularity, while the bicycle racing "craze" declined. In addition, races received much less attention from the press. An announcement of a twenty-mile handicap race in November 1927, for example, received only two short paragraphs in the Washington Post.[66]

Nevertheless, the fading popularity of bike racing did not dissuade cyclists in the District from trying to make a mark on the sport. In August 1927, sixteen-year-old Milton Albert Smith set out to break the bicycle world endurance record by riding continuously for at least twenty-five hours (the previous mark had been twenty-four hours and 163.6 miles). Fueled by coffee, ice cream, "liquid nourishments," and chocolate bars that he planned to consume while riding, the Eastern High student repeatedly circled the track at Potomac Park and the Polo Fields.[67] Smith succeeded in breaking the record by riding 250.4 miles in twenty-four hours and fifteen minutes.[68] Smith's record did not last long, however. Five days after the new mark had been set, bicycle messenger Eugene Fish, also sixteen years old, mounted his bike on the same Potomac Park track and rode the full twenty-five hours. According to press accounts, he could have gone on longer, but at 10:35 in the morning, his mother stepped in front of him on the track and forced him to stop, yelling, "That's enough, Eugene."[69]

The reasons why Washington, DC, struggled to establish itself as a bicycle-racing hub are complex, but they seem to have more to do with marketing miscalculations than with lack of local interest. In fact, the stories of Smith and Fish indicate that throughout the early twentieth century, cycling remained a vibrant activity in the District. The history of cycling in the city is one activity that grew increasingly into a widely popular sport. What began as an exclusive pastime for affluent white men evolved into a recreational activity enjoyed by a diverse population, as well as a spectator sport that thrilled thousands of fans.

Moreover, the history of cycling in the nation's capital is one that has always been a blend of recreation, transportation, and competitive sport. In the urban landscape of the District during the early twenty-first century —one lined with miles of bicycle paths, buzzing with commuters and an occasional messenger, and interrupted by fast-paced races with world-class cyclists—these trends continue. They also continue to reflect the vibrancy, diversity, and even the struggles among the District's dynamic and ever-changing population.

2

Less Than Monumental

The Sad History of Sports Venues in Washington, DC

Ryan A. Swanson

In a city full of monuments, Washington's stadiums and sports venues serve as reminders of the District's failures and limitations. Uninspiring architecture, pervasive racism, and crippling debt have characterized the city's places of athletic competition. This chapter will not be a nostalgic celebration of Washington's "green cathedrals."[1] From the antebellum period to the turn of the twenty-first century, three venues in particular—the White Lot, Griffith Stadium, and DC Memorial Stadium (later renamed the Robert F. Kennedy Memorial Stadium)—have dominated the sports landscape in the District. At these places, Washingtonians gathered to play and watch athletic contests. Baseball and football dominated the schedule, but horse racing, ice-skating, running contests, and cricket were mainstays as well.

In terms of aesthetic design, Washington's facilities are hardly worth remembering. The White Lot was more an open expanse than a carefully developed sporting venue. But it did sit squarely in front of the White House, making obvious to anyone who set foot on the grounds the relationship of sports, land, and politics. Griffith Stadium, located about two miles from the White Lot, was similarly uninspiring. Visiting clubs and fans made fun of the facility. Opposing players often complained about the lights, the field, the warning track, and the proximity of the stands to the bullpen. As one player whined, fans "look right down your throat."[2] RFK Stadium, by contrast, was a modern venue, one of the first in the now-derided, multiuse stadium movement of the 1960s and 1970s. A financial disaster from the start, RFK never paid for itself—one of the reasons why the District and the federal government passed it back and forth over the years. It also had the misfortune of losing the tenancy of the Redskins, and all but prevented

Major League Baseball (MLB) from returning to the District. Longtime *Washington Post* sportswriter Thomas Boswell later called RFK "a big old beautiful dump of a park"—a disapproving yet nostalgic view that balanced the sports memories that had occurred inside the stadium's confines with its nondescript architectural style and lack of amenities.[3]

Clearly, none of Washington's sporting places are as venerated as Chicago's Wrigley Field, as widely hailed as Baltimore's Camden Yards, or as memorable as Green Bay's Lambeau Field. But they are immensely informative for understanding the District's history. Investigating the places where Washington's sports have been played and watched reveals the historical and cultural issues that were unique to the city.

Almost since its inception, the District has struggled with federalism. The city and its stadiums have had jurisdictional challenges brought on by tensions between the federal government and local authorities unlike those of other American cities. While Massachusetts senator Charles Sumner might have hoped that the District would "set an example for all the land, and most especially for the South," on matters of race in the nineteenth century, the city has instead often been an incubator of oppression.[4] Although significantly shaped by its sizable African American population, Washington, for most of its history, has been divided between "black Washington" and "official Washington."[5] Indicative of these two worlds, the District had white baseball's worst team in the Senators and the best from the Negro Leagues in the Homestead Grays. Both played at Griffith Stadium.

Land in the District

The Residence Bill of 1790, signed into law by President George Washington, created a unique type of property in the embryonic United States. The "Seat of the Government of the United States" was not to be part of any individual state. Instead, the federal government took control of the land upon which its physical structures were built. Because of this law, many of the District's stadiums and sporting venues were, at their very root, different from their counterparts in other American cities.

Land policy in the District was, and still is, complicated. The struggle to control the development of the city intensified after the Civil War. Not surprisingly, race relations figured prominently. Census data from 1870 shows that each of the two cities within the District—Washington and Georgetown—had roughly two whites for every African American.[6] Though clusters of black Washingtonians did exist, strict spatial segregation did not. Many blacks lived in present-day Foggy Bottom, as well as in neighborhoods immediately to the north and west of the White House, and in areas southwest and southeast of the National Mall.[7]

Politically, Washington has enjoyed only a few periods in its history in which decisions about land and property were made at the city level. Mostly, the federal government has been in charge. In 1791, the newly created government assigned Pierre L'Enfant the task of designing the nation's new capital. His plan created numerous recreational spaces, and afforded the District flexibility to adapt over the years.[8]

In June 1868, Washington, DC, held its first postbellum mayoral election. Land policy was a central issue. Sayles J. Bowen, elected mayor in no small part because of the new black vote, was committed to making the District a better place for its growing African American population (Bowen was white).[9] The fear among whites was that the city's land policy—especially when it came to venues of recreation and entertainment—would not keep the races apart. A Washington correspondent for the *Philadelphia Sunday Mercury* in 1869 reported bitterly:

> The ordinance compelling all licensed places of amusement to admit all persons, without distinction of color, to every part of such places of public entertainment, has passed both branches of the City Council and will, undoubtedly be signed by our republican Mayor. The pure and immaculate Sayles J. Bowen on being asked whether he intended to give his autograph to the pro-African bill, he smartly responded, "Well, sir, I see no reason why I should not do so." A White man is, evidently, as good as a nigger in Mr. Bowen's estimation.[10]

Local governmental control, however, lasted only a short time. The Organic Act, which became law in 1871, drastically curtailed "home rule" in the District. It would not be until 1973 that Congress began relinquishing control over the region.

The White Lot

Washington's struggle over recreational space began on the doorstep of the president's house. Often referred to as "The President's Grounds," the White Lot was located on the southwest grounds of the White House, between the executive mansion and the Washington Monument. Beginning in the 1920s, the space acquired its familiar name, the Ellipse.[11] Because of its proximity to the White House, presidents from Andrew Johnson to William Howard Taft visited the facility.[12]

Baseball games had taken place on the grounds behind 1600 Pennsylvania Avenue even before the Civil War.[13] In May 1860, before a large and appreciative crowd, a game between the Nationals and Potomac Clubs was played on the White Lot. By 1866, the area was prime baseball real estate. Half a dozen baseball clubs, including the Nationals, Union, Potomac, and Jefferson Clubs, regularly used the facility. The city's Washington and American Cricket Clubs also played there. Adding to the confusion, a half dozen junior ball clubs used "all the spare ground on the margin." The shared field was a chaotic example of public space enjoyed to its fullest. Wrote one baseball reporter, "What a crowd of ball players there are on the field every day. . . . The way the balls fly in every direction is enough to remind a veteran of the army" of battle.[14]

The White Lot was located in a neighborhood that had one of the highest percentages of African American residents in the city. The First Ward encompassed the ten-block area immediately to the north and west of the White House, and was an area in which many of the city's affluent black families lived.[15] In its formative years in the District, then, baseball was played not only in the White House's front yard, but also in part of the city where many black ballplayers resided.

After the Civil War, the battle for control of the White Lot brought baseball firmly into the struggle over civil rights. The grounds, because of their proximity to the White House, lent credibility to the activities that took place upon them—much as the Lincoln Memorial would come to do for civil rights demonstrations during the 1960s.[16] The tussle over the space began almost immediately after the Civil War. Restrictions came incrementally. Then, in 1869, authorities ordered that baseball cease being played on the White Lot, ostensibly for security reasons.[17] Although there was little enforcement of the edict, it did signal the jousting to come.[18] By 1873, the situation for black clubs using the White Lot became even more tenuous: Closed-door negotiations named the white-run Creighton Base Ball Club as the primary tenant of the White Lot.[19]

Black Washingtonians could not have been prepared for what came next. On September 6, 1874, the *Sunday Herald* announced: "The White Lot has been closed to all ball players except the Creightons. The gangs of lazy negroes and other vagrants infesting the grounds made this action necessary."[20] No longer could the city's other baseball clubs—black or white—rely on public space to carry out their craft. In the District's desire to expel the "gangs of lazy negroes" from the highly prized White Lot, the District had awarded a white baseball club of the second-tier full control of the city's most powerful baseball address.

Over the next four decades, Washingtonians argued with the federal government over the usage of the White Lot, while Congress considered how much money to earmark for developing the grounds. Meantime, usage policies vacillated as concerns about security changed. By 1880, the White Lot—largely closed to the city's ballplayers and athletes—had fallen into disrepair. The *Washington Post* termed it a "dumping ground" dominated by "vagrant boys and dogs."[21] Builders throughout the city used it as a repository for excess soil and gravel.

Unlike such cities as Boston or Chicago, whose leaders would have overseen the improvement of recreational grounds, in Washington the task of developing the White Lot fell to the United States Army and Congress. In 1877, President Grant appointed Colonel Thomas L. Casey to be the commissioner of public buildings for the District of Columbia. Casey, to say the least, was a busy man. During his twenty-year tenure, he oversaw the completion of the Washington Memorial, the Library of Congress, and the Executive Office Building.[22] Casey's Army Corps of Engineers would be in charge of Washington's sporting venues for more than five decades. It would not be until 1934 that the task of overseeing the District's parks and other open spaces was shifted from the Corp of Engineers to the National Park Service.[23]

Security and jurisdictional concerns influenced the operation of the White Lot. On at least three occasions, officials considered closing it to the public altogether. In 1885, a group of revelers on the White Lot fired off several shots from their cannons in the wee hours of the morning. "Hundreds of people believing that [former president] Grant was dead or that some unusual event had occurred . . . came down town" following the incident, reported the *Washington Post*.[24]

In 1901, an interesting proposal arose: why not build two baseball diamonds on the grounds of the White House—one for white baseball teams and another for black ones? A letter to the editor of the *Washington Post* supported the idea. It urged that the White Lot should remain open to all baseball clubs. But Jim Crow policies prohibited black and white teams from playing each other. So ball clubs waited their turn to use the field. The sight of ballplayers doing nothing fed negative stereotypes:

> It might save the slight annoyances which occur occasionally if the white men and colored were each allowed "to have and to hold" their own diamond. . . . One will sometimes find white or colored teams sitting around disconsolately because the other color has the only diamond which is in good order. If that little point could be settled, each color would keep his ground in good condition, cutting the grass and throwing out the stones.[25]

The two-field proposal was ignored. A DC statute declared that federal land could not be reserved, even though the Creighton Club had enjoyed such a designation previously.[26] The statute also defined the racial lines along which sport in Washington was contested, even when it took place upon the grounds controlled by the federal government.

Two years later it was Theodore Roosevelt's turn to decide the fate of the White Lot. In the 1890s, the White Lot had been used for tennis and "trotting contests." Bike races and running events took place there as well. More than any other president before him, Roosevelt was an advocate of athletic competition. Football, wrestling, and wilderness adventures took up much of his free time. Unlike most of his contemporaries, though, Roosevelt did not play or follow baseball.[27] Nevertheless, the remodeling of the White Lot—which included the construction of three separate baseball diamonds—was carried out under his administration. Initially, anyone could use the diamonds. As the *Post* reported in spring 1904, "Three first-class ball fields are to be thrown open to the amateurs in the White House ellipse."[28] Teams from the Sunday-school Athletic Association and the Departmental League, among others, took to the White Lot during the hot summer months of 1904.

But as was always the case in the District, the federal government stood poised to intervene. Between 1905 and 1907, baseball clubs were required to apply for permission just to play ball on the White Lot. In 1906, it seemed that the baseballers might have to look elsewhere for a place to play. "The most serious question which confronts the [Departmental] league this year is the securing of grounds," noted the *Post*, in March 1906. "It has been reported that the league would not be allowed to use the White Lot ellipse."[29] In the end, the Army Corps of Engineers allowed the league to use the fields.

Access to the White Lot would continue to ebb and flow. In 1905, promoters interested in bringing the vaunted Army-Navy football game to the District suggested that a massive grandstand be constructed on the White Lot. The game "would not injure the Ellipse," advocates promised. Moreover, "the only natural battle ground for [the Army-Navy] contest is here at the National Capital," argued the *Post*. But the military game in front of the president's house never came to fruition.[30] A successful track and field event staged on the White Lot in 1910 hinted at open access.[31] Such accessibility never happened, though. As the 1920s dawned, fewer organized athletic contests took place on the White Lot. Part of the reason was because the grounds had become more closely guarded territory. Politics and governmental concerns trumped athletics—a reality Washingtonians would see repeated throughout the twentieth century.

Griffith Stadium

Although the White Lot served as Washington's premier athletic facility in the 1860s and 1870s, it was not the only venue available. The Olympic Grounds, in the northwest quadrant of the city, was also a widely used field. In the last decade of the nineteenth century, another facility, the "Swampoodle Grounds," which was located near today's Union Station, provided ballplayers with a basic—and often wet—field. The grounds had rickety bleachers, which could accommodate 6,000 spectators.[32]

The field that would become Griffith Stadium was staked out in 1891. Located at Seventh Street and Florida Avenue, Northwest, the grounds took shape gradually. During its lifespan, the facility had a variety of names, including National Park, Boundary Field, American League Field, and, finally, Griffith Stadium. The development of the park followed the traditional pattern of early sports stadiums: In 1891, ballplayers claimed the plot of land, then fences went up, and finally permanent stadium seating was erected. The quality of construction was not the highest priority. Like many early stadiums, Griffith Stadium was razed and rebuilt. In 1911, the original wood structure burned to the ground, leading to the construction of the modern—or, at least, more modern—Griffith Stadium.

A key characteristic of Griffith Stadium—like that of the White Lot— was the neighborhood in which it was built. Griffith Stadium sat squarely in one of Washington's most vibrant and affluent black communities. Located two and half miles northeast of the White Lot, the stadium bordered Washington's U Street corridor, home to "one of the largest, wealthiest, and best-educated African American communities" in the United States during the first half of the twentieth century.[33] The U Street community pushed for both control and use of the facility. Watching baseball games was only one activity for black Washingtonians. Church revivals, high school and college football games, and drill competitions brought many of the city's African Americans into the stadium.

Clark Griffith, the stadium's namesake, deserves both credit and blame for what the venue became and how it operated. In 1919, after becoming majority owner of the Washington Nationals, Griffith also acquired control of the stadium. Unlike many sports venues throughout the South, Griffith Stadium featured racially desegregated seating, which garnered Clark Griffith some positive press from black newspapers. "Long Live King Baseball: The Only Monarch Who Recognizes No Color Line," trumpeted a *Daily American* headline after the Senators won the World Series in 1924.[34] Baseball was still segregated when the headline appeared, but Griffith

Stadium was not. Indeed, the stadium was one of the few integrated public spaces in the District during the Jim Crow era.[35]

The integration, though, was far from codified or thorough. There were no specific standards at the ballpark as to where a black patron could sit. Nor were there signs reserving certain areas for white spectators. Nevertheless, at Griffith Stadium racial assumptions still prevailed: African Americans were expected to sit in the right field pavilion.[36] Although there were some exceptions to this unwritten rule, black and white Washingtonians understood that everybody would be admitted to Senators' games and that most everybody knew where to sit. In this way Griffith Stadium was not all that different from the White Lot. De facto, and not de jure, segregation held sway.

During the early 1920s, Clark Griffith invested heavily in his stadium. He expanded the seating capacity by nearly 50 percent, pushing the number of seats to more than 30,000. The stadium's second deck was reinforced with steel and concrete, and workers dug up the infield and replaced it. A "green monster" was added to right field, replicating Fenway Park's signature feature.[37] An infield replanted with new sod drew comparisons to a finely manicured golf course.[38]

The expansion and improvement of Griffith Stadium was the result of a misreading of the city's baseball future. During the 1920s, Walter "Big Train" Johnson led the Senators to a short-lived stay within the upper echelons of baseball. The rise culminated with the 1924 World Series, particularly game 7, hosted at Griffith Stadium. At this one juncture, the relatively small confines of Griffith Stadium left thousands of Washingtonians shut out of the most important baseball game ever played in the District. Some 25,000 fans had lined up to get the few remaining available tickets on October 9, 1924, the day before the series' pivotal game. The lines stretched along U Street, connecting, once again, the stadium to the District's "Black Broadway."[39] Throughout the series, the *Post* hinted at the inferiority of the small stadium in light of the team's largess. "Thousands of Washington baseball fans, unable to obtain tickets for the World Series games because of the *limited capacity of the ball park*, are listening in on the games by radio," the paper reported disapprovingly.[40]

The Senators won game 7, defeating the New York Giants. The game had stretched into extra innings, providing Washingtonians with even more excitement. After the victory, the city basked in the glory of the Senators' triumph. But the next eight years produced only a handful of successful seasons. Meanwhile, Griffith Stadium was expanded and improved. In 1933, the Senators returned to the World Series, but lost to the Giants in five games. Washingtonians would soon appreciate how lucky they had been. Of the Senators' next twenty-seven years in the city, the club finished last or second to last thirteen times, and never made it to the postseason again.

The lack of success led to a precipitous decline in attendance. During the 1930s and 1940s, the team finished second to last in attendance eight times, and from 1955 to 1960 the club ranked last in the American League in attendance. The decline had been swift. In 1930, more than 614,000 fans attended Senators games. In 1935, the team drew approximately 255,000 spectators. To be sure, the Great Depression had wreaked havoc at the turnstiles. But the Senators' struggles had impacted attendance as well.[41]

The Senators and football's Redskins alone could not keep Griffith Stadium afloat. Largely because of each team's feeble drawing power, the venue became home to a team from the Negro Leagues. The stadium also hosted activities that served Washington's African American citizenry. The stadium's location near U Street made it accessible for many black Washingtonians. Griffith Stadium had desegregated to the pay the bills, but even then not completely. It was, as one scholar has described it, a "mercenary desegregation."[42]

Griffith Stadium hosted black baseball and football consistently throughout the first half of the twentieth century. It also hosted boxing matches, high school events, religious gatherings, and military maneuvers. While these types of events often failed to attract large crowds, the fact that Griffith Stadium offered more than just football and baseball games elevated it in the eyes of Washington's African American community. For instance, two of black Washington's signature cultural events—the Thanksgiving Day Lincoln-Howard football game and the Colored Washington High School's annual drill competition—often took place at Clark Griffith's venue. Each event drew tens of thousands of people.[43] In addition, Elder Lightfoot Solomon Michaux of Washington's Church of God, an African American congregation, held several events at Griffith Stadium. In 1937, for example, more than 7,000 attended a baptismal service overseen by Michaux. The *Washington Post* headlined the next day: "Candidates from Near and Far Dipped in Tank at Griffith Stadium."[44] Such events transformed a white-owned facility into sacred ground for black Christians in the District.

But while African Americans paid to use Griffith Stadium, rarely were they given priority over white groups in procuring the grounds. One important exception was the Lincoln-Howard Thanksgiving Day game. After the game had shifted to other venues several times during the 1930s, Griffith Stadium administrators in 1940 gave priority to the Lincoln-Howard contest, even bypassing bids from other District colleges trying to secure the traditional Thanksgiving Day slot. The African American *New York Amsterdam News* proudly noted:

> Howard University football officials won a prize package from all the colleges of Washington DC, when they signed a recent contract for Griffith Stadium, Thanksgiving afternoon. . . . This is the only large football plane in Washington and is usually sought by George Washington, Georgetown, Maryland, American, or Catholic University for their Thanksgiving game. But Hilltop officials got the jump on them and procured the field for the annual Howard-Lincoln gridiron struggle.[45]

Clark Griffith's staff never found a marquee event equivalent to the Lincoln-Howard game for white Washingtonians. This failure was not due to a lack of effort. For instance, communications with Notre Dame to secure the Fighting Irish for an annual game were begun in 1923. Authorities even tried to lure the Fighting Irish by hinting that a "new Griffith Stadium" would be built.[46] However, Notre Dame's annual game in DC failed to take hold. Washingtonians also heard periodic reports that college football's most prestigious annual matchup—the Army-Navy game—might become a fixture in the city.[47] Instead, Griffith Stadium hosted football's less-prestigious "President's Cup," a yearly game between the US Marines and the Coast Guard.[48]

But Griffith Stadium did host some events that had a distinct Washington flavor. The Congressional Baseball Game began at American League Park—which would become Griffith Stadium—in 1909, and it was played in the venue numerous times in subsequent years. The annual matchup, pitting Republicans against Democrats, raised funds for charity.[49] Those who couldn't play watched. The crowds for the games regularly included senators and congressmen, Supreme Court justices, and a "social list" that rivaled DC's other marquee events.[50]

Griffith Stadium was open to black patrons and their events as long as the events could draw a big enough crowd to make money. Thus the stadium, like the District itself, was simultaneously a step ahead of, and thoroughly mired in, the segregationist tendencies of the South. Moreover, many important events created by segregation itself found their start at Griffith Stadium. For example, on May 19, 1933, the East-West Colored Baseball League's inaugural game was played in the stadium.[51] In addition, the Homestead Grays were the most important African American baseball club to call Griffith Stadium home. The Grays had formed in 1919 in Homestead, Pennsylvania, bringing together black steelworkers to play baseball. The club began splitting its games between Pittsburgh and Washington

Philadelphia Athletics manager Connie Mack (*left*), United States vice
president Alben Barkley (*center*), and Clark Griffith at Griffith Stadium on
Opening Day, 1950. The Senators won, 8–7. Courtesy National
Archives, photo no. 306-PS 50-9245.

in 1937—playing in Forbes Field when the Pirates were out of town, and at
Griffith Stadium when the Senators traveled. During the club's twelve-year
tenure in the District, the Grays won nine straight Negro National League
(NNL) pennants and a pair of Colored World Series.[52]

The Grays got a boost during World War II, after one of their best
players was determined to be unfit for fighting. The American war effort had
snagged many of the era's best ballplayers. Ted Williams, Joe DiMaggio, and
Stan Musial left the Major Leagues, while Larry Doby, Connie Johnson, and
Buck O'Neil left the Negro Leagues. With many of its stars fighting overseas,
Major League Baseball dipped in popularity. The Negro Leagues, however,
prospered—partly because the leagues' two most famous players, Satchel
Paige of the Kansas City Monarchs and Josh Gibson of the Homestead
Grays, were both declared "4-F." Paige had flat feet, and Gibson creaky

knees. Washington's black fans, with more disposable income than ever because of increased employment opportunities in war-related industry, flocked to such venues as Griffith Stadium to see their heroes play. During the early years of World War II, Negro League franchises were bringing in revenues of more than $2 million a year, making them among the largest black-owned and -operated businesses in the country.[53]

Sadly, Griffith Stadium did not age well. By the 1950s, as the stadium entered into its fifth decade of consistent use, its edges began to fray. Players increasingly complained about the field. What had once been brushed off as the stadium's quirky peculiarities now fell into the category of serious failings. Bill DeWitt of the St. Louis Browns expressed what many had long thought when, in 1950, he called Griffith Stadium "one of the most run-down excuses for a ballpark in the majors."[54] Not even the end of the stadium's fifty-five-year ban on selling beer appealed to fans.[55] When it became clear that the proposed DC Stadium project would proceed, the Senators considered "exchanging a landlord's role at Griffith Stadium for a tenant status at the District Stadium."[56] The Redskins, who in 1944 had signed an exclusive lease to be the only professional football club using Griffith Stadium, were more blunt. They planned to bolt as soon as the new DC Stadium would have them.

The legacy of Griffith Stadium proved to be bittersweet. The venue had been the scene of the city's biggest sporting triumph, including the Senators' 1924 World Series victory. The stadium had also served the District's growing African American population. The city's "Black 400," the upper crust of Washington's black community, had frequented stadium events. Ballplayers like Josh Gibson and Satchel Paige had provided momentary relief from the hard edge of segregation, while sports journalists like Art Carter, who covered the Negro Leagues for the *Washington Afro-American*, pushed for racial integration in the sport.[57] The stadium's final years suggested that social progress was coming. In 1961, Howard University—a longtime beneficiary of Griffith Stadium's space—bought the facility from the Senators, who had left town to become the Minnesota Twins. In 1965, the stadium was razed, and Howard University built a hospital on the site. When big-time sports moved two and a half miles away to the newly constructed DC Stadium in the early 1960s, few Washingtonians looked back.

DC Stadium

The venue that replaced Griffith Stadium had not even opened its gates before it was co-opted in the fight against racial segregation. Because of the Stadium Act of 1957, the Department of the Interior had ultimate jurisdiction over the yet-to-be-built stadium. It mandated that no tenant of the newly constructed DC Memorial Stadium could employ segregationist practices. Since Washington Redskins owner George Preston Marshall signed only white players, the measure targeted the Redskins. It worked. In 1962, Marshall traded for future Hall of Famer Bobby Mitchell, an African American running back who starred for the Cleveland Browns. (The player Marshall traded was Ernie Davis, also an African American running back. Winner of the 1961 Heisman Trophy and the Redskins' number-one draft in 1962, Davis refused to play for Marshall.) Mitchell would play for Marshall's team that season, making the Redskins the last team in the National Football League (NFL) to integrate. In large part, the DC Memorial Stadium had effected the change.[58]

The idea of the DC Stadium was born in the 1930s. In 1945 Senator Theodore Bilbo of Mississippi pushed through an appropriations request for a "National Memorial Stadium Commission." The move came not only as the United States was experiencing the economic boom of wartime production, but also as the nation's leaders were beginning to ponder how best to honor those who served in Europe and the South Pacific. The Joint Resolution suggested organizing a commission "to consider a site and design for a National Memorial Stadium to be erected in the District of Columbia."[59]

Chairman of the Committee on the District of Columbia, Bilbo led the effort to build a national stadium in Washington. Building the venue was to be a project of the federal government, not unlike constructing the Washington Monument during the nineteenth century, or even the earlier commissioning of the L'Enfant plan. A staunch segregationist who argued for the disenfranchisement of African Americans in the District, Bilbo could have never envisioned that his project would be used in the struggle for civil rights. But he did recognize the need for a new stadium in the District. At a hearing in 1945, he added his voice to the growing chorus that was deriding Griffith Stadium. "Do you not have a stadium [in the city] already?" Bilbo was asked. "No," he replied. "We have no stadium. We have a little ball park owned by Mr. Griffith."[60]

Bilbo's commission reported back to Congress on November 1, 1945. It recommended that the stadium should be among the largest ever built. It also recommended that the facility be built near the DC Armory, on East Capitol Street in Southeast Washington, alongside the Anacostia River. The commission envisioned that the stadium would host a variety of events, from "Boy Scout jamborees" to "4H Club meetings" to "International Olympics." The commission also envisioned that different modes of transportation would bring spectators to the ballpark: automobiles and trains were to provide easy access, while a "landing strip for private planes" was to be used as well. In what would prove to be the most farfetched idea of all, the commission demanded that the stadium "be operated on a sound business" basis, and that all building loans be satisfied out of the first year's profits. The project was also to be exempted from all federal and local taxes.[61]

Bilbo never got his "behemoth" stadium.[62] Instead, a smaller venue was built. Plans for a scaled-down stadium were discussed as early as the mid-1950s, several years after Bilbo had died. The *Post* featured editorials that derided Bilbo's vision:

> We trust that the present effort will be more successful than that of the late Sen. Theodore G. Bilbo just after World War II. Mr. Bilbo, in his capacity of unofficial "mayor" as chairman of the Senate District Committee, campaigned for a 200,000 "all-weather" stadium roofed with aluminum supported by air pressure. Engineering advice that the roof would "take off like a kite" in a heavy wind, and the obvious impossibility of handling either the traffic or seating for such a crowd seemed not to dismay him.[63]

During the hearings on H.R. 1937, the House bill that would eventually become the DC Stadium Act of 1957, Congress attempted to secure assurances from both the Senators and the Redskins that they would play in the federally backed stadium. John Powell, representing the Senators, promised only that his club would consider switching venues. "I think you recognize, as does all of the world, that we have great problems at Griffith Stadium," Powell confessed. But he would not commit to the stadium. In contrast, George Preston Marshall of the Redskins expressed his full support for the project.[64]

The District of Columbia Stadium Act became law on September 7, 1957. It limited the cost of construction to $6 million, and it selected the East Capitol Street site, near the National Armory. The federal government was to cede the necessary property to a newly formed District of Columbia Armory Board. The board was then given the right to issue bonds for funding, with the payments on all debts to be satisfied on a monthly basis by using the operating revenues of the stadium.[65] A plan that had been discussed for more than twenty-five years had finally come to fruition.

Ground for the stadium was broken on July 8, 1960. It was a joyous ceremony. Obscured by the joy, however, was the fact that many Washingtonians had already started to complain about the stadium's cost, which had ballooned to nearly $20 million. Because the original bids lacked specific details, hundreds of changes to the original plans had had to be made, dramatically increasing the budget.[66] Perhaps more worrisome, the Redskins still remained the new stadium's only lined-up tenant. Even though Calvin Griffith, president of the Senators and the nephew of Clark Griffith, had attended the ceremony for the stadium, he remained tightlipped about his views of the facility. "I'm here because this stadium is a good thing for the city of Washington," Griffith said. Asked about the possibility of the Senators playing in the new stadium, he demurred, "I wouldn't even comment on that, at this time."[67]

The stadium opened in 1961. Despite the cost overruns, reactions from Washingtonians were generally positive. There were some minor complaints about the bathrooms and the slow installation of stadium seating. Even so, the *Washington Post* deemed the stadium "magnificent."[68] A wire story from United International Press (UPI) was not so kind. It criticized the price tag—an estimated $23 million—and the fact that there were no restrooms near the press box. The UPI story also pointed out that the sole team committed to playing in the sparkling new facility was still lousy. "The cynics are saying that puting [*sic*] the oft-beaten Redskins (they're [*sic*] lost 15 consecutive games) into such plush surroundings is like renting the Taj Mahal to a hobo convention."[69]

For Washington baseball fans, the timing worked out. After the Griffith-owned Senators left for Minnesota, an expansion franchise—also called the Senators—began play in the District in 1961. The new club played its initial season at Griffith Stadium, but moved over to the DC Stadium the next season, securing revenue for eighty dates each year. The Senators' home opener at DC Stadium caused an epic traffic jam, even by DC standards. President John F. Kennedy threw out the first pitch.[70]

Alas, the DC Stadium enjoyed only the briefest of honeymoons. Financial concerns dampened Washingtonians' enthusiasm. Because of the nearly $20 million sale in bonds, the Armory Board was saddled with an annual bill of $832,600 in interest alone. Revenues produced by the stadium did not even come close to covering the cost. As a result, the stadium's initial season produced a net operating loss of more than $600,000. For fiscal year 1963, when $179,632 in rental income was collected from the Redskins, and $83,226 from the Senators, losses topped $1 million.[71] The DC Armory Board suggested that the federal government make a hefty payment toward satisfying the debt or the city would have to raise taxes.[72]

What was supposed to be a boon to the District became a burden. According to some estimates, the Senators needed to increase their average attendance three-fold, just for the stadium to break even.[73] Making matters worse, rental and concession income declined, from $705,981 in 1963 to $390,314 in 1967.[74] Some Washingtonians wanted the Department of the Interior to take the property back.[75] Calls for federal intervention made sense. After all, it was Secretary of the Interior Stewart Udall who had told Marshall that the Redskins would have to integrate before the club could move into the new stadium. In addition, the federal government had always been intimately linked to the DC Stadium project. Senator Bilbo had created momentum for it, while other federal officials had lent their support.[76] Besides, it was unreasonable to assume that the stadium's dire financial situation could be solved by the District of Columbia alone.

There were also claims of graft. Critics argued that backroom deals and sweetheart contracts had led to many of the stadium's cost overruns. In 1964, Congress began investigating the matter. The hearings marked a new low point for the stadium. A handful of scandalous theories emerged: under-the-table payments had secured less-than-optimal bids; the secretary to the Senate Majority Leader had taken bribes; "party girls" and prostitutes may have been privy to government negotiations.[77] The hearings produced thousands of pages of documents and many titillating rumors. In the end, no legal charges were filed.

In 1966, the comptroller general of the United States issued a report on the stadium controversy. The report found that the stadium had been poorly planned, and that authorities had made ill-informed decisions, which drove up costs even more. The report also condemned 234 change orders that had been approved without consent of regulatory agencies so that an illegitimate deadline—the beginning of the Redskins' 1961 season—could be met. "The Redskins would have been able to lease Griffith Stadium for the 1961 football season," the report noted. "There was no apparent urgent need for the Board to agree to make the stadium available" earlier.[78]

By 1973, the District of Columbia Stadium, which was renamed the Robert F. Kennedy Memorial Stadium in 1969, was not producing enough revenue to pay even the tiniest of portions of the interest due on its debt. That the baseball Senators had left for Texas after the 1971 season did not help the situation. Even though the Redskins made it all the way to the Super Bowl in January 1973, the Armory Board claimed that it had almost no capital available to meet its obligations. As was outlined in the 1957 Stadium Act, any debts left unmet were to be relegated to the city. Frustration over the stadium's finances boiled over. The *Washington Post* in 1973 seethed: "Since the stadium was built, not a penny of the $19.8 million actually borrowed has been raised."[79] Ultimately, the federal government ended up having to pay off most of the debt. Once the debt was cleared, the federal government reclaimed the stadium.

The transfer, however, did not end the ownership odyssey of RFK Stadium. By the 1980s, the venue had become outdated and unwanted. Congress again held hearings to discuss its fate. House Resolution 6697, which was introduced in 1982, intended to give the stadium back to the District, which by then had assumed a greater level of "home rule." The hearings underscored one thing: RFK Stadium had failed. "The stadium never paid for itself," Senator William Gray declared at the hearings. "The city should own and operate the stadium."[80] Finally, in 1985, the transfer to the city went through. The District government now assumed "all right, title, and interest" of RFK Stadium.[81]

Twelve years later, RFK stadium lost its primary tenant—the Redskins. In fact, the team fled the District altogether, moving into a new stadium, FedEx Field, in suburban Maryland. Hoping to keep the team, authorities had proposed building a new stadium within the District limits. But there were some who wanted to make the construction of the stadium conditional upon the Redskins changing their name, which critics viewed as a slur against Native Americans. This time the Redskins would not be leveraged. After nearly a decade of negotiating, team ownership failed to reach an agreement with the District. A new stadium would not be built adjacent to RFK, as had been discussed, or elsewhere in the city. In 1997, the Redskins left RFK for FedEx Field in Landover, Maryland. The franchise kept its name.

The failures of the White Lot, Griffith Stadium, and RFK did not stop the District from building sports venues. Abe Pollin, owner of hockey's Capitals and basketball's Wizards, opened the Verizon Center (initially the MCI Center) in 1997, the same year RFK lost football. By all accounts the privately financed arena has revitalized the downtown area of Chinatown. The arena, instead of the futile teams that have played there, might be Pollins's most lasting legacy.[82]

Then, in 2005, baseball returned to the District. The move of the Montreal Expos to Washington hinged upon the city's promise to build a baseball-only stadium. This time the federal government had little say in the matter. Mayor Anthony Williams staked his administration's legacy on pushing the deal through. In 2008, a $600 million stadium called Nationals Park was built alongside the Anacostia River. Both the Verizon Center and Nationals Park are comfortable venues to watch a game. One can only hope that these new sporting venues will continue to serve Washingtonians better than the facilities that preceded them. It would seem that there is no place to go but up.

3

The Biggest "Classic" of Them All

The Howard and Lincoln Thanksgiving Day Football Games, 1919–29

David K. Wiggins

African Americans established a number of successful and important separate sports programs during the latter half of the nineteenth and first half of the twentieth centuries. Banned from most predominantly white organized sport during this period because of racial discrimination, African Americans organized their own teams and leagues behind walls of segregation at the amateur and professional levels, in small rural communities and large urban settings, and among both men and women of different social and economic backgrounds. Some of the most important of these separate sports programs were those established at historically black colleges and universities (HBCUs). Since the latter stages of the nineteenth century, HBCUs have competed at a relatively high level in football, basketball, and a number of other sports.[1]

The annual Thanksgiving Day football games played between well-known HBCUs drew a great deal of attention and much enthusiasm from African Americans. Arguably the most popular and significant of these games were those pitting Howard University and Lincoln University from 1919 to 1929. Described in 1922 by *Chicago Defender* sportswriter Frank Young as "the most important game in the country as far as we [African

Americans] are concerned," the Howard and Lincoln Thanksgiving Day matchups during the 1920s, a decade commonly termed the "golden age of American sport," garnered some attention in the white press, voluminous coverage in the black press, and attracted great interest among upper-class African Americans in Philadelphia, Washington, DC, and other black communities across the country.[2]

The Howard and Lincoln annual Thanksgiving Day football games, along with the accompanying social activities were, like the creation of black All-American teams and naming of mythical national champions, a way for two of the most prestigious HBCUs to exhibit a much-needed sense of racial pride and self-determination while at once measuring themselves against the standards of predominantly white university sport and its attendant rituals. The "classic" was also important in that it enhanced the already elevated prestige of Howard and Lincoln, which, in turn, contributed to intangible strategic advantages for two institutions that were becoming more entrepreneurial and commercialized. The games and their accompanying social activities, moreover, played an important role in the identity of upper-class African Americans in Philadelphia, Washington, DC, and other locales. For many African Americans, the "classic" was both a salve and a symbol of status, bringing them together while cordoning them off according to their respective social station. And things were in flux. Social changes, resulting from the northern migration of southern blacks during the early decades of the twentieth century, cast racial identity in a new light. With alternative modes of social advancement becoming possible in black communities, and toleration of whites toward upper-class African Americans being diminished because of the geographical expansion and more economically mobile pattern of the black population following the great migration, the "classic" was more than just a test to determine athlete superiority. It was "a social competition between the black populous of Washington, D.C. and Philadelphia" and a highly visible way to help keep African Americans of like kind together.[3]

The first football game between Howard and Lincoln took place in 1894 on Howard's campus in Washington, DC. Characteristic of the sport in the late nineteenth century, the game was a vicious and bloody affair. Lincoln's right tackle James Harper suffered a broken jaw after colliding with Howard's star halfback "Baby" Jones. This incident, along with several other unfortunate confrontations during Lincoln's 5–4 victory and following the game, including a Lincoln player having a pistol drawn on him by a white man on a Washington, DC, street, were so serious that the schools did not play each other again until 1904. The games played between 1904 and 1918 attracted relatively little fanfare. During this period, Lincoln won seven games, and Howard four; three games ended in 0–0 ties. No games were played between the two schools in 1906 and 1915.[4]

In 1919 the Howard and Lincoln Thanksgiving Day football game, which was played at National League Park in Philadelphia and ended in a 0–0 tie, was advertised and promoted as the "classic" and "greatest event of the season."[5] It would prove to be an apt descriptor as the game, which attracted a reported 10,000 mostly black fans, the usual composition of the crowds for these contests, was transformed into a grand social affair that combined the traditional gridiron battle between the two institutions with elaborately organized dances, visitor receptions, dinner parties, musical productions, breakfast socials, and alumni gatherings held over a frenetic three- to five-day period.[6]

In 1920 Howard crushed Lincoln, 42–0, in front of what was described as "the largest crowd regardless of race, that ever attended a football game in the capital city."[7] The Lincoln Lions, coached in the game by former Harvard University star Clarence Matthews and Paul Robeson, the great athlete, actor, singer, and civil rights activist, were completely outclassed by the Howard Bison at American League Park (renamed Griffith Stadium that year in honor of Washington Senators owner Clark Griffith) in Washington. Matthews and Robeson were brought in as replacements for Fritz Pollard, the former Brown University All-American running back who had spent the last two years splitting time as head coach of Lincoln and playing professionally with the Akron Pros. Opting to stay in Ohio to play for his professional team rather than returning to coach the Lions effectively ended Pollard's controversial tenure at Lincoln. Officials of the school, who had become increasingly upset with Pollard's absence from practices and games, decided to part ways with him following the 1920 season.[8]

The "classic" produced a far different outcome in 1921, the Lions defeating the Bison, 13–7, at the National Baseball Park in Philadelphia. Approximately 10,000 rain-soaked spectators attended the game. Lincoln's victory was due in large part to the outstanding coaching of John A. Shelbourne, former Dartmouth star,[9] and to captain James Law, who played the "greatest game of his career." Law threw for one touchdown and made several other crucial plays in a game where all "the players were plastered with mud and their features rendered unrecognizable by the brown ooze."[10]

In 1922, at the American League Park in Washington, Lincoln squeaked by Howard, 13–12. The star of the game was Franz "Jazz" Byrd, the speedy and elusive running back considered by many to be the greatest player in Lincoln history. Among Byrd's many great plays at American League Park that day was a seventy-yard run for a touchdown.[11] The 1922 game was the first "classic" to be covered by a rain insurance policy. A year later, Howard and Lincoln battled to a 6–6 tie in front of approximately 16,000 spectators in Philadelphia. In a game marred by a highly publicized but unsubstantiated ticket scandal in which receipts supposedly came up some $10,000 short, "Jazz" Byrd dazzled fans with an eighty-yard kick-off return that set up his one-yard plunge for a touchdown three plays later. Howard matched the touchdown, but, like Lincoln, missed the extra point. The *Chicago Defender* reported that "the great and only Charles P. McClane, manager of the Royal (referred to as 'America's Finest Colored Photoplay House') and Olympic Theaters and President of the Universal Advertising Company in Philadelphia" planned to film the "full game in action and close-ups of the grandstand and box parties."[12]

In 1924, a reported crowd of 27,000 at the American League Park in Washington watched Lincoln humiliate Howard, 31–0, in perhaps the most ballyhooed of all the "classics." Lincoln was once again led by "Jazz" Byrd, dubbed by the black press as the "black Grange of football," a reference to Red Grange of the University of Illinois, white college football's boy wonder.[13] Sportswriters were rarely at a loss for words describing Byrd's exploits. "Like a drop of mercury, Howard men put their fingers on Byrd only to find out he had slipped to one side," wrote the *Baltimore Afro-American*, in its coverage of Lincoln's 1924 victory. "He sidestepped, dodged, skipped, jumped and twisted from the grasp of eleven men as if they never existed."[14]

The drubbing of Howard was the least of the great black institution's worries. Prior to the 1924 contest, Lincoln threatened to cancel its game against Howard unless the Washington, DC, school kept one of its players, Robert Miller, out of the game since Miller had not sat out a year stipulated by Central Intercollegiate Athletic Association (CIAA) guidelines following his transfer from Virginia Union the previous season. Part of a national discussion regarding eligibility requirements, professionalism, and increasing number of "tramp athletes," Howard balked at keeping Miller out of the game, but eventually acquiesced to Lincoln's demand, all the while claiming it had done nothing wrong. The depth of Howard's anger over the Miller affair was so strong that its Board of Athletic Control, chaired by Dr. Edward P. Davis, unanimously voted to withdraw from the CIAA.[15]

The 1925 game was held at Philadelphia's Shibe Park. In front of a reported 16,000 fans, Lincoln and Howard tied, 0–0. Despite its success, the "classic" was marred again by controversy. In a strange and ironic turn of events, Lincoln was expelled from the CIAA sometime before the contest having disobeyed the conference's wishes to cancel the "classic" because

Howard was no longer a CIAA member.[16] Lincoln would be reinstated two years later, but not before incurring the wrath of other CIAA schools, because the Lions had refused to discontinue the series against Howard and thereby seemed to condone the use of ineligible players. Reluctant to sever ties with its archrival because of the money it would have lost, Lincoln in truth was convinced Howard played "tramp" athletes. Many "Lincoln alumni" noted that Howard "would have used Red Grange if he were black."[17]

In 1926, with approximately 10,000 spectators on hand in the new Howard University Stadium, the home team demolished the visitors, 32–0. The game's star was Howard quarterback Jack Coles, who repeatedly weaved his way through the Lincoln line for huge gains.[18] Much was made of the new stadium, with an elaborate dedication ceremony held prior to the game. With first-year president Mordecai Johnson presiding, the celebration began with a speech by Representative Martin B. Madden of Illinois, chairman of the House Appropriations Committee. Madden's committee had approved the $301,000 needed for the building of the new Howard stadium and gymnasium-armory project. Madden used the occasion to talk about the "progress of the negro in America and the contribution of Howard University to his advancement." Following Madden at the podium was Dr. Emmett J. Scott, Howard's secretary-treasurer and business manager, who was presented a plaque "in appreciation of his efforts to give to Howard University a larger program of athletics, health, and recreational activities." Albert Cassell, university architect, spoke next, followed by Howard football coach Louis Watson.[19]

An indication of the importance of the 1926 game was the elaborate program published to commemorate it. Although all the programs for the "classic" were detailed and lengthy, perhaps none included as many images, specific information about the two institutions, and number of advertisements as the one from 1926. With a cover depicting both a male and female student from Howard sitting in the grandstand cheering on their team, the forty-six-page program included photographs of President Johnson and Secretary-Treasurer Scott; listings of the various social activities accompanying the game; rosters and pictures of the coaches, support staffs, and players representing the two institutions; and a wide assortment of ads from Nail and Parker Real Estate in New York City to the Pryor Press in Chicago to the Capital Awning Company in Washington, DC, to the law offices of Raymond Pace Alexander in Philadelphia. The program also included a layout and directions to the new stadium, the "songs and yells" for Howard, alma maters of both schools, and a historical assessment of the "classic."[20]

In 1927, Howard, with one of its strongest and deepest teams, defeated Lincoln, 20–0, at Philadelphia's Shibe Park in front of an announced 15,000 spectators. The game followed by almost two months a temporary strike by the Howard football team, which protested the decision of President Johnson to eliminate athletic scholarships and the customary free training table and living quarters provided to players during the football season. Extending some of the policies of his predecessor, Stanley Durkee, who was forced to resign after confrontations with professors and alumni over the direction of the university, Johnson strove to improve the academic reputation of the school while also de-emphasizing highly competitive athletics in favor of a more expansive exercise and physical activity program for the largest majority of students on campus.[21]

In 1928 Howard again beat Lincoln, 12–0, much to the pleasure of some 10,000 spectators at Howard Stadium. The Howard team received an added boost from the expertise of coach Charles West, the former Washington and Jefferson College football and track star who had taken over for Louis Watson after Watson failed to reach a contract extension with President Johnson—a falling-out perhaps caused by Watson's support of the players' strike from the year before. Similar to the previously mentioned Clarence Matthews, Paul Robeson, John Shelbourne, and a host of other outstanding African American athletes who competed at predominantly white institutions but who could not coach at those same institutions, West helped support himself by coaching the team while attending Howard's medical school.[22]

In 1929, the final year of the "classic," Howard and Lincoln played, just as they had ten years earlier, to a 0–0 tie. Approximately 10,000 spectators attended the game, which was held at Municipal Stadium in Philadelphia. The Howard faithful were disappointed in the performance of the Bison team, claiming that the football program in particular and the athletic program more generally had deteriorated significantly since the "classic" began a decade earlier. Ralph Matthews, writing in the *Baltimore Afro-American* in 1938, contended that the downfall of the Howard football program was partly attributable, ironically enough, to the new stadium built on campus in 1926. Obviously pining for the days when the game was played at the American League Park, Matthews wrote:

> The circus-like bleachers, the absences of boxes, the lack of a foyer, where women could show off their new styles, where old grads could prove how successful they had become, the inability to move about and mingle with old friends and acquaintances, removed the most important elements from the classic. Without these opportunities it was just

another football game. And who in the old days really paid any attention to the game?[23]

Much of the blame for the faltering football and athletic program at Howard was laid at the feet of President Johnson for abolishing athletic scholarships, limiting players' access to the training table, and reducing their board and lodging privileges.[24] For many observers, Johnson's handling of the school's athletic program was a result of his efforts to adhere to the recommendations provided in the famous 1929 report by the Carnegie Foundation for the Advancement of Teaching. Originally titled "American College Athletics," the report was a condemnation of the increasing commercialization of college sport and its attendant professionalism and corruption.[25] In truth, Johnson, who was no doubt influenced by the Carnegie Foundation report, was being criticized by football-loving fans for trying to bring some sanity and more balance to the school's athletic program while at once elevating the academic integrity of the institution. B. S. Baskerville, a 1926 alumnus of Howard, summed up the feelings of many of the school's avid supporters of football when he wrote in the *New York Amsterdam News* of 1927 that

> President Johnson alone is to be blamed for the miserable football team that represents Howard University this year. He cut out the training table a couple of years ago because he feared the survey being made by the Carnegie Foundation. Then he began to ballyhoo clean sportsmanship in order to justify his act. I believe, however, that he was sincere in what he did, but sincerity or no sincerity, the effect is just the same. The miserable showing of his mediocre team has created a spirit of sullen indifference among the students and of sour indignation among the alumni.[26]

As evident from the comments by B. S. Baskerville, the end of the "classic" was difficult to bear for the alumni and other followers of the Howard and Lincoln Thanksgiving Day game. Ending the "classic" was hard to take because for the previous ten years it had been so important and meaningful to African Americans in Washington, Philadelphia, and much of the eastern portion of the United States. How did it come about? Who was responsible for the "classic" and what significance did it hold for African Americans?

The "father" of the Thanksgiving Day football "classic," according to former president and historian of Lincoln, Horace Mann Bond, was Dr. Charles A. Lewis, a 1905 graduate of Lincoln and medical doctor from Philadelphia by way of the University of Pennsylvania. A lifelong supporter of all things Lincoln who regularly traveled with the team and sat on the bench tending to injured players, Lewis realized the monetary and intangible strategic advantages that could potentially result from a more highly publicized and commercialized football contest between his beloved alma mater and Howard.[27] And the time was right for such a series of contests: northern blacks were experiencing an increasing number of southern blacks making their way north; a relatively higher standard of living was becoming a reality for many blacks in northern cities; and a consumer culture and national obsession with sport were in their early stages—and destined to become much larger.[28]

Emmett J. Scott was highly supportive of Lewis's idea and perhaps the man most actively involved in marketing "the classic" and its ultimate success. A native of Houston, and former editor of the city's black newspaper, the *Texas Freeman*, Scott had been a close friend, advisor, and private secretary to Booker T. Washington and the man in charge of the "Tuskegee Machine," an elaborate system in which Washington controlled and manipulated African American leaders and the press.[29]

These experiences would bode well for Scott as he set about promoting the "classic." Encouraged by the success of the first designated "classic" between Howard and Lincoln in 1919, Scott took much of what he had learned while working for the *Texas Freeman* and while at Tuskegee to ensure that the following year's game in Washington, and subsequent contests between the two institutions, were just as successful and generated the same amount of attention and publicity from the African American community. Just as he strove to improve the academic programs and bring financial stability to Howard, Scott worked tirelessly, called in favors from old friends, and utilized his professional contacts in an effort to provide as much publicity as possible for the annual Thanksgiving Day football "classic" between his institution and Lincoln. He was successful in his efforts, making the public aware of the contest—with the notable assistance of Dr. Charles A. Lewis and Dr. W. G. Alexander, Lincoln's graduate manager of athletics—through public announcements and press releases and other media initiatives.[30] "Everyone present realized the tremendous possibilities of the game," wrote the *Chicago Defender* in 1929, recalling the first classic played ten years earlier. "It remained, however, for the business sagacity of Dr. Emmett J. Scott, secretary-treasurer of Howard University, to perfect the details whereby the occasion might be financially profitable to both institutions as well as occasions worthy to be recorded in the annals of our history."[31]

What Scott helped to create was a recurring athletic and social ritual that allowed Howard and Lincoln to exhibit important feelings of self-pride and determination while at the same time comparing themselves against the standards of white college sport. Like the East-West All-Star Game in black baseball that had its beginnings in 1933 and any number of other sporting events organized behind walls of segregation, the Howard and Lincoln Thanksgiving Day football games between 1919 and 1929 attested to the strength and vibrancy of the two institutions and the African American community more generally, while also providing an opportunity to measure themselves against the more nationally known and famous football contests between predominantly white institutions. Tellingly, the comparisons made were not with just any predominantly white institutions, but typically with one or more of the Big Three universities: Harvard, Yale, and Princeton. Although beginning to be challenged for football superiority by other institutions across the country, Harvard, Yale, and Princeton still represented the very best in higher education and college football, and the black press was quick to point out the relative merits of the "classic" and by extension the quality of Howard and Lincoln as institutions in comparison to the Big Three.[32] "Dr. Scott has perfected arrangements to such a degree," noted the *Chicago Defender* of 1928, "that the classic takes first place in the games of our schools and to our people it is the Yale-Harvard game of our group."[33] "The football classic of the year is the title justly ascribed to the annual game between Howard and Lincoln Universities," wrote the *Philadelphia Tribune* in 1928. "The importance attached to the game has been likened to the annual classics between Yale and Harvard, Cornell and Penn or Princeton and Yale."[34]

Such heady comparisons could be more readily achieved if the annual Thanksgiving Day black "classic" was hyped, helping create a much-talked-about rivalry. Black weeklies heightened interest by filling a voluminous amount of column space that preceded each of the contests and then followed with additional coverage once the games had been played. Commentators particularly devoted much energy in detailing the rich history and traditions of the "classic." They made clear that each upcoming "classic" was going to be more spectacular, colorful, and exciting than the one preceding it. "Two years ago," wrote the *Chicago Defender* in 1921, "when the Lincoln management announced that the annual football game between the two ancient rivals, Howard and Lincoln, would be held in Philadelphia at the big National League Park, the pessimists began to shout 'this will be nothing less than athletic suicide,' but the move was without a doubt the most popular venture ever attempted in this country. It was the greatest athletic and social success that has ever been witnessed."[35] "With only seven days intervening, much interest in the annual Turkey Day clash involving the Lincoln and Howard game is being exhibited in Philadelphia and adjacent regions," wrote the *Philadelphia Tribune* in 1928. "As a spectacle and a colorful event little doubt exists that this year's game will rival and perhaps excel in splendor and grandeur those of the past."[36]

Representatives from Howard and Lincoln welcomed the build-up because it added to an already burgeoning rivalry. A rivalry—especially an intense rivalry—these representatives understood, enhanced their respective institutional interests and ensured that the African American community would more closely identify with them and their various constituents. The intense rivalry between the two institutions was born out of the same requisite qualifications for all rivalries; namely, similarities, differences, and contrasts.[37] While Howard and Lincoln were two of the most prestigious HBCUs and both in the business of educating the African American community's "talented tenth" and fielding strong athletic teams, they had different histories, different geographical settings, different student enrollments, different philosophies, and different academic specializations. White Presbyterian minister John Miller Dickey founded Lincoln University, located in the small town of Oxford in Chester County, Pennsylvania, in 1854. During the 1920s it charged $110 in tuition, which was one of the highest of any HBCU in the country. It had a white president, sixteen white faculty, and an all-black male enrollment that by 1927 had reached only 305. The university offered a four-year bachelor of arts degree in liberal arts, a three-year bachelor of sacred theology degree, and a three-year diploma in theology. A committee made up of faculty, alumni, and students administered all athletic activities.[38]

Howard University was founded in 1866 in Washington, DC, and named after General Oliver Otis Howard, a philanthropist and commissioner of the Freedmen's Bureau. Although a privately controlled institution, Howard since 1879 has received a subsidy from the federal government for both maintenance and capital outlay. It hired its first African American president, Mordecai Johnson, in 1926, employed 171 faculty members (the majority of whom were black), and had a coed enrollment that by 1927 had reached 2,118 students representing thirty-six states and ten foreign countries. The athletic program was governed by a board of athletic control, consisting of faculty, alumni, the secretary-treasurer (Emmett J. Scott), and the director of physical education.[39]

The differences between the two institutions were symbolically displayed on the football field and through distinctive songs, colors, ceremonies, rituals, and logos each Thanksgiving Day during the 1920s. These activities did not simply mimic those that took place in white college sport and in the white sporting world more generally. Students, alumni, and other followers of the "classic" refashioned these activities, like so many other things during this era of the "new negro," in a style and manner that reflected the black experience in Philadelphia and Washington, as well as that of Howard and Lincoln. A ritual of the Lincoln alumnus was to march en masse to the game, which was recorded in the *Chicago Defender* of 1922: "The Lincoln Alumni will hold a get together meeting tonight. Tomorrow morning, headed by a 60 piece band, the alumni headed by Drs. Cannon and Alexander of New Jersey, Prof. Saunders of West Virginia, with their pet lion cub sent from Liberia by the United States minister, an alumnus of Lincoln, will head for the park from the Whitelaw hotel, bedecked in Lincoln's colors, singing their 'Alma Mater' as they go. All Lincoln adherents will follow in the line."[40]

An example of a representative song from the game was recorded in an undated issue of the *Lincoln News*:

Howard has a quarterback,
Who thinks he's mighty cute;
But when he hits the Lincoln line,
He'll do the loop the loop.

He'll ramble off the tackle,
Ramble around the end,
Ramble through the center,
Then ramble back again.

Chorus:
He'll ramble, ramble, ramble all around,
Hey! In and out the town.
Oh! ramble, ramble, ramble 'til ole Lincoln cuts him down.[41]

One of the most original and regular features of the "classic" were the "rabbles," a pregame, halftime, or improvisational dance in which students climbed out of the stands and marched around the field carrying their own musical instruments and singing songs praising their own institutions and denigrating their opponents. The *Howard University Record* of 1921 reported on the "rabble" that took place at halftime of that year's game between Howard and Lincoln: "The ending of the first half was the cue for 'rabble' exhibitions. The rabbles of both schools pounced upon the field in spite of its mud-soaked conditions and the continuous rain. The 'blue and white' rabble headed by its band, executed a wild snake dance while the Lincoln horde did its serpentine dance."[42] One example of a rabble yell appeared in the 1926 game program. Titled "Nine Rahs Yell," the shout had the Howard faithful perform a call-and-response cheer:

Rah, Rah, Rah,
Rah, Rah, Rah,
Rah, Rah, Rah,
Team! Team! Team!
Leader—Who?
Rabble—Team!
Leader—Who?
Rabble—Team!
Leader—Who?
Rabble—Team! Team! Team![43]

Historian Patrick Miller, in his oft-cited essay, "To 'Bring the Race Along Rapidly': Sport, Student Culture, and Educational Mission at Historically Black Colleges During the Interwar Years," initially brought attention to the "rabbles," citing the above-mentioned quote from the 1921 *Howard University Record*.[44] Historian Michael Oriard elaborates further on the "rabbles" in *King Football*. Using the work of William Pierson on "African American Festive Style" and referencing accounts of the Howard and Lincoln games of the 1920s from the *Chicago Defender* and the *Baltimore Afro-American*, Oriard makes the point that "rabbles" were representative of "Black Expressive Culture" in that they emphasized improvisation, spontaneity, and the close interplay between performers and spectators. The "rabbles," like various types of dances, funeral processions, and celebrations in the African American South (including different activities in the slave-quarter community, it should be added) can also be seen as a way to satirize the "more formal celebrations" of the ruling class in the country, in this case the "precision marching bands of the big-time football universities." Quoting Pierson, Oriard notes, moreover, "that the marching bands at historically black institutions in the 1990s still retained a 'cake-walking heroic (and comedic) quality' very different from the style at say, the University of Michigan or Ohio State."[45]

Additionally, the annual "classic" was just as much, in the words of sport historian Raymond Schmidt, "the centerpiece of a social competition between the black populace of Washington, D.C. and Philadelphia" as it was a football rivalry between Howard and Lincoln.[46] Washington, DC, referred to by historian Willard B. Gatewood as the "capital of the colored aristocracy," was a segregated southern city with a black population that had reached more than 132,000 by 1930.[47] Among this population was a

Halftime of the 1922 Howard-Lincoln game. Students and fans celebrate on the field at American League Park in DC performing the "rabbles." Sport: 25, Moorland-Spingarn Research Center, Howard University Archives, Howard University.

relatively large and influential black elite made up of civil servants, schoolteachers, college professors, lawyers, and doctors who had made their way to Washington, DC, to take advantage of the jobs available with the federal government and because of the superb educational opportunities provided by Howard. Though Seventh Street housed important business and entertainment establishments and was the center of social life for the black masses, the U Street corridor harbored the very best in Washington's African American community. Sometimes referred to as the "Black Broadway" and with many famous African Americans living within its confines, the U Street corridor included, in addition to Howard University and Griffith Stadium, such landmarks as the Howard Theatre, M Street School, True Reformer Hall, Lincoln Theatre, Meridian Hill, Café De Luxe, and Freedmen's Hospital.[48]

Philadelphia had a black population of more than 219,000 by 1930, which ranked it third behind only New York City and Chicago. Unlike African Americans in Washington, who were largely confined to limited segregated areas, African Americans in Philadelphia lived in several large integrated districts in the north, south, and western parts of the city. Perhaps the most wealthy and prestigious integrated neighborhood in Philadelphia during the 1920s was located west of Fifty-Third Street and north of Market

Street in an area now known as Haddington. Black Philadelphians, both alumni and those who were not, adopted Lincoln University as their own. Located some forty-five miles from Philadelphia, Lincoln became the hometown college team for the city.[49]

Each year of the "classic," the black upper crust in the host city vied for social supremacy by staging elaborate dances, parties, receptions, and other affairs. Chartered trains would bring the very best of black America to Washington and Philadelphia to watch the game and to participate in the many accompanying social activities. For upper-class blacks of both cities, prestige was at stake as well as bragging rites and reputations. Those who arrived in Philadelphia or Washington to attend the "classic" were some of this country's most prominent African Americans. The game and social activities that complemented it attracted distinguished African Americans from the worlds of education, business, medicine, politics, entertainment, and a host of other professions. The society pages of all the major black newspapers regularly listed, in addition to notable faculty and administrators from both institutions and local dignitaries, the elite African Americans from out of town who attended the "classic." Among the many prominent African Americans listed as having attended one or more of the Howard and Lincoln games were William Henry Lewis, United States assistant attorney general; Walter White, civil rights activist and future leader of the National Association for the Advancement of Colored People (NAACP); authors James Weldon Johnson and Mary McLeod Bethune; Henry Binga Dismond, noted Harlem physician; Robert Abbott, founder of the *Chicago Defender*; and E. C. Brown, banker and owner of the largest black realty corporation in New York City.[50]

William H. Jones, in his 1927 study *Recreation and Amusement Among Negroes in Washington, D.C.: A Sociological Analysis of the Negro in an Urban Environment*, wrote that the annual Thanksgiving football game between Howard and Lincoln "has given to the negro life of Washington a prestige among other cities and a magnetic influence over vicinal districts which no other field of negro life in the capital can approximate. Every day for approximately a week scores of important social affairs are held. These consist of breakfast, matinee and evening dances, poker games, bridge parties, slumming, cabaret parties, and numerous other entertainments."[51] "The visitor within our gates," noted the *Philadelphia Tribune* in 1929:

> will evidently go home wondering who was the person that invented the saying "Philadelphia is a slow town," for with the Chi Delta Mu dance on Wednesday night, the breakfast and dance given [by] Mrs. George Deane and Mrs. Hobson Reynolds on Thursday morning, the

game, cocktail parties, followed by dinner and the Japelmas dance on Thursday night, not to mention the Frogs and innumerable "official dances," the matrons matinee dance on Friday afternoon, the second annual supper dance of the cosmopolitan club which distinguished itself last season by giving the finest affair of the year on Friday night, a matinee dance given by the Frogs on Saturday when Mrs. Lawrence Christmas and Mrs. Julian Abele will also give a dance in the afternoon for their friends and visitors followed by several parties on that night there will be, very little sleeping. For while dances are over at 2 o'clock, one immediately transports himself to somebody else's home or his own home where the merriment goes right on.[52]

Writing in the *Chicago Defender* in 1924, a busy Frank A. Young provided a detailed account of the variety of social affairs accompanying the "classic" that year in Washington, DC. "[I] have a minute or two to get a tabulated list together before I beat it to the nearest telegraph station," Young penned. "Here it goes."

List of Events

Wednesday evening, Nov. 26
5:30—Reception to the press, Howard university.
8:00—Grand reunion reception. Howard university dining hall.
8:00—Student demonstration, Lincoln Colonnade.
9:00—Chi Delta Mu Frat dance, Murray Casino.

Thursday morning, Nov. 27
Thanksgiving Day
9:00 to 11:30—Arrival of special trains from New York, Philadelphia, Baltimore, Atlantic City and the South.
9:00—Breakfast promenade, Lincoln Colonnade.
9:00—The Ambassadors' dance, Murray Casino.
11:00—Meeting of executive council, Howard university alumni.

Thursday afternoon
1:30—Awarding varsity letter "H" to veteran football players.
2:00—The football classic of the year—Howard university vs. Lincoln university.
4:00—Matinee dance, Murray Casino.

Thursday evening
Allied Collegiate Dance, Convention hall, with Ford Dabney's Zeigfeld Frolic orchestra of New York. Grand reunion reception, Howard university (this event is backed by the committees representing both Howard and Lincoln universities and is the official event of the evening).

Friday morning, Nov. 28
10:00—Breakfast dance, Murray Casino.
Friday afternoon
3:00—Interfraternity dance, Armstrong high.
Friday evening
8:00—Alpha Phi Alpha reception, Murray Casino.
Omega Psi Phi fraternity dance, Lincoln Colonnade.[53]

The competition between Howard and Lincoln, as well as that between Washington and Philadelphia, should not blind us to the fact that the "classic" was more than just one large party. Like present-day golf outings for corporate executives, the time before, during, and after the games were opportunities for representatives from the two schools, members of the black press, and other prominent African Americans to conduct business and establish connections that could prove beneficial to their professional success. In addition, the "classic" played a supportive role in both the coalescence of the campus communities at each institution and upper-class blacks more generally during the early decades of the twentieth century, when many poorer southern blacks migrated to northern cities. The annual Thanksgiving Day contests between Howard and Lincoln, while important in bringing additional monies into institutional coffers, were particularly significant because they provided occasions for fostering school spirit and helped bind students, alumni, and to a much lesser extent faculty, closer together on both campuses. The *Howard University Record* of 1921 provided its assessment of the significance of the "classic" when it wrote that the game served not only "to dispel any doubt that may have previously existed as to the high place of football as the most popular sport among American college and university students, but also showed that such contests are the best means of indicating the true coefficient of college alumni loyalty. . . . On no other occasion probably do all unite with one mind, one heart and one voice. The whole college gives a striking instance of group psychology and thousands of students act as one man in urging their struggling heroes on to victory."[54]

The need to unite the campuses of each institution was perhaps never so important than during the decade of the 1920s. Although able to maintain their prestige and national reputations, Howard and Lincoln both experienced well-known internal dissension and turmoil during this crucial ten-year period. As Raymond Wolters writes in *The New Negro on Campus: Black College Rebellions of the 1920s* (1975), Lincoln experienced its share of internal dissension during the decade, particularly concerning its all-white faculty and administration. Influential and angry alumni, including the likes of Langston Hughes and Frances Grimke, made concerted efforts to ensure that African Americans were added to the faculty and the board of trustees and also fought to have more voice in all decisions pertaining to the operation of the university. The situation was so bad that on three separate occasions presidents-elect ultimately decided to turn down offers to lead the university when determining that life would be made miserable for them because of the disgruntlement of alumni who believed they had not been adequately consulted on the new hires.[55]

Life on the Howard campus was not much better and, in some cases, perhaps even worse. For much of the decade, white president Stanley Durkee faced bitter opposition from students, faculty, and alumni who questioned his leadership and the direction in which he was taking the university. Carter G. Woodson, the "father of black history," and Kelly Miller, the distinguished professor of sociology and dean of the College of Arts and Sciences, were just two of the Howard faculty who wrote scathing denouncements of Durkee and bitterly opposed his presidency. In 1925, 1,200 Howard students went on strike in protest over president Durkee's decision to expel anyone who missed a minimum number of courses in ROTC. Two years later, the football team, as previously mentioned, went on strike after President Mordecai Johnson, who would serve the university in that capacity from 1926 until 1960, abolished the football training table and severely reduced the athletic budget. Students walked out of their classrooms to show support for the players, and the Thanksgiving Day game with Lincoln was canceled until Johnson persuaded the strikers to give him more time while he considered their demands.[56]

The annual Thanksgiving Day games between Howard and Lincoln were important not only for fostering school spirit and binding the campuses of each institution together, but also for assisting in uniting upperclass African Americans during the social disruption brought about by the northern migration of southern African Americans during the post–World War I period. Upper-class African Americans were being challenged for their special place in society as the great migration came into existence and as alternative modes of social advancement became possible within the black community. In addition, white America's toleration of upper-class African Americans rapidly diminished as the larger African American population became more geographically and economically mobile.[57]

The Howard and Lincoln Thanksgiving Day football "classic," while drifting toward tribal display and exclusivity and a social competition between upper-class African Americans of Washington, Philadelphia, and other parts of the East and Midwest, also helped to keep these same African Americans together. This is evident in the recurrent descriptions of the succession of parties, dances, and other social gatherings that accompanied the games. These descriptions make clear that the annual contests between the two famous institutions was to a great extent about upper-class African Americans reaffirming their special place in society, distancing themselves from lower-class blacks—whom they blamed for the rising tide of racism—and creating an occasion to join with those of similar thoughts and values and mutuality of interest in sports and other social and cultural rituals. "The 1919 game between Howard and Lincoln was augmented," noted the *Philadelphia Tribune*, "by the presence of thousands of fashionable and ultrafashionable visitors from Washington, Baltimore, New York, Atlantic City, and other neighboring cities, the latter coming in several days ahead in order to secure the choicest hotel and private accommodations and to participate in the numerous festivities and social functions preceding the open football classic in the afternoon of turkey day."[58] "It will be the eighteenth meeting of the two elevens," wrote Frank A. Young of the *Chicago Defender* before the 1922 game in Washington. "Every incoming train brings its quota. The vanguard of the hosts who will watch tomorrow's struggle are busy renewing acquaintances. The 'Flapper Special' from New York City is due in early in the morning as is a special from Pittsburgh and one from Philadelphia and early morning trains will bring the balance who will help to make up the gayest throng that ever witnessed a football game anywhere and the largest that has ever witnessed a struggle between any two institutions representing our people."[59]

Unfortunately, by 1929 the "classic" had lost much of its luster, though many fans and university leaders continued to believe that the Thanksgiving Day game was still the highlight of black football and would continue to garner national attention. In 1931, for instance, the *Lincoln News* announced, "Thanksgiving brings us down to that classic of Negro football, the Howard-Lincoln game. Other schools advertise their games as classics but this one is not only advertised, but is, the classic of classics."[60] Notwithstanding this pronouncement, the overwhelming evidence makes clear that by 1929 the games generated far less media coverage, experienced a decrease in attendance, and was devoid of much of the great gridiron talent that had marked the previous nine contests between the two institutions. The weakening financial condition of Howard and Lincoln's football programs specifically, and of their athletic programs more generally, contributed to this state of affairs. Though the two schools would continue to play each other regularly until Lincoln dropped football after the 1960 season, the Howard-Lincoln game would never be as popular or meaningful as it was during the 1920s. In its heyday, the "classic" was an athletic and social event that provided upper-class African Americans the opportunity to exhibit racial pride, measure themselves against the standards of white universities, and come together as a distinct group. In the process, African Americans reaffirmed their place in a country that had undergone unprecedented geographical and economic changes wrought by the northern migration of southern blacks. To African Americans, the Howard and Lincoln Thanksgiving Day football "classic" during the second decade of the twentieth century was just as important as the annual games between Harvard and Yale and any number of other famous gridiron contests between predominantly white institutions. Maybe more so.

Epilogue

On September 10, 2011, Howard University and Morehouse College played each other in what was billed as the "First Annual AT&T Nation's Football Classic" at RFK Stadium. Rekindling a rivalry that had been scrapped some fifteen years earlier, the game was advertised in the *Washington Post* in much the same way the black press advertised the Howard and Lincoln Thanksgiving Day games between 1919 and 1929.[61] The *Post* suggested that the game could potentially provide a financial boost to both institutions, would contribute to a sense of kinship and camaraderie among the students, friends, and faculty from both institutions, and furnish these same individuals an opportunity to watch outstanding football and enjoy the marching bands that "compete with a unique flair."[62] The game was supplemented with many parties, joint fundraiser dances, a student debate, and an assortment of other social gatherings. To some, the game between Howard University and Morehouse College was less about football and more about the accompanying social activities and the opportunity for alumni to "join students to backslap and trash-talk, holler and rally in maroon and white or blue and red on the campus of Howard University and the streets of Washington."[63]

There appear to be many similarities in the descriptions of the Howard University and Morehouse College AT&T Nation's Football Classic with that of the Thanksgiving Day football games between Howard and Lincoln during the 1919 to 1929 period. In actuality, however, because of the strict racial segregation in this country during the 1920s, the Howard and Lincoln Thanksgiving Day "Classic" was decidedly different in regard to organization and probably far more meaningful and culturally significant to the African American community. With only a very select number of African American athletes able to participate in predominantly white college sport during this period, the Howard and Lincoln Thanksgiving Day games included extraordinarily gifted athletes whose names today would undoubtedly dot the rosters of Division I football powers. But because they participated behind the walls of racial segregation, the Howard and Lincoln games received little coverage in the white press and no sponsorship from major corporations. Finally, with the hopes of highlighting their athletic accomplishments and by extension their sense of black pride and ability for self-organization and independent business acumen, the Howard and Lincoln Thanksgiving Day Football "Classic" was particularly significant in that it was part of a burgeoning black national sporting culture that would eventually include other well-known Thanksgiving Day games between other HBCUs and such events and organizations as the East-West All-Star Game, Gold and Glory Sweepstakes, American Tennis Association, National Negro Bowling Association, and Interscholastic Athletic Association Basketball Tournament. This black national sporting culture, which was fueled by a consumer culture that was a boon to the growth of sport more generally in the United States, brought African Americans from across the country a great deal of pleasure and sense of satisfaction and accomplishment that was not easy to come by during the era prior to integration.

4

Teeing Off against Jim Crow

Black Golf and Its Early Development in Washington, DC

Marvin P. Dawkins and
Jomills Henry Braddock II

The introduction of golf to America's socially elite and the game's rapid growth in the United States at the turn of the twentieth century have been well documented.[1] Although much of golf's early development was concentrated in and around such cities as Boston, New York, Philadelphia, and Chicago, the nation's capital also became a focal point for the sport because of its popularity with a handful of sitting presidents. William Howard Taft, who began playing as vice president under Teddy Roosevelt, was the first president to take up the game after he assumed office in 1909. The growth of golf in the District can be largely attributed to him. According to golf historian Richard Moss, Taft urged "the creation of more public golf courses in 1913," argued "for the installation of courses in public park space," and believed that the game should be available to all social classes.[2] Despite such support, it would not be until 1921 that the nation's capital got its first public course. Built at Hains Point, the East Potomac Park Golf Course was a popular venue. Among the first who played there was President Warren G. Harding.[3]

While golf's appeal in the nation's capital grew, Jim Crow segregation forced local African Americans to assume the role of caddies, since they were prohibited from playing the city's public and private courses. In response to such exclusion, black Washingtonians drew upon a network of social connections to create a golfing community that served the interests of local African Americans. During the first half of the twentieth century, this community organized golf clubs for men and women, produced talented players, ran local tournaments, and provided officers for important national organizations that governed the sport. DC's black residents also played a significant role in persuading the federal government to build a golf course in the District for African Americans and fought successfully to ultimately gain access to public golf courses citywide. Perhaps more important, the methods used by black Washingtonians became a template for African Americans in other cities who were seeking to dismantle Jim Crow golf. Simply put, the nation's capital deserves much more credit than sports historians have given for advancing the cause of black golf in the United States.

Golf's popularity during the early decades of the twentieth century was largely due to white elites playing the game. To meet the demand, municipalities nationwide constructed public golf courses. By the early 1920s, private golf clubs and country clubs run by whites had also built golf courses. Access to these venues, of course, was restricted to white members only. For African Americans in Washington, DC, the courses at the city's white-operated golf and country clubs were strictly off limits, as were the five public courses (although blacks who caddied at the public venues were permitted to play on Mondays). Just to play a round of golf, black Washingtonians had to travel outside the District.

And yet DC produced a number of talented African American golfers. In fact, the city was critical to the overall development of black golf. In 1925, for instance, a group of African American golfers meeting in the District formed the United States Colored Golf Association (USCGA), the first national organization of African American golfers.[4] At the time, the United States Golf Association (USGA) and the Professional Golfers Association (PGA) did not allow black members. Later that year, the USCGA held the first International Golf Championship at the Shady Rest Country Club, a black resort in Scotch Plains, New Jersey. Tied for the lead after the first day were two golfers from the District of Columbia—Harry Jackson and John Shippen. Jackson would go on to win the tournament. Shippen finished second.[5] Over the next quarter of a century, several black golfers from DC would leave their mark on the game, including Jackson, who won the first "Negro National Open" championship, which was sponsored by the United Golfers Association (UGA), a national group of black golfers, in 1926. But it was Shippen who had the greatest influence.

John M. Shippen Jr. was the best-known black golfer from Washington, DC, and possibly the most influential African American golfer in the first decades of the twentieth century. Golf historian Herb Graffis, author of *The PGA: The Official History of the Professional Golfers' Association of*

America, called Shippen one of the "pioneer personalities" in golf's earliest years in America. Graffis viewed Shippen's golfing achievements with great appreciation, believing that Shippen was part black and part Native American. Given the barriers Shippen would have faced as a person of mixed ethno-racial heritage, Graffis was correct to have extolled the golfer's feats.[6]

In his groundbreaking book, *Forbidden Fairways: African Americans and the Game of Golf,* Calvin Sinnette corrected many of the misconceptions surrounding Shippen's life. He was born in the Anacostia neighborhood of Washington, DC, in 1879. In 1888, his father, who was a Presbyterian minister, was assigned to a mission on the Shinnecock Indian reservation in Southampton, on Long Island, New York. In 1889, the elder Shippen moved the family there. In no time, young John was well integrated into Shinnecock culture. He played with many Shinnecock children, including Oscar Bunn, who became his close friend. When wealthy Southampton residents decided to build a golf course in the early 1890s, Shippen and Bunn were among those recruited as caddies by the well-known Scots golfer Willie Dunn Jr., who had been hired to oversee the completion of the eighteen-hole course at nearby Shinnecock Hills. Taught to play by Dunn, Shippen displayed a knack for golf. Soon, he was encouraged to play competitively. According to Sinnette, "Dunn [also] made him an assistant and permitted him to give lessons to some of the [Shinnecock] club members."[7]

When the seventeen-year-old Shippen applied to enter the USGA national open championship tournament in 1896—only the second to be held by the young organization—some of the white participants threatened to withdraw. While the USGA tournament did not have an official whites-only policy, this type of objection was not unusual for the 1890s (the same year that the tournament was held, the United States Supreme Court, in *Plessy v. Ferguson,* reaffirmed the constitutionality of the race-based principle, "separate but equal"). The matter was swiftly resolved. After declaring that the organization did not discriminate based on race, USGA president Theodore Havemeyer said the competition would be held even if Shippen and Bunn were the only entrants. The announcement ended the dispute and the tournament proceeded. Shippen tied for fifth, the best showing of any American entrant. He later competed in at least four additional USGA national open championships—in 1899, 1900, 1902, and 1913.[8]

By the time Shippen returned to the District in the early 1920s, he was a well-established golf instructor. In DC, he played and taught golf and eventually organized tournaments at the Lincoln Memorial Golf Course, the first black golf course in the city.[9] Seeking their own playing space, elite blacks in the District had persuaded the federal government, under the Jim

Crow principle of "separate but equal," to build the nine-hole course, which was finally completed in 1924. Despite the obvious milestone, African Americans who had fought for the construction of the venue were criticized for having bowed to segregationist norms. The *Afro-American* wrote in 1925: "Casting aside their much vaunted self-respect, men in high business and professional circles have adopted 'Jim Crow' golf as a sport and are submitting gleefully to segregation on account of race and are making ineffective the protests of others against other forms of segregation and discrimination."[10] Shippen, though, must have considered himself fortunate to have daily access to a golf course—particularly in a city whose public venues were walled off from African Americans.

Given his talent, Shippen was a golfer in high demand. When Riverside Golf Club, the District's first African American golf club, opened in 1924, he was "retained by the new organization to render professional advice and help," according to the *Washington Afro-American*.[11] Later, he became an instructor at the Citizens Golf Club, another black club in DC. Then, in 1931, he moved to New Jersey and became the club pro at Shady Rest Golf and Country Club in Scotch Plains. Although recognized as the first black golf pro, Shippen more rightfully deserves to be known as the first American-born golf professional.[12]

In 1924, the Riverside Club held a golf tournament at the Lincoln Memorial course. Although the white press did not cover the event, the *Washington Afro-American* noted that Riverside was "the first [club] to hold a colored golf tourney in the U.S."[13] Actually, the first black golf tournament in the United States was held by the Alpha Golf Club of Chicago in 1915. Alpha's founder, Walter Speedy, was instrumental in overseeing the tournament. In 1921, Speedy organized the well-known Windy City Golf Association (WCGA). Along with the *Chicago Defender*, one of America's most famous black weeklies, the WCGA sponsored black golf tournaments in the city.[14]

Initially consisting of one hundred members—mostly attorneys, doctors, businessmen, and civic leaders, including such prominent black professionals as Dr. Charles Wesley of Howard University and Dr. W. A. Warfield, surgeon-in-chief at Freedmen's Hospital—Riverside was short-lived. Soon after the club opened, newspapers reported that some members were displeased by the way in which Riverside's founder, Victor Daly, a former Cornell University athlete and local businessman, ran the club, especially his year-end financial accounting. As a result, several members left the organization and formed the Citizens Golf Club. Like those at Riverside, the officers at Citizens consisted of Washington's black elite. For a time, Shippen taught golf at Citizens and maintained the greens.[15]

In contrast to Riverside, Citizens was better organized and, in electing a bank president as its treasurer, particularly sensitive to the desire of members to have an accurate accounting of club finances. The leadership was also more representative of the city's black elite, men who were better able to emulate their white counterparts in promoting golf and showing off the social status that normally accompanied the game. The *Washington Afro-American* reported that in his acceptance speech, club president Dr. M. L. T. Grant "point[ed] with pride to Bobby Jones and Walter Hagen as Golf Champions," and then stated, "I see no reason why the Citizens' Golf Club should not become the most wealthy Colored Golf Club in the world and produce champion players as well."[16] In 1927, Citizens changed its name to the Capital City Golf Club. Six years later the club was renamed the Royal Golf Club.

The Royal Golf Club promoted golf locally and nationally, including an annual citywide golf championship tournament. By promoting the game and holding tournaments, Royal was not unlike the growing number of black-operated clubs in other cities. But no African American club, with the possible exception of Chicago's Windy City Golf Club, had as avid and active a leadership as Royal's. The club's president, Dr. George Adams, a prominent physician, and Dr. Albert Harris, a local dentist, guided the organization through its early years with great skill. Both were conscientious and fair-minded, and both cared deeply about the game. As a testament to their prominence in the black golfing community, the two would go on to help found the United Golfers Association, after the USCGA disbanded in 1926. Although some sources list Robert H. Hawkins as the initial UGA president, Adams was actually the first after the organization had become a legally constituted body in 1927. In addition to New York's St. Nicholas and New Amsterdam golf clubs, and the Fairview club in Philadelphia, Royal was one of the four African American golf clubs on the east coast that comprised, in the words of Sinnette, "an important power bloc in black golf circles . . . [whose] combined influence would be felt for years to come."[17]

The leaders and rank-and-file members of the Royal club were people from diverse socioeconomic groups. Such a wide difference in class was particularly important when attempting to field a strong team for intercity matches. Many African American clubs included caddies on their rosters. Caddies were often the most talented golfers, but they came from the poorest families. Unlike white clubs, Royal was similar to other African American golf clubs because it encouraged and supported participation from all social classes. But like white clubs, most black clubs—Royal included—were dominated by men.

Although women-only golf and country clubs were part of the American golfing landscape as early as 1894 when a group of affluent women in the exclusive village of Morristown, New Jersey, formed the Morris County Golf Club, no such parallel club existed for African Americans until the formation of the Wake Robin Golf Club in the District in 1937.[18] Founded largely by women whose husbands were members of the Royal club, Wake Robin was the "first formal organization of African American women golfers," according to Sinnette.[19] Some of the club's founders had been introduced to the game by their husbands, and began playing among themselves. Ethel Williams, one of Wake Robin's founding members, recalled:

> My husband and I used to play tennis and he had a condition with his legs that prevented him from jumping. So the doctor recommended that he take up walking. So he started playing golf. He was working at night and it was very difficult for him to get anybody who could play with him in the morning. So that's when I came with him to the course with a 5 iron and a putter so that he would have someone to play with. I started playing in 1936 but I had no formal lessons. I had two young children so I didn't have much time. I got very interested in golf when we had [golf] meetings. I could hardly wait to get out to play [golf], especially with the women.[20]

The women of the Wake Robin club were not only instrumental in promoting and facilitating local golfing activities, but, like the leaders of the Royal Golf Club, were also important in promoting the game among African Americans regionally and nationally. Helen Webb Harris, for instance, Wake Robin's first president, was later elected president of the Eastern Golf Association (EGA), and Paris Brown, who joined the Wake Robin Club shortly after its founding, was selected as the club's delegate to the UGA. In 1941, Brown was elected vice president of the UGA, becoming the first woman to hold an executive position in the organization's history. Brown would later serve as UGA national tournament director. Over the years, she improved the efficiency of UGA tournaments and other events, while staying involved in golf-related activities in her native Washington, DC.[21]

Unfortunately, the District's African American golfers—at least initially— were little competition for Jim Crow. During much of the first half of the twentieth century, black Washingtonians were prohibited from playing white-owned, private courses, and the five public golf courses in the city were restricted to whites only. Although the Lincoln Memorial course had provided access to black golfers under the pro-segregation, "separate-but-equal" principle since opening in 1924, it was poorly maintained and consisted of only nine holes. It was clearly inadequate to meet the needs of the District's growing African American golfing community. Located on the grounds of the Lincoln Monument, the course was described by Sam Lacy, legendary sportswriter of the *Baltimore Afro-American*, as "a tiny layout which had sand putting greens no wider than a modern compact car."[22] When Wake Robin member Ethel Williams played there in 1936, she remembered having to walk across streets to go from one hole to another.[23] By 1938, following the construction of the Jefferson Memorial, the Lincoln course was considered outdated. Soon thereafter, it closed, its land becoming part of the new Mall development.

The opening of the Langston Golf Course in 1939 represented an important step in addressing the needs of African American golfers in DC. Langston was the result of the dogged effort by the District's black leaders, including members of the golfing community, to have federal officials build a course for African Americans in the city. The origins of the Langston course can be traced back to a letter written by John Langford, a prominent African American architect from Washington and a member of the Capital City Club. In 1927, Langford requested that the Department of the Navy construct a public course for black golfers as part of the recreational area under consideration in the city's Anacostia area.[24] Although there was some sentiment in the African American golfing community to push for access to racially segregated courses, attention was primarily focused on the immediate goal of building a better course for African Americans. In 1934, a delegation of local black leaders, including Langford, and Drs. George Adams and Albert Harris of the Royal club, met with authorities from the Navy's Department of Public Buildings and Grounds to discuss the construction of a public golf course. A site was selected, and construction soon began. Finally, in 1939, the John Mercer Langston Golf Course was opened. John Mercer Langston occupied a vaunted position in local African American history. In 1888, he was the first African American to be elected congressman from Virginia. He also served as dean of Howard University's Law School and became the first president of Virginia State College in Petersburg.[25]

The opening of the nine-hole Langston course was greeted with much fanfare. Announcements in the black press were made weeks in advance, with depictions of it as a beautiful and scenic golf venue. The course was described as having "several hundred trees arranged to outline the fairways, providing background for the greens. The trees selected were varieties all native to this area and collected in nearby Maryland [including] willow and red oaks, tulip poplars, sweet gums, sycamores and American elms."[26] The dedication ceremony was held on June 11. Among those who attended were officials from the US Department of the Interior and the National Park Service; former Royal Golf Club president Dr. George Adams; Royal member and black golf trailblazer Dr. Albert Harris; Royal president Dr. Harold A. Fisher; and Mrs. Helen Webb Harris, founder of the Wake Robin Golf Club. Royal Golf Club member and president of the United States Government Employees Union, Edgar G. Brown, served as master of ceremonies.[27] Attendees were greeted with an exhibition match between John Thompson and Beltran Barker, who were paired against Willie Jones and Clyde Martin. Coverage in the black press included a photo of Thompson teeing off, "as a large crowd looks on in admiration."[28] Thompson and Barker won.

By the time of the exhibition match at Langston, Clyde Martin had made a name for himself among black golfers in the District. Shortly before the venue's debut, Langston manager Clarence Pollard had selected him to become the course's first pro.[29] Martin was born in southern Maryland. As a boy, he began caddying at the esteemed Congressional Country Club in Bethesda, Maryland, where he was first exposed to the sport. Several notable golfers noticed that the young Martin had a knack for the game. In 1941, *Washington Afro-American* sportswriter Nat Rayburg observed that Martin had "worked as clubmaker, golf instructor, and caddy for such stars as Walter Hagen, Tommy Armour and Ton[ey] Penna over 18 years. . . . In many quarters, Martin is rated as the country's most outstanding [black] golfer."[30] According to golf historian Calvin Sinnette, Tommy Armour, who was the club pro at Congressional, "recognized Martin's golfing talents and before long he began to pit the young caddie against visitors looking for (betting) 'action.' Martin rarely lost in those head-to-head matches but . . . was never given the opportunity to play in national competition."[31] In 1940, Martin left DC to become the personal golf tutor of world heavyweight boxing champion Joe Louis, who was an accomplished golfer himself. Louis had stopped by Langston almost a year after it opened and was so dazzled by Martin's play that he asked Martin to travel with him and teach him golf, "in an effort to improve his game."[32] In 1941, Martin won the first Joe Louis Open golf tournament.

African American women golfers were also excited about Langston. Wake Robin members Ethel Williams and Adelaide Adams were the first women to play the course. Williams recalled, "One of the charter members of Wake Robin, Adelaide Adams, was the first woman to tee off at Langston and I was playing with her so I was the second."[33] Within two months after Langston opened, the Wake Robin Golf Club held the first of many Scotch Foursome tournaments on the new course.[34]

The opening of Langston generated much excitement, but its obvious shortcomings led to persistent dissatisfaction. For example, the course on

Clarence Pollard (*left*), manager of the Langston Golf Course in
Washington, lines up a putt during a round of golf with the club
pro, Clyde Martin. Art Carter Papers, Box 170-41, Folder 5,
Moorland-Spingarn Research Center, Howard University.

opening day appeared to be hastily prepared. More obvious, the federal
government had not constructed an eighteen-hole course as it had promised. Other deficiencies included overcrowding—due mostly to Langston's
popularity—and a dearth of shelters (by contrast, the East Potomac Park
course had ten). Visiting Langston to inspect the grass in 1941, officials from
the Departments of the Interior and Agriculture "declared it [the grass] was
in a terrible condition."[35] Furthermore, the nine-hole Langston course, like
the Lincoln Memorial venue, was ill suited to host major golf tournaments.

Despite the need for corrective measures to improve the Langston
course, many black Washingtonians instead pressured authorities to desegregate DC's public golf courses. On June 29, 1941, three African American
golfers from the Royal Golf Club—president Asa Williams, Cecil Shamwell,
and George Williams—went to the racially segregated East Potomac
Park course to play a round of golf. A week earlier, the three had been
refused admission, but now they had returned to play the game they loved.
They were accompanied by Edgar Brown, president of the United States
Government Employees Union and director of the National Negro Council;
Brown's wife, Paris, who was a member of Wake Robin; and two other

black community activists.[36] A light-skinned black man had purchased the golfers' tickets in advance. When they presented the tickets to the attendant to enter the course, however, the three were denied entrance. The golfers entered anyway, leaving the tickets at the doorkeeper's desk. Fearing possible trouble, the DC police department had assigned officers to escort Williams, Shamwell, and Williams around the course. The trio played without incident until they reached the tenth hole. There, white onlookers started harassing them. The black golfers played two more holes before a storm forced them to stop.[37] Reactions to this "invasion" by "colored" people onto public golf courses, long regarded as spaces reserved for whites, were instant and received coverage nationally in both the black and mainstream press.[38]

Jim Crow golf was under attack on other fronts. In 1941, Edgar Brown, with the backing of both the Wake Robin and Royal clubs, and other prominent local black organizations, appealed to Secretary of the Interior Harold Ickes to grant African Americans permission to play East Potomac and any other course under the jurisdiction of the National Park Service. In July, Ickes ordered the opening of the East Potomac venue and other public courses in Washington, noting that since black Washingtonians also paid taxes, they "had the right to play on the city's public courses."[39] The secretary of the interior was no stranger to the fight against racial segregation. Two years earlier, he and First Lady Eleanor Roosevelt had allowed Marian Anderson, a noted African American contralto, to perform on the steps of the Lincoln Memorial after she had been barred from singing in nearby Constitutional Hall.[40] Ickes even introduced Anderson to the 75,000 spectators who attended the concert.[41]

Importantly, all federally controlled land, *including* golf courses at parks run by the National Park Service, fell under the control of the United States Department of the Interior, and were thus subject to Ickes's authority. Even though Ickes made the bold decision to grant the request allowing African Americans to play East Potomac, he was initially critical of the methods used by the protesting golfers. He realized that the presence of African American golfers on the course would probably elicit negative reactions from whites—regardless of how blacks conducted themselves. In *The Secret Diary of Harold L. Ickes*, which was published posthumously, Ickes wrote on July 20, 1941, three weeks after the incident involving the black golfers at East Potomac Park:

> Late Tuesday morning a delegation of Negroes, headed by Edgar Brown and Dr. George W. Adams, the latter of Freedmen's Hospital, came in to talk to me about Negroes playing on the East Potomac golf course.

I told them that when the issue had been raised I announced, as policy of the Department, that Negroes were entitled to the privileges of the course just as whites were. There had been an incipient riot the preceding Saturday afternoon. Some twenty Negroes had gone to the course in a body, although only eight or nine of them wanted to play golf. I protested that going to the golf course in a mob was likely to provoke trouble. I said that we would protect these people in their rights as citizens but that they ought to go to the course in a normal way, pointing out that their use of the course would be more likely to come to be accepted if this procedure were followed than otherwise. They agreed with me and said that they would do this. Later in the week, on Friday, Dr. Brown and his wife went over to this course to play golf. They were followed by a jeering, booing group of whites. When I learned of this I called [Arthur] Demaray [director of the National Park Service] and told him to have enough police there to protect the Negro players and to lose no time in making arrests of those who were conducting themselves in an improper manner.[42]

Sadly, such white resistance would continue, helping keep many African Americans off the city's better-maintained courses. Timmy Thomas, a member of the Royal Golf Club and its tournament director for more than thirty years, ran into problems on more than one occasion. Because of threats from white patrons, Thomas almost always brought along several other black golfers whenever he played the city's public courses. Sometimes fights broke out. A particularly ugly incident occurred when he and several other black golfers tried to play the course at East Potomac two weeks after the incident there had prompted the desegregation order from Ickes. "That particular day," Thomas recalled, "was a little cloudy, but the [course vendor] sold us tickets and we were getting ready to tee off when all of a sudden a big rain squall came up. We rushed to get back in the clubhouse but they had locked the screen door on us. We were pretty belligerent and someone hit on that screen door and it went flying." Then things turned nasty. "We had a real free-for-all down there," Thomas remembered. "I carried marks on my chest as we got to fighting. They called the police, the reserves, and everything else, which didn't stop some of those blows."[43]

Coverage of the incident in the white press was consistent with the firsthand account given by Thomas. The Washington Post reported: "Park and Metropolitan police answered a call to the East Potomac golf course yesterday morning after some 40 Negro golfers had sought refuge at the clubhouse from the downpour and were prevented from entering by white golfers." The article further stated that "blows were exchanged but no one was injured and order had been restored when the police arrived."[44]

Interestingly, black newspapers played down the incident, perhaps not wanting to discourage African Americans from playing the course. The *Washington Afro-American* reported that in an attempt to seek shelter from the rainstorm, "Colored golfers were impeded in their frantic attempt to enter the clubhouse as a few white hoodlums, such as whom even an Ickes will find hard to completely civilize, successfully barred entry." The paper, though, failed to mention the fight and that police had been called, simply noting, "The players retired to their autos until the rain ceased."[45] The contrasting headlines in the *Washington Post*—"Negroes Prevented from Entering Clubhouse"—and the *Washington Afro-American*—"Golfers Take Advantage of New Courses"—supports the argument that black leaders wanted black golf patrons to continue playing racially desegregated courses, especially those at East Potomac and Anacostia, the two venues located closest to black communities in the city. The ultimate goal of desegregating the courses, then, may have dictated the type of coverage the black press gave to the incident.

While the black press encouraged black Washingtonians to play the newly desegregated public golf courses, some whites were opposed to the idea. Indeed, so menacing were threats from a handful of groups that the Wake Robin club had to withdraw its application to use East Potomac as the site for its annual club tournament in the fall of 1941. The decision was made even after the women's club had received a permit to hold its tournament at that location.[46] Using such methods as tampering with cars left in parking lots by black golfers and other bullying tactics, hostile whites tried to prevent African Americans from playing the District's public courses.

White resistance was not confined to the East Potomac course. The Fairlawn public golf course in Anacostia was the scene of another incident. In late July 1942, four members of the Wake Robin club—Helen Harris, Frances Watkins, Banita Harvey, and Kelly Snowden—had just reached the third green when approximately forty whites, including children and soldiers, started hurling sticks and stones as well as using abusive language. Some of the whites picked up the black golfers' balls in an attempt to prevent the foursome from continuing. The *Washington Afro-American* reported, "Two friends of the players, Cecil Shamwell"—who had been one of the three golfers to initiate the desegregation of East Potomac the previous year—"and William Morris, seeing [the women's] plight summoned police assistance, but the mob's response to the policeman was only to continue to attempt to throw stones at the golfers, and to yell, 'What do we care about the law?'"[47] Sensing trouble, the officer called for reinforcements. Eventually, additional policemen, including the sergeant of the park police, arrived. Escorted by the officers, the foursome completed their round while continuing to be taunted.

To most black Washingtonians, the desegregation of DC's public courses in 1941 was an illusion. Even after the superintendent of the National Capital Parks assured the black community that public golf courses would continue to operate on a nonsegregated basis following the venues' transference from the Department of the Interior to the DC Recreation Department in 1951, white resistance did not cease. The white-dominated board of the DC Recreation Department, for instance, "tried to insist that facilities under [the DC department's] direction be segregated."[48] As late as 1954, such resistance was still prevalent. The result was that many blacks viewed Langston as the only golf course where African Americans were welcomed. So ingrained was this perception that some black commentators were of the view that they needed to remind readers that, unlike cities in the Deep South, public golf courses in DC were open to all citizens, regardless of race. In 1954, Earl Tasco of the *Washington Afro-American* wrote: "[It is] True [that] most of our golfers play at Langston [Oklahoma Avenue and Benning Road], which is the reason for the reference to 'our' course, but it is only one of the many public courses . . . It is your privilege to play at any public course in the District of Columbia."[49] It is also possible that the concentration of black golfing activities at Langston reflected the efforts of African Americans to support their "own" course. Either way, direct-action tactics like those used at East Potomac and Fairlawn probably created the greatest impetus for the acceptance of desegregated golf courses in Washington and other cities. Although Langston was expanded to eighteen holes in 1955—which meant it could finally stage national black golf tournaments—its significance began to fade as desegregation took hold and opened up public courses in the city. Moreover, Langston continued to lag behind the District's other public courses, which were better suited for daily and tournament play.

While the desegregation of public courses in DC had technically been in effect since the order issued by Ickes in 1941, the desegregation of golf courses in the city and elsewhere was not fully implemented until after the rulings of the Supreme Court in *Brown v. Board of Education*, in May 1954, and *Holmes v. Atlanta*, in late 1955.[50] The Holmes decision was particularly significant because it applied directly to golf course segregation. Seeking legal action through the courts to address racial discrimination in golf was not new. Robert "Pat" Ball, a highly successful black golfer who sought entry to play in public links tournaments in Chicago and other cities, filed an injunction in Philadelphia's Common Pleas Court to gain entry to the national public links tournament held in the City of Brotherly Love in 1932.[51] But seeking action through the courts or higher authorities *after* using direct-action tactics first occurred in 1941, when appeals were made to interior secretary Ickes to desegregate the District's golf venues. The direct action of the three black golfers at East Potomac served as a model for golf course desegregation fights in other cities and ultimately led to the 1955 ruling of the Supreme Court in *Holmes v. Atlanta*. The pioneering efforts of black Washingtonians paved the way for African American golfers in other locations seeking admission to public courses in the face of continued white resistance.[52]

After DC's public courses were made available to everyone, the historical significance of Langston and its location near a heavily black-populated area of the city made it a relatively important venue for staging African American golf-related events. The course became home to several local clubs that hosted local and national golf tournaments—the Royal and Wake Robin golf clubs, to name a few. Also based at Langston were the Oxon Blades, which hosted the annual Capitol City Open Golf Tournament, and the Postal Golf Club, which staged the yearly Postal Golf Club Championship. The Arlington Divots of Arlington, Virginia, used Langston as well. In 1957 and 1959, Langston hosted its first and second UGA Championship Tournaments, which attracted the best and most famous black golfers from around the country. Among those who played in one or both of the tournaments as amateurs were Joe Louis (the ex-heavyweight boxing champion), Bill Wright, Alfred "Tup" Holmes, and local resident Rafe Botts (who would soon enter the professional ranks). Professionals included Ted Rhodes, Charlie Sifford, Richard "Dick" Thomas, Howard Wheeler, Ben Davis, William Bishop, and Bill Mays of the District. Also taking part were several well-known amateur women, including Ann Gregory, Vernice Turner, and Ethel Funches. In 1959, Rafe Botts and Ethel Funches won the amateur men's and women's divisions; Dick Thomas captured the professional title.[53] In 1963, the UGA championship returned to the District. Ethel Funches won the women's amateur championship again, and Lee Elder, a rising professional, claimed the pro division, defeating such established players as Pete Brown, Ted Rhodes, Willie Brown, Cliff Brown, Nat Starks, Howard Brown, and Junior Walker.[54] In addition to staging the UGA, Langston hosted tournaments organized by African American fraternities, physician groups, and college athletic conferences.[55]

The most widely publicized black golfers with DC area ties were those who crossed over to the world of white professional golf and competed as PGA players after the PGA lifted its infamous "Caucasian-only" clause in 1961. Among the PGA players with Washington connections were Rafe Botts, Richard Thomas, and Lee Elder. Without question, Elder was the most successful and most celebrated. A native of Dallas, Texas, where he learned the game as a young caddy, Robert Lee Elder moved to the District in 1961 after he turned pro. He soon became the most notable African American golfer with ties to Washington and the Langston course. In addition to competing in the Capitol City Open each year at Langston, Elder played, and won, numerous UGA national tournaments, including several Negro National Open titles before joining Charlie Sifford, Pete Brown, and other first-generation black golfers on the PGA tour in the 1960s. In 1975, Elder became the first black golfer to play in the prestigious Masters Tournament at the Augusta National Golf Club in Georgia.[56]

Success never spoiled Elder. Even at the peak of his career, he always remembered that the Langston course had provided countless opportunities—not just for him, but also for other black golfers. Whenever he had the chance, he returned to his adopted city and visited Langston. In the late 1970s, he and his wife, Rose, launched a variety of golf-related programs at the storied course that attracted both blacks and whites.[57] For many years, black golf in Washington was identified with Elder, whose national recognition soared after his first of seven appearances at the Masters. But Washingtonians—black and white—had recognized his greatness years before. In 1974, Lee Elder Day was declared in the District of Columbia.

DC's contributions to black golf are numerous and great. Yet few people know about them. That situation is slowly changing, however, as a younger generation of golf enthusiasts learn about what the sport's black pioneers overcame. In 1997, after winning his first Masters championship, twenty-one-year-old Tiger Woods paid special tribute to Lee Elder and to Charlie Sifford and Ted Rhodes, two of black golf's greatest legends who also played the District's courses during the tumultuous days of racial integration. According to Vartan Kupelian, author of *Stalking the Tiger: A Writer's Diary*, Elder "visited briefly with Woods on the putting green before the final round." Reacting to the visit by Elder, Woods commented after capturing the tournament:

> That meant a lot to me because he [Elder] was the first, he was the one I looked up to. Because of what he did I was able to play on the PGA Tour. When Lee came down that really inspired me and reinforced what I had to do. I wasn't the pioneer. Charlie Sifford, Lee Elder, Ted Rhodes, those are the guys who paved the way. All night I was thinking about them, what they've done for me and the game of golf. Coming

up the 18, I said a little prayer of thanks to those guys. Those guys are the ones who did it.[58]

While Woods's tribute to Elder is certainly laudable, many other black golfers, administrators, activists, caddies, and instructors from the District also played an important role in popularizing the sport and making it accessible to African Americans nationwide. For too long, the accomplishments of these men and women have existed in the shadowed recesses of history. It is time their contributions see the full light of day and are celebrated.

5

Shirley Povich and the Tee Shot That Helped Launch DC Sportswriting

Dennis Gildea

"Everything depends upon a red wheelbarrow," William Carlos Williams claimed poetically.[1] Maybe, then, it is no great stretch to claim that just about everything associated with Washington sportswriting depended upon an errant tee shot.

It was a hot summer day in 1920, and teen-aged Shirley Povich thought he might beat the heat with a quick swim. The caddy master at the Kebo Valley Golf Course in Bar Harbor, Maine, had other ideas, though. There was a man, a summer visitor, a "rusticator," as the locals called the wealthy summer people, waiting to tee off, and he needed a caddy.[2] The caddy master nabbed Povich just as he was heading to the swimming hole. "It turned out over the years that on that day in 1920 I was trying to run away from my destiny," Povich would write decades later.[3]

The "rusticator" who needed a caddy proved to be Edward B. McLean, the owner of the *Washington Post*; enter, in other words, the opening stages of Povich's destiny. McLean, a big man whose strength sometimes overwhelmed his golf game, stood on the second tee, measured his shot, and drove the ball clear over the green, over a road, and into the woods beyond the hole. "Give me another ball, Shirley," he said. "Nobody will find that ball." Nobody, that is, but Shirley Povich, who "knew every root and tree trunk and leaf in that woods," and, after a dash into the woods and much to McLean's amazement, came back with the ball in hand. "Shirley," McLean said, "I've never seen anything like it."[4]

From that point on, McLean insisted on having Povich caddy for him, and when Povich graduated from high school, McLean invited him to come to Washington and work for his newspaper. Young Shirley, who had seldom ventured beyond Bar Harbor, accepted McLean's offer and went to the "unreal world of Washington" and to the newsroom of the *Washington Post* where he began work in 1922 as a copyboy for twelve dollars a week.[5]

However, his first job for McLean was anything but mundane. Almost immediately upon arrival in the city, Povich reported to McLean's private golf course where he was to caddy for a foursome that included President Warren G. Harding. "Mr. President," McLean said by way of introduction, "this is the greatest caddy in the United States and he's going to caddy for you today." Povich's reaction could not have been more greenhorn. "I didn't know what the hell Mr. McLean was talking about. When he said 'President,' I didn't realize it was President Harding. And so help me, Harding and the secret service men got rid of the caddy he had and I took Harding's bag."[6]

Caddying for the president of the United States, getting acclimated to life in a big city, and beginning work on a major metropolitan newspaper were all tasks Povich approached exactly as he had finding the errant tee shot in the Maine woods: They were challenges he would not back down from. And it was a destiny most definitely about to be fulfilled.

Povich rose from copyboy to police reporter and night rewrite man to the sports department in 1924, becoming in 1926—at the age of twenty-one —the youngest sports editor of a major newspaper in the country, although in terms of circulation and reputation the *Post* at the time ranked below other DC papers, such as Cissy Patterson's *Washington Times-Herald*, the *Washington Star*, and the *Washington Daily News*.[7] Povich, though, paid little heed to his newspaper's lowly reputation. In fact, he thought he was on top of the journalistic world. He tells a story of borrowing sports department colleague Walter Haight's car for a date with a young lady. Povich was cruising along Rock Creek Park when Haight's car ran out of gas. "While pondering our fate and avoiding the scornful stare of my fair lady, I was surprised by a soldier who approaches our car and says, 'Are you from the *Post*?'" Povich admitted that he was, and in just a few minutes another soldier returned with gas. "How much do I owe you?" a grateful Povich asked. "Nothing," the soldier replied. "For anybody from the *Post*, it's free." Povich was thrilled by "the stature of my paper," but then he told Haight the story and confirmed the location where he ran out of gas. "No wonder those soldiers were good to you because you were from the *Post*," Haight said. "This is the Walter Reed Army Post."[8]

Povich wrote sports for the *Post* from 1924 until his death in 1998, and he played a huge role in transforming the paper into the most widely read daily in the District of Columbia and one of the most respected papers in the nation.[9] "Shirley Povich was why people bought the paper," *Post* editor Ben Bradlee said. "You got the *Post* for Shirley and the sports section. For a lot of years, he carried the paper, and that's no exaggeration."[10]

While other noted sports reporters in the business abandoned the sports beat for various literary and journalistic pursuits, Povich remained faithful to his calling, and in doing so, he shaped not only the sports journalism of his paper but the work of other papers, especially those in Washington. "Herbert Bayard Swope called the creation of a daily journalistic endeavor 'the curse of everydayness,'" the *Post*'s Bob Considine wrote. "Shirley Povich has turned that dour evaluation into 'the joy of everydayness.'"[11]

Eventually, that would be the case, but Povich's learning curve in the newspaper business was a process that took him over the course of a few years from being an effusive Gee Whiz sportswriter to a more balanced, keen observer of the sports world whose writing was uncluttered and effective. In *City Editor*, Stanley Walker grouped sports reporters into two categories he called "Gee Whizz" (Walker's spelling) and Aw Nuts. The Gee Whizz writers, Walker argued, romanticized and even mythologized athletes and their games. Grantland Rice was the foremost Gee Whizz writer in the business. Aw Nuts writers, on the other hand, tended to regard sports as a business and athletes as human beings with enormous physical talent and often accompanying character flaws, failings these writers would not overlook in print. W. O. McGeehan, writing in San Francisco and later in New York, and Westbrook Pegler, writing in Chicago and then New York, best exemplified the Aw Nuts school.[12]

As a rookie writer, Povich tended to imitate the already-established Rice. "I was a young sportswriter in thrall to the times," he would write about his salad days in the 1920s.[13] One of his greatest thrills in covering the 1924 World Series that the Senators won was sitting next to Babe Ruth in the press box.[14] But with experience, he abandoned his hero worship of athletes. "Despite the fact that I was a precocious young sports editor, I would describe myself as a late bloomer. . . . I was about thirty when I discovered I wasn't a clear thinker. I was a hero worshipper, a romanticist, highly sentimental, and highly impractical. I was constantly overwriting, often attempting to make the event and the game more exciting and dramatic than it was."[15]

Nevertheless, he noted that he began as a sportswriter in 1924, an especially glorious time for Washington sports. "The Senators were about to win two American league pennants in a row and in August of that year I saw my by-line on a story for the first time." The Senators were taking the train back to Union Station after beating the Yankees in three straight games to take the lead in the American League, and sports editor Norman Baxter assigned Povich to write a story on the reception the team would receive upon arriving home. Povich stood among five thousand fans on hand to greet the Senators, and his story accurately captured the euphoria of the day. "I handed the story to Mr. Baxter, who on reading it, said simply, 'I'm going to put your name on this.'"[16] Over the ensuing decades, of course, his name appeared on countless stories and columns.

Even though the *Post* under McLean's ownership was experiencing huge financial difficulties that would culminate in his selling the newspaper, Washington in the Roaring Twenties was "a sports-hungry town and McLean at least recognized that," *Post* historian Chalmer Roberts has written. "He sent Povich to cover the World Series when he was cutting down on all other out-of-town assignments."[17]

Baseball reigned supreme in the nation's capital. The Senators were the biggest draw in Washington sports in Povich's early years in front of the typewriter, and no player on the team was bigger than pitcher Walter Johnson. The Senators' ace was in the twilight of his career when he faced the Detroit Tigers on August 2, 1927, the twentieth anniversary of his Major League debut against the same Detroit franchise. That day, a crowd of 20,000 showed up at American League Park in Washington to honor Johnson. He held the Tigers hitless for four innings, rekindling momentarily memories of his sparkling past. But Detroit got to him for six hits and four runs in the fifth inning, and Johnson was pulled for a reliever in the ninth. Detroit won, 7–6.

Povich covered the game, and his lead sentence in the next morning's paper read: "Walter Johnson pitched, and he didn't win, but who cares if he didn't win?" The game, Povich argued convincingly, was on that day a secondary concern.

> Win or lose, Walter Johnson was hero to the 20,000 persons who assembled in homage to the greatest of all pitchers, and no mere ball game could rob him of the esteem in which admiring fandom of a generation has learned to regard him. . . . It was Johnson the man more than Johnson the pitcher whom the 20,000 chose for their tribute. His pitching deeds, written indelibly in the record books, were open evidence of his physical achievements but written even more indelibly in the minds of fandom throughout the nation was his worth as a man, a family man, and a citizen and the sterling qualities that have endeared him to the people of a generation.[18]

True to his angle, Povich didn't get around to the play-by-play reporting until near the end of a long game story. He concluded: "But Johnson, his speed ball gone and his cunning insufficient, was unable to hold the Tigers at bay in the ninth, and he didn't win."[19]

It was years later when Povich picked up Johnson at his farm in Germantown, Maryland, and drove him to Griffith Stadium to see a rising speedball pitcher, a young Bob Feller, pitching for the Cleveland Indians against the Senators. Johnson watched Feller for a while, and said, "My, my, he's fast." Povich, always the inquisitive reporter, asked the "question which had long concerned me. 'Is he as fast as you were, Walter?' It was then that Johnson's complete honesty collided with his complete modesty. His honesty won. 'No,' he said."[20]

The Senators remained the top story in Washington sports, but following Johnson's retirement and into the 1930s, their days on or near the top of the American League became almost distant memories. Branch Rickey's implementation of the farm system "with far-flung minor league empires owned by major league teams and stocked with players who were the property of the parent club" was changing the game's power structure. Clark Griffith, running the Senators, and Connie Mack of the Philadelphia Athletics, two pioneers of the game, "were running a general store in a super-market era," Povich wrote, and other clubs were signing young players, grooming them in the minors, and bringing them up to the big leagues while leaving the Senators and the A's to languish near the cellar.[21]

In 1937 a new hero and a new professional sport emerged in DC when George Preston Marshall, who turned out to be anything but a hero to Povich, moved his Redskins football team from Boston to Washington. The new hero to emerge on the scene was a first-round draft choice that year from Texas Christian University, Sammy Baugh. Baugh played for the Redskins from 1937 until 1952, but it was the decidedly unheroic 1940 National Football League championship game that gave Washington sportswriters the chance to unleash some of their most delicious zingers. When the hometown team loses a championship game—and a rematch of an earlier victory, no less—by the outrageous score of 73–0 to the Chicago Bears, the typewriter keys glow red hot.

Of those scribes covering the football debacle, the *Post*'s Walter Haight took top honors for acerbic, funny lines. He led his first-day game story with: "You readers are lucky. You don't have to admit you were there. The boss told me to write something, so I'll have to admit I saw the Vanishing Americans yesterday. . . . As soon as I can get this out of the way, I'm going to sneak back to Charles Town, where the horses don't lose by 73 lengths."[22] Haight confessed to leaving the track reluctantly and going to the title game "only to see if football had changed since 1912, when I bit down

on my nose guard at left tackle for the Little Potatoes (We're Hard to Peel)."
With the Redskins down 21–0 early in the game, a score that included a
sixty-eight-yard touchdown run by Bill Osmanski on the second play from
scrimmage, Haight allowed as to how his Little Potatoes eleven would have
had the good sense to have "called it a game and made it a double-header."
Not the Redskins, though, they were "gluttons for punishment." As were,
he noted, the Redskins fans. "Why at one stage the crowd was so quiet you
would have thought prohibition had returned. And if it hadn't been for
George Marshall's sizzling, you could have heard a pin drop."

Haight, if not the Redskins, was having a lot of fun.

> A little boy sitting near me said, "Look, Pop! There's a dirigible." His
> father raised his head, looked back at the field and discovered the Bears
> had scored three touchdowns during the interval. . . . The Chicago
> coach was letting everybody and his cousin try for the extra point. I
> expected to see Mrs. O'Leary's cow out there for that last one. Well,
> she kicked over a lamp, didn't she?[23]

Bob Considine, who started at the *Post* in 1930 but by 1937 was writing a nationally syndicated column for the International News Service, preferred to cover baseball. But he could not resist returning to his hometown
to cover the NFL championship game. And he could not resist addressing
the Redskins' embarrassment in his "On the Line" column.

> Washington is recovering from the worst sports hangover in its his-
> tory. The loss of the Senators to the baseball Giants in 1933 four
> games to one aroused little or no woe here. The tragic loss of the 1925
> Senators to the Pittsburgh Pirates, when Walter Johnson came to the
> end of his career, was softened by the fact that the final game was
> played in Pittsburgh. But the Bears' unbelievable 73–0 victory hap-
> pened right under the township's collective nose, and some of the most
> rabid Redskin fans—who have been known to march up Broadway
> caroling the club's praises—were just as rabid the other way as the
> score mounted. An announcement concerning next year's Redskin
> tickets was hooted into incoherency, instead of laughed at as comically
> ill-advised.[24]

A day later, Considine observed that several of the Bears' players said they
felt sorry for Redskin coach Ray Flaherty as they were running up the score.
"But apparently they didn't feel sorry enough. . . . We're mighty glad that
the Redskins got that dry field they hoped for, or that game Sunday might
have resulted in a runaway," Considine concluded.[25]

Povich, conversely, played the story journalistically straight. The devastating defeat, he wrote, "reminds us of our first breathless visit to the Grand

Canyon. All we could say is: 'There she is and ain't she a beaut.' When they hung up that final score at Griffith Stadium yesterday, all we could utter was: 'There it is and wasn't it awful.'"[26]

Before too many more football seasons passed, the most awful thing about the Redskins, at least for Povich, was the team's owner. "Marshall," he wrote, "was easy to dislike. He bullied many people. He bragged about being big-league, but he deprived his players of travel comforts while reaping huge profits."[27] Marshall barred Povich from the team's dressing room, an annoyance Povich was easily able to overcome. The Redskins' owner insisted on being directly involved in coaching, a practice that invariably found him on the sidelines during games. One Sunday in a game in Pittsburgh, Marshall kept edging closer to the actual playing field. Povich took note, and he wrote in his column the next day: "If Marshall takes one more step, the Redskins will be penalized for having eleven and a half men on the field."[28]

Marshall was married to a former actress, Corrine Griffith, and in the early 1940s she wrote a book titled *My Life with the Redskins*. Povich reviewed it for the *Post*, noting that the best part of the book was the appendix that detailed the Redskins' all-time records and Sammy Baugh's passing marks. "This was one operation," Povich concluded about the book, "in which they should have thrown away the body and preserved the appendix."[29]

In 1942, the Povich-Marshall feud came to a head when Marshall sued him for libel. The Redskins played an exhibition game in Los Angeles, and Marshall announced that the proceeds would go to the widows' and orphans' fund of Army Relief. Povich felt that Marshall would be the primary beneficiary of the profits realized from the game, and wrote as much in his sports section. Marshall demanded a retraction and a formal letter of apology from Povich. He got neither. Consequently, Marshall sued Povich and the *Post* for $200,000. The case went to trial, and Povich was cleared. The last line of his column the next morning read: "The jury, in fewer than 20 minutes, brought in a verdict for the defendants."[30]

More than anything else, though, Povich objected vigorously to Marshall's refusal to sign an African American for his team. Just as Griffith's refusal to embrace the farm system in baseball hurt the Senators, so, too, did Marshall's racist stance hurt the Redskins. It also led to some of Povich's most powerful lines. For example, he once wrote that Redskins' colors "are burgundy, gold and caucasian." Following a decisive win for the Cleveland Browns over the Washington team, Povich wrote one of his most famous lines: "Jim Brown, born ineligible to play for the Redskins, integrated their end zone three times yesterday."[31]

Shirley Povich, the elder statesman of Washington, DC, sportswriting, was still going strong in the 1990s. *Washington Post* photo courtesy of the Shirley Povich Center for Sports Journalism.

Povich's was not a lone voice raised in protest of the Redskins' racism. In 1959, Art Carter of the *Afro-American*, a weekly that covered Baltimore and Washington, wrote a story in which he quoted Lawrence A. Oxley, president of the Washington Pigskin Club, expressing anger at a Marshall policy. "When 'Dixie' is played instead of the Star-Spangled Banner at a football game or any other place, we know what the score is." African Americans, Oxley said, "await the day when Marshall comes to a realization of what democracy in sports means."[32]

In 1937, Carter devoted much of his "From the Bench" column to the case of Wilmeth Sidat-Singh, a Syracuse University football player who was a victim of Jim Crow racism after he was not permitted to play in a game against the University of Maryland and who was also discriminated against by his own university and Syracuse city sportswriters. "Syracuse sports-writers have always styled the youth as a Hindu," Carter wrote, explaining that, in fact, Sidat-Singh was a black man who grew up in Washington. The University of Maryland imposed its Jim Crow ban on the player's participation and Syracuse shamefully acquiesced, Carter wrote.[33]

It was not until 1961 that Redskins owner Marshall relented and signed his first African American. The team drafted Heisman Trophy winner Ernie Davis, and then traded him to the Browns for Bobby Mitchell and Browns draft-pick Leroy Jackson. "Davis was the first Negro picked in the draft by the Redskins in their 25-year history here," Jack Walsh of the *Post* wrote, adding, "Both Mitchell and Jackson are Negroes." Walsh quoted Marshall as saying, "I think the fans will agree [the trade] should mean immediate victories for the Redskins."[34]

Mitchell proved to be a legitimate star for the Redskins, but his role in integrating the team came about because of Davis's reluctance to do so. Povich wrote:

> George Marshall's deal with the Browns didn't happen overnight. He had early doubts that the Redskins would be able to sign Davis, and not merely on a money basis. That Davis was resisting the Redskins was known a month ago when Paul Bixler, Cleveland personnel man-ager who had visited the Syracuse player, made comment that "Davis is uninterested in pioneering as the Redskins' first Negro player." This happened after the Redskins made plain that at long last Marshall was ready to claim Davis in his new decision to make an Alliance for Progress with Negro players. There were pressures from Secretary of Interior Stewart Udall and also from Washington fans, wearying of the performances of the Redskins' segregated peace corps which could win only one game in two years.[35]

Needless to say, Povich had applied pressure on Marshall to integrate for decades.

One of the most commendable and successful efforts to integrate Washington sports occurred in the 1940s when Edwin Bancroft Henderson—an African American physical educator, writer, civil rights activist, and community leader—forced Michael Uline to integrate his arena, the showplace for all-indoor sporting events in the District. Under Uline's orders, the Uline Arena restricted African American spectators to certain events. African

Americans could attend boxing, wrestling, and other "low cultural" contests, provided, of course, that they seat themselves in Jim Crow sections
of the stands. Basketball, ice hockey games, and the Ice Capades, in which
scantily clad white women would skate, were off limits.[36] The *Washington
Tribune*, an African American newspaper, observed: "Mr. Uline thinks
Negroes are savages, that they enjoy those events that display muscular
strength. The white people who attend cultural shows are of a high type
and do not wish to attend cultural programs with Negroes is his theory."[37]

Henderson launched action against Uline by organizing the Citizen's
Committee Against Racial Discrimination in 1945, by instituting a boycott
against the arena, and by deluging newspapers with his letters to the editor
arguing against Uline's discriminatory policy. As early as 1937, Henderson
led a successful attempt to open the DC Golden Gloves Tournament to
African Americans. The Amateur Athletic Union (AAU) event was supported financially by Cissy Patterson's *Washington Times-Herald*, and
Henderson urged her to cease the newspaper's support until the tournament
was integrated. However, it was not until 1947 when Patterson stopped supporting the tournament, and that decision came about only after the *Post*
announced it would no longer support segregated boxing in the District.

While the Golden Gloves boxing tournament was fully integrated,
Henderson's boycott against the Uline Arena was still in effect. Consequently,
the African American community refused to attend the boxing championships, which led tournament promoter Dick O'Brien to vow he would move
the 1948 tournament to another venue. Faced with the loss of the tournament and the loss of further revenue because of the boycott, Uline relented,
declaring in a news conference that people of color could attend all subsequent events in his arena.[38]

The integration of the Redskins came seven years after *Brown v. Board
of Education* and seven years after the District of Columbia's public schools
integrated. As a result, and following a pattern that had occurred and would
occur in other cities, notably Boston in the 1970s, white parents pulled their
children out of the integrated schools and sent them to private schools.[39]
For years, the *Washington Post* and the DC Touchdown Club sponsored the
annual Thanksgiving Day city championship high school football game that
pitted the winners of the Public League against the winners of the Catholic
League. In 1962, the game would match Eastern, a predominantly black
school, against St. John's College High School, a predominantly white school
that drew many of its students from the suburbs. In a pregame story, Bob
Addie of the *Post* wrote that the game would attract approximately 51,000
fans. "It's a tribute to this game that a new D.C. Stadium [later to become

RFK Stadium] attendance record probably will be set. It is a tribute to the brand of high school football now being played in the District." The title game, Addie noted, would top the attendance record of 49,888 who turned out earlier that season to watch the Redskins face the Dallas Cowboys.[40]

In fact, on Thanksgiving morning a stadium record crowd of 50,033 saw St. John's beat Eastern, 20–7. But neither the turnout nor the game rated the biggest headlines. Instead, fighting broke out immediately following the game when disappointed Eastern fans, all African American, attacked St. John's fans, all white. "At least 33 persons were injured yesterday in widespread fighting that erupted after the annual city high school championship football game in D.C. Stadium," a front-page story in the *Washington Post* observed. In the fourth quarter with the game out of reach, two Eastern players were ejected for throwing punches. "When the game ended, hundreds of Eastern followers left their seats on the south side of the stands and raced across the field in the direction of the section in which St. John's rooters sat." It took more than a hundred police to quell the ensuing fight. Nine people were arrested. The *Post* quoted deputy police chief George R. Wallrodt as saying that he would not call the fight a racial incident, but "some other officials thought the racial element was involved."[41]

The *Post*'s sports reporters treated the incident gingerly, avoiding mention of the racial nature of the postgame riot. Byron Roberts wrote the game story, and he did a masterful job of burying the lead. Roberts devoted twenty-one paragraphs to play-by-play before he got around to mentioning the fights, which he covered in four paragraphs.[42] In his column, Addie focused on the record crowd and the details of the game before reaching for a rationalization for the incident. "It must be remembered that some of the college rallies often are more violent. For all of their tradition of dignity and learning, Harvard students, for example, have been involved in dozens of battles with the police."[43]

The *Baltimore Afro-American* praised Addie's coverage while blasting WTOP-TV, a *Washington Post*–owned station, for describing the postgame fight as a "race riot."[44] Longtime *Afro-American* sportswriter Sam Lacy wrote in his "A to Z" column: "The disorders were unfortunate, but the conclusions that they were influenced by racial animosity was even more so." Lacy noted that he did not attend the game, but *Afro-American* sportswriter Art Carter and his son Carlton were on hand. "Art was one of the first to recognize the fallacy in the 'race riot' rumor," Lacy wrote, adding that "few legitimate students of either school" were involved in the fights. He quoted Carter as insisting that the people involved "were individuals of the type which usually comprise the 'trouble-making rabble.'"[45]

The *Post* eventually produced a sports section that commented on race and athletics more intelligently than any other mainstream daily in the land. Tennis great Arthur Ashe, who grew up in racially segregated Richmond, Virginia, began writing a column for the paper in the 1980s, and Ashe charged, not tiptoed, into racially sensitive issues, including intercollegiate sports' tendency to use and discard African American athletes rather than provide them with a meaningful education.[46] Ashe also was honest enough to criticize historically black universities for protesting that the NCAA-mandated SAT scores under Proposition 48 were culturally biased. Ashe's take on the inadequacy of Proposition 48 spawned an editorial in the paper headlined, "These Are Tough Standards?" "Those who have been the most vocal in their criticism of test-score placements and Proposition 48 would do better to devote their time and interest to tutoring sessions, test-taking skills and career counseling. As standards go, Proposition 48 simply isn't very tough."[47]

Ashe, obviously, was a far cry from being the stereotypical dumb jock, but a bit of an irony exists in the *Post*'s engaging him to write a column. As the 1933 World Series was drawing near, the *Washington Star*, more established and more widely read than the *Post* at the time, touted the fact that Ty Cobb and novelist Charles Francis Coe would cover the Series, a journalistic ploy used by a number of papers in those days. Povich countered with an advertisement of his own:

> The *Post* takes pleasure in announcing that Mahatma Gandhi, Aimee Semple McPherson, Prof. Moley, Col. Lindbergh, "Machine Gun" Kelly and "Sistie" Dall will not cover the world series for *The Post*. This newspaper will cover the year's greatest sports spectacle with sports writers, which seems fairly logical . . . Reach for a *Post* instead of a Ghost.[48]

As Ashe's columns suggested in several ways, the times had, indeed, changed.

As had the composition and quality of the newspaper's sports staff. Povich retired, after a fashion in 1974, although he continued to write his column, producing another six hundred columns before his death in 1998.[49] Aside from Povich's quasi-retirement that year, 1974 proved to be a significant time of change for the sports section. Donald Graham, the eldest son of publishers Philip and Katherine Graham, became the assistant managing editor for sports. "In his year in that job, [Graham] spruced up the page design, revamped the staff, and tore down a glass partition that symbolized the long-time separation of sportswriters from the rest of those in the newsroom," an historian of the paper noted.[50] The sports department was no longer the "toy department," as it was widely known in journalistic circles; it was a department at the *Post* that was staffed by first-rate reporters.

Moreover, the sports department, under the management of Donald Graham and the overall influence of his publisher mother Katherine, no longer was the exclusive domain of white men. Joan Ryan, who had written for the *Washington Star*, and Nancy Scannell were covering sports by 1977. Nevertheless, some of the veteran male reporters had to run interference for them to ensure they gained acceptance into press boxes. According to one *Post* historian, "The first time Scannell went to Kennedy Stadium it took a combined escort of Shirley Povich and sports editor James Clayton to break the all-male tradition."[51]

Donald Graham stayed in sports for just a year, but during and immediately following his time there the newspaper's sports pages included the bylines of some of the nation's best sportswriters. Thomas Boswell's piece on the ending of Cal Ripken's consecutive-game streak, a story that ran during the 1998 season, was included in the 1999 edition of *The Best American Sports Writing*. Boswell's opening line read: "Cal Ripken and his inspiring streak of 2,632 consecutive games ended in the one way that few within baseball expected. Perfectly."[52]

The sports section also employed some of the best-known and most widely read writers in the field. Dave Kindred, Ken Denlinger, John Feinstein, William Gildea, Michael Wilbon, Paul Attner, and Tony Kornheiser all covered sports at some point. Throughout the 1991 football season as the Redskins were downing foes on their way to a 37–24 win over the Buffalo Bills in the 1992 Super Bowl, Kornheiser wrote columns that eventually became known as the Bandwagon columns. If Povich's writing, as Considine suggested, celebrated the "joy of everydayness" in sports, Kornheiser's weekly Bandwagon columns celebrated the fun and hilarity of sports. The fact that the Super Bowl was played that year in the Humphrey Metrodome in Minneapolis, rather than a sunny, balmy location ("Get your parkas, it's cold as a moose in Minnesota"), was ideal for Kornheiser's satiric prose.[53] As the regular season ended and the playoffs were beginning, Kornheiser vowed to winterize his Bandwagon.

> Assuming nobody's jumping off, The Bandwagon welcomes Dave and Betsy Hansgen, whose chicken wings are hot enough to melt Minneapolis snow, Anna Burchick, Bradley R. Freiss, Kurt and Kathleen Grimwood, who pledge to make up a batch of Snowshoe Grog.[54]

The genesis of the Bandwagon came from the notion of "having a little fun with Coach Joe Gibbs, who saw doom at every stop on the schedule, and Redskins followers, who took every bad play as a sign of disaster or every good play as a sign of greatness."[55] Kornheiser was shrewd enough to recognize how deadly serious the Redskins' fortunes were being considered, and he was intelligent enough and funny enough to spoof the seriousness of a game.

The columns became so popular that the *Post* brass decided to go all out and capitalize on Kornheiser's creation. They bought him an actual "bandwagon," a thirty-eight-foot recreational vehicle painted in such a way as to turn Kornheiser's fantasy into a garish reality that took to the highway for the trip to the Super Bowl.[56]

Meanwhile, newspaper competition for the *Post* sports section was both evaporating and emerging. Time, Inc., had purchased the *Washington Star*, an evening paper and at one time a major rival of the *Post*, but Time management found it too financially draining to keep the paper publishing. After losing $85 million over a three-year period, Time gave up the venture. The end for the 130-year-old newspaper came on August 7, 1981.[57]

Washington remained a one-paper town for just a short time. In 1982, the *Washington Times*, taking its name from the defunct *Washington Times-Herald* (absorbed by the *Post* in 1954), began publication. The *Times* was launched by New World Communications, a media conglomerate directly related to Sun Myung Moon's Unification Church, and editorially, it was more conservative than the *Post*.[58] Regardless, the "Moonie paper," as it came to be derisively known, proved to be a worthy competitor. Observed one historian of Washington journalism: "[The *Times*'s] local and sports coverage in particular often gave the *Post* tough and badly needed competition."[59]

One of the first sportswriters hired by the *Times* was a throwback to Povich when he began reporting and writing in the 1920s. Dave Fay was a veteran newsman and an accomplished writer who had only a high school education. Fay covered the Redskins on occasion, but his primary beat for which he won most acclaim was hockey. Fay covered the Washington Capitals from the early 1980s until his death in 2007, including the team's trip to the Stanley Cup finals in 1998 when they lost to the Detroit Red Wings. "He was the last of a dying breed," according to his obituary, "a guy who embraced his beat in workmanlike fashion and who always had his finger on the pulse of what was going on."[60]

Throughout the 1980s, Washington area hockey fans were kept abreast of their sport's news through the efforts of Fay and Robert Fachet of the *Post*. Shortly before his death, Fay received word that he would receive the Elmer Ferguson Memorial Award given "in recognition of distinguished members of the newspaper profession whose words have brought honor to journalism and to hockey."[61] Fay is enshrined in the Writer's Wing of the Hockey Hall of Fame.

In the final decades of the twentieth century, television became the dominant medium in sports coverage, and many print reporters went with the prevailing current. Most notably, Wilbon and Kornheiser of the *Post* gained new popularity and profit by cohosting "Pardon the Interruption," a daily sports commentary show on ESPN. Feinstein produced several books on sports topics, with his books on golf achieving particular success. Sally Jenkins cooperated with basketball coaches Dean Smith of North Carolina and Pat Summitt of Tennessee to produce successful books, and her effort with Lance Armstrong, *It's Not About the Bike: My Journey Back to Life*, became a *New York Times* best seller in the years before the Tour de France champion was stripped of his titles because of his use of performance-enhancing drugs.

As 2012 was beginning, the *Post* scooped the world on a story that had people both fascinated and horrified—the Jerry Sandusky sexual abuse case and legendary Penn State football coach Joe Paterno's knowledge of it. Because her father, Dan Jenkins, wrote a 1968 *Sports Illustrated* piece on Paterno as he was in the throes of his first undefeated season, and because the story painted Paterno as the director of a Grand Experiment that featured true student-athletes who also happened to be first-rate football players, Sally Jenkins got the call from the Paterno family to conduct his first interview after the coach had been fired and what turned out to be his final interview before his death.[62]

Jenkins's story ran on January 14. She interviewed Paterno in the kitchen of his home in State College, Pennsylvania. Paterno was eighty-five, weakened by radiation and chemotherapy treatments for the lung cancer that would kill him. Surrounding him during the interview were his wife, Sue, four of his children, an attorney, and a public relations man. The heart of the interview and the ensuing story came down to a question of what Paterno knew about Sandusky's preying on young boys and when did he know it.

Jenkins asked him how it was possible that nobody at Penn State, including Paterno, knew anything about Sandusky's actions. "'I wish I knew,' Paterno said. 'I don't know the answer to that. It's hard.'" Paterno told Jenkins that he had "no inkling" that Sandusky was a sexual predator. Moreover, she wrote, "Paterno insists he was completely unaware of a 1998 police investigation into a report from a Second Mile (Sandusky's charity established to aid troubled boys) mother that Sandusky had inappropriately touched her son in a shower . . . 'You know, it wasn't like it was something everybody in the building knew about,'" Paterno told Jenkins. "'Nobody knew about it.'" Jenkins reported Paterno as saying, "I never heard of, of, rape and a man."[63]

When the Freeh Report, an investigative effort commissioned by Penn State and conducted by former FBI director Louis Freeh, was released months later, it provided evidence that Paterno knew about Sandusky's actions and kept them under wraps. Jenkins knew that as a reporter, she had been used. She led a July 12, 2012, story with: "Joe Paterno is a liar, there's no doubt about that now." Her story, an angry admission that she had been duped into providing a rationale for Paterno's inaction, uses lines and quotes from her interview with the Penn State coach and refutes his claims, using the judgment, "Guilty," as a way of undermining her initial source—Paterno—and as a way of expressing her contrition for producing a one-sided account of a complex situation.[64]

The temptation is to conclude that the world of sports and writing about games and athletes have become in recent years a more challenging and difficult undertaking than it was almost a hundred years ago when Shirley Povich began at the *Post*. But maybe not. About his craft and the writing game that he loved, Povich wrote: "It's a great challenge in the sense that there it is—it has happened in front of you and now you must sit down at the typewriter. It's a task . . . And if you don't recognize how tough it is, I'd say you're hopeless, because if you think it's easy, your product isn't going to be much good."[65] For decades, Povich's sportswriting products, and the products of those who followed him on the sports desks of DC papers, were nothing if not genuinely good.

6

Between the Lines

Women's Sports and the Press in Washington, DC

Claire M. Williams and
Sarah K. Fields

Press coverage of women's sports in Washington, DC, varied widely during the twentieth century. Although women and girls—white as well as black—participated in sport and physical activity in a variety of ways in the early 1900s, newspapers focused almost exclusively on men's sports, reflecting cultural attitudes toward women's position in society. But beginning in the 1920s, as more sporting opportunities presented themselves to women and girls, the local press increased its coverage of women's athletics, even employing female columnists. Such reporting did not mean newspapers had shed their biases. But it did suggest that cultural norms were changing.

As relatively extensive as these opportunities were, they still lagged behind those available to boys and men. And as the United States became more culturally conservative in the 1950s, these modest gains were increasingly curtailed. However, the passage of Title IX in 1972 gave supporters of women's athletics a legal instrument to redress gender inequities in sports. As a result, more women began participating in athletics, and newspapers in the nation's capital and other cities expanded their coverage accordingly. But it was just not the playing of sport that garnered sportswriters' attention. Battles over gender equality found their way onto the sports page as well. The result helped reshape the perception of women's sports, and, ultimately, women's roles in society.

DC Newspapers and Women's Sports, 1900–1910

Historically, women in the United States have been discouraged from participating in competitive sports and from performing rigorous physical activity. Medical discourse during the turn of the twentieth century helped justify
such limitations. Doctors, the vast majority of whom were men, "utilized
pseudo-scientific theories about the effects of the reproductive life cycle upon
women's physical capabilities . . . to rationalize the life choices of middle-
class women and define limits for their activities," one scholar of women's
history has written. Prescriptions for physical activity were restricted to
those deemed "necessary for improving the health of women as mothers
of the race," and to those that could be accomplished while wearing long
dresses and socializing. According to the then-popular vitalist theory, people
had only a limited amount of energy to use in their lifetime. Women especially, it was argued, had to conserve energy for the bearing and rearing of
children. Because working-class women and women of color were held to a
lesser standard of feminine propriety, restrictions on participation in sport
and physical activity, including the types of clothes worn for such participation, were less rigid. Still, these women "too had clearly demarcated lines
they were not to transgress."[1] This form of social control had a lasting effect
on society's perception of women and their physical capabilities.

Opportunities for women to participate in sports in the DC area were
similarly limited, as was the press coverage of what sporting pursuits actually existed, thus giving only a narrow view of the physical activities girls
and women took part in. In 1905, for example, Miss Gladys Lawson's
accomplishments as a horsewoman and athlete were touted in the African
American weekly, the *Washington Bee*, but the information was published
as part of her "matrimony notice."[2] Based on the accounts available, each
new decade brought additional opportunities, but each decade also reaffirmed notions about the proper place of women in the sporting world.

From the turn of the century until the 1920s, references to women's participation in sports were brief, but when mentioned, discussed such diverse
activities as canoeing, field hockey, golf, polo, tennis, and, on at least one
occasion, craps. Women's sportswear was also discussed. In an early, and
rare, example of the potential benefits of participation in sports for girls
and women, a *Washington Bee* article from 1899 chronicled Miss Charlotte
Dunphy's transformation from a "physical wreck"—an inevitable consequence of her gender in relation to the energy she spent on school, the article
argued—to a "strong woman," after she trained three months with a professional male athlete. A 1902 photo spread in the *Washington Times* entitled
"How the Summer Girl of 1902 Is Enjoying Herself" included shots of

women lounging on the beach, holding a golf club, captaining a yacht, and riding a horse. Advertisements for "women's sports wear" and "women's sports suits" were common in local papers. Sports hose was advertised as a holiday present. Signaling that women were entering the world of sport while simultaneously underscoring the navigation required of them in this previously male-dominated sphere, an article in the *Washington Post* asserted that lace and hand embroidery were inappropriate on the golf links, as were "mannish" blouses originally designed for sports participation. Another article, however, suggested that sports clothes were not just for athletic activity, but could be worn on other occasions. References to sportswear appeared regularly in the fashion section.[3]

While most reports of girls and women in sport were published in the mainstream press, articles about girls and women of color partaking in physical activity also appeared in African American newspapers. That the black press devoted attention to such activities undercut the widely held belief that only African American men and boys played sport. One of the places where African American girls initially participated in organized physical activities was high school. Founded in 1870, M Street High School—originally called the Preparatory High School for Negro Youth but now named Dunbar High School—was one of the first high schools for African American students in the nation. In 1911, M Street began developing a Public Schools Athletic League, mirroring the sports league that had been established in the city's white schools five years earlier. The aim of the program was to aid boys' development in the realms of the "mental, moral, and physical." Girls, too, were included. Linking athletics to female empowerment, one author believed that "girls on playgrounds are being taught to play team games that the co-operative lessons learned thereby may further add to [a] woman's power in modern civilization. Let us encourage physical sports for girls along with the attainments at whist and society." During the winter months, girls at M Street played indoor baseball and basketball.[4]

Women's Sports Columnists

In the 1920s, several sports columns focusing on women's sport and physical activity were published in DC newspapers. In the summer of 1925, the *Evening Star* had two columns that appeared semiregularly: In "Water Nymph," columnist Merze Marvin Seeberger focused on different swimming skills, each accompanied by a sketch of a female swimmer performing a particular stroke, while Corinne Frazier's column, "Women in Sport," covered local women's sporting events and reported the results.[5] Also in the mid-1920s, Dorothy Greene of the *Washington Post* maintained a regular column, "The Sportswoman," and between 1938 and 1940 Margaret Davis wrote a regular column sponsored by the DC Board of Women's Athletics entitled "D.C. Women in Athletics." In the *Washington Times*, the androgynously named "Jerry" Martin (quotations are original) also reported on local women's sport.

Whereas Merze Marvin Seeberger's *Evening Star* columns concentrated exclusively on swimming, Corinne Frazier's included reports on local tennis, swimming, and golf. Frazier also wrote about the success of women at a field day in Maryland in which participants competed in races and traditional track and field events, rifle, volleyball, and fire making. In addition to sharing information about swimming pool openings and upcoming competitions and field days, her columns gave the results of more unusual games, too, such as Schlag Ball, a German game, and Block Ball, whose matches in 1925, apparently, had to be canceled because of a diphtheria outbreak. Frazier also reported on playground championships in girls' basketball and national meetings on women and girls in sports. In addition, she wrote about celebrated events in women's sports outside the DC area, including Gertrude Ederle's preparation for swimming the English Channel in 1925. Ederle would not accomplish the feat until August 1926—and she did it by shattering the mark previously held by a man.[6]

Dorothy Greene's columns in the *Washington Post* were particularly notable for their breadth, depth, and quality of coverage. For example, in July 1926 Greene wrote about the tennis, rifle, volleyball, swimming, wood craft, and folk dance contests at a local private camp; commended an eleven-year-old girl who swam three miles in the Chesapeake Bay; and, presumably for fear of being called a poor sport, allowed space for a male reader's humorous views on the rise of women's participation in golf. In a five-part series in 1925, Greene covered the status of girls' physical education in Washington high schools. In the last article of the series, she explained that, under the direction of a Wellesley College graduate, a physical education program at McKinley Technical High School had been started so that girls could develop "the best possible physical condition in order that they may derive the greatest benefit from their intellectual and social opportunities both in school and after graduation." In another article from 1925, Greene lamented the fact that championship swimming was not on par with championship tennis and golf, attributing the problem to swimming's association with bathing beauty contests. "There are," Greene wrote, "few people who will not concede the respect for the ability of the good swimmer and as soon as we divorce the idea of the swimming meet from the bathing beauty contest and realize that there is a difference in wearing a one-piece suit in a meet and in a parade, then, and only then, will swimming find its merited position on the sports map." Greene also applauded the improved physical condition of local Girl Scouts at Camp Fort Foote's summer program, which featured "vigorous athletics."[7] Greene's advocacy for women in sport was evident in her writing, and her regularity as a columnist suggested Washingtonians' demand for coverage of women's sports.

Also writing in the *Post*, Margaret Davis chronicled events related to the Amateur Athletic Union (AAU), the governing body for amateur athletics in the United States for men and women; the American Association for Health and Physical Education; the District's Jewish Community Center; and physical education at George Washington University. Davis's broad coverage reflected the growing number of local organizations and institutions providing sports programming for girls and women.[8]

Readers of the *Washington Times* during the mid-1920s relied on "Jerry" Martin's periodic reports on women's sport—be it local or national. Martin covered girls' basketball league expansion and results and wrote about the only girls' basketball team in the DC area to play male rules (five-on-five, full-court basketball rather than the half-court, six-on-six game that was typically played by women and girls). According to Martin's reporting, the girls' team had lost to a boys' team, but were preparing for a rematch. The article was positive, noting that the girls had only played under male rules for a month and that they were collecting the "best feminine athletes in the city," possibly allowing them to become a "championship aggregation." Martin also included updates on local swim meets, reported on an interclass girls' baseball game at Western High, and described the training of Lillian Cannon, a Baltimore woman who was preparing to swim the English Channel. The article included four action photos of Cannon. Martin called her a "plucky young American mermaid" and wrote that she "had wonderful endurance and determination to win against the odds." Cannon had accompanied Gertrude Ederle on part of Ederle's historic swim across the Channel in 1926, but never succeeded herself.[9] Importantly, all of the aforementioned columnists covered women's sports in such a way that gave credibility and respect to those who participated.

Greater Participation, Greater Press Coverage: The 1920s

The 1920s saw a surge in the coverage of women's sports that would not be surpassed until the 1970s, when women's participation in athletics dramatically increased. Just as it does today, press coverage of men's sport in the 1920s dwarfed that of women's. But when the press did cover women's sports, it was often—but not always—positive. The stories and topics varied widely.

Much of the coverage reflected a complicated understanding of the benefits and drawbacks of sport for women and girls. In 1925, for instance, the *Washington Sunday Star* reported two upcoming sporting events for local junior high girls. The significance of the article lay in part in the distinction between the two events. The first, hosted by the Girls Scouts, was described as "traditional," while the second, hosted by the Physical Education Department of the city's junior high schools, was "a decided departure from the stereotyped meet both in respect to program...and the atmosphere." PE department members had just returned from national conventions espousing "athletics for women and not women for athletics." Consequently, they agreed to limit the number of events girls could enter to "avoid undue strain upon an individual girl" and to promote greater participation in games like volleyball and dodge ball. The Girl Scouts' event was more of a traditional track and field event, with ribbons given to winners. Over the next few decades, the PE view would become the dominant philosophy, thus limiting the competitive opportunities for schoolgirls. This transition slowly played out in the DC school system. By 1921, white high schools in the city— following the general lead of M Street High, ironically enough—required all freshmen to enroll in a Physical Culture class. The requirement was waived for older boys and girls involved in a supervised sport.[10]

Physical activity, sport, health, and beauty were often linked on the city's sport pages. For example, one article reported that a foreign doctor had warned that smoking was bad for women's health, particularly for their voices. The article mocked the doctor, suggesting that someday equally dubious claims about tobacco's deleterious effects on women's stamina, heart, and lungs would become popular. Ironically, the article proudly suggested that the success of American female athletes like Gertrude Ederle proved that their use of tobacco was not debilitating. Taking a similarly quasi-scientific approach, a different article suggested that sport had helped make women "taller, more agile, svelte of style"—in other words, more like Amazons. Still another article promoted "water push ball," with photos of women in bathing suits carrying large, inflatable balls. The article argued that this was "how to build up healthful and vigorous muscles and beauty." Even an ad for a bicycle event, which was described as being "not a race," encouraged women and girls to participate in the "bicycle ride for health and pleasure." Health was very much a justification for female sport.[11]

Not all the articles regarding women's sport were laudatory or positive. Indeed, some articles, photos, and cartoons in the 1920s were less than flattering. In 1926, the *Washington Times* published an article entitled, "This Photo Started Row." The picture showed a local woman in a bathing suit posing next to several silver cups she had won in swimming and life-saving competitions. The article explained that the United Daughters of the Confederacy in Richmond, Virginia, had condemned the woman for posing in her bathing suit. That the *Times* chose to reprint the photo and focus on the United Daughters of the Confederacy's outrage, rather than the woman's athletic success, gave credence to the organization's complaint, thus reflecting the relatively prudish attitude of the era. That same year, the *Times* ran a series of photos of the Arcadian, a girls' basketball team, which was preparing to play against boys. Published two days after a positive article by columnist Jerry Martin about the event, the photos showed the girls in playful nonbasketball poses. The first showed a girl having her make-up done. The caption stated: "'Mickey' Whaley helps 'Shockey' Hatton get her eye brows on." Others showed players wearing a nose guard, football helmet, and shoulder pads. None showed the girls playing or even holding a basketball. The pictures trivialized and disparaged the Arcadian team, as if the club was unworthy of playing against boys.[12]

Cartoons mocking women were a source of amusement in local sports pages. The *Washington Herald* sometimes published cartoons by Robert Ripley of *Believe It or Not Trivia*. On August 2, 1929, Ripley's cartoon included a reference to the shortest letters ever written; the fact that the "zick-zack bird picks the teeth of crocodiles"; a report of a Cuban man who could dislocate his eyeballs; and the news that that July Dorothy Hale had "pitched and won 4 games."[13] While not particularly problematic unto itself, placing Hale's feat next to the zick-zack bird and the dislocated eyeballs served to portray her accomplishment as unusual, even freakish, thus belittling her baseball talent. Similarly, the *Washington Times* periodically ran an International Features Services cartoon by the single-named Tad called "Indoor Sports." Some of Tad's cartoons referenced women's shopping as a sport, and generally cast the shop girls and the women in the stores in uncomplimentary ways. In one cartoon from November 1926, Tad drew shop girls making fun of the yammering shoppers behind their backs.[14]

Some articles reported the results of school-aged girls' sporting events. Such simple reporting can be read as being positive. In 1921, one article reported that hundreds of schoolgirls had participated in class and inter-class competition—carefully noting that there were no interscholastic girls' competitions in the District. The competitions took place in rifle, basketball, swimming, tennis, and field hockey. In the summer, swimming and diving competitions were popular, and in the winter, according to one paper, forty-seven girls competed on the rifle team at Western High School. Among school-aged girls, basketball and tennis was also popular. One local girls' tennis tournament was described as "intensely interesting."[15]

By 1924, high school girls in DC were competing against one another interscholastically in rifle—apparently the sole sport in the city that allowed for head-to-head competitions among high school girls. According to G. Harris "Doc" White, DC Central High's athletic director, rifle "[was] the only athletic interest in which the girls of the high schools are permitted to compete as an interscholastic activity, and it is conducted with a great amount of true sportsmanship and enthusiasm." Central High especially fielded a strong team. The *Washington Post* reported that in a victory over Western High in February 1924, Central's squad "made a score of 622 [points] out of a possible 625." The article added: "The . . . team has no professional coach. Two former Central students, who had been leading members of the girls' rifle team, are the only coaches the girls have." As sport historian Robert Pruter noted in *The Rise of American High School Sports and the Search for Control, 1880–1930*, part of the reason why girls' (and boys') rifle in the District was so popular was because the National Rifle Association had its main office in DC, and the organization encouraged interscholastic competition locally and nationally. The press too ratcheted up interest, reprinting pictures of local high school and university squads. One photograph in 1922 showed team members from McKinley Manual Training School pointing their rifles straight ahead at readers, the butts of their firearms firmly planted against their shoulders. A picture of the University of Maryland squad in 1924 carried the caption: "Maryland Girls' Rifle Team Includes Many Crack Shots."[16]

Perhaps the strongest indication of the acceptance of girls' sports was the *Washington Herald*'s 1926 poll regarding the most popular athlete. The poll closed on August 30, and early reports listed several female athletes in the lead. On August 19, nationally renowned female athletes like Helen Wills, Gertrude Ederle, and Aileen Riggin, as well as baseball superstars Walter Johnson, Ty Cobb, and Babe Ruth, were ranked in the top ten. By August 26, Johnson was in second place, Ederle in third, and Wills in fourth. In the lead, though, was a local "14 year old Virginia Avenue playground lassie," who was photographed throwing a ball in the air. On September 1 the *Herald* reported that the young lassie, Mary Ellen Totten, a tennis and swimming whiz, had won the contest largely because "Miss Totten's friends worked manfully for her and won the honor in a final four-day drive."[17] Totten received an engraved silver cup commemorating her honor. Washington Senators' pitching ace Walter Johnson came in second. The paper did not report if he too got a cup.

Members of the girls' rifle team at Central High School take aim in front of a
hard-earned trophy, November 1922. Library of Congress, LC-F8-21092.

Local women's sporting events were also covered. Determining which
events involved girls—as opposed to women—is a challenge. Although some
reports noted that the participants were school- or college-aged, others had
no such description. It is likely that women and girls crossed over and participated in any event open to them. One exception was local golf clubs,
which held open tournaments for adult men and women. At times, newspapers extolled women golfers' skills. On November 26, 1926, for instance,
the *Washington Times* ran several photos of local golfer Dorothy White—
"District Golf Champ," according to the caption—demonstrating her tech-
nique. In addition, women's results in local tennis and bowling tournaments
were sometimes reported in great and positive detail. Again, most of these
newspaper accounts, though less frequent than accounts of men's events,
were generally positive. For example, a photo spread of seven female basketball players under the title, "Fair Members of the Undefeated Jewish

Community Center Basketball Team," in the March 11, 1929, edition of the *Washington Times*, showed the women holding basketballs in action-type poses. The captions simply gave names and positions, showing respect for the women as athletes.[18]

During the 1920s, DC sports pages also acknowledged some national and international women's sporting events and athletes. On July 29, 1925, the *Washington Evening Star* published an extensive North American Newspaper Alliance article by Captain Alec Rutherford about Gertrude Ederle's upcoming attempt to become the first woman to swim the English Channel. Although the article included a photo of Ederle in her swimsuit flexing her muscles, most of the article focused on Ederle's male coach and the technicalities of her preparation and plan for the swim. A year later, on August 7, 1926, the *Evening Star* reported in a laudatory article that Ederle, in her second attempt, had successfully swum the Channel, noting, "America is proud." Similarly, several months earlier, on December 17, 1925, the *Evening Star* reported that Eleonora Sears had completed a "forty-four-mile walk between Providence and Boston" in just over eleven hours. The paper called this a "truly remarkable feat"—pun likely intended—and also noted that Sears had great success in a number of sports other than pedestrianism. The *Washington Daily News* on July 9, 1928, praised the United States women's Olympic team, including photos of all seven athletes. Less singular but still important women's events were also described, including the women's results at a tennis tournament in New Jersey and the results of the British Open golf tournament.[19] Like the articles reporting District events, the majority of these articles were supportive in their depiction of women's sports.

Title IX, Women's Sports, and the Press

Between 1930 and 1972, press coverage of women's participation in athletics suggested a general support for female involvement, as long as it remained at an "appropriate" level. Criticism, however, could be biting. An author from 1927 asserted that "women have gone too far" in pursuing "the records and accomplishments of men"—perhaps a swipe directed at Gertrude Ederle—while an article from 1933 posed the question as to whether "sports subtract from feminine charm." The author of the latter piece mentioned women's participation in bowling, golf, tennis, track, and trapshooting, and concluded that femininity was ultimately left up to the "individual girl," not determined by the sport she played. In the 1940s, field hockey began to be mentioned frequently, likely due to the city's proximity to Maryland and Virginia, important hotbeds of lacrosse and field hockey. A feature story in 1958, for example, highlighted the accomplishments of a female field hockey player from Gallaudet University. As far as school-based sport was concerned, articles noted that women physical educators continued to discourage girls from taking part in varsity competition. Instead, "play days"—in which fun, cooperation, and good sportsmanship (but not winning) was the goal—were offered. Particularly among women's colleges in the Northeast and the South, female students participating in play days could take part in physical activity while simultaneously upholding virtues of femininity, modesty, and restraint.[20]

In 1972, President Richard Nixon signed into law Title IX, which prohibits discrimination in educational institutions receiving federal financial assistance. While originally intended to combat the discriminatory admissions practices ubiquitous in institutions of higher education, women physical educators adopted the law as their own, marking a significant transformation in the sporting opportunities for girls and women in school-based sport. Now supported with the force of law, girls and their parents in Washington, DC, and other cities nationwide began demanding more sporting opportunities. In the nation's capital, American University coordinated one such effort in the form of a pro-Title IX rally held at the White House and the Capitol in April 1979.[21]

Due in large part to the rising number of female athletes, press coverage of women's sports in the DC area in the 1970s expanded significantly. A great deal of coverage examined the growth of women's sports in relation to the number of teams, availability of funding, and struggle for control over women's athletics. Newspapers noted that within the women's sporting community, some women's athletic programs sought equal treatment with those that existed for men. However, some women's sports advocates, such as Dorothy McKnight, the coordinator of women's athletics at the University of Maryland in the mid-1970s, opposed the male sports model. McKnight and three of her colleagues resigned because they did not approve of the university's decision to grant athletic scholarships to female athletes. Nevertheless, high-school-aged female athletes in the Washington metro area pursued athletic scholarships as a path to a subsidized education rather than as a path to professional sports, since women's professional leagues did not exist at the time. Local female athletes earned athletic scholarships in a variety of sports, including basketball, field hockey, and softball. Local institutions such as American University, Catholic University, Georgetown University, and George Washington University recruited many of the city's best athletes.[22]

In addition to athletic scholarships being offered to female athletes for the first time, other changes in women's sports at the college level during the 1970s were evident. For instance, according to the city's sporting press, both the women's tennis coach at Georgetown University and the women's volleyball coach at George Washington University began requiring weight training for both athletic improvement and injury prevention. Fears surrounding too much weight training for women were still prevalent. A weight-training instructor at the University of Maryland, for instance, lauded the accomplishments of his female powerlifters, but assured readers that they "don't look like Magilla Gorilla's girlfriend. . . . The girls who compete in the fighter classes are gorgeous . . . they have nice figures and look like models." However, a weight-training instructor at Howard University explained that women were increasingly enrolling in his general weight-training class for strength and conditioning purposes. A 1974 article focused on the "'unfeminine' stigma" of sports participation, but rather than using such stigmatization as a scare tactic, the author encouraged continued participation by women. In 1979, Byron Rosen of the *Washington Post* reported that Jackie Frazier, daughter of former boxing heavyweight titleholder Joe Frazier, had decided to attend American University to play basketball, thus signaling that daughters as well as sons were, at last, able to capitalize on their fathers' athletic genes. Also in 1979, Washington, DC, native Karen Leslie Stevenson received a Rhodes scholarship—the first African American woman to earn the prestigious honor. Stevenson was also the first woman to win the Jim Tatum Memorial Award, which recognized the most outstanding athlete at the University of North Carolina.[23]

Coverage of women's sports in DC continued to increase during the 1980s, echoing many of the cultural themes found throughout the nation. For example, features related to the growth of girls and women's sports were tempered by the recognition that funds for women's athletics were lacking; that press coverage of women's sports was substantially less than the coverage of men's; and that sexism was common in sports reporting. In terms of growth, newspapers noted that the District—at 41.3 percent— ranked fifth in the nation for the highest percentage of girls participating in high school sports. By the Olympic year of 1984, the press reported that the increase in both participation and success was attributed to the implementation of Title IX. In 1987, Congress designated a National Women in Sports Day—a story that newspapers widely reported. Efforts on behalf of women to play sports otherwise offered only to men were reflected in the efforts of Nancy Bonura, a female student at Gallaudet University who won the right to play on the university's men's soccer team. The *Washington Post* covered Bonura's achievement.[24]

Old assumptions, however, were hard to erase. Two *Washington Post* articles from 1989 illustrate the contrast between the ideas of Victorianism and modernity prevalent in women's modern sporting experiences: one piece recommended a resource for evaluating home exercise videos, while the other reported on allegations of steroid use in both women's and men's Olympic-level track and field. Another *Post* article, titled "Sweat, Pain, and Grace: Meet the Women of the 1990s," predicted the continued increase in sports participation into the next decade and century, specifically highlighting women's participation in the Washington metro area. At George Washington University, Lynne George, the director of women's athletics, saw "the women's sports program evolve from what was basically an intramural club program to a nine-sport intercollegiate program." Yet even then, it still lagged far behind that of the university's men's program. At many DC area colleges and universities, the budgetary strain of adding opportunities for female athletes represented an ongoing concern. Linda Ziemke, the women's basketball coach at American University from 1978 to 1988, understood all too well the harsh reality of being constrained financially. Though Ziemke played in the first Association for Intercollegiate Athletics for Women (AIAW) basketball tournament in 1972, participation had been in doubt until the very last moment because of the lack of available funding for transportation to the event.[25]

Howard University provides an illustrative example of the impact of Title IX on women's participation in athletics in general, and on women's sports in Washington, DC, in particular. Although women have been admitted to Howard since it was founded in 1867, female student-athletes and coaches have struggled to gain equal footing with their male peers. On the positive side, as early as 1941 Howard hosted an interschool play day for its female athletes, and in 1981 and 1982 the Bison women's swimming team won the Black National Swimming and Diving championship (particularly notable because African Americans are not usually associated with swimming). In 1988, three Howard graduates participated on the United States Women's Olympic taekwondo team. Local newspapers covered these accomplishments.[26]

However, not everything linked to the women's athletic program was to be celebrated. In 1979, and again in 1991, Howard faced Title IX complaints from its female coaches. In 1979, the women's volleyball coach, Jackie Cody, filed a Title IX complaint against the university, alleging that Howard discriminated against its female athletes by failing to provide athletic benefits—training space and time, meals, quality of coaching—equal to those afforded to the school's male athletes. Cody explained: "Howard can't call itself the mecca of black freedom, it's not that way there. When you talk about a black school which should know what discrimination is like and it's treating women like that." Cody was fired, she claimed, in retaliation for her complaint. Echoing popular sentiment, Leo Miles, Howard's athletic director and an unabashed critic of women's athletics, stated that providing women's sports with support equal to that of men's would have "a serious impact" on the athletic program as a whole and "would be a severe curtailment of our program."[27] Clearly, Miles's interest was in preserving support for men's athletics rather than complying with Title IX.

In 1991, Sanya Tyler filed another Title IX lawsuit against Howard, this time in the wake of the United States Supreme Court's ruling in *Franklin v. Gwinnett* (1991), which, for the first time, allowed monetary damages to be awarded to Title IX plaintiffs. Tyler, a Howard graduate, had been the women's basketball coach since 1980. By 1985, however, she was only one of two NCAA Division I women's basketball coaches employed on a part-time basis. Working full time as a radiologist and raising her daughter, Tyler struggled to keep up with the hectic pace of Division I athletics. She lamented that "many of the Washington area's top prospects [chose] colleges away from home" because she was unable to devote more time to recruiting. In her complaint, Tyler alleged that Howard had not provided the women's team with enough office space, adequate locker room and training facilities, and sufficient resources to hire a complete staff. Moreover, despite having been promoted to a full-time coach in 1990, Tyler earned about half of what the men's coach made. In 1993, she was awarded $1.1 million, and $54,000 for defamation.[28]

Local press coverage of female athletes during the twentieth century varied in quantity and scope. Generally, it was more positive than negative, and reflected that even as far back as the early 1900s, women and girls in the nation's capital participated in sports. That participation, mirroring the growth of women's sports nationwide, expanded during the last quarter of the twentieth century, so much so that female athletes not only had coaches, they also had coaches who were now willing to fight for their athletes' rights.

For much of the twentieth century, the press coverage of women's athletics in the nation's capital paled in comparison to the attention sports journalists showered upon men's sports in the city. But after the enactment of Title IX, which saw a significant increase in female athletic participation, the press began to devote more space to women's sporting events. It was still not commensurate with the dramatic jump in female participation —between 1971 and 2001 the number of women playing college sports nationwide increased five-fold, while more than 85 percent of newspaper space nationwide remained devoted to men's sports—but it did represent a shift in perception, signifying that many more women and girls were play-ing sports. The development of professional women's team sports during the 2000s would be the next step in the evolution of women's sports in the DC region, and the press, much like it had done throughout most of the twentieth century, covered the highs and lows. Yet the amount of cov-erage continued to fall far short of what the men's professional franchises received. "The more things change, the more they stay the same" might best describe the relationship between major women's professional sports teams in Washington and the press during the turn of the twenty-first century.[29]

Epilogue

The genesis of these professional clubs is found in primarily two events: the 1996 Atlanta Olympics and the 1999 Women's Soccer World Cup in the United States. The success of the American women's basketball team at the Atlanta Summer Games—the squad won the gold medal and featured such stars as Rebecca Lobo, Lisa Leslie, and Sheryl Swoopes—convinced promoters that the time was right to start a women's professional league. Actually, two leagues were established: the American Basketball League (ABL) and the Women's National Basketball Association (WNBA). Offering higher sala-ries yet lacking the media attention and organizational sophistication of the WNBA, the ABL struggled. In December 1998, the league disbanded.

That same year, Washington Sports and Entertainment Limited Partner-ship, which also controlled a majority stake in the Washington Wizards of the National Basketball Association (NBA), was granted one of the WNBA's two expansion teams. Named the Mystics, the club experienced immedi-ate success at the box office, averaging almost 16,000 people per game. Through 2004, the team remained popular. But in 2005 attendance declined by 20 percent, and the Mystics were sold to Lincoln Holdings LLC, which owned the Washington Capitals of the National Hockey League (NHL). Sheila Johnson, cofounder of the Black Entertainment Network, was named president. Johnson became the first African American woman to own a large stake in three major sports franchises (the Wizards, the Capitals, and the Mystics). Through 2013, the Mystics' overall record was an uninspiring 208-324. Nevertheless, since 1998 eight Mystics players have been named to WNBA All-Star teams, including Chamique Holdsclaw, a six-time All-Star; Alana Beard, who was voted onto four squads; and Monique Currie, a District native and 2010 team member.[30]

The enthusiasm with which Americans embraced the Women's Soccer World Cup in 1999 similarly persuaded investors to organize a professional soccer league for women. Two years after the World Cup, the Women's United Soccer Association (WUSA) commenced play. The league's primary backer was a group led by John Hendricks, founder of the Discovery Channel, which is headquartered in the Washington suburb of Silver Spring, Maryland. The District, in fact, has played a large role in advancing world-class women's soccer. RFK Stadium, for instance, hosted several matches of the 1996 Atlanta Olympics and the 2003 Women's World Cup. A quarter-final match of the 1999 Women's World Cup was played at FedEx Field in Landover, Maryland.

The WUSA consisted of eight teams. The District's was called the Freedom. Before the start of the inaugural season, it was decided that three "founding" players from the 1999 World Cup championship squad would be assigned to each club. These players, league officials hoped, would help build local interest, due to their status as hometown or college stars. The Freedom got Mia Hamm—arguably the most popular women's soccer player of all time—largely because she had played a year at Lake Braddock High School in nearby Burke, Virginia (that year, Lake Braddock won the state title). Known for her prolific goal scoring, Hamm would twice win the World Player of the Year. In April 2001, more than 34,000 people attended the Freedom's opening game at RFK Stadium.

But the large gate was an illusion. WUSA officials discovered that maintaining such popularity could not be achieved. In 2003, the league folded—but not before the Freedom won the last WUSA title. In 2009, the Freedom returned to the nation's capital as a member of Women's Professional Soccer (WPS). Two years later, however, the team was sold to Dan Borislow, the inventor of MagicJack—which allows users to interface their telephone service with a computer—and moved to Florida. In April 2013, the Washington Spirit of the National Women's Soccer League (NWSL) kicked off its inaugural season at the Maryland SoccerPlex in Boyds, Maryland, where the WPS Freedom had played its home games. With a record of 3-5-14 in 2013, the Spirit finished last in the eight-team NWSL.[31]

7

Exercising Civil Rights

*Public Recreation and Racial Segregation
in Washington, DC, 1900–49*

Martha H. Verbrugge

In a message to the National Recreation Association in 1947, Julius A. Krug, secretary of the US Department of the Interior, emphasized the responsibility of local, state, and federal agencies in providing recreational services for the American public. Urging government officials to bring "more joy, happiness and richness of living to [their] communities," Krug stressed the dual need for "recreation in our democracy" and "democracy in our recreation."[1] As interior secretary from 1946 through 1949, Krug had many opportunities to implement his philosophy. In particular, he oversaw the National Park Service (NPS), including National Capital Parks (NCP)—the unit responsible for federal land, buildings, and facilities in Washington, DC. Throughout his tenure, Krug advocated nondiscrimination at federal recreation sites around the District and vigorously opposed the city's policy of racial segregation at facilities operated by the municipal Department of Recreation.

Racial incidents in 1949 dramatized these conflicting approaches to "recreation in our democracy" and "democracy in our recreation." In late June, several racial disturbances occurred at the Anacostia swimming pool, a federal recreation facility. On June 29, for instance, a mêlée ensued when white swimmers harassed some black teenagers who tried to use the pool, while hundreds of spectators looked on. Four individuals were injured and police made five arrests. Secretary Krug ordered the pool closed, and it remained so for the rest of the summer.[2] Why did events at Anacostia draw so much attention from government officials, civic organizations, civil rights groups, staunch segregationists, local newspapers, and ordinary citizens? More generally, why did questions of race and recreation collide in Washington, DC, at midcentury?

One explanation relates to the District's unusual status as a federal and municipal entity. Part of a federal recreation complex, the Anacostia pool was operated during afternoons and evenings by a private company under contract with the Interior Department. Many recreation sites in the District—including various parks, tennis courts, golf courses, and swimming pools—fell under federal jurisdiction, primarily through National Capital Parks and its concessionaires. The city government also had a claim over the Anacostia facility. The municipal Department of Recreation ran free swim programs at the pool (for whites only) during morning hours. Besides "borrowing" Anacostia and other federal spaces, the department managed city facilities through agreements with the District commissioners and Board of Education (which controlled schoolyards). Thus, many recreational facilities in the District, including Anacostia, were part of a jurisdictional web comprising both federal and municipal stakeholders.[3]

Racial attitudes and policies also affected the incidents at Anacostia. Since the early 1930s, federal recreation sites were technically open to the general public, regardless of race, creed, or nationality. However, de facto segregation prevailed because most federal facilities were used by white or black residents, either routinely or at specific times. In the 1920s, for example, African Americans typically gathered at Rock Creek Park on the Monday after Easter; most whites, one contemporary noted, "seem to understand that this is the Negroes' day and either remain at home or go elsewhere."[4] Similarly, four of the Interior Department's six pools, including Anacostia, were patronized in the 1930s and 1940s solely by whites, while African Americans frequented the other two.[5] By contrast, the city's Jim Crow arrangements were formal administrative decisions. From the early 1900s through late 1940s, municipal parks, playgrounds, and schoolyards operated on a dual system; one set of facilities was designated "white" and the others were "colored." Black citizens could not participate in the city's free morning activities at the Anacostia pool or use any municipal site reserved for whites.

These restrictions applied to all local African Americans (as well as to black visitors and foreign dignitaries), regardless of social class. By 1910, African Americans constituted more than one-quarter of the District's population, and a distinct hierarchy had emerged, from the back-alley poor to a fair-skinned aristocracy.[6] Well-to-do African Americans leveraged their wealth and status to create special forms of leisure and recreation, both interracial and black only.[7] For example, because many private clubs and establishments (such as Glen Echo Amusement Park in nearby Montgomery County, Maryland) were restricted to whites (and some light-complexioned blacks who "passed"), middle-class and elite African Americans bought, operated, and patronized their own sites, including the Suburban Gardens Amusement Park. Similarly, many affluent blacks purchased residential beachfront property in the exclusive Highland Beach area during the 1920s. Most black Washingtonians, however, had no such opportunities. Excluded from sites reserved for or used primarily by whites, less privileged black families were confined to public facilities that were limited in number, hard to access, and inferior in terms of programs, equipment, and maintenance. Discrimination forced many blacks to swim in polluted rivers and streams, play in dangerous streets and alleys, and make do with dilapidated baseball fields and tennis courts.

These jurisdictional and racial problems were interconnected. Every argument over control raised questions of racial policy. Conversely, every conflict over Jim Crow entailed disputes about authority. Which government body controlled a particular site and its rules of use? In Krug's terms, which agencies were responsible for "recreation in our democracy," and which regulations were or were not consistent with "democracy in our recreation"? The answers had real consequences for average citizens. Municipal and federal policies determined who had access to various facilities and who did not. Similarly, patterns of daily use affected which citizens were welcome or unwelcome, based on race and class. Simply put: Who could play, relax, and socialize with whom at which public spaces?

To be sure, recreation was not the only domain of segregation and discrimination in Washington, DC, before midcentury.[8] Following the abolition of slavery in the 1860s and the demise of Reconstruction in the 1870s, the nation's capital joined many cities, northern and southern, in formalizing racial separation, both de facto and de jure. During the first half of the twentieth century, a sharp color line ran through the District, demarcating where white and black citizens typically lived, worked, studied, shopped, dined, got medical care, played, and relaxed. Although transgressions were common, a general understanding existed about who could occupy which spaces and how they were expected to behave. African Americans who trespassed onto "white only" spaces often faced intimidation and physical violence.[9]

The ubiquity of Jim Crow in Washington, DC, illustrates "how racism takes place," to borrow a phrase from George Lipsitz.[10] The relationship of race, power, and "place" is two-fold. On the one hand, racial identities and inequities are "inscribed in the physical contours of the places where we live, work, and play"—in other words, space becomes racialized. Conversely, racism is spatialized. Throughout the twentieth century, segregation privileged whites while teaching blacks to, literally, "take their place" as subordinate citizens. As this chapter shows, discriminatory regimes were especially effective at spaces intended for physical activity.

Parks, playgrounds, and pools, though, were also contested spaces. The efforts of African Americans and their white allies to overturn Jim Crow in housing, employment, education, and public accommodations (such as retail stores and restaurants) are well known. Historians are just beginning to examine, however, the critical role that recreational resistance played in race relations and the civil rights movement. This chapter describes some of the individuals and groups that opposed recreational inequity in Washington, DC, before midcentury.

After summarizing general developments in recreation in the District from the early 1900s through the 1930s, the analysis focuses on the bitter struggle over racial segregation at public facilities between 1942 and 1949. The chapter addresses primarily two questions: Why was recreation such a powerful arena for both discrimination and progress? How did fights over jurisdiction and racial policy both preserve and overturn recreational injustice in the District?

Public recreation in Washington, DC, reflected national trends.[11] Noteworthy developments before midcentury, especially in metropolitan areas, included more numerous facilities of more varied types; the diversification of both supervised and unsupervised programs; increased bureaucratization and administrative oversight; a more prominent role for trained recreation professionals; and divergent perspectives on urban planning, child development, and the value of "play" as cities experienced economic, demographic, and social change.

Two features, however, complicated public recreation in Washington, DC. The first was the District's unique management. On the one hand, it was a ward of the federal government. Many aspects of local recreation, from land acquisition to site development and usage, fell under the aegis of executive branch offices, plus congressional committees overseeing the District's business and other senators or House members who meddled in the city's affairs. On the other hand, because Washington, DC, was also a municipal entity, the city's District commissioners, Board of Education, and Recreation Board (established in 1942) had a stake in recreation as well.

Coordinating these many bodies, much less harmonizing them, proved virtually impossible. Federal and municipal officials wrangled over every feature of public recreation, from jurisdiction to daily operation.[12] Political rivalries, though, were inseparable from racial disputes. Where could white and black residents play, at which times, and with whom? Were facilities in black and white neighborhoods not only separate, but also unequal?[13]

The complexity of recreational use and authority had a long history. Development of the District's physical space dated back to 1791, when President George Washington appointed Major Pierre Charles L'Enfant, a French engineer, to design the nation's new capital. Although L'Enfant's scheme determined the basic layout of avenues, open spaces, and major buildings, progress on recreational sites languished until the late 1800s and early 1900s. As the capital's centennial approached, various projects related to public recreation and tourism got underway, including the national zoo and Rock Creek Park. Shortly thereafter, Senator James McMillan (R, Michigan) proposed a special commission charged with planning a comprehensive system for the capital, ranging from office buildings and national museums to outdoor spaces for leisure and recreation, especially in the city's core. The commission's administrative work was handled by the US Army's chief engineer, who, as the Officer in Charge of Public Buildings and Grounds (PB&G), oversaw all federally owned "reservations"—that is, public spaces—in the District. Political disputes and financial difficulties hindered full adoption of the commission's recommendations, especially those affecting recreation. Moreover, the group's emphasis on the "City Beautiful" slowed progress on neighborhood parks and playgrounds for regular citizens.[14]

Nevertheless, residents and visitors found ways to play and relax outdoors in the early 1900s. As one historian idyllically recounts, children played "Prisoners' Base while their governesses and nursemaids gossiped" in Lafayette Square, and fashionable ladies, gentlemen, and dignitaries strolled by. Rock Creek Park attracted everyone from famous government officials pursuing "the strenuous life" to "boys armed with sticks and pillowcases" in search of chestnuts. Children and adults sought relief from the summer heat at the bathing beach along the Tidal Basin. Residents picnicked at the zoo, played tennis at municipal courts, and organized games on public baseball diamonds. Less fortunate youngsters played hopscotch and marbles in alleys or competed in ball games on vacant lots.[15] Clearly, leisure opportunities varied widely by social class. Affluent and middle-class whites and blacks had better options than did their working-class counterparts.

Private philanthropists and civic leaders filled in some of the gaps. Among the most important initiatives were the playground for young non-school-aged workers, founded in 1901 by Raymond Riordan, principal of

the Greenleaf School; the Neighborhood House playground established in
the Southwest section by Charles F. and Eugenia Weller; and the creation
of the Public Playground Committee (PPC), which took over the Weller
site and developed many others between 1902 and 1904.[16] After receiving
congressional funds in 1905 to equip and manage outdoor playgrounds,
the PPC tapped Henry S. Curtis to be the District's first supervisor of playgrounds.[17] A professional administrator and a leader of the national playground movement, Curtis believed that facilities "should be segregated by
age and sex" as well as race.

In 1906, the PPC was succeeded by the Washington Playground Association (WPA).[18] When the Board of Education took over the city's schoolyards
in 1908, jurisdictional fights ensued among the board, the WPA, and the
federal government. To remedy the situation, in 1912 Congress created the
Department of Playgrounds (DP), a municipal agency under the District
commissioners with responsibility for nonschool playgrounds. Shortly
thereafter, Congress also established the Community Center Department
(CCD). Housed under the Board of Education, the CCD ran recreation programs for adults. Instead of solving jurisdictional problems, however, these
changes exacerbated them.

During the 1920s, major disagreements emerged within and between
the federal and municipal entities handling recreation in the city. In 1925,
Congress transferred the functions of the PB&G to a new office of the director
of Public Buildings and Public Parks of the National Capital (PB&PPNC).
As the effort and expense of managing public areas grew, the PB&PPNC
decided in the late 1920s to outsource day-to-day operations to private
companies. The first contractor was the Welfare and Recreation Association
of Public Buildings and Grounds, or WRA (later known as General Services,
Inc., or GSI).

Another significant development was Congress's establishment in 1924
of the National Capital Park Commission (NCPC), with the full support of
the District's influential Board of Trade, which was an association of businessmen, civil servants, architects, and other leaders.[19] The NCPC's charge
was to provide "for the comprehensive, systematic, and continuous development of the park, parkway, and playground system of the National Capital" and surrounding areas, as well as to purchase land for future sites.
Despite its illustrious name and membership, the NCPC had limited funds
and power. In 1926, Congress approved broader responsibilities for the
group and renamed it the National Capital Park and Planning Commission
(NCPPC).[20] The NCPPC was an independent entity housed in the executive
branch and, until 1933, its chief executive and disbursing officer was the
director of the PB&PPNC (an overlooked conflict of interest).

Although the "monumental city" flourished under these federal initiatives, the "constituent city" attracted far less attention. Moreover, ongoing confusion over authority inspired numerous plans for public recreation. The resulting clutter of federal and municipal reports led the local press to opine that what local residents needed was more parks, not more plans.[21] The federal Capper-Cramton Act seemed a promising solution.[22] Passed in 1930, the legislation provided for "the acquisition of lands in the District of Columbia and the States of Maryland and Virginia requisite to the comprehensive park, parkway, and playground system of the National Capital." Although major projects came to fruition, progress on neighborhood centers and playgrounds was slow.

What did these developments mean for ordinary Washingtonians? How did bureaucratic conflicts and reorganization affect the children and adults who simply wanted to play? To be sure, from the early 1900s through the 1920s public facilities and activities were plentiful. These included municipal playgrounds with recreational spaces and athletic fields; schoolyards that usually were open for general use during after-school hours and summers; golf courses and tennis courts; bathing beaches, wading pools, and swimming pools; areas for boating and fishing; "play stations" and day camps; bridle paths and walking trails; centers for indoor activities; and large public spaces where people gathered for recreation, picnics, civic events, cultural performances, meetings, and parades.

Availability, however, did not mean access. The right and ability to use certain areas between the early 1900s and 1920s varied dramatically by age, sex, class, and race. Few residents had the time or resources to apply for permits, pay fees for lessons or lockers, lease or buy athletic equipment, or travel by public or private conveyance to recreational sites. Racial restrictions were even more systematic, encompassing all municipal and many federal facilities.[23]

City officials sanctioned segregation through willful neglect or by codifying it via formal policies. In 1905, for example, the city operated nineteen playgrounds: twelve for white children (including six schoolyards) and seven for "colored" children (including five at schools). As these figures suggest, the District had a dual system of public education, running separate schools for white and black pupils. This discriminatory setup had little, if any, basis in law. The authorizing legislation for the school system in 1862 implied, but did not mandate, dual operation. Ordinances to prohibit racial discrimination at public accommodations (specifically, licensed businesses) passed in 1872 and 1873; in the early 1900s, however, these statutes mysteriously "disappeared" from the city's official register, without being invalidated or repealed. Finally, it appears that no official decree required the municipal Department of Playgrounds to operate racially segregated sites in the early 1900s.

During World War I and the following decade, municipal facilities and programs remained racially segregated, either by common practice or administrative design.[24] Playgrounds at neighborhood schools adhered to the dual system of public education. During summer months, schoolyards typically were open for general use, but black children could play only at those designated "colored." Similarly, the Board of Education's community centers for adult activities were divided by race. Racial segregation also prevailed at nonschool municipal playgrounds, which typically served the residents of nearby neighborhoods. In 1927, only "six of the twenty-five grounds supported and supervised by the city government" were for African Americans.[25] Upon moving to other neighborhoods, some whites tried to retain control over their former playgrounds. The city also ran two play stations and one day camp for black children in the early 1920s, as well as segregated bathing beaches and swimming pools.

Importantly, "separate" did not mean "equal." Municipal facilities assigned to the "colored population" did not benefit from the degree of accessibility, space, equipment, or maintenance evident at sites reserved for whites. To be sure, the overall lack of recreational space in the District affected both whites and blacks, especially residents of congested areas. As a 1917 report observed, "Some neighborhoods with a population as big as many towns have no play spaces for children and no means of recreation for adults except motion pictures, pool rooms, and saloons."[26] Little children of both races were forced to use sites designed for their older brothers and sisters. To reach a playground, many white and black youngsters had to venture more than one-half mile, often across busy streets and unsafe terrain. Still, the report suggested that black citizens suffered particularly severe burdens. For instance, because African American children were twice as likely as white youngsters to work on Saturday, they presumably could not relax or play on that day. Likewise, factors such as work, distance, and dilapidated facilities probably explain why black youngsters five to fourteen years old were far less likely to use municipal playgrounds than were whites in that age range. Saddled with hardship and inequities, black Washingtonians had to find alternate places. Black children and teens swam (and sometimes drowned) in the District's polluted rivers. They played on vacant lots, crowded sidewalks, and dangerous streets—although using the latter two spaces was illegal.[27]

Many federal sites in the District were also off-limits to African Americans. Enforcers of segregation from the late 1910s to early 1930s included the Office of PB&G and its successor, the PB&PPNC; the heads of the NCPC and its successor, the NCPPC; and various members of Congress. Their decisions won enthusiastic support from the District's white establishment and civic organizations. Black activists and political groups worked just as diligently to expose and disrupt the white elite's discriminatory schemes.

This struggle was not confined to recreation; it occurred on many fronts around the District in the early twentieth century. For many Washingtonians, though, the question of where and with whom white and black residents played had special resonance. Because physical activities were informal, they seemed more intimate and unpredictable than other daily interactions. Above all, the freedom to *literally* exercise one's civil rights was at stake.

Conflicts over public bathing beaches and swimming pools during the 1920s illustrate people's differing racial attitudes and agendas.[28] Opened in the summer of 1918, the bathing beach along the southeast side of the Tidal Basin welcomed white children and adults for swimming as well as aquatic meets, canoe regattas, bathing beauty contests, and other activities.[29] The site became part of a large amusement park along the Potomac for "rich and poor" whites, featuring tennis courts, baseball diamonds, a speedway, and picnic grounds.[30]

In summer 1921, Lieutenant Colonel Clarence O. Sherrill, superintendent of the PB&G, proposed a federal beach for "colored people" on the Anacostia River, east of the old James Creek canal.[31] Although Congress eventually endorsed the basic idea, members suggested an alternate location (Jones Point), but the beach was not constructed.[32] The plan resurfaced in 1924–25 during Congress's perennial debate over money for the District. Although the House and Senate raised few objections when approving other projects for the city, the question of a beach for black residents inflamed racial politics in the two chambers and became entangled in their customary squabble over District appropriations.[33]

The proposed site was the western shore of the Tidal Basin—opposite the existing beach for whites. Despite recognizing that all residents would welcome relief from the city's notorious summer heat, members of Congress and the local press voiced concerns about a beach for the "colored population." How would operational costs be covered? Could pollution from sewage and other sources be properly managed, at either the new facility or the current one for whites?[34] Would the beach for black bathers require removal of the Japanese cherry trees, planted only a decade earlier?[35] Would such a facility compromise the city's overall health and beauty?[36] One senator assured his colleagues that the area for blacks "would be screened and would not be offensive."[37] Since white and black bathers would occupy the same body of water, however, a separate, "screened" area might not prevent interracial encounters. Even more terrifying was the possibility of a shared interracial beach. If "a colored bathing place was not provided," one senator warned, "the colored population of Washington would insist on using the beach for whites."[38] With this prospect looming, construction of a Jim Crow beach got underway.

Ongoing fights over the beach's location and District appropriations, though, sabotaged congressional funding for maintenance of the white beach. In February 1925, Congress ordered that both beaches be closed and dismantled by July 1, 1926. This action prompted many schemes to preserve bathing for whites. For instance, the District commissioners and some white citizens rallied to keep the Tidal Basin area available, perhaps through subscriptions.[39] Various congressmen, too, favored the continuation of the white beach, while exploring an alternate site for blacks.[40] Proceeding very slowly in demolishing the white beach, Superintendent Sherrill of the PB&PPNC also suggested legal grounds on which to reopen it.[41] If that option failed, Sherrill said, two new beaches could be developed: an area "for the white people at the down-stream end of the Georgetown bridge on the Virginia side of the river and [another] for the colored people at Jones' Point east of the Washington barracks."[42]

Although this idea gained traction, a different plan appealed even more to Congress and Lieutenant Colonel U. S. Grant III, Sherrill's successor; perhaps segregated swimming pools (rather than beaches) could be constructed.[43] After a southern senator inserted language requiring racial segregation, Congress approved two "artificial bathing" facilities, and locations were chosen.[44] Black residents immediately objected that the remoteness of the "colored" pool would greatly inconvenience them and "overtax the single street railway line in that section."[45] The PB&PPNC countered by proposing "several smaller bathing places for colored residents in various parts of the city."[46] The idea garnered broad support from the white establishment, including the Board of Trade, the newly formed NCPPC, and its executive officer, Lieutenant Colonel Grant III (who also directed the PB&PPNC).[47] Although multiple sites would improve access, black leaders understood that the scheme's real intent was to "thrust upon them . . . a segregated recreational unit on Federal territory."[48] Arguably, the plan for separate pools signified even more virulent discrimination than did segregated beaches. By establishing neighborhood pools for black residents, white supremacists could literally confine the "inferior race" to small spaces and preclude any interracial encounters.[49]

Supported by some progressive congressmen, black protestors successfully delayed the construction of Jim Crow pools for several years. After
a black pool eventually was built near the Francis Junior High School,
black civic groups opposed Lieutenant Colonel Grant's decision to hire a
white man (former athletic director at a white high school) as its supervisor, because his appointment violated the long tradition of black personnel
at Jim Crow facilities.[50] When Congress failed to underwrite maintenance
costs, the PB&PPNC contracted with the WRA, the private concessionaire, to operate the site. However, black citizens objected that no African
Americans served on the WRA board and the imposition of admission fees
disadvantaged the very community the facility was meant to serve.[51] When
the Francis pool's first season concluded in 1928, Grant proudly declared it
a success: attendance was large, sanitary conditions had been inspected and
maintained, and "disorder" had been avoided.[52] As his remarks of "appreciation" suggested, Grant measured success by Jim Crow criteria: the site
had been filled to capacity with black youngsters (and them alone), and their
bodies and behavior posed no threat to themselves—or to anyone else.

During the Great Depression, local and federal resources for recreation
shrank around the country, and officials in Washington, DC, turned their
attention from long-term planning to the immediate crisis.[53] Reorganization
of the federal bureaucracy renewed jurisdictional questions about recreation
in the District. In 1933, the Office of PB&PPNC was abolished, and control of federal land in the city was transferred to National Capital Parks,
a new unit of the National Park Service within the Interior Department.
The NCP's Recreation Division was "charged with the construction, maintenance, and operation on a permit basis of all recreational facilities in the
parks of the National Capital," ranging from athletics to cultural events and
celebrations.[54] In the mid-1930s, the NCP's authority encompassed about
13 percent of the District's total land (excluding property purchased by or
assigned to the District commissioners).[55]

   With NCP in ascent, other groups tried to reassert their authority.[56]
The NCPPC, for example, had become little more than "a land-purchas-
ing agent for other government bodies."[57] To revive its planning function,
the NCPPC commissioned the National Recreation Association in 1934 to
prepare a comprehensive analysis of recreation in Washington, DC. Led by
Lebert Howard Weir, a national expert on playgrounds and recreation, the
group's final report offered a scathing indictment of the status quo along
with four possible plans for more effective, unified administration of public
recreation in the District.[58] With criticism mounting, Franklin D. Roosevelt

established the President's Committee on Recreation in 1935. Each key player—the NCP, District commissioners, and the Board of Education—was represented, with an NCPPC delegate serving as nonvoting chair.[59]

Despite ongoing animosity, some coordination developed. In summer 1939, the Board of Education's Community Center Department merged with the District commissioners' Playground Department. The new body—the Community Center and Playgrounds Department (CC&PD)—was run by a central coordinator and received a single appropriation from Congress. In 1940, National Capital Parks agreed to transfer 178 recreational and athletic sites to the CC&PD.[60] NCP continued to maintain and improve the properties, while CC&PD supervised the sites and issued permits. Although many questions remained, the interwar period ended with credible signs of cooperation.

How did structural changes affect the public's access to recreation in the 1930s? The answer differed sharply between municipal and federal facilities. The color line remained firmly intact at city-operated sites managed by the schools and the commissioners' Department of Playgrounds. The creation of the CC&PD did nothing to lessen racial segregation, in theory or practice.

By contrast, federal policy changed significantly. From the outset, NCP promised to operate facilities on a "non-segregated, non-discriminatory basis," with the full support of Interior secretary Harold L. Ickes (1933–46).[61] Ickes's most famous action for civil rights occurred in 1939. When the Daughters of the American Revolution barred Marian Anderson, the famed black contralto, from performing at Constitution Hall (the city's most prestigious venue), Secretary Ickes, along with Eleanor Roosevelt and the NAACP's local branch, was instrumental in finding an alternate site on federal land. On Easter Sunday, 1939, before a crowd of some 75,000 at the Lincoln Memorial, he introduced Anderson with a rousing speech about race and justice.

Ickes and his staff also furthered civil rights through many lesser-known decisions. In August 1935, for example, some parents objected to interracial play at the sand boxes in Lincoln Park on East Capital Street; the NCP, however, declined to interfere with black and white youngsters' habit of playing peaceably together. By 1939, Ickes opened the "picnic ground in Rock Creek Park to biracial use." In 1940, he ordered that black players be admitted to "the lighted tennis courts in West Potomac Park and on the Mall." In 1941, he made "the federally operated golf course similarly available to everyone."[62] These steps had both practical and symbolic meaning in a city still divided by race.

As the interwar period closed, a concerted effort was underway to centralize the administration of recreation. Another pressing issue was the contradiction between city-mandated segregation and federal nondiscrimination. These questions came to a head during the 1940s.

In 1942, Congress passed Public Law 534 (H.R. 5075), establishing the Recreation Board of the District of Columbia. The bill authorized the board to "determine all questions of general policy" and to appoint a superintendent of the new Department of Recreation (superseding the CC&PD). Together, the board and superintendent were expected to design "a comprehensive program of public recreation," ranging from games and sports to cultural and creative activities. Congress also instructed them to take advantage of public properties assigned by NCPPC to the District commissioners as well as work out agreements with the federal government and the Board of Education for using facilities under their jurisdiction.[63]

The Recreation Board comprised seven members: a representative of the Board of Education, a delegate from the District commissioners, the chief officer of National Capital Parks, and four residents selected by the commissioners. Harry S. Wender, one of the community representatives, chaired the board for its first decade. Despite his relative youth, Wender, who was born in 1908, was an established lawyer and prominent civic leader, having been active in the Federation of Citizens' Associations (an umbrella organization for whites), the Southwest Citizens' Association (his neighborhood group), and advisory councils concerned with traffic law and transportation. The lone black member during the 1940s was Alice C. Hunter, president of the Federation of Parent-Teacher Associations. Other members who played key roles during the 1940s were James E. Schwab, a real estate mogul and staunch segregationist who chaired the Board of Trade's recreation committee, and Irving C. Root, who steadfastly supported the Interior Department's nondiscrimination policy during his tenure as NCP superintendent (1941–50).

Racial segregation permeated the new structure. The Recreation Board's original By-Laws, Rules, and Regulations referred vaguely to "separate programs" organized by "regions."[64] The Department of Recreation clarified the intent; its personnel and activities were arranged according to twenty-six residential areas grouped into regions: A–F (a code for "white") and G–K (a code for "black"). Challenging this veiled form of discrimination, some blacks insisted that more African Americans be appointed to the board.[65]

This suggestion was the opening salvo in a long, bitter struggle. For the next ten years, the Recreation Board was embroiled in controversy: Which federal or municipal body controlled which recreational sites? Should racial segregation or nondiscrimination prevail? Conflicts arose among board members as well as between the board and other entities, including the Board of Education, District commissioners, the Interior Department, the NCPPC, and Congress. Local newspapers kept close track of the board's every move, as did political and civic organizations. Among these were the Federation of Citizens' Associations and its neighborhood groups for white citizens; the Federation of Civic Associations (a coalition of neighborhood organizations representing African Americans); the District branch of the Progressive Party; the League of Women Voters; plus labor unions, veterans' organizations, and ministerial and church groups.

Civil rights organizations were especially vigilant. These included the Citizens Committee on Race Relations (CCRR), a coalition of white and black leaders founded in 1943; the National Committee on Segregation in the Nation's Capital, an interracial group established in 1946 as "a vehicle for united action for full civil rights for all Americans"; and the local chapter of the NAACP.[66] The NAACP's membership and activities overlapped with those of the Committee for Racial Democracy in the Nation's Capital (CRD) and its successor, the Council for Civil Rights in the Nation's Capital (CCR). The NAACP's Committee on Recreation helped organize the Citizens Committee Against Segregation in Recreation (CCASR), which existed from 1945 to 1948. Edwin B. Henderson, a physical educator in the black public schools and prominent civil rights leader, chaired both committees.[67]

The public spotlight remained on the Recreation Board throughout the 1940s. In 1943, the NCP transferred to the board the responsibility of issuing permits to use various federal facilities. Seeking more authority, some board members proposed taking over the Interior Department's public golf courses. Lasting more than a decade, this effort underscored the two bodies' divergent racial policies.[68]

In 1945, the Recreation Board formally attached racial designations to each site under its control.[69] A majority voted to replace the bylaws' vague references to "separation" with explicit language: "Recreation programs for white residents shall be conducted in regions A–F and in designated city-wide centers. Recreation programs for Negro residents shall be conducted in regions G–K and in designated city-wide centers."[70] Arguing strenuously against the amendment, Irving C. Root and Alice C. Hunter cast dissenting votes.

Supporters and detractors promptly descended on the board. While some white citizens and congressional Dixiecrats hailed the change, civil rights advocates condemned its codification of racial discrimination. Labor unions, the Progressive Party, the Federation of Civic Associations, the

NAACP's local chapter, and the newly founded CCASR mobilized. They testified before government bodies, organized petition drives and mass meetings, prepared action letters and resolutions, distributed leaflets, delivered radio addresses, and issued press releases.[71]

After World War II, the Recreation Board focused again on civilian programs, with public swimming pools quickly taking center stage. The Recreation Board ran two free municipal pools, while the Interior Department's NCP contracted with Government Services, Inc., to operate six outdoor pools that assessed fees for swimming, lockers, suits, and other services. (During morning hours, the city's Recreation Department conducted free programs for whites at the sites.) In theory, the federal pools were open to everyone, regardless of race, creed, or nationality. In practice, they were de facto segregated: four federal pools were patronized exclusively by whites, while blacks typically used the other two.[72] Accusing GSI of financial mismanagement and lax supervision, the Recreation Board's special investigatory committee set out in 1946 to gain "full responsibility" for all pools in the District.[73] The Interior Department and the local NAACP recognized that municipal control would entail racial segregation. Federal officials therefore rejected the board's move and awarded GSI a five-year extension.

Conflicts continued into 1947 and 1948.[74] Segregationists and desegregationists passed resolutions, attended public hearings, and wrote letters to officials and local newspapers. Although CCASR folded in May 1948, other civil rights groups, especially the NAACP, increased their pressure on municipal agencies. Demographic changes also sparked concern. As white and black residents moved to different areas, the racial composition of many neighborhoods shifted. Nevertheless, local schools and playgrounds often retained their original racial designation. Some citizens and officials puzzled over the illogic (and injustice) of "white only" facilities in increasingly black neighborhoods.

The convergence of grassroots activism and demographic trends is well illustrated by the Park View playground in the District's Northwest section.[75] In 1921, Congress authorized that a vacant lot near the local white elementary school be purchased and developed as a community playground for white residents. Although some playing fields appeared, major improvements did not come about until 1932, when a wading pool, tennis court, and field house were added—making Park View one of the best-equipped playgrounds in the District.

By the late 1940s, Park View had become a fairly mixed neighborhood. Its school and playground, however, remained officially "white"—a situation that forced black children to play in alleyways and streets. In 1947, several local and national organizations confronted the Recreation Board about its discriminatory policies and recommended that Park View be reclassified as an "open" facility. Although the board refused, it did agree to investigate six playgrounds (five "white" and one "colored") in areas where the population was changing.

After the study's completion and bitter public hearings, the board decided in July 1948 to transfer the Park View playground from "white" to "black." However, "as long as the adjacent school remain[ed] white, the playground [would] be used by white children during school hours."[76] This dual arrangement meant that, despite a 66 percent decline in the number of local white children between 1942 and 1947, the site was still reserved for them during the day, whereas blacks could only use the facility after school was dismissed. This plan satisfied no one. White civic groups decried the usurpation of "white" space, while black organizations insisted on immediate desegregation. Meanwhile, black children in the Park View neighborhood took direct action, by simply using the wading pool and playground as they wished. Facing a logistical headache, the Recreation Board emptied and closed the pool. Once the NCPPC approved dual use, the board reopened the pool in July 1948. One year later, when the elementary school was transferred from white to black, the playground also became officially "black."

Other developments in 1948 proved equally significant. In the fall, Mastin G. White, solicitor general of the Interior Department, issued an opinion about the District's recreational sites. Who had jurisdiction, he asked, over property that NCPPC purchased under the Capper-Cramton Act and then assigned to the District commissioners as playgrounds?[77] The use of such spaces, White concluded, was "contingent upon the making of an agreement or agreements between the National Park Service and the D.C. Recreation Board."[78] These arrangements could include "any provisions that [were] mutually satisfactory" to the two bodies. In White's view, neither Congress nor the NCPPC had any say in the matter. His statement clarified the crucial distinction between jurisdiction and control. The NPS held jurisdiction over real property, whereas the Recreation Board merely acquired a provisional right of use. By White's reasoning, the Interior Department could demand nondiscrimination as a condition for using federal land and facilities in the District's park system. Not surprisingly, both the NCPPC and the Recreation Board responded with open hostility.[79]

The decibel level then rose even higher. Scores of citizens confronted the Board of Education and the Recreation Board at public hearings in the fall of 1948. In November, the National Committee on Segregation in the

Nation's Capital issued its final report. Referring to the District as "the capital of white supremacy," the document pointed to citizens' natural habit of playing together harmoniously, regardless of race, and sharply contrasted the Recreation Board's Jim Crow system with the Interior Department's policy of nondiscrimination.[80]

These controversies came to a head in 1949. Conflicts between the Interior Department (led by Julius A. Krug, 1946–49) and the Recreation Board (chaired by Harry S. Wender) proved especially volatile and decisive. Between January and March, the two bodies focused on federal tennis courts. The board agreed to stop designating eighteen courts as white, colored, or open, and to issue permits for use on a first-come, first-served basis.[81] The dust had barely settled on the tennis courts when conflicts over public golf courses resumed. Because the government's contract with its concessionaire would soon expire, the Recreation Board renewed its effort to take over the courses—even offering to run them on a nonsegregated basis. The board also accepted, with conditions, a proposal from the American Friends Service Committee to conduct interracial activities at some public playgrounds during the coming summer.[82]

Partial solutions, though, rarely satisfied Secretary Krug. In April and May, he broached the possibility of transferring *all* federal facilities to the Recreation Board if it abolished its race-based policies in toto. Seizing the moment, civil rights groups and progressive congressmen intensified their campaign. Meanwhile, the NCPPC removed all racial designations from its District of Columbia Recreation System Plan. This decision undercut the Recreation Board's stated rationale for segregation. As critics gathered and friends disappeared, pressure mounted on the Recreation Board. In early summer, its bylaws committee began considering amendments on racial policy—none of which met Krug's condition of system-wide nondiscrimination. The committee's deliberations were just underway when racial "disturbances" occurred at the swimming pool in Fairlawn Park.

A federal facility, Fairlawn featured baseball diamonds, a golf course, the No. 11 Police Boys Club, and the Anacostia swimming pool.[83] During morning hours, Recreation Department employees conducted free instruction and swimming for whites only. During the afternoon and evening, Government Services, Inc., the private contractor, operated the pool for the Interior Department. Theoretically, *any* citizen could use *any* federal pool in the District. In practice, however, Anacostia was patronized exclusively by whites.

Trouble began at the facility on Saturday, June 25, 1949, when about thirty black youth arrived for a swim.[84] Fearing that "trouble might start" if black patrons were admitted, the lifeguards refused to work—whereupon the manager closed the pool for several hours. These developments prompted a majority of Recreation Board members to threaten withdrawing the city's morning staff from Anacostia if racial segregation were not maintained.[85] According to a local newspaper, Harry S. Wender was "indignant 'about the whole thing.' He charged [that] the colored children coming to the pools [had] been 'inspired by radical elements who know full well [that] elimination of segregation at the pools is a very explosive thing.'"[86] Adhering to the principle of nondiscrimination, GSI offered to handle morning activities if the Interior Department covered the cost.

While leaders held meetings and exchanged memos, average citizens once again took to the streets. Although Anacostia's morning swim on June 28 was fairly calm, police "responded to a 3 p.m. 'trouble' call during the GSI paid swimming period."[87] Following an interracial "melee" that caused minor injuries and attracted a crowd of two or three hundred youngsters, police took several people into custody. Among those detained was Ida Jane Galpert, a white female who, representing the Young Progressives, wanted to see that "'Negro rights were made available to them and under protected circumstances.'" During her interrogation, police reportedly asked Miss Galpert if she "approved of interracial marriage" and "whether she was a Communist."[88]

On the afternoon of June 29, GSI employees again admitted a group of black teenagers to Anacostia, in accordance with federal policy.[89] White swimmers began harassing the black youth, chasing them out of the pool and forcing some to scale a barbed-wire fence to escape. Drawn by the commotion, nearly five hundred people gathered around the pool's perimeter. The crowd comprised both blacks and whites, including representatives of the Young Progressives, who distributed handbills encouraging biracial use of the pool. As the disturbance escalated, mounted police tried to disperse the crowd, nearly trampling a white female member of the Young Progressives. When the fracas subsided, at least four persons had been injured and another five arrested. Citing the incidents at Anacostia, the Northwest Council of [white] Citizens' Associations reiterated its support for segregation and warned of imminent threats to public health and safety. "Among the foremost duties of the Government of the District of Columbia," the group declared, "is the protection of the health of its citizens and prevention of the spread of readily communicable and transmissible diseases."[90] Unwilling to forsake federal policy, but wanting to avert further violence, Secretary Krug ordered the Anacostia pool closed, pending a plan that ensured all citizens safe and equal use of the facility. It remained closed for the rest of the summer.

The manager of the Anacostia swimming pool "looks over his hot, dry domain" after the US Interior Department closed the facility due to racial disturbances. (Quote from *Washington Evening Star*, July 27, 1949.) Reprinted with permission of the DC Public Library, Star Collection, © Washington Post.

Against this backdrop, federal officials and the Recreation Board continued negotiating, while board members wrangled over possible policy revisions. In July 1949, a majority on the board agreed to "make every possible and realistic effort toward the removal of racial segregation in public recreation in such sequence and at such a rate of progression as may be consistent with the public interest, public order and effective administration."[91] Segregationists predicted that racial chaos would ensue. Siding with Hunter and Root (the board's reliable dissenters), civil rights groups deplored the change as a feeble gesture lacking a clear timetable and action plan.

On July 20, 1949, the Recreation Board and the National Park Service reached an agreement.[92] The Interior Department would transfer control of five golf courses, more than fifty tennis courts, the Hains Point bicycle concession, and the Tidal Basin boating concession. In exchange, the Recreation Board would add its new statement on gradual desegregation to its bylaws and remove "all references to segregation designations at recreation facilities." Subsequent meetings produced an additional agreement.[93] Besides transferring more federal facilities to the Recreation Board, the pact of August 29 allowed the city to run programs at about twenty other federal areas, if the NPS consented. The agreement permitted the board to "determine all questions of general policy," as long as its decisions conformed to federal regulations that sites be "open to use by all people irrespective of their race, creed, color or national origin." The accord stipulated that supplementary arrangements be worked out for golf courses, tennis courts, and other sites under concession management. It said nothing about the federal swimming pools.

Knowing that official promises might falter without grassroots pressure, local citizens and civil rights groups continued their efforts. In September 1949, for example, several black parents filed a civil lawsuit on behalf of their children, alleging racial segregation and discrimination at some neighborhood playgrounds. The action named the Recreation Board, the superintendent of Recreation, the Board of Education, District commissioners, and Interior secretary Krug as defendants.[94]

Events in 1949 by no means ended the District's struggle over public recreation and racial segregation.[95] Conservative and progressive members of the Recreation Board remained at odds, as illustrated by debates over municipal playgrounds. To fulfill its gradual desegregation pledge of 1949, the board formed a "transition committee" that evaluated city facilities for possible reclassification from "white" or "black" to "open" (that is, without racial restrictions). Before finalizing any change, the board typically invited input from the general public, especially the affected neighborhoods.

A clear pattern emerged. In July 1951, the board tentatively approved the conversion of the Raymond and New York Avenue playgrounds (used by local blacks) from "white" to "biracial use." However, it "decided to continue Turkey Thicket and Edgewood playgrounds in the northeast section as white," after "white organizations in the area objected" to desegregation.[96] In November 1951, the board converted the Hoover playground from "white" to "open." The facility served a neighborhood that was 87 percent black.[97] In spring 1952, the transition committee suggested that Trinidad and Wheatley playgrounds be transferred from "white" to "open" and Park View from "black" to "open." All three were located in increasingly or predominantly black neighborhoods. By contrast, the committee "recommended no change in restricted use" of four white playgrounds "because they were well used by white children, and other facilities [were] available to Negro children in the area"—a claim that blacks vigorously disputed. White groups also regarded desegregation as unfair because the playgrounds in question did not have "enough equipment for the white children alone."[98]

The board's racial calculus was evident. As one civic leader aptly observed, the board "designated as 'open' only those playgrounds whose naming evoked little or no opposition from white citizens." Such facilities "already served a large or completely Negro neighborhood."[99] Overall, the board's concessions to white opinion and privilege hindered democratic recreation. Between June 1949 and June 1952, only twelve play areas in the District were reclassified as "open," while more than seventy remained segregated.[100]

Civil rights activists challenged the board's logic and authority at every step. In 1952, for example, Park View residents urged the board to formally desegregate the community playground because the facility "should serve the recreational needs of all the people" and both black and white children already used it.[101] In 1952, the plaintiffs in *Camp v. Recreation Board* challenged the board's right to operate the Trinidad playground on a segregated basis. The District Court dismissed the case, arguing that the board had authority to "determine all questions of general policy relating to public recreation" and private plaintiffs had no standing to bring the suit.[102] Finally, the Congress of Racial Equality (CORE) played a key role in desegregation efforts at the Rosedale playground and swimming pool (a municipal site) after racial clashes in 1952 and 1953.[103]

Swimming pools remained especially controversial. The fate of federal pools (still under concession management) had not been settled. The Interior Department consistently reiterated its policy of nonsegregation.[104] Meanwhile, the Recreation Board was determined to gain the "transfer of these public facilities to its authority" on the board's own terms—a smokescreen for racial segregation.[105] Consequently, negotiations over swimming pools (and golf courses) stalled in the early 1950s.

Major court cases soon altered the landscape. In *District of Columbia v. Thompson*, a landmark suit in 1953 concerning discrimination at a local restaurant, the US Supreme Court ruled that the city's civil rights statutes from the 1870s (the "lost laws") were still valid. Hailing the decision, many civil rights advocates believed that it also applied to hotels, barbershops, and places of amusement. The Supreme Court's twin judgments on May 17, 1954, in *Brown v. Board of Education* and *Bolling v. Sharpe*—which dealt specifically with public schools in Washington, DC—were decisive blows to the longstanding principle of "separate, but equal" and unambiguous calls for desegregation. At a special meeting the next day, the Recreation Board voted

> That in accordance with the policy . . . adopted on July 20, 1949, the Board issued orders to the Superintendent to immediately put into effect a nonsegregated program for all units under the control of the Board; that the Board's Administrative Control Plan adopted on July 20, 1949, which contained designated units, be immediately abolished;

and that the Superintendent be directed to expedite the reorganization of the Department necessitated by this action.[106]

Within days, the Recreation Board announced success. On May 20, a spokesman declared that desegregation had not affected the "general pattern of attendance" at city facilities and that "no incidents were reported."[107]

The board's call for prompt action sounded transformative. Its claim of instant success seemed impressive. Nonsegregation on paper, however, did not signify desegregation, much less integration, in daily life. Nor did the elimination of racial designations ensure equity at every public playground and pool in the city. Racial prejudice and discrimination remained entrenched, further legal remedies were necessary, and advocates of democratic recreation continued their fight through the 1950s and beyond.[108]

This survey of public recreation and racial segregation in Washington, DC, during the first half of the twentieth century suggests three conclusions. The first relates to the confluence of governance and race. By definition, public recreation falls under the aegis of governments. Inevitably, the city's dual status as a federal district and municipal entity complicated every decision about recreation. Similarly, racial issues were ever-present, whether the topic was site development, facility management, or rules of use. These jurisdictional and racial questions were inseparable. Conflicts of authority were, simultaneously, disputes over segregation. Conversely, every struggle over racial policy brought together agencies with disparate political agendas.

The legal technicalities can seem so thick that they obscure the story's human participants: the federal and city officials who weighed decisions, the members of local civic groups who spoke out, and the ordinary citizens, black and white, who were eager to play, compete, relax, and socialize; in particular, the African Americans who wanted, literally, to exercise their civil rights at public facilities. Black Washingtonians defended this right, individually and collectively, in courtrooms, government offices, recreation sites, and the local media. Civil rights groups were the city's most persistent and well-organized advocates of justice. Their efforts suggest a second general conclusion: The campaign for equitable recreation mirrored key features of the local civil rights movement.

Instead of inventing the movement anew, recreational activists in Washington, DC, took advantage of existing strategies and machinery. Rather than work in isolation, they built on the know-how and coordination already present within the city's civil rights community. Finally, they learned to adapt after each apparent failure. Rebuffed by the Recreation Board after it codified segregation in 1945, civil rights advocates pursued democratic recreation via other centers of power, including the Interior Department, Justice Department, District commissioners, and the city's Board of Education. These efforts kept the struggle alive and, arguably, built momentum for the Recreation Board's commitment to desegregation—however imperfect—in 1949. Although the District's battle for civil rights had unique characteristics, it reflected similar campaigns in communities around the country.[109]

These observations raise a final question: Why was public recreation so contentious? After all, white supremacists defended segregation on many fronts, and civil rights activists targeted numerous injustices. Why did both sides consider recreation such a critical domain—one deserving as much energy and perseverance as did conflicts over fair housing, employment, and voting rights? Some answers emerge through a broader consideration of the connections between racial politics and physical activity.

Segregated recreation was commonplace before midcentury.[110] As African Americans demanded a "level playing field," legal battles arose in New Orleans, Nashville, Cincinnati, Los Angeles, and communities in Illinois, Missouri, Kansas, and Florida. Riots and police brutality occurred in Chicago, St. Louis, Philadelphia, Detroit, and Buffalo. To avoid integration, many white communities resorted to subterfuge. Some turned their public swimming pools into parking lots and their playgrounds into landfills. Others leased or sold their public tennis courts and golf courses to private operators, who felt no moral or legal obligation to be fair and inclusive.

The range of these examples suggests the important role of physical activity in discrimination and equity. As a corporeal experience, recreation automatically elicits questions about human bodies, movement, behavior, and "worth." Whether accessible to everyone or restricted by age, ability, sex, and/or race, recreational sites deliver immediate lessons about "where we belong" and "how good we are," in both an athletic and social sense. At playgrounds and swimming pools, ordinary Americans experience fairness or injustice in immediate, physical ways. Recreational spaces are also fluid and unpredictable; activities tend to be unscripted and unregulated; and people's interactions can be casual, direct, even intimate, to a degree not evident in more structured settings.

Washingtonians considered these attributes of recreation through the lens of racial politics. Segregationists believed that regulating "lesser" people by controlling space would maintain white privilege. Few sites institutionalized blacks' physical "inferiority" and social subordination as decisively as did separate playgrounds, athletic fields, and swimming pools. These spaces did ideological work as well. White supremacists contended that being in intimate contact with blacks by sharing recreational facilities with them was unfair, unsanitary, and abhorrent. By contrast, advocates of justice understood that spaces for leisure and physical activity had to be reconfigured for racism to be challenged and social inequities dismantled. The opportunity to play wherever and however one chose represented an exercise of civil rights—a premise as compelling today as it was decades ago.

8

"The Greatest High School Basketball Game Ever Played"

DeMatha vs. Power Memorial, 1965

Chad Carlson

Lew Alcindor sat in the locker room, dejected. Teammates around him were crying. Outside the visitors' locker room, his mother was in tears, too. It was January 1965, and Alcindor and his Power Memorial teammates had just lost to DeMatha Catholic High of Hyattsville, Maryland. The raw emotions of the visiting Panthers indicated that this was no ordinary game. Indeed, DeMatha's legendary coach, Morgan Wootten, would call it "the greatest high school game ever played." Alcindor's coach, Jack Donohue, would come to believe that it represented a seminal moment in the history of high school basketball.[1]

Alcindor, who later changed his name to Kareem Abdul-Jabbar, would go on to become one of basketball's greatest players. The six-time National Basketball Association (NBA) champion won six Most Valuable Player awards, played on nineteen All-Star teams, was named one of the NBA's fifty greatest players, and ended his career as the league's all-time leader in points scored, games played, field goals made, blocked shots, and defensive rebounds.[2]

In college, Alcindor was equally impressive. He won three National Collegiate Athletic Association (NCAA) championships while playing on UCLA's varsity team, and claimed three Player of the Year awards *and* three Most Outstanding Player awards in the NCAA tournament. Incredibly, his Bruin teams compiled an 88-2 record. One of those losses—a 1968 regular-season defeat to Elvin Hayes and the University of Houston at the Astrodome in

Houston, known as "The Game of the Century"—was the first nationally televised regular-season college basketball game.[3]

At Power Memorial Catholic High School in New York City, Alcindor's teams fared just as well. Following Big Lew's freshman year, in which the Panthers lost five games, Power was defeated only once during the rest of Alcindor's prep career. His teams amassed a record-setting seventy-one-game win streak over the span of three seasons. The loss to DeMatha in 1965 ended the string of victories.[4]

Amazingly, this epic hard-court battle was one of only three losses Alcindor experienced between the end of his freshman year in high school and the start of his rookie season in the NBA—a period that covered almost the entire 1960s. DeMatha's victory was arguably the most important in the school's distinguished basketball history. The triumph even seemed to rise above social boundaries. Wootten and the rest of the DeMatha team remember a racial inclusiveness that may be more remarkable than the defeat of Alcindor and Power Memorial. Indeed, race seemingly played no part in the game.

The January 30, 1965, matchup between consensus 1964 national prep champion Power Memorial and 1963 high school national champion DeMatha provides insight into attitudes toward race in the nation's capital during the 1960s.[5] Generally, race relations in Washington have played a significant role in carving out different existences for black and white residents. But DeMatha's and Power's racially integrated teams, as well as that night's desegregated standing-room-only crowd in attendance at the University of Maryland's Cole Field House, site of the famous 1966 "racial statement" championship game in which an all-black starting five from Texas Western University beat an all-white squad from the University of Kentucky, symbolized an unusual moment of racial tolerance, reflecting important advances in civil rights at the time. The sportsmanship and respect exhibited by both teams suggests that the game was mostly about basketball, and not racial division.

DeMatha's victory also became a source of pride for Washingtonians. It proved to local fans that Washington could produce prep basketball teams as good as, or even better than, those from larger cities. After DeMatha beat Alcindor and Power Memorial, DC basketball gained more respect among Washingtonians. As Alcindor's fame grew, so too did the significance of DeMatha's triumph, thus embedding it further in Washington's collective sporting memory. DeMatha's win and the prestige it accrued helped popularize DC high school basketball, while simultaneously promoting the city's prep basketball scene nationwide.

The 1965 game between DeMatha and Power was not the first time the two teams had met. Morgan Wootten, who ended his forty-six-year coaching career at DeMatha in 2002 as one of the most respected basketball coaches in history, had scheduled his squad to host Power during Alcindor's junior season. Believing that the game would attract a crowd too big for DeMatha's modestly sized gym, he proposed that the school rent out the University of Maryland's Cole Field House, a substantially larger arena near DeMatha. But DeMatha's athletic moderator, Father Louis Amico, believing the financial risk of such a venture was too great, declined. Undeterred, Wootten got his close friend, Washington Redskins Pro Bowl linebacker Rod Breedlove, to cosponsor the game. Inspired by Wootten's belief that the game would draw a large crowd, Amico finally accepted the revised plan with the provision that the school would receive a portion of the proceeds. The game was set for February 1, 1964. "I knew that we had a good team . . . with good players," Wootten recalled, "and, of course, never before had I ever heard of a [high school] player [except for] maybe Wilt [Chamberlain who was] . . . quite like [Alcindor]."[6]

By the start of his prep career, Big Lew had already made a name for himself. Much of his fame was because of his height. He was literally head and shoulders above his peers. In December 1962, Manhattan College coach Ken Norton mentioned Alcindor—then a high school sophomore—to a group of sportswriters and coaches at a pregame luncheon in Chicago. Believing he was the first to tell the Windy City basketball brass about the Big Apple's prized athletic pupil, Norton was surprised to find that many of the coaches in attendance had already heard of the young seven-footer. Averaging nineteen points and sixteen rebounds in his sophomore year, and playing on an undefeated Panther team, Alcindor attracted a wide following. In April 1963, just after Big Lew's sophomore season ended, the *Chicago Defender* commented that the New York underclassman "is the most discussed young sports figure of modern times." The black newspaper also remarked, tongue-in-cheek, "By the time Lew hits one of the many professional teams bidding for him he may be 8 feet tall."[7]

By the middle of Alcindor's junior season, his national reputation had skyrocketed, with Power playing games in Rhode Island, upstate New York, and New Jersey. Big Lew's twenty-eight-point average generated "more excitement than any prep cager since Wilt Chamberlain," according to the *Philadelphia Tribune*. The newspaper also noted that Eddie Gottlieb, former general manager of the Philadelphia Warriors, a team for which Chamberlain had played, thought Alcindor looked "as good or better than any basketball player I have seen at his stage of development." The next year New York Knicks general manager Eddie Donovan said, "We could use Lew Alcindor right now, even though he's only a high school kid." Commented Baltimore Bullets coach Gene Shue: "I'll trade two first round draft choices for him right now."[8]

Therefore, when Alcindor and his teammates traveled to Maryland to face DeMatha in February 1964, they did so with Alcindor as the marquee attraction. The "giant center"—he measured 7'2"—was accustomed to drawing large crowds wherever he went. The DeMatha players, taller than average themselves, remembered first seeing Alcindor at a hotel restaurant for a pregame banquet. The Stags gawked as they saw Big Lew lower his head just to get through the large doorway leading into the dining room. After the meal, the players continued to stare as Alcindor ducked under the balcony that extended all the way down the corridor to his room.[9]

Alcindor was just as extraordinary in the game against DeMatha, scoring 35 points and grabbing 17 rebounds. Even though Bob Whitmore, DeMatha's junior center, gave up six inches to Big Lew, he managed to play good defense on the Power star before fouling out with 4:36 remaining and the score tied at 53. When the Stags tried double-teaming Alcindor in Whitmore's absence, Big Lew's classmate, Charley Farrugia, was often left unguarded. The junior guard hit three crucial jumpers down the stretch—two of which came in the final minute. Power went on to win, 65–62, in a game that included fifteen lead changes and twelve ties.[10]

The shootout produced Cole Field House's first sell-out crowd, even though the arena had hosted Atlantic Coast Conference (ACC) basketball games since its debut in the mid-1950s. While many of the estimated 12,500 fans came to see Power's standout center, there were other reasons contributing to the large gate.[11] According to Wootten, "At that time . . . none of the colleges were really doing much, basketball-wise. So . . . high school basketball became *the thing* in the sixties in Washington, D.C. In popularity [the prep game ranked] almost ahead of the colleges."[12]

Interest in local basketball may not have necessarily translated into undying partisanship for the local team. As three-time defending Catholic League and City champions, DeMatha was the envy of many local schools. DeMatha guard Bob Petrini, who played on the 1963–64 squad, recalled, "A lot of people came to see DeMatha lose." While that may have been true, Petrini, who would go on to play at the University of Pittsburgh, noticed that the crowd's allegiances shifted during the course of the game. Petrini later explained that "as the game went on and [the fans] saw how competitive we were with [Power], and how good Lew Alcindor and the rest of them were, [attitudes] changed." Although the home team lost, DeMatha players could sense by the end that fans were cheering them on.[13]

The victory over DeMatha was Power's forty-eighth in a row, and tied the New York City high school basketball record for consecutive wins. Alcindor and his teammates continued the streak by finishing the season undefeated—their second straight unbeaten campaign. Between his junior and senior year the introspective Alcindor gained a growing sense of racial and personal identity in what he called "my black and independent summer." Living in Harlem afforded Alcindor the opportunity to witness racial discrimination and see white business owners moving to "safer" neighborhoods. Living in Harlem also gave the seven-footer a chance to learn the ways of the world from Wilt Chamberlain—a man with whom he was frequently compared. "I got close to Wilt that summer," Alcindor later acknowledged, having interacted with Chamberlain at the NBA star's summer residence. The 2 seven-footers also spent time together socially, listening to jazz music, sharing clothes, and hanging out in VIP sections of lounges. "Wilt was the only star I knew, and I stood in awe of him," Alcindor wrote in his memoir, *Giant Steps*. Chamberlain taught Big Lew how a famous and confident black athlete should act. But Alcindor's personality was different from Chamberlain's. Big Lew never quite felt comfortable following Chamberlain's public and glamorous life.[14]

In contrast, many of DeMatha's players spent the summer playing ball on DC's more popular playgrounds. Some frequented neighborhood courts like Turkey Thicket and Kelly Miller on the city's predominantly black east side. Like many of his teammates, DeMatha forward Sid Catlett, an African American and sophomore-to-be, felt comfortable in these urban settings. "Most of us were raised in the city and traveled to DeMatha in the suburbs," Catlett recalled, adding that he and many others on DeMatha's team had "inner-city experience." Catlett, who later played at the University of Notre Dame, did not see his teammates so much through the lens of race as he did through the lens of basketball ability. Mickey Wiles, a white point guard on DeMatha's team, remembered, "I would go over to . . . Kelly Miller at night and I'd be the only white guy there. And I never had any problems . . . I never thought about race." These halcyon memories of playing basketball on the city's playgrounds, however, are at odds with the social injustices that black Washingtonians confronted at the time. Likewise, Wiles's experiences of playing pickup ball in black neighborhoods were an exception to the numerous racial barriers that remained in the city. "You just didn't want to steer too far away from 'home,'" Catlett remembered, adding that the 5'9" Wiles was a kind of "social hero" who was "not afraid to go wherever the competition was in spite of the potential for racial tension."[15]

That DeMatha's integrated squad played pickup games in both predominantly white and black neighborhoods suggested that sport, when played well and fairly, could rise above racial barriers. But the strident battles being waged over civil rights must have reminded the players that they moved within an insular world. Basketball at DeMatha, it seems, was relatively immune to racial issues—at least according to players and coach. "We just looked at everybody the same," Petrini recalled forty years later, "you played if you were good enough to play." According to Wootten, *Sports Illustrated* sent a correspondent to DeMatha in the mid-1960s to write a story about race and the school's basketball program. The writer found nothing negative and left. The story was never written.[16]

Such a colorblind attitude was consistent throughout DC area prep basketball. DeMatha players remember playing intense games against predominantly white St. John's High School, predominately black archenemy Mackin High, and several integrated teams. Overt acts of racism largely eluded the racially integrated basketball program at DeMatha. "Whenever we played, I never saw any disrespect to any DeMatha players," Petrini remembered. "I think that if we would have heard [racial taunting], [Wootten] would have pulled us off the court." Fortunately, the coach never had to make that decision.[17]

Still, there is no denying that the Baltimore-Washington region has had a wrenching history with race relations. A century before the DeMatha-Power showdowns, President Abraham Lincoln preceded his famous "Emancipation Proclamation" with the lesser-known April 1862 "Emancipation Compensation," which freed almost 3,000 slaves in the District by remunerating their owners with local funds. The legislation encouraged many African Americans to move to the integrated capital, which increased the city's black population from 11,000 in 1860 to 40,000 by the end of the Civil War. Fifty years later, southern-raised president Woodrow Wilson officially recognized what had become de facto policy by segregating federal facilities and the accompanying workforce in the capital—a policy that lasted for three decades and reinforced the acceptability of segregation in Washington.[18]

Wilson's term in the White House coincided with the beginning of the period known as the Great Migration, which saw hundreds of thousands of African Americans move from the South to cities in the Northeast, Midwest, and West. Interestingly, the capital's black population actually decreased as a percentage of its overall population in the early decades of the Great Migration. However, from 1940 to 1970, a period encompassing the modern civil rights movement, the number of African Americans living in DC soared, going from 28 percent to more than 71 percent of the city's population.[19]

While the District's southern neighbor, Virginia, would retain much of its former Confederate views throughout much of the twentieth century, the city's northern neighbor had a more ambiguous history. It was Maryland secessionists who drew the first official blood of the Civil War in what became known as Baltimore's Pratt Street Riot of April 19, 1861, but the Old Line State cast its lot with the Union several days later. The clash between sentiment and policy perpetuated racial uncertainty along the Mason-Dixon Line that existed well beyond Reconstruction. In 1936, the University of Maryland, located within only a few miles of the District of Columbia, became a pioneer of sorts by integrating its Law School. The progressive overture occurred largely from the prodding of Thurgood Marshall, a Baltimore native, civil rights activist, and, later, first African American to serve as a United States Supreme Court justice. But at the undergraduate level, things were much different, the university not opening its doors to African Americans until 1951, when a single black student was reluctantly admitted.[20]

The Washington-Baltimore area also had a checkered past with race and sports. Jackie Robinson, for instance, encountered more resistance when he visited Baltimore in 1946—his lone minor league season and the prequel to his rookie year with the Brooklyn Dodgers—than any other city in which he played during the tumultuous early years of professional baseball's "Great Experiment." In DC, African Americans were forced into segregated seating for boxing matches and were excluded from many other events at Uline Arena (later renamed Washington Coliseum) until 1948. The stadium's owner, Michael Uline, believed that blacks were incapable of appreciating "high culture" sporting events like ice-skating exhibitions and basketball games.[21]

In October 1950, Earl Lloyd became the first African American to play in the NBA when he took the court on opening night for the short-lived Washington Capitols. The following season, the NBA's Baltimore Bullets integrated its squad by signing former UCLA teammates Davage Minor and Don Barksdale. Both Minor and Barksdale experienced Jim Crow conditions off the court, while in games they were sometimes told to guard the opposing teams' black players—regardless of size or position. A 1947 collegiate All-American and 1948 Olympic gold medalist, Barksdale became the Bullets' highest-paid player in 1952. The next year, he became the NBA's first black All-Star.[22]

The 1954 *Brown v. Board of Education* ruling ended segregated sports in the District's high schools. However, more than a decade later, the most prominent collegiate athletic conference in the area, the Atlantic Coast

Conference (ACC), had yet to open its doors to black basketball players. In late 1965, Billy Jones, a native of Towson, Maryland, became the first African American to play basketball in the ACC when he suited up for the University of Maryland—the conference's northernmost member. Norwood Todmann, who played alongside Lew Alcindor in both of Power Memorial's matchups against DeMatha, followed Jones as an ACC pioneer by becoming the first black player for Wake Forest University—also an ACC institution— in 1967.[23]

While several cities across the nation continued to struggle with civil rights, Power and DeMatha seemed to thrive with squads featuring black and white starters. By the time of the 1964 game, Power had run off forty-seven straight wins, and DeMatha had won both the Catholic League and City championships three times in a row. DeMatha versus Power seemed to offer a glimpse into the possibility of racially integrated sports, its focus remaining steadfastly on basketball rather than the skin color of players.[24]

DeMatha's loss in 1964 also offered a glimpse into the immense popularity of high school basketball in the District. Leading up to the 1965 rematch, Power coach Jack Donohue said that he preferred to have the game played in Washington rather than in The Big Apple. "We never get these types of crowds in New York," remarked Donohue, who went on to become head coach at Holy Cross College after Alcindor's season year at Power. "We probably wouldn't draw more than six or seven thousand if we played in Madison Square Garden." Apparently, New Yorkers had enough entertainment options to keep them from attending big-time high school basketball games. By contrast, Washingtonians had fewer distractions and were perhaps bigger fans of the prep game. As Wootten recalled, "[T]he community . . . took great pride in their high school basketball."[25]

"I think anyone who loved basketball was there that night," Petrini would later say about the 1965 rematch. Most who attended had little or no affiliation with DeMatha, since there were not nearly enough DeMatha fans to fill Cole Field House, which sat 12,500. Given the relatively long distance Power had to travel, the New York school brought even fewer supporters. Crowds for both the 1964 and 1965 games consisted of many spectators who had no direct connection to either school.[26]

Later, many members of DeMatha's team learned that players from rival high school teams had attended both games. Springarn, Dunbar, Archbishop Carroll, St. John's, and Mackin provided top-notch competition for DeMatha in what had become a bloc of local elite high school teams in the DC region. Squads from these schools had produced such standouts as Elgin Baylor, John Thompson, and Dave Bing. Mackin, runner-up to DeMatha in the 1964 Catholic League championship, also played Power in both the 1963–64 and 1964–65 seasons, thus serving as the only mutual opponent for the Panthers and Stags. In 1963–64, Mackin lost by 14 points to Power, and by 9 to DeMatha. The following year, Power beat Mackin by 3 points, and the Stags defeated Mackin by one. A perennial DC runner-up, Mackin competed with each team as closely as any squad in 1964–65. By January 1965, Power and DeMatha entered the rematch as undefeated kings of their own basketball world, having beaten all opponents.[27]

Leading up to the rematch, Washington newspapers found little difficulty in stirring up excitement. Taken together, DeMatha's "Fabulous Six"—guards Mickey Wiles and Ernie Austin; forwards Sid Catlett, Bob Petrini, and All-American Bernard Williams; and center Bob Whitmore—and Lew Alcindor were a big enough attraction to draw fans.[28] Recognizing the great interest in the contest, the *Washington Daily News* allocated a one-page preview on the day of the game. The feature section carried an article titled, "Nation's Best Clash Tonight." Reporter Neal Bobys wrote that the game "will decide the top high school team in the nation—New York City's Power Memorial or Our Town's DeMatha." Comments from Mackin coach Paul Furlong ran throughout much of the article. "Neither team can be favored," the coach remarked, diplomatically, "DeMatha is too good a team to underrate. They can bounce back better than any other team. Power has Lew Alcindor, and he's the cool type. He just doesn't choke in the clutch." Furlong also told fans "to keep your eye on DeMatha's Sid Catlett. He'll be the key man. Sid will pull down the rebounds, and that could make the difference in the game."[29]

The *Daily News* feature included a cartoon of a Lilliputian DeMatha player climbing a pole to reach a ball held loosely by a giant, caricaturized as Alcindor. This was nothing new. Similarly exaggerated stories about Big Lew often peppered the pages of papers across the country. Both the black and white press lauded his success, and even claimed to know where he was going to college from the more than one hundred scholarship offers the seven-footer had reportedly received. Black newspapers in particular noted that seven of these offers came from southern schools in all-white conferences. In late January 1965, just days before the rematch, the *Daily News* reported that Alcindor planned to attend Fairleigh Dickinson University in New Jersey because his high school coach, Jack Donohue, was to be named the school's next head coach. Three weeks later, the paper circulated a New York–based rumor that Alcindor would be attending St. John's University.

After the season, news sources reported that Donohue would be taking his star pupil with him to Holy Cross.[30]

Most of this reporting was hearsay, since Donohue kept his prized player from the media. In fact, Donohue allowed no college recruiters to talk to Lew without going through him first. Dennis Galbraith, an employee at Power, justified the arrangement, arguing, "boys who are any good don't need publicity, especially when they are as good as Alcindor. There's no real reason for a kid to be bothered by sportswriters. It just takes up time." Such restrictions may have helped form what was to become the frosty relationship Alcindor had with the media—one that he maintained throughout most of his collegiate and professional career. Unlike many popular athletes, Big Lew never became an outgoing or charismatic media darling, much to the dismay of many journalists. *Washington Daily News* columnist Mike Kiernan observed on the day of the DeMatha rematch that "Lew has progressively become a god, whom the newspapers and magazines will write about whether he's co-operative or not."[31]

Look magazine reinforced Kiernan's claim, producing an article on Alcindor that appeared the week before the 1965 game and one that also had no quotes from the schoolboy star. Though the article failed to mention the upcoming encounter against DeMatha, it did offer an analysis of the apparently more tolerant racial climate reflected by the integrated squads of Power and DeMatha. Adding to what appeared to be racial tolerance, an article preceding the story on Alcindor reported the unprecedented achievement of African American actress Diana Sands, who was starring in a "white" role opposite Alan Alda in the Broadway hit, "The Owl and the Pussycat."[32]

While Alcindor and his teammates may not have been aware of Sands's groundbreaking performance, they probably would have remembered the precarious racial climate in the Big Apple. As late as 1964, the New York City public school system had yet to reach a level of racial equality acceptable to the city's black population. Two days after Power faced the Stags in 1964, more than 450,000 students, along with thousands of adults, protested the school system's lack of action vis-à-vis African American students, demanding that the city improve the conditions of the 165 de facto segregated elementary and junior high schools across all five boroughs.[33]

Despite such headlines, interestingly enough, when the Power players returned to the federal capital for their rematch against DeMatha, press coverage of the contest rarely mentioned race. For its part, the black press exerted little effort in building up the rematch and discussing the interracial composition of the teams. In fact, while many black papers printed stories about Alcindor's fame and potential selection of college, all but a few even cared to mention the Power-DeMatha game.[34]

Alcindor also garnered far more attention in the white press than did matters of race. Newspapers in DC and New York covered the lead-up to the rematch, while national magazines, such as *Time* and *Newsweek*, sent reporters to cover the game. On the evening of the game, a standing-room-only crowd braved blizzard conditions—eleven local high schools canceled their basketball games that night—to join the host of sportswriters already inside Cole Field House. Numerous television reporters also made the trek through the snow. The atmosphere was electric.[35]

The media frenzy surrounding the rematch produced various predictions about the outcome of the game. While the previous year's loss to the Panthers may have placed the Stags in the position of underdogs, DeMatha's players did not see it that way. They, like Power, had played in enough important games not to be concerned by hype and speculation. Wiles, a senior point guard on the 1965 team, recalled, "I thought we could've beaten them in '64. In '65 . . . there was no doubt that we were going to win." Perhaps more importantly, the game carried significance beyond two top-ranked teams playing each other. It was New York versus Washington, with status implications for other cities along the east coast and for high school basketball more generally.[36]

Until the DeMatha-Power rematch, New York City had long been considered basketball's Mecca. It produced top-flight high school, college, and professional talent, and was the home of Madison Square Garden. Ever since James Naismith invented basketball in 1891, countless young New York schoolboys had played the game. They learned it on the city's heralded playgrounds and in its armories. They refined their techniques in the Big Apple's high schools, and joined local college teams, some of which were the best in the country. Beginning in 1934, Madison Square Garden hosted the nation's first college double- and triple-headers, pitting local teams against top-ranked squads from schools around the country. Before the early 1950s, metropolitan teams, for the most part, excelled. In the years to follow, New York continued to produce outstanding prep talent, but an increasing number of players left the city to attend colleges outside the five boroughs.[37]

The Big Apple was not the country's only basketball hotbed. Indiana had developed a longstanding tradition of high school basketball excellence dating back to before the interwar years. Often, attendance at rural Indiana high school basketball games far exceeded the combined populations of the towns represented by the competing schools. Another place where basketball thrived was Kansas City, which benefited from the dedicated efforts of the game's founder, James Naismith, who taught and coached at nearby University of Kansas. During the early decades of the twentieth century, Naismith labored tirelessly to promote the sport. As a result, Kansas City became a basketball Mecca itself, hosting the Amateur Athletic Union (AAU) national championship tournament from 1921 to 1934 and the National Association of Intercollegiate Athletics (NAIA) national championship from 1937 to the present.[38]

In the late 1940s, basketball slowly increased its regional popularity and became more of a national game. The growth of the NCAA and National Invitation Tournament (NIT) championships, the emergence of viable professional leagues, and the growing media exposure of the game in the 1950s granted basketball more of a national structure and following. Still, there were several cities that continued to stand out as exceptional breeding grounds for the sport. Philadelphia, for instance, had a rich basketball history. Wilt Chamberlain, basketball's best-known prep player before Alcindor, learned the game on the city's playgrounds and played his high school ball in one of the city's formidable prep leagues. The City of Brotherly Love was also home of college basketball's Big Five: La Salle, Penn, Villanova, St. Joe's, and Temple. In 1964 the *New York Herald-Tribune*, taking note of the Big Five's winning record against New York universities, questioned whether Philadelphia was becoming a better city for basketball than Gotham.[39]

While Washington may not have had the kind of basketball tradition of Philadelphia or New York, it did begin to emerge as a high school basketball power in the decade leading up to the Power-DeMatha duels. By the early 1960s, the nation's capital had sent a number of prep standouts to successful college programs around the country. "The unbeaten [Archbishop] Carroll teams (of the late 1950s) started us on the road to being recognized," Wootten later said.[40] As a result, DC high school basketball began to develop a national reputation. "In the late '50s," Wootten remembered, "New York and Philadelphia [teams] were better—we couldn't beat them." But in a matter of just a few years, DC area squads were able to compete with, and sometimes even beat, top teams from the Big Apple and the City of Brotherly Love.[41]

When Power traveled to Washington for its rematch with DeMatha, many of the Stag players and fans understood the relevance of the game for DC's basketball reputation. "We always played for DeMatha," Petrini bluntly explained. Yet he also could not ignore "a feeling . . . that it was DC versus New York." That sentiment was built upon the successes of DeMatha, Archbishop Carroll, Mackin, and several other DC area teams, such as public schools Springarn and Dunbar, during the 1950s and early 1960s. The success of these squads attracted more national attention for DC high school basketball, elevating the city's basketball status closer to that of New York's and Philadelphia's. Interestingly, this recognition was attained in spite of these teams not having the kind of difficult schedules that DeMatha's squads had between 1963 and 1965. By the early 1960s, Wiles recalled, Wootten "wanted to take on all comers."[42]

No other opponent on DeMatha's schedule was more highly touted than Power. The Panthers carried with them Gotham's reputation for high quality and rugged prep basketball. In truth, not every Panther was representative of the stereotypical New York playground player, but each seemed to be rugged and ready for action. Catlett would later note that New York had a reputation for producing "aggressive" and "intimidating teams." The city had "trash-talkers" and "inner-city players [who were] tough." By comparison, DeMatha's players "were perceived as nice Catholic school guys."[43]

Surprisingly, DeMatha center Bob Whitmore, who at 6'8" was roughly half a foot shorter than Alcindor, won the opening tip of the rematch. From that moment on, both teams understood that they were in for a battle. However, no DeMatha player recalled any overly aggressive behavior or intimidation from the New Yorkers. In fact, the game was played as if it had been diagramed from a coaching manual and conducted according to the highest expectations of good sportsmanship. Flashy New York playground moves never appeared. "I don't recall that much trash talking," recalled Catlett, looking back on the famous matchup. "It was a quiet game. And other than the stands going [wild], I think there was respect" shown by both teams.[44]

If the 1964 game displayed both teams' striking offensive talents, the rematch showed their defensive prowess. DeMatha's goal was to limit Alcindor—in all facets of the game. Wootten and his players devised a number of strategies to disrupt the rhythm of the seven-footer. Wiles, for instance, noticed that almost every time after Alcindor made an outlet pass, the Panther star would bow his head and begin running up the floor. So the DeMatha point guard, sacrificing limbs and body, tried to draw an offensive charge from Alcindor, or at least make the tall center stumble or slow down. Another strategy was to have DeMatha's big men prevent Alcindor from getting the ball. In the game, Catlett and Williams assisted Whitmore by rotating off their men and alternately double-teaming Alcindor, depending on which side of the floor the Panther center set up.[45]

The strategy worked. Alcindor did not score until a dunk late in the first quarter. A reporter for the *Baltimore Sun* noted that the schoolboy star took only eleven shots for the game, and most of his successful attempts were "of the 'stuff' variety." Mike Kiernan of the *Washington Daily News* offered a slightly harsher assessment: "Alcindor looked like a man asleep. Everyone in the house expected him to suddenly awake in all his fury. . . . But Alcindor never awoke."[46]

From tip-off, the game was tight. Both teams seemed affected by the momentousness of the game. Early on, neither could find the mark. Combined, they made just 6 of 35 first-quarter shots. With 12,500 screaming fans looking on and many others listening to the game on DC's WMAL radio, Power jumped out to a 4–0 advantage. But DeMatha quickly bounced back, and moved in front, 6–5. Almost two minutes later, Big Lew netted his initial points of the game, throwing down a dunk. By the end of the first quarter, Power led, 11–8. The second quarter was a reverse of the first: Players shook off their jitters and started popping in shots, while DeMatha, not Power, was the more offensively productive squad. Late in the second stanza, the Stags clung to a 23–17 lead. Scoring 5 straight points, Power guard Charley Farrugia trimmed the margin to 23–22 by halftime. Although the first half was low scoring, excitement was near fever pitch.[47]

As the second half opened, it looked like DeMatha would pull away. Whitmore then Catlett tallied a basket. Momentum seemed to be on the Marylanders' side. But Alcindor, who had been held to just 5 points in the game, scored three baskets in the last minutes of the third quarter to even the score, 30–30. The Stags' Wiles notched a foul shot and then slithered through New Yorkers' defense for a layup. With a quarter remaining, DeMatha held a 3-point lead.[48]

In the final period, the Stags, taking time off the clock, stretched their advantage, 37–32. Power countered with two baskets by reserve Ed Klimkowski (he would be the only substitute from either team to play in the game), bringing the visitors to within one point. Catlett, however, would not be denied. He drained a shot from the outside and then sank two foul shots. With the clock showing 1:40 to play, the Stags led, 41–36. A quick basket by Farrugia sliced 2 points off the margin. After being fouled by Whitmore, Alcindor was presented with an opportunity to whittle it down even more, but he missed the foul shot. Two free throws by Wiles and a put-back dunk by Catlett with forty-three seconds left put the home team out of reach. DeMatha went on to win, 46–43. Catlett scored 13 points, while his teammate, Bernard Williams, whom the *New York Post*'s Jack Lynn had termed in a preview of the much-anticipated matchup, "probably . . . the best-all-around high school player in the Washington area," added 12.[49]

But the most-discussed statistic was Alcindor's 16 points—roughly half his season average, and less than half of what he scored the previous year

DeMatha's Bob Whitmore shoots a free throw under the watchful gaze
of a sold-out Cole Field House. In the foreground, Power Memorial's
Lew Alcindor and DeMatha's Sid Catlett jostle for position.
Courtesy of DeMatha Catholic High School.

against the Stags.[50] One reason was that DeMatha's double-teaming strategy forced Alcindor to pass more often to teammates, some of whom were
less-talented players than the previous year's supporting cast. Big Lew had
not experienced defeat in almost three years. Yet after the game he graciously
led his teammates into the Stags' locker room and offered his congratula-
tions. "He was quiet . . . [and] professional in his demeanor," DeMatha
reserve Ned Merchant remembered, adding, "He came into our locker room
after the game and shook our hands and all [he said] was, 'good game, good
game' and [then he was] out." Despite having just been beaten in arguably
the biggest game of his life, Alcindor exhibited class and sportsmanship,
according to Merchant. "There was nothing antagonistic from him at all
that I remember." Power coach Jack Donohue also visited the locker room
and praised DeMatha's win.[51]

Over the following days, commentators provided their take on the game.
Local headlines shouted: "DeMatha Proves It's the Greatest"; "DeMatha
Topples Power, 46–43; Alcindor Held to only 16 Points"; and "DeMatha
Snaps Power's Streak." The *Washington Sunday Star* included two pictures

from the game. One, featured prominently on the front page of the sports section, showed Alcindor in midflight, stuffing the ball. The other captured Wiles lofting a shot over the outstretched arm of Power's seven-foot star. Most New York newspapers highlighted the fact that Power's 71-game undefeated streak had been snapped. Mike Kiernan of the *Washington Daily News* quoted an elated Wootten after the game: "It's just like the old West. There's always one gun slinger just a little bit faster than the one which is supposed to be the fastest."[52]

While many postgame comments focused on Alcindor's grace in defeat and his obviously abundant talent, there were those that found fault with the seventeen-year-old star. Some reporters wrote that Alcindor had brushed aside a young boy seeking to shake his hand as Big Lew left the Cole Field House court. Though no writer mentioned the boy's poor timing—after all, Power had just lost—Alcindor collected more than his share of criticism for what was most likely an unintentional gaffe. Also criticizing Alcindor was Villanova assistant coach Jack Devine—a strange occurrence, given that Villanova still had a chance of landing the coveted high school recruit. "He showed me he is a lazy ball player," Devine remarked after the game, drawing upon a stereotype commonly applied to black athletes. While noting a key play in which the shorter Catlett beat out Alcindor for a critical rebound, the coach said, "He lost that game for them. If he had shown a little hustle, they [Power Memorial] would have won." Unlike numerous press reports, Devine did not discuss Big Lew's many exceptional plays during the game or that Alcindor was a marked man playing an excellent DeMatha team.[53]

After beating Power, DeMatha players felt as though they had targets on their backs. "Once we beat [Power], everyone wanted a piece of us and so it became tougher to win," Merchant remembered. Even with opponents gunning for them, the Stags continued their winning ways, losing only once to the University of Maryland freshman team. DeMatha and other elite high school teams sometimes played college freshman teams (the NCAA did not allow freshmen on the varsity). For DeMatha and other elite high school teams, these games often provided the season's biggest challenges. In 1964–65, DeMatha won most of these matchups, beating highly touted freshman squads from such universities as Georgetown and Penn.[54]

DeMatha's victory over Power reflected the high quality of DC basketball. "I think [the game] put a stamp on D.C. basketball," Merchant later said. "It elevated [the city's] high school basketball." Washingtonians took pride in DeMatha's win and increasingly became interested in the prep game. The Stags' triumph also signaled to basketball enthusiasts nationwide that the high school game in the nation's capital was among the finest and most popular of any American city. As Wootten later recalled, "Our win over [Alcindor] and Power then gave us the reputation as a basketball area." Wootten often mentions the comments of Hall-of-Fame Boston Celtics coach and one-time District resident Red Auerbach, who once said that "the best high school basketball in the country is played right here in Washington, D.C."[55]

In his postgame remarks after DeMatha's emotional victory, Wootten, the imaginative force behind the two DeMatha-Power matchups, referred to the 1965 game as "the greatest high school game ever played." While it might be easy to view Wootten's statement as hyperbole, that sentiment reverberated well beyond Cole Field House. The 1965 win "took high school basketball [in DC] to a whole new level," Wootten remembered. He also noted that "it was the game that put Washington basketball on the map." That January evening in 1965, possibly the greatest high school basketball player ever squared off against a DeMatha squad with six future Division I standouts and a coach who became one of the most successful at any level in basketball. What followed altered not only the landscape of DC high school basketball; it also changed how local and national fans viewed the prep game in the Washington area.[56]

The 1965 game helped create a deeper national awareness of high school basketball. "In California people didn't really know what was going on in Indiana or New York or Florida," Wootten later said, recalling the regional divisions of early 1960s prep basketball. In 1965, neither Alcindor nor New York was the only story in high school basketball. Largely because of DeMatha's victory in 1965, Washington and its high school players attracted attention and proved they could match up with the best any city had to offer. "The greatest high school game ever played" helped breakdown the divisions that had cordoned off the country into basketball regions.[57]

After 1965, DC high school basketball grew in prestige. Each of DeMatha's "Fabulous Six" received athletic scholarships to major colleges, thus continuing a streak that lasted for three decades in which every senior from the school earned a basketball scholarship.[58] Such phenomenal success greatly impacted the DC region. Just to keep pace, DeMatha's rivals were forced to recruit and produce top talent. As players from rival teams also went on to star at colleges around the country—some with the help of Wootten—the prominence of DC prep basketball grew even more.

Following his team's loss to the Stags, Alcindor went on to become one of the greatest players in the history of basketball. And with every achievement he earned and championship he won, DeMatha's triumph in 1965 acquired even greater status, adding to the ever-increasing prestige of DC high school basketball. Importantly, the Power-DeMatha game of 1965 was played fairly and without incident. In large part, the game became what it was because of the many talented players on the court that night. But the racial composition of the respective squads and the sportsmanship exhibited by the players reflected the central purpose of the civil rights movement—which was to have a more equal and racially integrated society. And that might be the game's greatest legacy of all.

9

Whips, Darts, and Dips

The Rollercoaster Ride of Men's Professional Soccer in Washington, DC

Charles Parrish and John Nauright

On a hot afternoon in July 1968, more than 20,000 soccer fans made their way to DC Stadium to catch a glimpse of "The King." Promoted as the highest-paid athlete in the world, and designated a Brazilian national asset not available for export, Pelé delivered roses to a few lucky ladies and then trotted out onto the field, eliciting enthusiastic cheers from the crowd. Although he failed to score, Pelé demonstrated his flamboyant ball-control skills and set up all three of his team's goals. A secondhand account of the game published in the *New York Times* erroneously credited two goals to him.[1] The confusion is understandable: Both goals were scored by his Brazilian teammate, Pepe.

The game featured the District's own professional team, the Washington Whips, and Pelé's Brazilian team, Santos. The exhibition was heavily promoted in local papers, and the Whips, who were struggling to attract fans, provided additional incentive for would-be spectators by offering a "Meet Pelé" contest. A throng of 20,189 people, approximately three times the size of a typical Whips crowd, endured the summer heat to watch the game, which was won by Santos, 3–1. Unfortunately for the Whips, the exhibition did not bolster Washingtonians' interest in their hometown club. A few months later, the Whips' rocky two-year journey came to an abrupt end.

Ever since the late nineteenth century, soccer has been an integral part of the District's sporting experience. In parks and on playgrounds, in schools and recreational leagues, Washingtonians have played and watched the world's most popular sport. The nation's capital has also had several professional clubs. In 1894, the "Soccer Senators" were one of six teams to compete in what is widely regarded as the first professional soccer league in the United States, the American League of Professional Foot Ball.[2]

Beginning in the 1960s, and continuing for much of the next five decades, Washington experienced the ebb and flow of professional soccer. New clubs were established, and then disappeared. Three teams in particular—the Whips, the Darts, and the Diplomats—reflected the tantalizing potential sports entrepreneurs believed the city possessed when it came to matters of pro soccer. Ultimately, the teams failed. But it was not for a lack of effort. All three teams marketed themselves vigorously and promoted the sport with equal intensity. All three teams, too, enjoyed success on the field. Yet their viability was almost always in question. The history of professional soccer in the District is largely a tale of futility. Despite the superb quality of play, Washingtonians have only halfheartedly supported their teams.

Although soccer has struggled to become a recognized national pastime in the United States, its second-tier status was not a predestined outcome. By the 1870s, many colleges in the northeast were playing the sport, and evidence suggests it was played as far south as the University of Virginia.[3] By the end of the decade, however, rugby had gained most of the attention of influential collegians. Subsequent modifications to the game—many of which were introduced by Walter Camp, "the father of American football"—made it less "British," and resulted in the birth of American football.

In 1905, President Theodore Roosevelt invited athletic officials from Harvard, Yale, and Princeton to the White House. Several players had recently been killed while playing football, and Roosevelt, much like many other Americans, wanted the brutality to end.[4] Even though the meeting resulted in pledges from collegiate authorities to make the game safer, the violence persisted. Consequently, a number of institutions dropped the sport. Soccer promoters were poised to fill the void.

Meanwhile, soccer was gaining popularity among the residents of an increasingly diverse Washington, DC. During the years immediately following the Civil War, the District experienced a large influx of people.[5] Though the flow of European immigrants was much larger in the industrial port cities of the northeast, the federal capital also experienced a substantial surge in émigrés from Europe. These newer residents brought their Old World ways and tastes, including their love for games.[6]

British expatriates were among the District's early soccer enthusiasts. Founded in 1872, the Caledonian Athletic Club (CAC), which was mainly comprised of immigrants from Scotland and northern England, played an integral role in the early development of soccer in *fin de siècle* Washington. For several years, the club had a monopoly on soccer in Washington, DC. In 1894, after just one month of competition, the American League of Professional Foot Ball folded, and the "soccer Senators" vanished. In 1907, the CAC organized its first soccer team and became active in promoting the sport citywide.[7]

The number of amateur and recreational soccer teams expanded rapidly in the District during the 1910s and 1920s. The Young Men's Christian Association (YMCA), for instance, began sponsoring indoor soccer in 1912, and by 1915 the city's Playground Department had successfully held a "schoolboy soccer championship." Fifty schools, with 1,135 participants, competed in eight divisions.[8] For the next fifty years, soccer in Washington was mostly played at the semiprofessional and amateur levels.

Founded in the early 1920s, the American Soccer League (ASL), a semi-professional league, featured the highest level of play in the United States until the late 1960s. Despite having a distinctly "foreign" label—teams were called the Brooklyn Hispanos, Kearny Scots, Newark Portuguese, New York Hakoah, and Ukrainian Nationals—the ASL proved to be a popular league. It disbanded (for the second time) in the early 1980s because of financial difficulties. That the league survived as long as it did is impressive.[9] During the Cold War years, soccer in the United States faced ideological and cultural barriers. Critics labeled soccer "un-American" and called it a communist sport for pansies in tight shorts. Such assumptions undercut efforts to promote the sport and draw people to games. When Americans did attend matches, soccer was usually relegated to a hyped-up novelty showcasing a "celebrity in cleats"—Pelé, for instance—or a high-profile international club. Americans, including those in Washington, DC, rarely appreciated soccer for soccer's sake.

The Britannica Soccer Club, the predecessor to Washington's first authentic professional club, the Whips, was founded in 1963 by British expats (most of whom were Scots) and initially participated in the city's amateur league, which consisted of a number of clubs whose names suggested a "foreign" heritage. In addition to Britannica, there were the British Lions, Trinidad All Stars, Hispano, Pan American Union, Italia Cadets, German Eagles, La Riviera, Surquilla, Schweigert, WSC Bavarians (I & II), Deportivo Peru, and the Washington Internationals.[10] In 1967, Britannica won the city championship. That same season, the club beat the powerful Irish Americans of Kearny, New Jersey, and appeared in the division final of the National Amateur US Cup. Britannica lost to the Hartford-Italian club of Connecticut.

Nevertheless, Britannica officials believed the team had progressed suffi-
ciently enough to make the leap to the ASL later that year. The decision was
really a leap of faith, given the club's fiscal difficulties and lack of support
from Washingtonians.

Playing its home games at Woodrow Wilson High School in Northwest
DC in the fall of 1967, Britannica dropped its first four games, prompting their new coach, Charles "Cannonball" Fleming, to put himself in
the lineup for the team's fifth match.[11] Following this apparently desperate attempt, the club acquired eight players from the Atlanta Chiefs of the
rogue National Professional Soccer League (NPSL). It was a smart decision,
since several had played for their national teams. (The most prominent was
Peter McParlend of Northern Ireland; at the 1958 World Cup, he netted five
goals.) Although the deal significantly improved Britannica's performance,
it drove a wedge between team members, resulting in the departure of several players and Flemming.

By joining the ASL, Britannica hoped to elevate itself in the eyes of
local fans and thus generate enough revenue to offset its operating costs.
Doing so, however, proved difficult. In its first year in the ASL, the club
averaged only a few hundred people per match. But Britannica had an even
larger issue: the emergence of a rival soccer team in the city, the Washington
Whips.

During the 1960s, professional sports in the United States became a highly
profitable venture. Operating in a booming post–World War II economy,
and taking advantage of lucrative television contracts, professional sports
leagues grew rapidly.[12] By the middle of the 1960s, the United States Soccer
Football Association (USSFA) began entertaining proposals from investors
who were interested in developing a national professional soccer league.
Several groups submitted plans. One proposal included the involvement of
American football investors Jack Kent Cooke and Lamar Hunt. Another
included the backing from Bill Cox, founder of the International Soccer
League (ISL).

Since 1960, the ISL had been bringing top European-based teams to the
United States to play a series of games, a gambit that was largely frowned
upon by the USSFA. Little surprise, then, that the USFFA selected Cooke
and Hunt's group to run the new league. Cox, though, disregarded the decision, and went ahead with his own league, the National Professional Soccer
League (NPSL). He aggressively promoted it, even signing a ten-year TV
contract with CBS. In 1967, the NPSL was launched. Cooke and Hunt's
group had originally planned to start its league, the North American Soccer

League (NASL), in 1968. However, not wanting to lose ground to the rival NPSL, the group was forced to start the NASL a year earlier.

Seeking to distinguish their league from the NPSL, organizers of the NASL changed the league's name to the more patriotic United Soccer Association (USA). Since the league had started a year ahead of schedule, USA franchises collectively decided to recruit foreign clubs to masquerade as American-based teams. As a result, the inaugural season of the USA not only featured an abbreviated schedule, it had no US-born players. The USA team in the nation's capital—the Washington Whips—consisted of players from the Aberdeen club in Scotland.

While Britannica was on its way to winning its first city league championship, the Whips were busy executing what one newspaper columnist termed a "skillful propaganda campaign."[13] Hoping to gain media exposure, the club organized a "name the team contest," which yielded the team's political moniker, the Whips.[14] The *Washington Post*'s announcement of the name featured a photograph of Senate Minority Whip Thomas Kuchel, Senate Majority Whip Russell Long, and House Minority Whip Les Arends, among others, holding whips behind an A-frame sandwich board emblazoned with the team's logo.[15]

Fresh off a runner-up performance in the Scottish Cup competition, the newest members of the Whips arrived at Dulles Airport three days before the opening match, amid the piercing sound of bagpipes.[16] Although the Whips had secured a lease agreement to play their home games at DC Stadium (soon to be renamed RFK Stadium), Armory Board officials prohibited practice sessions at the venue. Instead, the Whips held workouts on the old polo grounds between the Jefferson and Lincoln Memorials.[17]

The Whips promptly worked to secure financial resources, hoping to offset what management believed would be $500,000 of expenses.[18] Team executives promoted the sale of season tickets and ran ads in newspapers. A mailer for tickets, which included a brief explanation of soccer and a description touting the European and South American teams that comprised the league, was also sent to 15,000 District residents.[19] Additional efforts included half-priced admission for children, "Department of Defense" and "Professional Dry Cleaners" nights, and a ceremonial season pass for President Lyndon Johnson.[20] Season tickets cost between $32.50 and $49, and included the Eintracht Frankfurt (West Germany) versus Cruzeiro (Brazil) exhibition match, as well as preferred parking. The cost of a single game ticket ranged from $3.50 to $7.[21]

In their first season, the Whips captured the Eastern Division title, but lost to the Los Angeles Wolves in the league championship, 6–5. Almost 18,000 fans attended the game, which was held in the Los Angeles Coliseum.[22] Though they excelled on the field, the Whips underperformed at the box office. To help attract English fans, Whips management organized British Isles sporting contests—cricket, hurling, and rugby—before several games. The idea yielded little dividends. With an average attendance of 6,200, the Whips' debt exceeded $300,000.[23]

Before the start of the 1968 season, the NPSL and USA merged. Called the North American Soccer League, the new league was made up of eighteen teams, including the Whips, and received sanctioning from both the USSFA and the International Federation of Association Football (FIFA). The most pressing issue for the Whips was assembling a roster. Rather than bring in a foreign club, team officials decided to sign individual players.

The owner of the Whips was Earl Foreman, a local attorney who had dabbled in the ownership of various sports teams, including football's Philadelphia Eagles and basketball's Baltimore Bullets. Initially, Foreman gave "semi-serious consideration to stocking the Whips on an ethnic basis—getting South American players to attract Latin fans, African players to attract Negro fans, etc." But eventually he abandoned the idea, and allowed Whips coach André Nagy to assemble the roster. Foreman established a budget of $8,000 per player.[24]

The 1968 Whips were stocked mostly with Danes and Brazilians. That several Brazilian players were included on the roster suggests that management was interested in the theatrical side of sport. Brazilian footballers were widely noted for their flair on the field. Furthermore, Brazilian players commanded respect, at least in the eyes of the average fan. Having won the World Cup in 1958 and 1962, the Brazilian national team was considered to be one of the best squads in the world. Foreman not only wanted to tap into this fame, he wanted his team to resonate with the District's diverse fan base. But the Whips soon discovered that it would take more than Brazilians and their flashy approach to gain a foothold in DC.

Hoping to boost ticket sales, the Whips announced that the price of admission would be reduced by 33 percent from the previous season. The club also offered further discounts for children, college students, and active military personnel.[25] In more of a PR stunt than a serious effort to build the roster, the Whips even held an open tryout on a cold February morning near what is now the Carter Baron Soccer Fields in Northwest DC. No future Pelé was discovered. Nagy joked that he was looking for pearls, but found only oysters.[26] Such comments hardly endeared the team to locals.

Both the Whips and the NASL started the season inauspiciously. In their first two games, the Whips failed to score, prompting general manager Jerry

Cooper to claim that the losses were the result of the erroneous decision to "stock the offense with South Americans, whose clever style of play . . . would provide goals and attract customers."[27] It soon became apparent that interest in the Whips—and the NASL in general—was ebbing. The psychological attachment between the Whips and fans was practically nonexistent, given that the year-old club had brought in an entirely new roster. Moreover, the Whips had no star player.

By midseason, Foreman's team was struggling to keep personnel issues at bay. Roberto Mauro, the Whips' top goal scorer, decided to return to his native Belo Horizonte, Brazil, so he could fulfill his duties as city council member. Zemario, another Brazilian, was released for being "out of shape" and missing practices. Finally, Henry Largie, who left to attend his father's funeral in Jamaica, failed to return to DC on the date that had been agreed upon by him and management.[28] The Whips were on the verge of collapse.

In June, a group of Maryland investors bought a large stake in the club and immediately assumed control. For professional soccer to survive in the District, they believed, the Whips needed to put more emphasis on youth soccer.[29] The future of the NASL itself was also on shaky ground. With all but two teams reportedly in debt, it was generally assumed that many clubs would fold by the end of the season. The high cost of signing quality players contributed to the league's poor financial health. The Whips, for example, spent approximately $10,000 per player, plus transfer fees. The total was well over the amount Foreman had allotted. No wonder he had been reluctant to pay the reported $27,000 one-time appearance fee for the exhibition against Pelé's Santos club that summer.[30]

Following the resignation of Jerry Cooper in June, Pete Haley was hired as the Whips general manager. Haley immediately began strengthening the club's grassroots development efforts. Soon it became his top priority. The Whips offered numerous youth soccer clinics and helped organize additional soccer leagues in the District. The hope was that such efforts would generate more interest in the team and benefit the franchise financially.[31]

Another way to promote the Whips was to have the world's most talented footballer play a match in DC. On July 14, 1968, just three months after the devastating riots in the city, Pelé and his Santos teammates defeated the Whips, 3–1, at DC Stadium. Realizing a solid showing against a world-class side could enhance the image of the team, Foreman, who still had a stake in the club, overturned Coach Nagy's decision to rest some of the Whips' key players.[32] Unfortunately for the Whips, the game proved to be a disappointment. According to Francis Stann of the *Washington Evening*

Star, Pelé hardly exerted himself—"Brazil's national treasure was like a man walking a dog," noted Stann—and the match itself ranked "right up there with Chinese water torture."[33] In league play, the Whips put on a much better show. Well past the season's midpoint, the club was in first place. Yet success on the field could not stop the Whips' downward financial spiral.

A series of run-ins between Nagy and management spelled the end for the coach. The Whips wasted no time in finding a replacement—Hacabi "Turk" Emekli, coach of Catholic University's soccer team. Despite declining fan interest elsewhere in the NASL, the Whips' sudden success actually increased their attendance. The NASL Atlantic Division title game, which was played between the Whips and the Atlanta Chiefs at DC Stadium, drew 14,227 spectators—the largest crowd to watch an NASL game in Washington that season.[34] The Chiefs were too strong, and beat the Whips, 1–0. Following a brief European tour in which the Whips tried to generate extra revenue, NASL officials voted to suspend the league. Given no choice in the matter, the Whips were done.

Meanwhile, the 1968 season proved to be somewhat of a renaissance for Britannica. The club changed its name to the Darts and, like the cross-town Whips, began engaging the community in hopes of garnering much-needed support. In early 1968, the Darts initiated a grassroots development program, which included the distribution of a soccer newsletter, the screening of a documentary on the 1966 World Cup, and the establishment of an award given to the city's top "American-born" amateur soccer player. The Darts even financed Woodrow Wilson High's inaugural soccer program.[35] Playing in the less-prestigious American Soccer League, the Darts were perceived as being inferior to the Whips. Nevertheless, the Darts persevered, which in a city saturated with sports teams—in addition to the Whips, there were baseball's Senators, football's Redskins, and a host of college teams—was no small feat. The Darts went on to win two consecutive ASL championships, in 1968 and 1969, and in March 1970 the DC City Council presented the club with the ceremonial "All-Purpose Trophy."[36]

In 1970 the Darts jumped to the NASL. To bolster the roster, the team signed several new players. Selris Figaro and Leroy DeLeon were brought in to play alongside fellow Trinidadian stars Gerry Browne and player-coach Lincoln Phillips.[37] The Darts also signed Argentinean Victorio Casa, who, while with the Whips in 1968, impressed fans but fell out of favor with the coach because of his "individualistic" style of play. Casa was "billed as the only one armed professional soccer player in the world." But the Darts signed the Argentinean because of his proficiency at distributing the ball. He was rewarded handsomely. According to the Darts' manager, Casa's

$15,000 salary made him "the highest paid professional soccer player in America."[38] Casa also possessed other skills. A native Spanish speaker, he was used as part of a grassroots effort to engage Washington's Hispanic community. The Darts may have exaggerated his value, however. In the early 1970s, the District's Hispanic population was relatively small, and it was made up of many immigrants who came from countries where soccer was a secondary sport. Casa's impact on the DC Hispanic population was probably minimal.[39]

Playing their home games in front of sparse crowds at Catholic University, the Darts finished the season in first place in the Southern Division.[40] Leroy DeLeon proved to be invaluable. He was the league's co-leader in the number of goals scored and third in total points.[41] The Darts advanced to the NASL championship, but lost to Rochester, 4–3.

Because of the limited number of franchises in the NASL, the Darts (and the other five teams in the league) supplemented their schedule with matches against touring international squads. In 1970, the Darts lost to Coventry City (England) and Hertha Berlin (West Germany), but beat Hapoel Petah-Tikvah (Israel) and Varzim (Portugal). No other NASL club had better results against foreign teams. For their efforts, the Darts earned the league's International Cup.

Although the international matches were relatively well attended, the arrival of Pelé and his Santos team in Washington at the end of the 1970 season generated the most interest. Several months earlier, Brazil had won the World Cup. Not surprisingly, all things related to Brazilian soccer were suddenly in high demand. For the game at RKF Stadium, Pelé and his Santos teammates attracted a crowd of 13,878 people. Showing a "boyish" enthusiasm, Pelé tallied four goals and set up two others, as Santos defeated the Darts, 7–4. Following the match, hundreds of fans streamed onto the field to get a closer look at "The King." Surrounded by admirers, the soccer legend "quickly took off his game jersey, tossed it to a couple of players and then waited for a rescue squad of 13 special policemen to escort him off the field," Mark Asher of the *Post* wrote.[42] Once again, Washington's soccer fans had turned out in large numbers—not because of a DC team but rather because of a "celebrity in cleats."

The 1971 Darts played much of the season uncertain about their immediate future. A New York–based real estate agent named John Bilotta was trying to purchase the club and move it to Miami. Financially, the Darts were in trouble. The club owed a reported $500,000, and given DC's apathy toward soccer, that sum most likely would grow. In a desperate effort to attract fans, team management even experimented with playing live rock-n-roll music during games. The music annoyed many in the crowd, and the experiment was quickly shelved.[43]

Norman Sutherland, the founder of Britannica, welcomed the idea of a sale. Moreover, he was pleased that the prospective owners were interested in retaining his services as general manager. Meanwhile, a group of DC businessmen was trying to keep the team in the nation's capital. But with Darts owners and team president Rudy Clemen eager to cut their losses, it appeared the club would be moving to Miami.[44]

One last effort to keep the Darts in the District came in the form of a public stock option. However, few Washingtonians bought the notes.[45] With this latest failure, NASL officials approved Bilotta's purchase of the club for $25,000. Despite winning two ASL championships and conducting more than 1,000 free lectures, clinics, and demonstrations, the Darts had failed to generate enough interest to support a pro soccer team in DC. The lack of a midsized stadium and competition from other sports teams undoubtedly contributed to the Darts' demise.[46] Following the 1971 season, the Darts shifted operations to Florida and were renamed the Miami Gatos.

The failure of two pro soccer franchises in DC, however, did not deter the establishment of a third. In early 1974, two Marylanders—insurance agent Mike Finci and construction company owner Nick Mangione—bought the Baltimore Bays of the ASL and moved the team to the District. The club was renamed the Diplomats. But most people called them the Dips, a name team executives disliked. The Diplomats retained several Bays players, and added four players on loan from England and Ireland. The team also picked up four area players in the 1974 draft.[47] Having locals on the roster, management hoped, would help undercut the perception that soccer was a foreigner's game, and thus attract more Washingtonians to matches. The coach of the Dips was former Bays coach and Manchester United striker Dennis Viollet. A talented player, Viollet was also known for having survived the 1958 Munich Air Disaster, in which the plane carrying the Manchester United team back from a European Cup match crashed during takeoff. Perhaps more familiar to Washingtonians was former Whips and Darts stalwart Joseph Gyua, aka Nana. Having already been a member of two unsuccessful soccer teams in the District, Nana maintained a "day job" at the United National Bank of Washington.[48]

The Diplomats practiced at American University and played their home matches at RFK Stadium. Team executives calculated that to break even, the Dips needed to average at least 12,000 spectators per match. Given pro soccer's recent history in the city, that would be a daunting task. But the increasing number of children playing soccer in the Washington area gave management hope.[49]

What the Dips owners could not have foreseen was the shift in local demographics. Heightened racial tensions, skyrocketing real estate values, and general social unrest during the 1960s resulted in the flight of many DC residents to the Maryland and Virginia suburbs. As the District's population declined, the challenge facing the Diplomats was enticing the large number of suburban youth soccer players and their parents to come to games in the city. Getting to RFK Stadium posed no problem. The Capital Beltway, finished in 1964, provided easy access, and the stadium had more than 12,000 parking spaces. To attract fans from the suburbs, the Diplomats scheduled all ten of their home games for Saturday afternoons.[50] Prices for discounted ticket ranged from $1.50 to $2, while general admission tickets cost between $3.50 and $6.

But Saturday games and affordable prices made no difference. A few weeks before the season was to begin, the Dips had sold only 173 season tickets.[51] The lack of interest prompted Viollet to increase the number of promotional events in the community. The hard work paid off. After Viollet made an appearance in Arlington, Virginia, two men who had attended the event bought a total of 1,000 tickets.[52] Unfortunately for the Dips, Viollet could not devote more time to promoting the club. As coach, he had to prepare for the season. Two weeks before the first game, the Diplomats traded their first pick in the 1975 draft for former Darts standout Leroy DeLeon, who was playing in Miami. George Ross, Alan Spavin, and Clive Clark—all on loan from clubs in England—were also brought in.[53]

After only a week of practicing together, the Diplomats opened the 1974 season against the defending NASL champions, the Philadelphia Atoms, before 10,175 fans at RFK Stadium. For Dips fans, the game was a letdown, as the Atoms won, 5–1. The loss was the least of the Dips' worries. With only three ticket windows open before the game, more than 1,000 fans had waited in line while DC mayor Walter E. Washington ceremonially kicked off the game.[54] The snafu did not bode well for the rest of the season.

Despite not having to compete with baseball's Senators, who had left the District in September 1971, the Diplomats struggled at the box office.[55] Not even clever promotions, such as weekly halftime penalty shootouts featuring some of the city's popular sports figures like Redskins running back Herb Mul-Key and WRC-TV sports personality Bud Kaatz, were able to attract fans.[56] As if things could not get any worse, the Dips gifted winger Clive Clark left the team in July to rejoin his wife in England.[57] After declining to enter a team in the NASL's indoor league for the winter, Dips executives were forced to reassure fans that the team was not planning to fold. The Dips' 7-12-1 record and their inability to draw fans—they averaged fewer than 5,000 spectators per game—did not inspire much confidence.

General Manager Steve Leipsner, trying to alleviate fans' concerns, stated that the Diplomats were "committed to staying in this area for at least three more years." Yet he also admitted that the club's lease at RFK Stadium was unsustainable.[58]

For the 1975 season, Dips officials figured that area families would be more inclined to attend if games were held on Wednesday and Friday nights. In addition, the Dips offered, for the first time, a package of family season tickets. The cost was $80 for eleven games. The team also held clinics, arranged speaking engagements, and screened instructional films for younger players.[59]

There was one thing the Dips could not control: the field at RFK Stadium. A few weeks before the home opener, club officials received word that the recently installed turf would not be ready. The bad news marked the second time in as many years that issues outside the Diplomats' control had disrupted opening day. As a result, the home opener was rescheduled, and the Dips' next two home games were played at W. T. Woodson High School in suburban Fairfax, Virginia.[60]

Moving the matches to Woodson High offered a glimpse into a brighter future—or so the Dips thought. Each game attracted more than 10,000 fans—a healthy number, no doubt. So when the matches returned to RFK Stadium, many fans complained. A supporter from Virginia summed up the Diplomats' inability to attract suburbanites to RFK. "Its too inconvenient to drive over there," the fan remarked. "Plus you gotta pay to park."[61] That kind of message resonated with Dips officials, who were more than eager to cater to the growing number of suburban fans. Even though their rent at RFK was subsequently reduced, the Diplomats decided to play most of their home games for the remainder of the season at Woodson High, whose field was ten yards narrower than the standard soccer field. The prospect of crowded stands and a cut from concessions revenue helped convince team officials.[62]

The Dips' fortunes also appeared to receive a boost from an unsuspected source. In 1974, Pelé left his native Brazil and agreed to play for the New York Cosmos of the NASL. Suddenly, soccer fans in the United States had a new superstar. As the popularity of the "beautiful game" in America grew, the potential for profit was not lost on sports entrepreneurs. In 1975, weeks before the Cosmos and Pelé were to play the Dips in Washington, DC, Joseph Danzansky and his associates at SJR Communications purchased the Diplomats for a whopping $650,000.[63] Scheduled field maintenance at Woodson High, and a desire to appeal to suburban Marylanders for the remaining five games of the season, forced the Dips back to RFK. The first of these games featured Pelé and the Cosmos. The King dazzled the crowd of 35,620, recording two goals and two assists, and leading the Cosmos to a 9–2 blowout. Yet again, the large crowd reflected Pelé's celebrity status, not the appeal of the local club. For the last four games, the Dips averaged a relatively meager 10,119 fans per game.[64]

Before the start of the 1976 season, the Dips changed course again and announced that eleven of their twelve home games would be played at Woodson High. With less money going to stadium rental, the front office hoped the club might be able to turn a profit. The Dips' fine season instilled hope. Fueled by the scoring of international striker Paul Cannell, the former Newcastle United star, the Diplomats surged to the front of the Atlantic Division. But the team's 8-3 record went unnoticed, and attendance declined.

Dips players had their own gripes. Playing games on a high school football field was, to say the least, a unique experience for the team's international players. In a radio interview, Cannell said, "I was used to playing at St. James Park in front of 40,000–50,000 people. [Playing at Woodson] was . . . culture shock." In England, Cannell explained, fans frequently invaded the pitch. But at Woodson "it wasn't much of a pitch invasion; it was more like a pitch saunter."[65] Despite such innovative promotional offerings as youth matches at halftime with Ronald McDonald and the Hamburglar tending goal, enthusiasm for the Diplomats waned, and crowds dwindled to a disappointing 6,500 per match.[66]

Following an adjustment to the schedule, the highly anticipated game against the New York Cosmos was moved from RFK to Woodson High. A capacity crowd of 11,004 saw the Dips defeat Pelé and his Cosmos teammates, 3-2.[67] The victory moved the Diplomats into first place in the Eastern Division. However, subpar play during the rest of the season hurt the Dips, and they barely made the playoffs.

As both a PR move and concession to fans who wanted to attend the Cosmos game but could not because of a limited number of tickets, the Diplomats helped organize an exhibition at RFK between Dynamo Kiev and Borussia Monchengladboch from West Germany, in July. With United States secretary of state Henry Kissinger looking on, the match was an utter farce. Early morning downpours had left the field so soaked that the ball died after long passes. The rosters did not list the names of players. And the players themselves did not put forth much of an effort. Their blasé attitude should not have come as a surprise. To them, the game was meaningless. It was played on an unplayable surface. The weather was muggy and hot. Making matters worse, both teams declined to play extra time after the game ended in a 2–2 draw. Upon hearing the decision, the crowd of 15,415 unleashed a chorus of boos. John Schulz of the *Washington Star* likened the match to "taking the Washington Redskins and Dallas Cowboys overnight to Uruguay to play a shirts-and-skins football game. Who would care?"[68]

Still, Danzansky and his partners remained hopeful. The 1977 season, they believed, offered a good shot at financial sustainability. Elevating their spirits was the hiring of sports promotions guru John Carbray. With soccer booming in northern Virginia and Maryland, Danzansky and Carbray were confident that the Dips would appeal to the area's 45,000 registered youth soccer players and, by extension, their parents. Team executives set a lofty goal of attracting 24,000 fans per match. Carbray insisted that the Dips needed to shed their "minor-league" image, which meant moving the team back—yet again—to RFK.[69] But by returning to DC, the Dips had to contend with the perception that, in the words of *Post* sportswriter Nancy Scannell, "the stadium on East Capital Street [was] located in a high-crime area."[70] Would suburbanites refuse to attend Dips games simply because the team supposedly played in a rough neighborhood?

A master of promotional "gimmicks," Carbray believed he had the answer. He began by modernizing the color scheme of the Dips' uniforms and by painting the penalty area black and red. He also had the team's mascot, Big Mike, and the club's cheerleaders, the Honey Dips, make numerous public appearances. Unlike his predecessors, he embraced the "Dips" moniker by featuring it prominently on the front of the club's jersey. In addition, the Diplomats, in partnership with the District's Metropolitan Police Department, established a youth soccer division; held parades on the field for youngsters before games; and permitted public access to practices. Interest in the Dips increased.[71]

But from the very first game, they underperformed. Fifteen matches into the season, Viollet was ousted and replaced by Dips player Alan Spavin.[72] It did not matter. The remainder of the year was equally uninspiring, and the Dips finished a disappointing 10–16. The average attendance of 13,058 was a cause for concern. Not only was it far below what Danzansky had hoped for, it was artificially inflated, since the game against the Cosmos had attracted more than 31,000 people. In addition, thousands of free tickets had been distributed over the course of the season—no doubt alienating season ticketholders who had paid full price.

The Dips' days appeared to be numbered. But in 1978, former New York Cosmos coach Gordon Bradley was brought in, and the team finished a respectable 16-14. Unfortunately, fan interest continued to decrease. Danzansky was convinced that the Dips needed a superstar. Carbray disagreed, insisting, "anyone who was not Pele or Beckenbauer"—the star defender from West Germany—"would not affect attendance significantly."[73]

But in October 1978, Joseph Danzansky and SJR Communications sold their stake in the club to the Madison Square Garden Corporation of New York for a reported $1.5 million. Over the course of the 1977 and 1978 seasons, the Dips had amassed debts of more than $1 million.

In 1979, the Dips reversed their fortunes, and posted a respectable 19-11 record. The club also garnered a small amount of additional revenue from playing indoor games at the DC Armory during the offseason. Financially, though, the franchise continued to suffer significant losses. In a last-ditch attempt at profitability, the Madison Square Garden group in 1980 acquired Dutch international superstar Johan Cruyff from the Los Angeles Aztecs for a reported $2.5 million.[74] Signed to a three-year contract, Cruyff was widely considered the top European footballer of the 1970s—indeed, perhaps of all time. Dave Kindred of the *Washington Post* called him "the Pelé of the Potomac." Dips general manager Andy Dolich, using terms more familiar to the average American sports fan, crowed that the standout from Holland possessed "the creativity of Dr. J., the grace of Lynn Swann, and the leadership abilities of Willie Stargell."[75] Cruyff, it seemed, was just what the Dips needed.

The Dips and Cruyff began the season with two road losses, but then won their first two games at home. More than 24,000 fans attended the home opener, while 15,273 went to the next match. Hoping to attract an average of 20,000 fans per game, the Dips were off to a good start. But a rash of injuries, a contentious relationship between Cruyff and Dips coach Gordon Bradley, and lower-than-expected attendance for some games caused the club's ownership group to panic. If Cruyff could not save soccer in Washington, no one could.

The game against the Cosmos in June suggested brighter days. The match drew 53,351 spectators—a record for soccer attendance in the District at the time. But the Dips lost, 2–1—their seventh in ten games. The match was an embarrassment. There was an assault on linesman Gordon Arrowsmith and a double yellow card ejection of Cruyff. Also, two goals by the Dips were disallowed.[76] Midway through the season, Cruyff hinted that he planned to opt out of his contract. A difference of philosophy with Bradley, an antagonistic relationship with teammates, and several nagging injuries—all took their toll on the Dutch superstar.[77]

The Madison Square Garden group was also feeling the pinch. In just two years, the Dips had accumulated more than $5 million of debt. It was more than Madison Square Garden Corporation's parent company, Gulf and Western, was willing to take on. Unfortunately for Dips supporters, no investors came forward to post the required $3 million to maintain the

Johan Cruyff, "the Pelé of the Potomac," confounds Dallas defenders
during a match at RFK Stadium in 1980. The Dips won, 4–2.
Announced attendance was 15,273. Reprinted with permission
of the DC Public Library, Star Collection, © Washington Post.

ailing franchise. In late 1980, the league had no option but to terminate the
Dips.[78]

Incredibly, three months later the District acquired yet another pro soccer club, the Detroit Express, which, upon moving to the nation's capital,
changed its name to the Diplomats. Despite welcoming back Cruyff partway
through the 1981 season, the new Dips were just as unsuccessful as the old.
With a number of financial debts to settle and lacking the necessary financial
resources, in September 1981 the Diplomats called it quits—for good.

Supporters of American soccer, once more, would find the nation's capital
too enticing to pass up. In 1983, the NASL, with the help of the United
States Soccer Federation (USSF), the successor to the USSFA, placed another
squad in the District. Team America, as the club was called, played its home
games at RFK and consisted of players whom American soccer authorities
had identified as potential members of the United States national squad. The

aim was to prepare the team for international matches by having it play in the NASL. While it may have seemed like a good idea, Team America turned out to be an utter failure. In its one and only season in the NASL, the club compiled a 10-20 record and finished with the least amount of points in the league. The NASL itself would survive only one more season. In March 1985, the league that brought Pelé, Johan Cruyff, and other international soccer stars to America ended operations.

Ten years later, another soccer club found itself gracing the friendly confines of RFK. Competing in Major League Soccer (MLS), an outgrowth of the United States' hosting of the World Cup in 1994, DC United has tread cautiously where its predecessors have failed. Despite success on the field, a conspicuous presence in the community, and a network of devoted fans, the club has often looked to the future with apprehension. Just as the executives for the Whips and Dips had done in the late 1960s and 1970s, DC United officials, including former president Kevin Payne, have argued that the lease agreement with RFK was harmful to the viability of pro soccer in the District. With assistance from MLS, a feasibility study was undertaken in 2011 to assess the possibility of moving the team to Baltimore. As recently as early 2014, the team's future in the District seemed uncertain after the city council balked at developing a new stadium at Buzzard Point in Southwest DC. However, after a series of amendments to the initial plan, the DC Stadium Act was passed in December 2014, marking the beginning of yet another new era for professional soccer in the District.

The stadium issue is just one of the reasons why pro soccer has struggled in Washington. Another reason is that many soccer enthusiasts in the region are spread across a large geographical area. Many do not want to watch DC United bad enough to make the trip into the city. Still another reason is that the majority of Washingtonians have yet to develop an appreciation for "the beautiful game." The average Washington sports fan at times has responded to the appearance of celebrity soccer players and high-profile international clubs. Despite clever marketing campaigns, innovative community relations programs, and a handful of winning seasons, pro soccer teams in Washington have never been consistently supported. The Washington metro area soccer market is fickle. If DC United were ever to leave, its exodus would represent continuity, not change.

10

Uniting a Divided City

The 1969 Washington Senators

Stephen J. Walker

On January 20, 1969, President Richard Milhous Nixon inherited a nation in turmoil. An unpopular, divisive war in Vietnam slogged on with no end in sight. At home, the passage of the Civil Rights Act had done little to end racial strife. Northerners and southerners alike raged against court-ordered busing to end public school segregation. Schools in Alexandria, Virginia, literally across the Potomac River from the nation's capital, were no exception.

In the wake of the assassination of civil rights leader Martin Luther King Jr., angry and frustrated African Americans rioted, burning large areas of cities across the nation, including Washington, DC. On Nixon's Inauguration Day, the ashes from the fires from the April 1968 riots, which were then visible from as far away as Arlington, Virginia, near Bailey's Crossroads, still smoldered. In the city, charred ruins of former homes and businesses remained. Raw emotions and dark, suspicious feelings festered throughout the Washington Metro area.

Fear and misunderstanding became so acute that some suburbanites even expressed reluctance to attend sporting events at DC Stadium, the seven-year-old, multipurpose home of the Senators and the Redskins. Hailed as a beautiful architectural marvel with its gleaming white concrete and unique cantilevered roof, folks who long ago had retreated from the city claimed that the stadium resided in a "bad neighborhood." During the traumatic spring of 1968, city officials had called in the National Guard to patrol the stadium and surrounding area to ensure public safety. In fact, guardsman Ed Brinkman, otherwise the starting shortstop for the Washington Senators, spent more time at the stadium that spring in his military uniform than in a baseball uniform.[1]

Whether suburban dwellers' concerns reflected legitimate fears or misguided racism, Washington's major sports teams gave folks little reason to watch them. Both the Redskins and the Senators took few steps to bridge the city's racial divide. While pot-bellied star quarterback Sonny Jurgensen rang up points on the scoreboard, the Redskins had not enjoyed a winning season since 1955. Worse, the self-proclaimed "Team of the South" was the last franchise in the National Football League to employ an African American player, Bobby Mitchell, in 1961. "Dixie," the jaunty unofficial anthem of the southern rebellion, was the bridge of one version of the fight song, "Hail to the Redskins."

The Senators' displayed a better, but still tepid, commitment to integration. Scout Joe Cambria signed numerous Cuban players, but all, until 1954, were light skinned. Washington's first person of color, Cuban outfielder Carlos Paula, debuted in September 1954, but performed poorly, and was gone by 1957. That season, pitcher Joe Black, who appeared in seven games in August and September, became the first African American to don a Senators uniform. Not until 1959 did the Senators employ an African American ballplayer who appeared regularly—Lenny Green. That season, Sam Lacy, the legendary sports journalist, wrote in the *Afro-American* that Green would be "accepted by colored fans as the first bona-fide member of their race on the home roster."[2]

The team's performance reflected the consequences of their racist policies. As bad as the Redskins played, the Senators fared even worse. Since 1953, the team had finished no better than fifth place—in 1960. After that season, owner Calvin Griffith, for financial reasons and to flee a city that was majority African American,[3] moved the team to Minnesota.

Washington's replacement team, often termed the "Expansion Senators," played poorly. The club, suffering from a hasty and restrictive expansion draft, and from naive, underfunded owners, lost one hundred games or more each of its first four seasons. In 1968, the team lost ninety-six games, worst in Major League Baseball (MLB). Between the lousy play on the field and the racial tension in the city, only 546,661 souls dared attend a ballgame in the District. No other team in the big leagues drew fewer fans that year.[4]

Nixon, a self-described avid baseball fan, found his local team offered cold comfort from the myriad challenges he faced as leader of the free world. Congress, however, provided a small bit of solace, voting to rename DC Stadium the Robert F. Kennedy Memorial Stadium, in honor of the fallen leader, a champion of civil rights. Almost immediately, fans and sportswriters began calling the venue "RFK."

After the 1968 debacle of a season, the forlorn Senators seemed more lost than ever. Majority owner James Lemon decided to sell the team. Few buyers expressed interest in the sports equivalent of a dilapidated fixer-upper. Eventually, Bob Hope and his partners found themselves engaged in a bidding war for the Senators with Minneapolis businessman Robert E. Short. Short, a former Georgetown University law student, was treasurer of the Democratic National Committee, and had his own political aspirations. Scraping up every penny he could borrow against his Admiral-Merchants trucking business that reported $40 million in gross assets in 1968, his four hotels in downtown Minneapolis, and his Los Angeles radio station KRHM, Short won the battle, nabbing the Senators for $9 million, in December 1968.

The Washington media reacted warily to Short's purchase of Washington's baseball franchise. Shirley Povich termed him "a bit of an exhibitionist."[5] His heavily leveraged bid left him in a financially risky position. Shortly after Major League Baseball awarded him the Senators he said, "I've got my economic neck stuck out for miles."[6] The last time Short owned a sports team he moved it. In 1957, he led a group that purchased the Minneapolis Lakers, a charter member of the National Basketball Association (NBA) and its first dynasty, winning five championships in six seasons between 1948 and 1954, behind legendary center George Mikan. In 1960, the Senators' new owner moved the Lakers to Los Angeles. Minnesotans would not see NBA basketball again for thirty-nine years, when the expansion Timberwolves arrived.

Worse, Short felt he had the leeway to move his team out of Washington if he desired. He scoffed at implied threats that Congress would never permit the national pastime to leave the capital city. "Congress doesn't keep baseball in Washington," he said, "Baseball keeps baseball in Washington."[7]

It was no idle threat. Multiple cities, including Milwaukee, Louisville, New Orleans and Arlington, Texas—a Dallas suburb—advertised their desire to lure an existing team to their cities. The Chicago White Sox planned to play eleven games in Milwaukee's County Stadium in 1969. In addition to Short, owners of the White Sox and Cleveland Indians both made it known they would move their teams elsewhere for the right price.

In his first two decisions—firing general manager George Selkirk so he could handle the job himself and raising ticket prices to become baseball's most expensive—he served notice that major changes loomed for Washington's beleaguered baseball fans.

A month later, at a dinner in his honor sponsored by the Touchdown Club, Short decried the state of his new team, its ballpark and its home city. He kept using one depressingly descriptive word—dismal. He said: "[Baseball in Washington] doesn't belong in last place in terms of a bankrupt club in a $20 million stadium in which people are afraid to watch games. When you are last in all respects—attendance, concessions and the won-lost column—you are a dismal last."[8]

Into this darkness the Redskins, Short's chief rival for the dollars and attention of Washington sports fans, injected a brilliant light. In the bone-chilling winter of February 1969, Washingtonians awoke one morning to the warm, smiling face of the city's new football coach—the legend of legends, Vince Lombardi.

While Washingtonians rejoiced, Short felt a desperation-induced tension headache. The Redskins had just sent his doleful little team to the middle of the newspapers' sports sections and to the back of fans' minds.

Short needed to make a splash. Fast. He called a press conference and announced that he had no interest in the mundane baseball lifers rumored to have the inside track on the job of Senators' manager. Plainspoken men like Nellie Fox and former Oakland Athletics' manager Bob Kennedy would never do for an owner described in his team's own media guide as "a man on the move; a stern foe of the status quo."[9]

Short had one man in mind to turn around his dismal team—a man who hit 521 home runs during his nineteen-year career with a .344 lifetime batting average; a man who walked 2,012 times; the last man to hit over .400 in a season; a first-ballot Hall of Fame member who many still name as the greatest hitter who ever lived; a baseball icon and American legend—Theodore Samuel Williams, Teddy Ballgame, the Splendid Splinter.[10]

Writers and fans scoffed at the rookie owner's quixotic quest. One fan, Jim Hartley, a teenager in 1969 and now publisher of *Nats News*, the quarterly newsletter of the Washington Baseball Historical Society, noted that Washingtonians, already suspicious of Short's motives, began to question his sanity. "When I first heard he was trying to sign Williams to manage the club," Hartley recalled, "I thought, 'Yeah, right. What a jerk!'"[11]

Undeterred, Short persisted. He tracked down Williams in the Florida Keys, arranged a secret meeting in Atlanta, and reached a tentative agreement with the Splendid Splinter. For all his faults, Bob Short possessed a silver tongue. In what, at the time, marked his greatest coup, Short achieved what Red Sox owner Tom Yawkey and legions of Red Sox management failed to accomplish—convince Teddy Ballgame to return to baseball and become the skipper of baseball's most bedraggled ball club.

After days of wrangling over legal and financial details, on February 21, 1969, Ted Williams became manager of the Washington Senators. Short paid him $75,000 a year, an astronomical sum for managers in 1969, to manage his last-place team. Williams also became a minority owner and received stock options for the club.

The ten-day delay between the announcement that Short had convinced Williams to manage the Senators and his arrival in Washington left initially shocked fans and sportswriters somewhat numb. During the delay, the brilliant Shirley Povich described how Short had landed his man. In the February 16, 1969, edition of the *Washington Post*, Povich wrote: "The Senators' bodacious new owner brought it all off by turning it all on—his native chutzpah, the brashness that had helped make him a millionaire at an early age, his perseverance that three times refused to accept the 'no' of Williams to his offers, and his persuasive charm that in the past had melted even skinflint bankers."[12]

With fewer than ten days before the beginning of spring training in Pompano Beach, Florida, Williams assessed the Senators' few strengths and myriad flaws. After meeting the men he would lead during the 1969 baseball season for the first time, Williams told the press, "There is much raw talent on this team, but a lot of guys here haven't been thinking in a baseball sense."[13] His players affirmed this comment in their first preseason game, a brutal loss to the New York Yankees. The Senators, courtesy of utility player Rich Billings, got a single hit. The team proceeded to lose their next eight exhibition games.

Sportswriters began to speculate on how long Williams would last. Few thought he would remain for a full season. Once salmon started running upstream in the rivers of the great Pacific Northwest, the thinking went, Teddy Ballgame would bolt the sorry Senators, fishing rod in hand. But Williams scoffed at such speculation. He said, "People think I'll quit if we get off bad, but I'm in this thing to stay."[14]

As his team struggled, Williams noticed that one player, while talented, seemed aloof and discouraged. One day, as Senators outfielder Hank Allen, older brother of Philadelphia Phillies' All-Star Richie Allen, practiced hitting, Williams and his fellow coaches stood behind the batting cage, watching. The Senators manager said to his assistants, intentionally loud enough for Allen to hear: "This guy, there's no reason in the world that he shouldn't be a better hitter than he is. I'd like to know the reason. I'd really like to know." Exiting the cage, Allen said to Williams, "There is a reason."[15]

Williams, brand new to Washington, had no way of knowing the pain and frustration Allen held inside. During the 1968 season, Allen, an African American, felt he had been denied a fair shot to make the club. Even before he put on his cleats and picked up a bat, Allen had two strikes against him, at least in his own mind.

First, the Washington Senators still offered a less-than-ideal environment for African American and dark-skinned Latino players. In 1968, six persons of color appeared in games for Washington: catcher Paul Casanova, of Cuban descent, and African Americans Frank Coggins, an infielder; Allen, who played infield and outfield that season; and outfielders Ed Stroud, Fred Valentine (traded to Baltimore in June 1968), and Sam Bowens. Of those six, only Stroud and Casanova played even semiregularly.

Second, Allen suspected that the reputation of his younger brother, Richie, as an eccentric malcontent held back his own career. Richie, who later went by Dick Allen, was the first African American to play for the Phillies' farm team in Little Rock, Arkansas. He rocketed to the major leagues, but became labeled as a troublemaker in Philadelphia by showing up late for practices and games, fighting with teammates, and writing provocative phrases in the infield dirt such as "Boo" when Philadelphia's infamous fans directed their ire at him. On June 24, 1969, Phillies' manager Bob Skinner suspended Allen for twenty-six games when he failed to show up for the first game of an afternoon doubleheader at Shea Stadium against the New York Mets.[16]

Ron Menchine, one of the Senators' radio broadcasters in 1969, was new to the Washington organization that year. He arrived wary of Allen. Menchine remembered, "I thought, because his brother was pretty much a head case, that he might not be an easy guy to get along with."[17] For his part, Allen resented being tarnished by his kid brother. Teammate Brant Alyea later said, "He would always tell people, 'I'm not Richie Allen's brother, I'm Hank Allen.'"[18]

Allen felt the Senators' 1968 manager Jim Lemon and the Washington organization treated African American players unfairly. He remembered: "In spring training, you had Ed Stroud, Fred Valentine, Sam Bowens and me all placed in right field. It was four of the black guys competing for one position. You were essentially eliminating yourself. All the guys talked about it." During a 1998 interview, Allen called the 1968 season under Lemon, in which he appeared in sixty-eight games and hit .219, "a season of disaster."[19] But other players on the team, albeit all white, felt that talent, not skin color, drove Lemon's decisions. One teammate of Allen's in 1968 and 1969 said, "Hank was looking for the race card to be played on him and it really wasn't played."[20]

A 1968 conflict between Lemon, Paul Casanova, and then general manager George Selkirk offers an inconclusive, but intriguing, perspective on race relations within the Senators' organization, and in sportswriters' treatment of Latino and African American ballplayers during that era. A player who often displayed emotion during an era when most acted like stoics, "Cazzie" usually bubbled with enthusiasm. When he performed well, he flashed a wide smile and played with reckless, but often effective, abandon. When Washington pitchers faltered, he rose from his crouch, took four or five steps toward the mound, and, in an unsubtle attempt to motivate, fired the ball as hard as he could back to the pitcher. Being a former pitcher himself who could throw a ninety-five-mile-per hour fastball, Cazzie instilled fear with his blazing throws. Catching a Casanova fireball stung. Pitcher Bob Humphreys said, "Me and the other pitchers used to brag that one day we'd bare-hand one of Cazzie's throws. But none of us had the guts to do it."[21]

An All-Star in 1967 and fans' second-favorite Senator behind Frank Howard, Casanova in 1968 was mired in a season-long slump. During his 1968 trials, he sulked as his outs and mistakes added up. Lemon tried benching him, but the Washington catcher rebelled. "Play me or trade me," he told George Minot Jr., the *Washington Post* reporter who covered the Senators for much of the 1960s. "I'm not getting enough money."[22]

Eventually, Lemon's and Selkirk's patience ran out. On June 24, the organization assigned Casanova to Washington's AAA club in Buffalo, another east coast city ridden with a poor economy, crime, and racial strife. The Buffalo Bisons played in weatherworn War Memorial Stadium. Thieves regularly pilfered valuables from players' lockers. For a week, Casanova refused to go, saying, "I'll never play for Washington again." But the young catcher forgot that, under baseball's reserve clause, he had nowhere else to go. According to Minot, Selkirk let out a sardonic laugh, and then said, "What else can he do?" Eventually, Casanova gave up and reported to Buffalo.

Included in Minot's article were descriptions of Casanova's role in the incident, many of which today seem condescending and inappropriate. He termed Casanova "super-sensitive," "unsophisticated," "unworldly," "much too valuable a piece of property," "immature," and "the carefree kid." By contrast, Selkirk, who, while seldom accused of racial prejudice, rarely had more than three or four African Americans on the Senators' major league roster, was a man "whose logic is clouded by lack of tact" and "an honest executive who tells it as he sees it. Diplomacy is not his bag." While Minot's article placed more blame on the Senators' organization than on Casanova, the sportswriter's words reflected the time's disregard for nonwhite ballplayers. Roberto Clemente experienced similar treatment in Pittsburgh.

Casanova returned to the Senators on July 23, a broken, dispirited player. His performance and mood improved in 1969 under Williams, but he never recaptured the promise of his 1967 season. He ended his career in

Atlanta as the Braves' back-up catcher and Hank Aaron's roommate, helping Aaron weather the pressure and racism he experienced while breaking
Babe Ruth's home run record.

Whatever the Senators' motivation for the treatment that Casanova
endured, his performance merited no favors. The same facts applied to the
other African American players Allen mentioned. Statistics provide, at best,
mixed evidence that a player's skin color was considered in determining
who played and who watched. In 1968, Senators left fielder Frank Howard,
who was white, hit 44 home runs, best in the American League and boasted
a "slash line" (batting average/on-base percentage/slugging percentage) of
.274/.338/.552. His .552 slugging percentage was the AL's best. Another
white player, starting centerfielder Del Unser, in his rookie season, turned
in a less-than-stellar performance (.230/.282/.277). Although he made the
Sporting News' All-Rookie team, Unser did so primarily for his excellent
defense and accurate throwing arm.

Allen (.219/.265/.289) and his fellow African American players struggled during 1968, the "Year of the Pitcher." Bowens had one of the worst
seasons of his career (57 games, .191/.262/.330). Valentine (.238/.291/.347)
was traded to the Baltimore Orioles after appearing in 37 games, and Stroud
(.239/.284/.376), who eventually won the right field competition, appeared
in 105 games and had 10 doubles, 10 triples, and nine stolen bases.

Arguably, any of these veterans could have outperformed Unser.
However, as a highly touted rookie with a $100,000 signing bonus, the
Senators felt self-inflicted financial pressure to give Unser the centerfield
job. He rewarded them in 1969 with a much better all-around season after
Williams adjusted his approach to hitting. In 1968, Unser, a left-handed
batter, tried to get on base with drag bunts and bloop hits to left field. The
next season, during spring training, Williams encouraged Unser to change
his approach. Unser recalled, "He said, 'You've got a good stroke to left
field and I don't want you to lose it, but you're going to hit some home runs
someday. You've got enough power to pull the ball once in awhile when you
get your situation, get your pitch.'"[23]

Unser, who had just a single home run in 1968, hit seven the next season and served as the catalyst for an offense that scored 694 runs under
Williams's tutelage, 170 more than 1968's dismal total of 524. Nevertheless,
in 1968, Allen felt that Lemon discriminated against him and his fellow
African American ballplayers. "If it walks like a duck and quacks like a
duck then it is a duck," he later said.[24]

In contrast, Allen believed that Ted Williams treated him and everyone else on the 1969 Senators with the utmost fairness. To explain the

differences playing under Lemon and Williams, Allen offered two anecdotes of how each treated him following a spring training moment of triumph. In 1968, Allen was languishing on the bench as a March game dragged into extra innings. With every other position player used, Lemon had only Allen left on his bench. The pitcher's spot in the order came up with a runner in scoring position. With resignation, according to Allen's memory, Lemon said, "You might as well go on in there."[25]

Allen lined a base hit, driving in the game-winning run, and freeing his teammates to the pleasures of Pompano Beach and the surrounding Florida coast. His peers, one by one, congratulated him, but not, apparently, Lemon. Of the incident, Allen later said: "When you win a ballgame, I don't care what type of game it is, the manager always congratulates you. So, then and there, I knew he was telling me, 'I'm not going to use you. You might as well get it firmly in your mind you will not be on this club.'"[26]

During spring training the next year, Allen drove a home run into howling Florida winds to give the Senators another extra-inning victory. This time, Williams moved to the top of the dugout steps to be the first man to shake Allen's hand. A gaggle of happy teammates followed. Allen won over Menchine as well. "Once I got to know him, I learned that Hank was a good guy. Hank was great."[27]

After the game, Williams found Allen in the Senators' locker room and told him, "Buddy, they told me I couldn't use you this year, but I can't do without you. You just keep doing what you're doing, bud, and you're on this club."[28] Years later, as Allen recounted this scene, his voice changed to an almost perfect impression of the Splendid Splinter's during that period. Such was the impact Williams had on Hank Allen's career and life.

With years of teaching from a stern, Bible-thumping mother who spent more time proselytizing for the Salvation Army than she did at home, young Theodore Samuel had it literally beat into him that all souls stand equal before almighty God. Williams was a man nearly devoid of prejudice. Years before Jackie Robinson broke baseball's color barrier, Williams advocated for the integration of baseball with players from the Negro Leagues. He played against men like Satchel Paige and Josh Gibson and knew that they, and many others, were as good or better than most of his Boston teammates.[29]

From his first day on the job with the Senators, Williams made his commitment to equal opportunity clear. Frank Howard said, "Ted Williams doesn't show favoritism. If you play hard and do your job right, Ted Williams won't say a thing to you. Shoot, he'll admire you."[30] Allen described Williams's innate fairness more eloquently. "Ted gave you an opportunity to focus on what you did best. It was up to you to accept that opportunity. Ted's job was to get the 25 best players that he could and get the most out of them. That's exactly what he did."[31]

Performance alone mattered to Williams. When it came time to select his opening-day roster, Allen was on the club. He and Stroud shared the right field position for most of the season. Stroud, a left-handed batter, started against right-handed pitchers, while Allen, a right-handed batter, played against lefties. Much to Allen's delight, every one of Williams's players knew they made the team only because they deserved it.

On the afternoon of April 7, 1969, on a splendid spring day in Washington, the cherry blossoms in full bloom, Allen, along with several players and coaches from the Senators and their opponents, the New York Yankees, stood in a disorganized mass around the RFK Stadium infield. The day marked the beginning of the 1969 baseball season, professional baseball's Centennial. Washington, per longstanding baseball tradition, hosted what had grown to become the Presidential Opener.

All these men acting like excited little children awaited three season-opening tosses from President Nixon. Unlike today, the nation's chief executive made his tosses from an honorary box seat behind the Senators' dugout. The DC Stadium Armory Commission marked the spot with a sign bearing the president's official seal, which read "Presidnt [sic] of the United States."[32] No one noticed the mistake in time to correct it. As if to herald the new beginning to his baseball career, Allen snagged two of Nixon's three tosses. Washington coach Joe Camacho, Williams's close friend from his Boston days, snagged the third. Nixon autographed both balls for Allen, who kept one and gave the second to his mother.

Allen's spirits ascended higher once the season began. The Senators rebounded from an 8–4 loss to the New York Yankees in the opener to win their next two games, both against the Yankees as well. Buoyed by his manager's confidence, Allen turned in the best season of his career in 1969. Near the end of April, his batting average hovered above .400. He led the Senators to a 9–3 win over the Red Sox in Teddy Ballgame's return to Fenway Park. Despite playing with aching ribs and little sleep (bad weather delayed the team's arrival in Boston for the afternoon game until 4:00 a.m.), Allen had two hits and made a superb catch to rob a Boston batter of a home run.

Allen's performance earned him an in-season raise. After a home game in May, Williams ordered Allen to remain in his uniform and report immediately to team president Joe Burke. Allen, thinking he had been traded, reluctantly made his way to the executive suite at RFK Stadium. He recalled:

Opening Day, April 7, 1969: Washington Senators manager Ted Williams (*left*)
watches the first of three ceremonial pitches from President Richard M. Nixon.
To Williams's immediate left is Commissioner Bowie Kuhn. To Nixon's
left is Yankees' manager Ralph Houk. Between Nixon and Houk is Senators'
owner Bob Short. Courtesy of the Richard Nixon Presidential Library
and Museum Staff (NLRNS), National Archives, College Park, MD,
Roll #C0702, Frame #21. Robert L. Knudsen, photographer.

"Burke tore up my contract and gave me a raise right then and there. I
thanked him, signed the contact and came back downstairs to the clubhouse." A smiling Williams greeted Allen. The Washington manager said,
"Didn't I tell you, you do what you've been doing, that I'd take care of you?
Don't you worry, bud, there's more where that came from."[33]

Many years later, the memories of 1969 filled Allen, now an advance
scout for the Houston Astros, with delight. He said, "It was a defining time
in your life when you were young and when you were doing the thing you
loved best of all. It had nothing to do with money, nothing to do with prestige. It was the best time of your life."[34]

Allen's teammates, regardless of their skin color, also enjoyed playing for
Williams, a man free from stereotypical thinking about African Americans
and Latinos that plagued baseball for decades thereafter, especially in

coaching and managing opportunities. Other African American players, Ed Stroud and Arthur Lee Maye, a veteran outfielder who joined the Senators in June via a trade with the Cleveland Indians, thrived under Williams's leadership.

Maye, in particular, savored the chance to play for Williams. He arrived in Washington with a reputation as a clubhouse malcontent. While he did have a well-publicized shoving match with Ed Stroud around the batting cage before one game, his veteran status, including being a former team-mate of Hank Aaron and Eddie Mathews, earned him instant respect in the Senators' clubhouse. Maye played a central role in bringing that long-awaited winning season to Washington. On Friday, September 26, 1969, at RFK Stadium, he hit a grand-slam home run against his former team-mate, Cleveland pitcher Stan Williams, to give the Senators a 4–1 victory, their eighty-second win of the season. Maye's blast provided one of the finest moments in a magical summer for baseball fans in the Washington Metropolitan area. Maye cherished his time under Williams. He would later say, "I really enjoyed playing with the Washington Senators in 1969. It felt good to be part of a winning team."[35]

In fact, the entire Washington metro area began to share Allen and Maye's warm feelings about Williams and his transformation of the Senators. When the team recovered from a slow start to win ten of eleven games and post a 16-11 record, fans became cautiously engaged. A twelve-game west coast road trip against some of the league's weaker teams promised a chance to close in on east division heavyweights, the Baltimore Orioles and Detroit Tigers, defending World Series Champions. But the swaggering Senators, forgetting their own humiliating past, proceeded to lose nine of the first ten games on the trip. The humbled club returned home and lost five of six games to the league's newest and supposedly weakest teams, the expansion-created Seattle Pilots and Kansas City Royals. The encouraging 16-11 start devolved into a 20-26 implosion. Fans began dreaming of Vince Lombardi leading Jurgensen and his mates to glory.

After the Senators' brief return to .500, the dynastic Orioles and their All-Star pitching staff laid a three-game sweep on Williams's upstarts, out-scoring the Senators, 10–2, and dropping their record to 31-35. With six-teen of the next twenty games on the road, all but four against the AL's three best teams—Baltimore, Detroit, and Boston—another lost season seemed imminent. Would the expected dismal showing lead Williams to break his promise and bolt downtrodden, divided Washington for the pleasures of the great outdoors?

With the city poised to forget the Senators, the team instead performed so well it sparked a love affair that many fans would cherish for more than a generation. Washington won thirteen of the next twenty games, the final victory a 5–0 shutout in Fenway Park courtesy of Dick Bosman. Bosman, so obscure that on opening day the Senators' official game program listed him as "Dave" Bosman, had become the team's ace. He even wrested the AL Earned Run Average (ERA) title from Jim Palmer during the last week of the 1969 season. Like his team, Bosman's success seemed to come out of nowhere.

Williams locked his fishing gear away until October. His "Battlin' Senators" now boasted a winning record (44-42) with less than half the season remaining. Having beaten the Red Sox, the team boarded a plane at Boston's Logan Airport bound for Washington. As the captain announced the flight's descent into National Airport, Bosman and his teammates watched the Washington Monument and the Capitol Dome gleam below. Williams and his men felt happy, but exhausted from three weeks on the road. All rested, oblivious to the welcome party awaiting their arrival.

The Senators' unexpected success had not just resurrected their season, it reenergized a city yearning for good news. Vietnam continued to rage. Young men continued to die in an increasingly stalemated conflict. Racial tension continued to fester. Schools in Alexandria, Virginia, remained largely segregated, prompting a federal city-wide desegregation order that compelled the city's leaders to convert T. C. Williams High School, in 1971, to the sole public school in the city for eleventh and twelfth graders. The movie *Remember the Titans* addressed these race-related tensions in the District's next-door neighbor.

The Senators' success allowed everyone to forget the things, real or imagined, that divided them. After the jet carrying the Senators touched down, players entered through National Airport's north terminal to retrieve their bags. More than 1,700 fans, African Americans and whites alike, cheered the team's welcome back. Many held aloft signs that read "Welcome Home, Team" and "We Love Hondo," a reference to Senators slugger Frank Howard.[36] For one evening of celebration, the Washington Senators had united the city. The togetherness lasted all summer long and into October.

When Williams, Howard, Bosman, and the rest of the players appeared, the cheers grew louder. Children, up far past bedtime, clamored for autographs. The wide-eyed players, not used to such adulation, obliged. One longtime Washington resident was quoted as saying, "It's the first time I've been excited about them since the days of Walter Johnson and Joe Cronin." A woman from Silver Spring, Maryland, remarked: "They're great, really great. Even when they lose they look great—and that's better than last year."[37]

For the remainder of the season, only once would the Senators' record fall below .500 (51–52), after a 4–3 loss in Oakland. On August 19, Casey

Cox pitched 8 1/3 innings and, with help from Darold Knowles, defeated the Chicago White Sox, 3–1, for the Senators' sixty-second victory in 123 games.

Fans who had long ignored the hapless team, began to cheer them everywhere. During the summer of 1969, Burn Brae Dinner Theatre, located in Silver Spring, Maryland, performed *Damn Yankees*, the musical composed by Richard Adler and Jerry Ross that was based on the novel *The Year the Yankees Lost the Pennant* by Douglas Wallop. The Senators' unexpectedly good season helped boost ticket sales for the fledgling theater, in its second season. One evening, Del Unser, his wife, Dale, and a few teammates, decided to attend a show. With the Senators having their best season in nearly two decades, Unser and his teammates went for a night on the town and, perhaps, to gain inspiration from watching their fictional counterparts win the pennant (albeit with devilish intervention).

During intermission, the house manager informed the audience that their ranks included some real Washington Senators. The patrons and actors, who were waiting on tables during intermission—as was the theater's custom—responded with a standing ovation. Recalled Unser: "People were euphoric in the area. I mean, they were fired up. This was the first flush that, golly Moses, this is what winning is. It was a special night. It was neat. It was really neat."[38]

Fans also displayed their affection for the Senators during the 1969 All-Star Game, which baseball decided to hold at RFK Stadium, to help celebrate its Centennial. It marked the second time in eight years that the nation's capital hosted the Midsummer Classic. The first was in 1962, to celebrate the inaugural season of DC Stadium. For the first time since the expansion team began operations in 1961, Washington boasted two players on the AL roster, Frank Howard and Darold Knowles. As an added bonus, AL manager Mayo Smith of the Detroit Tigers added Williams to his coaching staff.

All-Star Game festivities throughout Washington included the naming of the game's all-time top lineups, as well as the greatest player ever and the greatest living player. Babe Ruth, to no one's surprise, was proclaimed baseball's all-time best. Williams, while named the greatest Boston Red Sox, lost to rival Joe DiMaggio for the honor of greatest living player. Nixon hosted a breakfast at the White House for Hall of Fame members, including DiMaggio, who traveled to the nation's capital for the festivities, and Washington's newest baseball hero, Williams, nattily attired in a brand-new black tuxedo that Bob Short purchased for him.

Senators' fans showed greater interest in the All-Star Game itself, but torrential rains nearly ruined the occasion. After hours of downpour,

Commissioner Bowie Kuhn on July 22 canceled the scheduled Tuesday evening game. That evening, Kuhn huddled with Short, players, coaches, and baseball officials. All emerged determined to play the game the following afternoon if the weather cooperated and Short's men could repair the field in time. The hearty crew, led by head groundskeeper Joe Mooney, worked all night and most of Wednesday morning to restore the RFK Stadium grounds. Optimistic Senators' fans who kept their tickets begged their bosses for the afternoon off. Late Wednesday morning, the sun appeared. Kuhn observed Mooney and his crew's work and declared it a success.[39] The game would be played. Washington rejoiced.

During pregame introductions, fans gave Howard and Knowles long standing ovations, and booed Boston shortstop Rico Petrocelli. Washington's rooters felt Petrocelli had usurped the spot from its rightful owner— Senators' shortstop Ed Brinkman, who was hitting .267 at the break and was in the top 10 in the AL in total hits.

In the second inning, Howard came up to bat against National League starter Steve Carlton. Carlton grooved a high fastball, right down the middle. Howard swung and connected, his massive, 6'8", nearly 300-pound frame moving in balletic grace and power.

The crack of the bat echoed above the crowd's sighs. The ball kept rising, farther and higher, toward the right centerfield fence. It cleared the wall, still rising, and clanged off the facing of the second deck, more than 450 feet away.

Washington fans, the majority of the sellout crowd of 45,259, thundered in joy. The deafening roar shook RFK's stands. The man nicknamed Hondo, the Capitol Punisher, the Washington Monument, and the Gentle Giant, jogged around the bases, head bowed so as not to show up Carlton. Anyone in the Washington area who followed baseball and had yet to fall in love with the Senators and Howard, succumbed in that moment, one of the highlights of Washington baseball history.

Already a Washington, DC, icon, Howard had achieved greater heights with his All-Star Game home run. The moment cemented his place as a local legend. Tales of his prodigious home run blasts grew taller with the years. When Howard, more than four decades later, threw out the ceremonial first pitch at Game 4 of the 2012 National League Division Series at Nationals Park, more than 45,000 strong stood as one and cheered the now-old man who forever remains a hero in the Washington Metro area.[40]

Knowles also appeared in the game, a 9–3 NL victory. The Senators top reliever faced two batters, retired both, and exited to his own standing ovation. He later said of the moment, "I was elated. It was one of the biggest thrills I ever had in baseball."[41]

In 1969, Knowles, Howard, Williams, and their teammates gave fans and the city of Washington the same feeling—pure elation. As the season progressed into the sweltering days of August and the cool evenings of September, the victories and special moments shared between friends and family continued. Jim Hartley, a teenager in 1969, watched numerous games with his younger brother in Section 422, on the second level of RFK, slightly to the right of home plate. To Hartley and his brother, the Senators were extended family. "You identified with them," he said. "They were like your cousins. You went to see their ballgames and they did so well."[42]

On October 1, the last day of the season, Washington celebrated a family reunion of sorts with their baseball team. A winning season secured, Williams let Howard bat first because he began the day tied with Harmon Killebrew, once a Senator himself (1955–60), for the AL home run crown. Alas, Howard went hitless while Killebrew homered, taking the title with 49 home runs to Howard's 48. Nothing, though, could quell fans' jubilation. Mike Epstein hit a three-run homer in the first inning, his thirtieth of the season. Joe Coleman pitched a complete game, surrendering two runs on a mere three hits. The Senators won, 3–2, their eighty-sixth victory, the highest total for a Washington team since 1945. When Petrocelli grounded to Brinkman to end the game, a small slice of ironic revenge for Washington's fans, the crowd of 17,482 rose and cheered like 100,000. They celebrated on behalf of an entire city. The clamor continued until every Senators player and, at last, Williams, left the field and disappeared into the Washington dugout.

For the first time in a long while, something felt right in the nation's capital. Things were, finally, looking up. A man had walked on the Moon. A new decade was about to dawn. And Washington's baseball club demonstrated itself to be a true team, a meritocracy under a strong, charismatic leader. Problems remained, to be sure, but the city had something to rally around—the Washington Senators. Years later, the unity and joy the 1969 team provided helped reignite the nearly extinguished embers of hope that, one day, brought baseball back to Washington.

Soon afterward, the goodwill surrounding the Senators disappeared. The team finished the 1970 season with fourteen consecutive losses. Rumors swirled that Short had no intention of renewing the team's lease, set to expire on September 30, 1971, which bound the Senators to RFK Stadium. He and Tom Vandergriff, mayor of Arlington, Texas, openly schemed to move the Senators to Texas. However, nearly everyone, including Kuhn, refused to believe that the AL's owners, President Nixon, and certainly not Congress, would permit the national game to depart the nation's capital city.

Like those who scoffed at his quest to hire Williams, Short made fools of them all. In late September 1971, ten of his fellow owners approved Short's plan to move Washington's team to Texas. Nearly three decades later, the pain of a city losing its baseball team, a civic institution since 1901, remained. Former RFK Stadium public address announcer Phil Hochberg would later say of Short: "He took away something that didn't belong to him—the tradition of baseball in Washington."[43]

Thus, Major League Baseball disappeared from Washington until April 14, 2005. Yet, somehow, as one Washington summer without baseball turned into another and more and more local residents gave up hope the game would ever return, memories of the 1969 Senators, and what they did for the city, endured.

One day, the thoughts of a man who remembered that season sparked the first meaningful rekindling of the desire to bring baseball back after the area again had its hopes dashed. In 1997, Houston voters, by less than a percentage point, passed a referendum for a publicly funded stadium (what is now Minute Maid Park). Their votes kept the Astros from being sold to a group led by northern Virginia businessman Bill Collins. After one more disappointment, many fans gave up.

But not Tom Holster.

In 1998, Holster, then president of the Washington Baseball Historical Society, remembered his heroes and those wonderful baseball nights at RFK Stadium. An idea percolated in his mind. He called his group's cohorts, including Hartley, together and said, "Let's have a reunion for the 1969 Senators."[44]

It would be a gargantuan undertaking, but all agreed to give it a try. After hard work and much good fortune, the event came together. Holster found the perfect venue at the beautiful Westfields Inn and Conference Center in Chantilly, Virginia. The inn's room for events had an opening—November 7–8, 1998. To help defray the costs, a promoter agreed to host an autograph show with the 1969 Senators and Hall of Famers Warren Spahn and Ernie Banks at the nearby Dulles Expo Center.

Holster and Hartley contacted team members. More than twenty-two players and coaches agreed to attend the autograph session, a private dinner in their honor, and breakfast with fans the following morning. The duo's friends eagerly volunteered to drive their childhood heroes from the airport to the event.

Hochberg, Menchine, and fellow broadcasters Shelby Whitfield and Johnny Holliday signed up. Best of all, Williams, although recovering from a recent stroke, promised to come, along with his son John Henry.

With nothing more than a hastily arranged flyer and no money left to hire a marketing firm, the breakfast event, available to the first 500 paying customers, sold out in less than a month. Holster soon learned that people throughout the local area shared his love for the 1969 Senators. Like Holster, they had not forgotten.

At the autograph session and in the hotel lobby before the doors opened for breakfast, fans shared their memories. "It goes back to your childhood," said Jeff Flippo, longtime Senators supporter. "These were the guys I looked up to, understanding that we've not had a baseball team in the Washington area for so many years. It's just something, as a baseball fan, I look forward to and hope that someday [a team will return]. It just means so much to see these guys who were a part of my youth. To see them again, it's just neat." Flippo, overcome with emotion, could not speak another word.[45]

Another supporter, Jerry Bush, said, "I got caught up in the excitement of finally having a team that was .500 or better the majority of the season. My favorite player was Frank Howard, no surprise.

"Being at that time a teenager, I knew all the different mannerisms of each hitter. The little ritual they would go through at home plate. [I remember] the excitement of the team and Ted Williams and the motivation he brought to them. These are just cherished, treasured moments and I'm glad to see people rekindling the spirit."[46]

When the doors opened and the crowd entered, some rushed to their tables to meet their childhood heroes. Many brought artifacts for their favorite players to sign, such as a ball presented by a fan for Mike Epstein to autograph to replace one lost in a house fire and a picture of Rich Billings making a leaping catch at the wall. Others, like Flippo, overwhelmed by the scene and the sadness of all the years that had passed since baseball truly mattered to them, broke down in tears. Charlie Gray, who attended twenty to twenty-five games in 1969 with his father, aptly summarized the feelings coursing through him and his fellow fans. "I can't even put it into words it means so much," he said.[47]

After breakfast, local media personalities past and present; Jim French, the team's back-up catcher; and one surprise VIP shared their memories and desire for baseball's return to Washington. Phil Wood, the current dean of Washington baseball history and host of the postgame show on the Washington Nationals radio affiliate, told the gathering, "In February 1969, I turned 18. I registered for the draft and declared my manhood. A week later, the Senators hired Ted Williams as manager and I was 8 years old once again."[48]

Looking at the giddy, smiling faces around him, Wood addressed the players, saying, "I doubt that a man who wore the Senators uniform that season can really appreciate the impact they had on this community. Today, maybe they can look around the room and get a better sense of it.

"That about 500 people would show up 30 years later to honor a fourth-place baseball team..." Wood's voice trailed off as he struggled to hold back tears. A moment later, he concluded his remarks. He turned to the players and coaches seated at the head table and said, "I thank all of you for the memories of a lifetime."[49]

After Hochberg introduced each Senator as if it were opening day, French spoke. Emotionally spent from the tears and laughter of reminiscing with his teammates into the wee hours of Sunday morning, he spoke for fewer than two minutes. He thanked the organizers for making the reunion possible and fans for their presence and enthusiasm.

After French, Menchine offered his remarks. He said: "Without a doubt the 1969 Senators were the greatest group of athletes I have ever been associated with. Before the season started no one ever thought they would wind up 10 games above .500, but they did. It's a memory that all of us will cherish." Giving voice to a theme underscoring the festivities, Menchine turned his thoughts to baseball's future in Washington. "I think this crowd here today is indicative of what a wonderful area Washington is for baseball. It's definitely a major league area."[50]

When it appeared the morning event had entered its final moments, the doors burst open and a wheelchair-bound Williams appeared, his son steering the chair through an aisle and up a ramp to the head table. A no-show for most of the morning, Teddy Ballgame summoned the energy to appear at the last minute. The crowd, fans and players alike, rose as one and gave Teddy Ballgame a standing ovation to praise the legend who transformed their baseball team in 1969.

The adulation enlivened Williams. On his own, he stood from the chair and approached the podium. He first thanked his players, saying many were better than anyone realized. He bantered with his son and took questions from the crowd.

Then, he gave the day its coda, saying, "I want to thank everybody for being here. I think that today has lit a little bit of a fire, possibly, in Washington, DC. about what a good place this is for baseball.

"Keep the faith about Washington. Because I can't think of a town right now that I would say ahead of Washington, DC, is as good a place and probably the best place for seeing major league baseball come back."[51]

Everyone stood and cheered once more. Williams, waving triumphantly, returned to his chair, and John Henry wheeled him back out the door. Few in the room would ever see him again.

Thirty years had come and gone, yet the 1969 Washington Senators, the team that brought together a divided city, had worked magic again. They brought more than memories of a happy, but lost time. They gave energy and hope to the wilting effort to restore baseball to Washington. It was a desire those thirsting, devoted fans in the room and across the Washington Metro area would see fulfilled seven years later.

11

George Allen, Richard Nixon, and the Washington Redskins

The Drive to Win in an Era of Stalemate

Stephen H. Norwood

During the early 1970s when George Allen became head coach of the Washington Redskins, pro football provided solace to large numbers of Americans confused and alarmed by challenges to traditional conceptions of masculinity, patriotism, and authority. Victorious in two world wars, the United States was bogged down in an inglorious conflict in Vietnam against what President Lyndon B. Johnson called "a raggedy-ass fourth-rate country," unable to deploy its formidable military resources in an all-out effort to force the enemy's unconditional surrender.[1] Vietnam was frustrating not only as a new form of "limited war," but also because the military objective no longer involved the conquest of territory. Unlike earlier wars, it was impossible for the public to discern how much, if any, progress United States forces were making. The increasingly unpopular Vietnam conflict caused an erosion of patriotic sentiment that greatly disturbed many Americans. Moreover, an emerging youth counterculture, the largest and most influential in the nation's history, bewildered and angered many mainstream adults by challenging the importance they placed on hard work, deferred gratification, and sharply demarcated gender roles.

President Richard M. Nixon used pro football to connect and communicate with a broad section of the American public. It allowed him to project a tough, determined stand against the Communist adversary in Vietnam and in America's Cold War conflict with the Soviet Union. Nixon's passion for the sport associated him with what became known in the late 1960s as Middle America, the conservative mainstream critical to his landslide victory in the 1972 presidential election over George McGovern, his Democratic opponent linked to the counterculture and antiwar movement.

President Nixon publicly cultivated a friendship with George Allen, the head coach of the Redskins from 1971 to 1977. Both were obsessed with winning, believed in the value of intense competition and discipline, and shared a mistrust of youth and the press. Nixon invited Allen to state dinners at the White House, where the coach mingled with royalty, prominent politicians, and foreign dignitaries. The president in turn visited the Redskins' training facilities, where he conversed with many of the players. He often telephoned Coach Allen to discuss Redskins games. *Washington Post* sports columnist Shirley Povich called Nixon George Allen's "self-appointed adviser."[2]

Nixon's obsession with the Redskins led him to recommend a play for their 1971 playoff game against the San Francisco 49ers. The play, a flanker reverse, proved disastrous when the Redskins tried it close to the San Francisco goal line, late in the second quarter. It resulted in a thirteen-yard loss, depriving the Redskins of a chance for a touchdown in a game they eventually lost, 24–20.[3]

Nixon became so involved with the Redskins that their starting quarterback Billy Kilmer, himself a Republican, complained that the president was hurting the team by creating distractions, and by criticizing Redskins' opponents, which angered them and made them "much harder to beat." Kilmer informed *Washington Post* staff writer Sally Quinn that President Nixon called Allen "all the time . . . even . . . on election night to talk about the game."[4]

Nixon went out of his way to accommodate and honor George Allen. After the Redskins hired Allen as head coach, Nixon assigned his two top White House advisors, H. R. Haldeman and John Ehrlichman, to help find a house for the coach and his family. Allen's wife, Etty, met with the two advisors at the White House and received their assistance. When the Redskins handily defeated the Dallas Cowboys to win the National Football Conference championship in late December 1972, the president invited Allen, his wife, children, and his in-laws to the White House. In the Oval Office, he showed the family a game ball Allen had given him at his inauguration. Nixon kept the game ball in the Oval Office in a desk drawer.[5]

George Allen brought to Washington, DC, an impressive record as head coach of the Los Angeles Rams, and a reputation as pro football's greatest defensive strategist. Although the Redskins enjoyed only three winning seasons between 1946 and 1969, they were still Washington's most popular sports franchise. From 1964 onward every Redskins game sold out.

Washington had introduced season tickets to the National Football League (NFL) in 1937, and from 1967 that was the only kind of ticket the Redskins sold.[6] By the time Allen assumed head coaching duties in the nation's capital, pro football had developed the largest following of any sport in the United States. He brought the Redskins into the playoffs in his first year as coach in 1971, and took them to the Super Bowl the next year. The Redskins reached the playoffs in five of his seven seasons in Washington. Allen never had a losing season with the Redskins, or with any other team he coached, professional or college.

When Allen began his first season in Washington, the Redskins faced little competition from other sports. The city did not have much of a nightlife or even notable restaurants that might distract people from pro football. Washington's major league baseball team, the Senators, was preparing to move to the Dallas-Fort Worth area. The nation's capital lacked professional basketball and hockey teams, and the college football teams in the metropolitan area were not particularly successful and attracted relatively little attention. Even when major league baseball was played in the capital, Redskins players received nearly all the commercial endorsements offered to Washington's athletes.[7]

The Redskins' consistent winning under Allen reinforced pro football's status as Washington's leading sport. Shortly before Allen began his last season as Redskins head coach in 1977, the *Washington Post* conducted a poll that demonstrated that pro football was "by far the favorite . . . [sports] pastime" in the District and its "close-in Virginia and Maryland suburbs." Pro "football stood alone" as the metropolitan region's most popular sport among all age, income, and education levels. The only exception was young African Americans, who showed a slight preference for basketball.[8]

A sizable segment of the capital's elite regularly attended Redskins home games and publicly proclaimed enthusiasm for the team, adding to the franchise's glamour. George Allen told the *Los Angeles Times* in November 1971 how "amazed" he was that so many people he met at a White House state dinner for the prime minister of Australia expressed serious interest in his team. He specifically mentioned national security advisor Henry Kissinger, Vice President Spiro Agnew, and various "admirals and generals." Allen reported that such dignitaries "were interested in the next game [and] asked me about the condition of the players."[9] Etty Allen invited Kissinger, Ehrlichman, and the Iranian ambassador to the United States to watch Redskins games in the Allens' box at Robert F. Kennedy (RFK) Stadium.[10] Prior to big games, the Redskins office was besieged by members of Congress requesting tickets.[11]

When *New York Times* columnist William Safire served on President Nixon's White House staff, the Redskins supplied him with free tickets, and Henry Kissinger accompanied him to games. Safire recalled that when a referee would call pass interference on a Redskins defensive back, former US Supreme Court chief justice Earl Warren, who was seated near him, would "shake his head and say, 'Poor judgment,'" while Kissinger "would leap to his feet, shake his fists and yell, 'On vot theory?'"[12]

The interest the foreign diplomatic community displayed in the Redskins was especially striking because American football had little or no following abroad. The *Washington Post* later reported that "countless foreign-born residents" of Washington were united by "Redskins mania," including diplomats and global business people. This phenomenon became particularly notable during the George Allen era, when President Nixon invited the coach to White House gatherings attended by foreign dignitaries. The *Post* quoted a Saudi Arabian diplomat who expressed support for the Redskins by denouncing their chief rival, the Dallas Cowboys: "I don't like Dallas; I like their cheerleaders only."[13]

Much of Washington was deliriously happy when Allen's Redskins began his first season as head coach with five consecutive victories, giving the capital its first prospect of a sports championship in decades. *Washington Post* sportswriter Kenneth Turan compared local fans' reaction to the Redskins' upset of their archrival, the Dallas Cowboys, in the season's third game to the frenzied welcome the citizens of Paris extended to Charles Lindbergh when he completed the first solo trans-Atlantic flight at Le Bourget airport there in 1927. After the Kansas City Chiefs handed the Redskins their first defeat, a crowd estimated at between 8,000 and 12,000 assembled at Dulles airport to display its passionate support when the team returned to Washington. So many Washingtonians turned out to greet the Redskins that airport traffic was backed up for ten miles. The airport public address system even interrupted its announcements of international flights by playing the team's song, "Hail to the Redskins."[14]

Allen's enormous popularity in the capital was apparent from the "thunderous ovation" he received at Duke Zeibert's restaurant every time he arrived with his family for dinner after Redskins home game victories. Duke Zeibert's had been a premier downtown dining spot since at least the early 1950s, when, as its proprietor recalled, "there wasn't much else to do" at night in Washington. Zeibert remarked that he had served "kings, queens, and presidents" in his restaurant but never had he "heard or seen anything close to the greeting these people gave George Allen."[15]

In 1969 Richard Nixon became the first American president to attend a regular-season pro football game, accompanied by his special consultant on youth affairs, former University of Oklahoma football coach Bud Wilkinson. That Nixon attended the game only contributed to his reputation as "the most avid football fan ever to inhabit the White House."[16] Drawn to Green Bay Packers coach Vince Lombardi's "strong leadership," Nixon considered Lombardi a potential vice presidential candidate when he ran for the White House in 1968.[17] After the Kansas City Chiefs won Super Bowl IV in 1970, Nixon made the first congratulatory telephone call by a president to the winning team, marking "a seminal moment in American sports."[18] Such calls became an annual ritual and underscored baseball's eclipse as the national pastime. The next year, major league baseball symbolically acknowledged its loss of status by abandoning the nation's capital. Not until 2005, when the Washington Nationals began playing in the District, would the longstanding ceremony of having the president throw out the first ball on Opening Day take place in Washington.

During the Nixon-Allen era, pro football appealed to many American men who viewed with distaste the transformation of gender roles provoked by the revival of feminism and an emerging androgyny. Pro football was, along with boxing, the most masculine and violent sport. It lacked college football's pageantry and connection to campus parties and dances, which turned game days into social occasions, attracting significant numbers of women. Moreover, the pro game was rougher than the college version. Attendance at pro football games, and the sport's television audience, was overwhelmingly male, just like the armed forces. The widespread lack of knowledge of football among women resulted in a proliferation of courses designed to familiarize them with it, a unique phenomenon in the sports world.

The violence intrinsic to football, a sport in which hard and potentially dangerous physical contact occurs multiple times on every play, caused most of the public to consider it inappropriate for women. NFL teams never sponsored Ladies' Day promotions, which major league baseball had used since the late nineteenth century to draw women to the ballpark.[19] Schools did not offer football as a women's sport or as an activity in girls' physical education classes. The gender divide over football was illustrated at a White House Thanksgiving Day dinner hosted by President Nixon for disabled Vietnam veterans in 1970. While the president discussed football with the veterans at his table, his daughter Tricia was "telling the guests at her own table that she did not like the game because it is too violent."[20]

Pro football reinforced male identity during a period when homosocial male leisure institutions like the pool hall and the neighborhood boxing club were disappearing. Even barbershops were being replaced by unisex hair parlors. The proliferation of suburbs and spread of television undermined the boisterous street corner society that had encouraged male combative-ness. The western film, which glamorized male courage and aggression, and in which violence provided the solution to problems, nearly vanished after the early 1960s. Pro football provided men the opportunity to vicariously identify with the players' strength, courage, and ability to inflict and with-stand pain.

For middle-class men employed in corporate management and the pro-fessions, watching pro football games permitted the release of aggressive impulses and thoughts they had to suppress in the bureaucratized work-place. Indeed, during the post–World War II period, corporations and school administrations and teaching staffs had stigmatized male anger, and considered any intense feelings a threat to group harmony. Corporations introduced personality tests to screen out hot-tempered job applicants, and trade unions became increasingly conciliatory, abandoning confrontational tactics like mass picket lines and paramilitary "flying squadrons" organized to protect them.[21] The strike that the United Auto Workers—once one of the nation's most aggressive unions—called against General Motors in 1970 was described as "a civilized affair" in which the two sides appeared to share "a greater community of interest than of conflict."[22]

Pro football celebrated traditional masculine qualities associated with the warrior and the hunter. The sport provided psychic release for men who lacked autonomy and felt emasculated in a modern bureaucratic environ-ment. The gridiron replicated the battlefield and the wilderness, where the warrior and hunter stalked his enemy or prey, relying on courage, fighting skill, and physical endurance. Duane Thomas, a star running back for the Dallas Cowboys who also played for Allen's Washington Redskins, noted that many of his Cowboys teammates spent their leisure time hunting. Thomas, however, did not join them because he preferred to hunt opposing linemen: "If you're going to kill something," he wrote in his autobiogra-phy, "kill the son of a bitch in front of you, not some helpless animal."[23] Redskins defensive tackle Diron Talbert, one of George Allen's favorite play-ers, boasted that he would take off Dallas quarterback Roger Staubach's ears as trophies.[24]

One of the NFL's greatest players of the 1960s and 1970s, Los Angeles Rams defensive end Deacon Jones, another Allen favorite, called pro foot-ball linemen "a bunch of animals." Jones's biographer, writing in 1970, implied a similarity between line play in the NFL and animal blood sports, in which people gathered around a pit to watch a bear or bull fight a pack of dogs to the death. The book was entitled *Life in the Pit*. Its dust jacket stated:

The few yards that lie between the line of scrimmage and the quarter-back are called the "pit." Here the biggest and toughest men in football confront each other in a battle of brute force that determines how—or whether—the ball will be moved. This book shows life in the pit through the eyes of the best player ever to pound, beat, scratch, claw, and tackle his way through it: Deacon Jones.[25]

Walter Camp, the "Father of American Football," who in the early 1880s devised the rules that made football a sport distinct from rugby and soccer, compared the game to war. During World War I, Camp declared: "The gridiron is the battlefield. The two teams are the opposing armies." He noted that in both football and modern warfare it was imperative that participants follow orders and operate in tight coordination. Yet each also provided some opportunities for individual initiative.[26] General John J. Pershing, commander of the American Expeditionary Force in France during World War I, attributed American soldiers' proficiency in throwing grenades in part to their experience playing football and baseball.[27]

During World War I, the American press used football metaphors in describing military action, a practice that reached its culmination during the Vietnam War, and was eagerly promoted by the Nixon administration. The *Washington Post* quoted an American soldier during the Meuse-Argonne offensive in August 1918 who implied that US troops gained an advantage from having played football, which had familiarized them with military tactics before they saw action. The American soldier reported that "Quarterback Foch," the supreme allied commander in France, had sent "some American substitutes . . . into the line" to "cut down the [German] interference." When the Germans responded by attempting "an end run" around the US forces, the American "tackles came through, messed up the interference, while the ends tackled the back so hard that he dropped the ball." The Americans then picked up "the fumble[d]" pigskin, and were now "on the offense, bound for a touchdown."[28]

During the Vietnam War, the Nixon administration often drew on pro football terminology in naming military initiatives and devising code names for top government officials. The Pentagon initially called the massive US bombing offensive against North Vietnam in April 1972 "Operation Iron Hand," but the White House changed it to "Operation Linebacker." (Linebackers, who attack quarterbacks and ball carriers with long running starts, are considered the most dangerous players on the gridiron.) Secretary of Defense Melvin Laird in 1972 compared the South Vietnamese army to an "expansion ball club" that would not win all its battles, but was nevertheless steadily improving. Nixon himself used the code name "Quarterback."[29]

Frustration with years of stalemate in Vietnam helped draw a large segment of the American male population to football, where each game ended in a team's unconditional victory, and where progress on the field was clearly discernible and could be measured precisely. In Vietnam, unlike in World War II or even Korea, the public could not trace the forward movements of American ground troops, and had no clear sense of what their territorial objectives were, if they even existed. American ground forces sustained significant casualties on "search and destroy" missions from land mines and booby traps, without ever encountering the enemy. Football presented a different situation: opponents were always in direct contact. The Vietnam War's seeming purposelessness was illustrated by the fiasco of Hamburger Hill, where US troops sustained significant casualties in twelve separate attacks between May 10 and June 7, 1969.[30] After finally seizing the hill from North Vietnamese troops, they abandoned it because it had no military value.

In football, by contrast, a team invaded and took possession of its opponent's territory. A team was also constantly in contact with the "enemy." Football was unique among sports in its military imagery: the quarterback was the "field general," the kickoff coverage team was the "suicide squad." Like soldiers from World War I onward, football players wore helmets. As in the army, they were expected to perform in any kind of weather, including heavy rain, snow, and bitter cold.[31] Deacon Jones's biographer described the Rams Hall of Famer as "durable as a tank and as fast as a jet plane." Jones's nickname was "the Secretary of Defense."[32] George Allen and Deacon Jones shared credit for inventing the term "quarterback sack," which became an important statistic in measuring line effectiveness in pass protection and pass defense. Previously, people referred only to "catching the quarterback behind the line for a loss." The "sack" brought to mind the pillaging and destruction of cities by invading armies.[33] In another military parallel, football players prepared for the season in spartan, often brutal training camps. Unlike in Vietnam, where a soldier, no matter how proficient a combatant, could be felled easily by a hidden booby trap, in football hand-to-hand fighting skill was critical, especially in line play and on defense.

NFL officials and teams promoted the Vietnam War in many ways, including staging patriotic displays in the stadiums at halftime and sending players to tour military bases and hospitals in the war zone. The Washington Redskins were particularly important in this effort because they represented the nation's capital during a time when it was the site of massive antiwar demonstrations. Significantly, pro football players were the first athletes to visit the troops in Vietnam. Arranged by the Defense Department in 1966, the first tour included Redskins middle linebacker Sam Huff. Redskins linebacker Chris Hanburger, who participated in the 1970 NFL tour, declared from Vietnam that he felt "especially good to see how much the soldiers really care about the war."[34] Hanburger returned home "more convinced" that US involvement in Vietnam was necessary.[35] Redskins tight end Jerry Smith, who visited sixty firebases in Vietnam in 1971 with sixteen other NFL players, told the press that US troops' morale was high.[36]

The Washington Redskins countered the antiwar demonstration of 250,000 people that was held in the capital on November 15, 1969, the largest such protest until that time, by staging a festival to honor the flag at RFK Stadium. Each person who attended the Redskins-Eagles game played the Sunday before the demonstration was given a miniature American flag upon entering the stadium. The Redskins invited the crowd to join in singing "America the Beautiful" at halftime, and a Korean War medal of honor winner recited the Pledge of Allegiance. The theme of the halftime show was "The Flag Story," a celebration of the American flag.[37] The Redskins head coach that year, Vince Lombardi, was prominent in the Tell it to Hanoi Committee, a conservative group organized to encourage support for the Nixon administration's Vietnam War policy.[38]

The Nixon administration's use of football to symbolize rejection of the antiwar movement was dramatized in the president's response to both the November 1969 demonstration and the May 1970 rally in Washington against his invasion of Cambodia. In November 1969, marchers gathered at the White House in an effort to attract President Nixon's attention, but he remained in his quarters watching the Ohio State football team defeat Purdue. Nixon then placed a congratulatory telephone call to winning coach Woody Hayes, an outspoken supporter of the Vietnam War.[39] During the May 1970 Cambodia demonstration, Nixon suddenly left the White House before dawn and was driven to the Lincoln Memorial to speak to demonstrators, who were largely college students. A twenty-year-old woman from Syracuse University told the press afterward: "Here we come from a university that's . . . on strike, and when we told him where we were from, he talked about the football team."[40]

Other conservative politicians explicitly associated football with opposition to the youth counterculture and antiwar movement. California superintendent of public instruction Max Rafferty in an October 1969 speech to a Rotary Club celebrated football for inculcating martial values. He denounced those who criticized the sport as "kooks, crumbums and commies" and "hairy, loudmouthed beatniks."[41]

The pro football establishment implicitly endorsed Nixon's Vietnam policy by presenting him with prestigious awards and by inviting him to deliver the keynote address at the Pro Football Hall of Fame banquet in 1971. The National Football Foundation and Hall of Fame (NFFHF) awarded the president its Gold Medal in November 1969, praising him for grasping one of football's "foremost lessons": not losing sight of your goal when you are "stopped for no gain."[42] The statement could be interpreted as praise for his political comeback and for his determination to pursue victory in Vietnam.

The pro-war symbolism of such occasions was dramatized about a month later when the NFFHF awarded President Nixon its Distinguished American plaque at a Pro Football Hall of Fame dinner at the Waldorf-Astoria Hotel in New York. Nixon had to enter the hotel from a side-street garage entrance because antiwar demonstrators were picketing the dinner outside. (Forty-eight demonstrators were arrested, many of whom were injured in clashes with the police.) In accepting the plaque, Nixon signaled to the highly sympathetic football audience his determination to break the Vietnam stalemate with an allusion to sports. He noted that tennis star Bill Tilden "once refused to congratulate a tennis winner because he said the player 'played not to lose' instead of 'playing to win.'"[43]

During the early 1970s, George Allen greatly assisted the NFL in forging the strongest relationship between a major sport and the presidency in American history. Sports served an important purpose during the Cold War, with the Americans and Soviets both extracting propaganda value from Olympic medal counts. Many Americans, including then vice president Richard Nixon, were deeply distressed in 1959 when a Swede, Ingemar Johansson, knocked out American heavyweight champion Floyd Patterson and took the title, a symbol of national power, out of the country. Nixon, a longtime football fan who attended regular-season Redskins games as vice president, considered the sport important in communicating not only national strength but also the will to win and the competitive drive associated with free-market capitalism, values both Nixon and Allen avidly embraced and promoted.

Allen was a longtime admirer and political backer of Nixon. They had known each other since the early 1950s, when Nixon was a US senator from California and Allen was coach at California's Whittier College, Nixon's alma mater. *New York Times* reporter Robert Lipsyte noted that the two men were drawn together by a shared belief that "competition is the true crucible of the soul." Allen praised Nixon for rebounding from his defeats in the 1960 presidential and 1962 California gubernatorial elections. He declared that the "determination to come back shows he is a competitor, and that is why he likes football."[44] In 1968, Allen joined a group of athletes formed to promote Nixon's presidential candidacy that included basketball star Wilt Chamberlain and tennis star Billie Jean King.[45] Allen called Nixon "a very knowledgeable football man."[46]

As Redskins coach, George Allen often spoke with President Nixon on the telephone. On December 26, 1972, the president called George Allen to discuss the Redskins 16–3 playoff victory two days earlier against the Green Bay Packers, which put Washington into the National Football Conference championship game against the Dallas Cowboys. Using the muscular language in which Nixon reveled, Allen declared that the Redskins had "dictated" to the Packers and given them "a lesson in how to play brutal defense." After the two men discussed the Redskins' injuries, they lashed out at the press. Allen mentioned that two reporters regretted that the Redskins had won, to which Nixon responded: "Some of these god-damn reporters don't want Washington to win." Allen proceeded to vent his hatred of his next opponent and archrival, the Dallas Cowboys, informing Nixon that the Redskins were "going to have to get physical with them." The coach confided: "I hate the state of Texas. I hate those big cowboy hats. I hate Dallas more than anything, more than any team in football. I want [my players] to feel that way. If you don't feel that hate, you're shaking hands with them."[47]

The next week, after Washington thrashed the defending Super Bowl champion Cowboys, 26–3, Nixon and his aide Charles Colson exulted on the telephone that the Redskins "hit hard" and "were out for blood." Colson said that the Redskins' crushing defeat of the Cowboys and post-game celebration reminded him of Nixon's landslide victory in the recent presidential election over George McGovern, who had won the electoral vote of only one state—Massachusetts—and the District of Columbia.[48]

Indeed, the outlook and demeanor of Nixon's campaign staff prior to the 1972 presidential election resembled George Allen's before a football game. Bryce Harlow, a counselor to President Nixon, recalled that as the campaign geared up, "everyone went macho. It was the 'in' thing to swagger and threaten." Charles Colson talked "about trampling his grandmother's grave for Nixon and showing he was as mean as they come."[49]

Nixon's vice president, Spiro Agnew, was also a great admirer of George Allen, and a football fan. The Touchdown Club of New York in May 1973 named Agnew Pop Warner Man of the Year and presented him with its first lifetime gold membership card. The club bestowed the honor not long before Agnew was forced to resign his office for taking kickbacks from building contractors as governor of Maryland and while vice president. In his acceptance speech at the club, Agnew praised George Allen as a role model for young people, and declared that adults should instill self-discipline in youth,

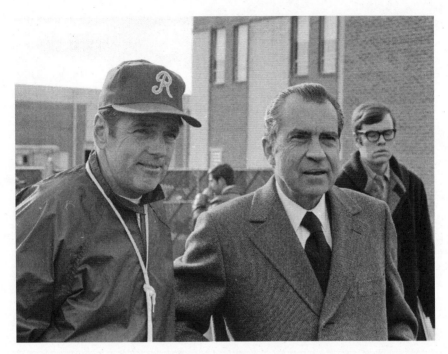

Washington Redskins head coach George Allen with President Richard M.
Nixon at Redskins football practice, November 23, 1971. Richard M.
Nixon Presidential Library collection, National Archives.

a quality football heavily emphasized. The vice president associated football
with free enterprise, telling the audience: "We are a competitive people, and
it is the spirit of competition that has made our economic system the envy
of the world."[50]

George Allen's paranoia and contempt for the press were evident when
he built an expensive office complex and training facility, known as Redskin
Park, in a remote area of northern Virginia, about twenty-five miles from
downtown Washington. Redskin Park contained two practice fields—one
on natural grass and one on artificial turf—along with weight and film
rooms, conference facilities, and numerous offices. One of Allen's purposes
in building Redskin Park was to prevent other NFL teams from spying on
his practices. The complex was surrounded by a high fence and woods.
Allen employed a former Los Angeles detective nicknamed Double O (after
James Bond) to patrol the complex's perimeter. During practices, Double
O positioned himself with binoculars on the roof of a nearby warehouse
to detect trespassers.[51] Allen feared that the Dallas Cowboys had infiltrated

his compound and that they had sent helicopters overhead to take infrared shots of practices.[52] Jennifer Allen, the coach's daughter, stated that Redskin Park "had the secrecy of the CIA with the aura of a mental institution."[53]

Both Nixon and George Allen were antagonistic to the press and suspicious of its motives. Nixon had bitterly denounced the newspapers in 1962 when he was defeated in his race for governor of California, informing reporters in an impromptu concession speech: "You won't have Nixon to kick around any more." He claimed that the press had been attacking him since the late 1940s, when he rose to political prominence through the Alger Hiss case.[54] While in the White House, Nixon held fewer press conferences than any president since Herbert Hoover. His press secretary, Ron Ziegler, was "tight-lipped with information and disrespectful of the reporters." In November 1969, Nixon had Vice President Agnew blast the media as elitist and being heavily biased against the administration.[55]

George Allen was similarly at war with the press. He complained to *Washington Post* editor-in-chief Ben Bradlee that his newspaper was divulging every play the Redskins practiced: "They're telling our enemy our plan of attack!" Jennifer Allen commented that her father considered the *Post*'s coverage "akin to announcing where we'd bomb next in Vietnam." She also noted that most teams offered journalists comfortable facilities in which they could work and socialize: "special heated and air-conditioned rooms, complete with a private bathroom, telephones and desks, hot coffee, and fresh doughnuts." Coach Allen, by contrast, provided reporters and broadcasters at Redskin Park only "an abandoned, unheated camper-trailer." When NFL commissioner Pete Rozelle told Allen to be more accessible to the media, he extended the time for post-practice interviews from five to eight minutes.[56]

Nixon and his staff appreciated Allen's contempt for the press. Jennifer Allen recalled a man in a three-piece suit personally delivering a letter from Vice President Agnew to the Allen home after some criticism of the coach had appeared in the Washington press. In the letter, Agnew encouraged Allen to disregard the opinions of "a few 'cry-baby' reporters" and "run your team as you see fit." He concluded by advising Allen, "Tell them all to go to hell." Allen framed the letter and placed it on the wall of his office in Redskin Park.[57]

Redskin Park, along with Allen's lucrative contract, was testimony to the exalted status pro football now occupied in the United States. In addition to an annual salary of $125,000, Allen was provided with a house and a chauffeur-driven limousine. He was also appointed general manager, a position that allowed him to make trades, negotiate player contracts, and sign and release players.[58]

Determined to quickly transform the mediocre Redskins into a winner, Allen immediately implemented drastic changes in the team. He greatly valued experience over youth, believing that seasoned players were much less likely to make mistakes and performed far better under pressure than rookies. Veteran players were also better able to grasp his complicated defensive schemes. Allen's outlook was not unlike that of military commanders, who preferred battle-hardened troops to green ones for the same reasons. He also disdained the draft, trading many of his choices for players who had proven themselves in the NFL, because the level of competition in professional football was much higher than in college.[59]

Using this approach, Allen had quickly turned the Rams, a perennial loser, into a top-flight team. In 1966, his first year as Los Angeles head coach, he moved the Rams above .500. In his second season, he achieved the best record in the franchise's history, 11-1-2. During the next three years, before moving to the Redskins, Allen's Rams finished 10-3-1, 11-3, and 9-4-1.[60]

On January 28, 1971, almost as soon as he joined the Redskins, Allen announced a trade that dramatically transformed the team and communicated that he was intent on immediately getting them to the playoffs. He sent the Los Angeles Rams seven draft choices, including that year's first- and third-round picks and one player in exchange for six Rams veterans, including the entire starting linebacker corps. The trade, which greatly strengthened the Redskins porous defense, brought them an outstanding defensive tackle, Diron Talbert, three highly regarded linebackers—Jack Pardee, Maxie Baughan, and Myron Pottios, all in their thirties—guard John Wilbur, and an excellent special teams man, Jeff Jordan. President Nixon, upon learning of the trade, telegrammed Allen: "Great trade. I am betting on the Redskins for the championship in 1971 or 1972."[61]

Allen had obtained eighteen veteran players in exchange for twenty draft choices by the time the Redskins began their training camp in July, and he never started a rookie that year. Washington fans fondly referred to Allen's Redskins as the "Over the Hill Gang." The acquisitions included defensive ends Verlon Biggs from the New York Jets and Ron McDole from the Buffalo Bills, who along with Talbert and Bill Brundige gave Washington arguably the NFL's best front four. Flanker Roy Jefferson came in a trade from the Pittsburgh Steelers, joining split end Charley Taylor to form one of the best wide receiver pairs in professional football. Allen also traded "a little-known linebacker and a pair of throw-in draft choices" for New Orleans Saints quarterback Billy Kilmer, a nine-year veteran signed as a backup for Sonny Jurgensen. When Jurgensen suffered a shoulder injury during the 1971 preseason, Kilmer took over starting duties and led the Redskins into the playoffs.[62]

Allen pioneered in giving high priority to special teams, probably the most violent and dangerous part of football. Under Allen, the Rams became the first NFL team to employ a special teams coach, Marv Levy, who followed him to the Redskins. Allen contended that kickoffs and punt returns, which involved high-speed collisions in the open field, and blocked field goals, determined the outcome of at least three games a season. By 1972, Allen's second season in Washington, the Redskins led the NFL in kickoffs and punt returns, and kickoff and punt coverage.[63] Kickoff plays resembled soldiers' charges in battle and carried significant physical risk. Vince Lombardi considered kickoff coverage "football's greatest test of courage." He declared: "It's the way we find out who likes to hit."[64]

Allen's strong preference for older, experienced players conflicted with the cult of youth that during the 1960s and early 1970s became more pronounced than at any other time in American history. Youth were the driving force and leadership in the antiwar movement. By contrast, middle-aged men in the government and armed forces were in charge of the US war effort in Vietnam. Historian David Hackett Fischer noted that during this period mature adults followed "fashions in books, music, and clothing which were set by their adolescent children."[65] In pro football, veterans clearly established and communicated their authority over younger players through hazing rituals and informal harassment of rookies. Dave Meggyesy, a St. Louis Cardinals linebacker from 1963 to 1969, stated that "rookies generally received constant abuse from the vets, designed to intimidate them and break their confidence."[66]

Salary inversion throughout the NFL in the 1960s, combined with fear of displacement by younger players, intensified veterans' hostility toward rookies. Many middle-aged Americans, who had suffered privation during the Great Depression, similarly resented a cohort of youth who had grown up during postwar affluence. Because the NFL had to compete to sign draft choices with the upstart American Football League from 1960 to 1966, rookies' salaries escalated dramatically, often surpassing those of longtime stars. Green Bay Packers all-pro guard Jerry Kramer recalled that his first NFL contract, in 1958, provided a salary of $7,750 and a bonus of $250. By contrast, running back Donny Anderson signed with the Packers in 1966 for a salary and bonuses of $600,000. Kramer noted that second-year Packers guard Gale Gillingham complained to him about his rookie contract because it provided a bonus of "only" $50,000. Kramer stated: "In 1958 I was very happy to get $250."[67]

Allen immediately put his imprimatur on the Redskins by drastically changing the type of football it played and marginalizing its star quarterback Sonny Jurgensen, the team's leader and most popular player with fans. The Redskins would no longer be Sonny's team, but Allen's team.[68] Jurgensen had been Washington's quarterback since 1964, when the Redskins obtained him in a trade with the Philadelphia Eagles. Many coaches, players, and sportswriters considered Jurgensen the best "pure passer" in football history.[69] Tom Landry, head coach of the Dallas Cowboys, called Jurgensen in 1966 the NFL's most accurate passer.[70] Los Angeles Rams defensive end Lamar Lundy explained the next year that it was exceedingly rare for a quarterback with Jurgensen's quick release to be so accurate.[71] *Washington Post* sportswriter Paul Attner later termed Jurgensen "the master of the two-minute drill, the architect of comebacks." Attner quoted Vince Lombardi, who coached the Redskins in 1969, as telling friends that if the Green Bay Packers had drafted Jurgensen they "never would have lost a game."[72]

After Jurgensen threw four touchdown passes against the Rams in 1967, Los Angeles safety Ed Meador stated that the Redskins were probably the "most explosive" offensive team he had seen in the NFL in his nine-year career.[73] In 1966, Jurgensen led the Redskins to a 72–41 victory over the New York Giants. Jurgensen loved the aerial game, and he had an outstanding receiver corps. Unlike most quarterbacks in the league, he often passed from thirty-five to fifty times a game.[74] Unfortunately, in the seven seasons prior to Allen's arrival, the Redskins usually played around the .500 level, primarily because of a weak defense and lack of a running game.

Not long after arriving in Washington, Allen replaced Sonny Jurgensen with Billy Kilmer, a far inferior passer, and revamped the offense to emphasize running and ball control, which gave the defense more time to rest. For Allen, the key to winning was minimizing mistakes as much as possible. In his view, teams that relied on passing were more prone to committing errors. There was a greater risk of a sudden turnover (through interceptions), as well as major loss of yardage (through quarterback sacks). While Allen appreciated Kilmer's toughness and leadership ability, many Redskins players and fans found the conservative offensive style dull. Jurgensen commented disdainfully that Allen's "Thou Shalt Not Pass offense" was "like driving a car in second gear instead of getting into high gear." Highly regarded *Washington Post* sports columnist Shirley Povich called Kilmer "pedestrian."[75]

Like other traditionally minded football men, Allen probably considered running the ball more macho than passing it. Offensive linemen are typically more aggressive when blocking on running plays than in pass blocking, which is largely reactive. Cal Hubbard, former Green Bay Packers tackle, once said: "only sissies throw the ball."[76] Similarly, combat infantrymen saw themselves as the most essential troops and often resented the greater glory attached to the flashier "flyboys" in the air.

Washington Post sportswriters Kenneth Turan and George Solomon maintained that Allen was threatened by the charismatic Jurgensen, who "can perform wonders all by himself," and did not want to share the stage with him. They commented that Allen seemed "positively hurt" when he had to bring the "freebooter" Jurgensen into a game, because he feared the man he had relegated to the bench offered a "better, more exciting" brand of football than his own.[77] In this sense Allen resembled Nixon, who felt diminished by the Kennedys' charisma.

Allen even went out of his way to humiliate Jurgensen. In an address at the National Press Club in Washington in February 1973, he called Billy Kilmer the second-best quarterback ever to play for the Redskins, behind only Hall of Famer Sammy Baugh. The coach disparaged Jurgensen for not delivering championships: "I know of Sonny Jurgensen's great records, but the big thing is to win. We're not interested in statistics, only winning."[78] When injury prevented Jurgensen from playing for most of the 1972 season, which culminated in a Redskins trip to Super Bowl VII, Allen refused to include him in the team photograph. Nor did Allen allow Jurgensen to stand on the sideline during the game, which the Redskins lost to the Miami Dolphins, 14–7. The Redskins offense under Kilmer had been flat, producing no points. Jurgensen was deeply hurt by Allen's disrespect. Forced to watch the Super Bowl from the stands, he felt "isolated."[79] Jurgensen was profoundly moved, however, when the Dolphins' Don Shula, one of the NFL's premier head coaches, approached him before the Super Bowl and said: "It's a shame you're not playing, it would have made it a better game."[80]

George Allen and Richard Nixon shared an obsession with winning and responded to defeat with an inordinate sense of shame. *Wall Street Journal* columnist Frederick Klein noted that football, the sport that most resembled war, where defeat is disastrous, produced the "most memorable (and absolute) quotes about winning and losing." Woody Hayes declared: "Without winners, there wouldn't be any goddamn civilization."[81] Vince Lombardi, referring to the Playoff Bowl, staged during the 1960s between second-place teams in the NFL's eastern and western conferences, told the Green Bay Packers: "There's only one place here, and that's first place. . . . There's a second-place bowl game, and it's a hinky-dinky football game. . . . That's all second place is: Hinky-dinky."[82] Significantly, in 1970, with the Nixon administration determined to break the stalemate in Vietnam, the NFL discontinued the Playoff Bowl. In 1974, after a frustrated US Government had withdrawn its forces from Vietnam without a victory, the NFL instituted a fifteen-minute sudden death period to break ties, enabling the first team to score to win the game.[83] In 1972, the Nixon campaign's Committee to Re-Elect the President posted a sign in its headquarters: "Winning in Politics Isn't Everything, It's the Only Thing."[84] This quotation, minus "in Politics," was widely attributed to Lombardi.

The intensity of Allen's drive to win was striking even in the football world. When asked how he wanted to be remembered, he replied, "That I want to win so bad I'd give a year off my life."[85] Anyone who could accept losing was "half-dead" and did not know it.[86] Redskins special teams coach Marv Levy recalled that Allen, meeting with his assistants before Super Bowl VII, declared: "I'd cut off my right arm up to here [the elbow] to win this game. Wouldn't you?" When no one reacted, Allen pointed to an even higher point on his arm. Again, none of the assistants voiced their agreement. Allen then went "all out" and announced: "I'd cut off my testicles to win this game." When that elicited no response, Allen "stormed out" of the room.[87] When in a tight game a referee ruled a Patriots' punt the Redskins blocked into the end zone a safety instead of a touchdown, Allen became hysterical. A Redskins player reported that Allen "looked as though he was about to commit suicide. . . . He appeared as if he might go completely insane."[88]

Allen was devastated when the Redskins lost Super Bowl VII. He told reporters after the game: "It doesn't do any good to play in the Super Bowl if you don't win." Jennifer Allen recalled that upon returning home after the Super Bowl loss in Los Angeles, her father isolated himself in "his dark, sorrowful bedroom."[89]

On the field, Allen gave the opposition no quarter. New York Giants linebacker Ron Hornsby compared Allen's Redskins to "a college team going for a national ranking by trying to run up the score." Giants head coach Alex Webster stated that Allen would not shake his hand before or after a game. Webster claimed that he had never met an NFL coach who would not do that.[90]

Driven to win, Allen considered anything other than football a distraction. Jennifer Allen wrote that her mother was proud she had raised four children without the help of a husband.[91] Etty Allen stated that during the football season her husband was "never home before 10 o'clock . . . 10 o'clock would be very early for him." She told the Los Angeles Times that her husband made many of his trades at night in bed, including the big deal that brought six Rams to the Redskins. Etty recalled that her husband began negotiating with the Rams at 3:00 a.m. She fell asleep while George was on the telephone, and "he was still [talking] on it when I woke up."[92] Jennifer Allen noted that her father always misspelled her name. Her mother told Jennifer that with forty players to coach and three hundred plays to practice, she was lucky her father even knew what her name was.[93]

George Allen maintained his friendship with Richard Nixon after he resigned the presidency in disgrace as a result of the Watergate scandal. In subsequent years Allen often visited Nixon at his home in San Clemente, California, where, according to Jennifer Allen, the two men "talk[ed] about the days when they both ruled the free world."[94] On the Fourth of July weekend, 1976, nearly two years after Nixon left the White House, Allen recited the Pledge of Allegiance at a special bicentennial dinner dance that wealthy sympathizers arranged in Nixon's honor.[95]

Nixon's successor, Gerald Ford, also praised Allen and pro football. In an article in *Sports Illustrated*, the conservative Ford asserted that "few things" were "more important to a country's growth and well-being than competitive athletics." The "competitive spirit," Ford maintained, had "made us great." It was "the guts of the free-enterprise system." Ford declared, "George Allen's principles are consistent with mine," highlighting the coach's "dedication to hard work."[96] In late September 1974, President Ford and the First Lady attended a Redskins game as Allen's guests.[97]

During the 1960s and early 1970s the passion for pro football reflected a strong undercurrent of conservatism that scholars of the period often neglect.[98] As the sport most similar to war, and with games that ended in clear-cut victory, pro football appealed to large numbers of Americans frustrated by a stalemated war in Vietnam. The highly popular Rambo films, released a few years after the Communist takeover of South Vietnam, featured a new "warrior hero" who resembles a pro football player in his bulk, violent aggressiveness and willingness to court danger. Before he begins his mission to locate American prisoners-of-war still held by the Communists in Vietnam, John Rambo asks contemptuously, "Do we get to win this time?" By killing hordes of North Vietnamese soldiers and safely extricating the prisoners, Rambo achieves victory and symbolically reverses the Vietnam War's outcome.[99]

In the post-Vietnam era, Allen could not command as much respect from the players and his authority eroded, as Vince Lombardi's would have, had he not died in 1970. Even though the conservative Ronald Reagan was elected president in 1980—benefiting in part from his Hollywood role as a Notre Dame football player, "the Gipper,"—a large section of the population was leaving traditional values behind. In his autobiography, Hall of Famer Deacon Jones expressed his strong admiration for George Allen and shared his priorities. Jones was even willing to have the Rams trainer inject his injured foot with a painkiller "game after game" to get him on the field and help the Rams win, "no matter what the long-term consequences." According to Jones, all of his teammates felt the same way.[100] This outlook became increasingly less common after the mid-1970s.

When Allen left the Redskins after the 1977 season to become the Rams' head coach for a second time, he did not last through the preseason. Rams owner Carroll Rosenbloom restricted Allen's authority by not giving him general managerial duties—something he had while he was coaching the Redskins. Curtailing his authority, though, did not stop Allen from demanding that front office executives in the Rams organization work on Saturdays. Allen also required players to practice three times a day—instead of the usual two—and would not allow them off the field until each play was perfectly performed. He awarded a prize of a gallon of milk, his favorite drink, to the player with the neatest notebook. Several front-line players walked out of camp, refusing to play for Allen, and he was dismissed before the season opened.[101]

Allen was never hired in the NFL again. Owners were unwilling to grant Allen the authority he coveted to make trades, and perceived him as too inflexible to relate to a new, more relaxed breed of player. Despite his phenomenal .712 NFL regular season winning percentage, he was repeatedly rejected for the Pro Football Hall of Fame. Allen was not elected until 2002, more than eleven years after his death.

George Allen was the only sports figure of the late 1960s or early 1970s, except for Vince Lombardi, who transcended athletics and came to symbolize major conservative cultural currents in a period of intense conflict. In embracing him, President Richard Nixon communicated his commitment to conservative values then under siege: the will to win; the importance of projecting power and the determination to use it against adversaries; and opposition to the countercultural celebration of leisure, immediate gratification, pacifism, and disregard for authority. Pro football's unprecedented popularity in the 1960s and early 1970s enabled Allen to become a leading representative of "traditional" American values, like John Wayne in celluloid.

12

A Little Big Man, a Fat Lady, and the Bullets' Remarkable Season

Chris Elzey

Washington Bullets coach Dick Motta was standing in a backroom of the Capital Centre in Landover, Maryland, surrounded by a platoon of reporters. His Bullets had just beaten the Philadelphia 76ers in game 4 of the 1978 Eastern Conference finals of the National Basketball Association (NBA). But Motta was in no mood to savor the victory, even if it put his team up three games to one. He had coached too many games, seen too many comebacks, to take anything for granted. In the NBA nothing was guaranteed.[1]

Motta, sporting a modish leisure suit, his wide-collar shirt partially unbuttoned, disco-style, calmly fielded questions. Having coached nearly ten years in the league, he knew the postgame routine. Courteousness, though, had not always been his forte. Once as coach of the Chicago Bulls he booted the ball into the stands after the officials refused to call goaltending against the opposing team. But since coming to Washington in 1976, his fiery side had cooled. Still, there was no telling when the old Motta might reappear. In fact, earlier that afternoon he had been whistled for a technical foul.[2]

It was sometime during the postgame interview that Motta's temper nearly got the better of him again. Luckily for the reporters in the room, the forty-six-year-old coach was able to suppress his ire, and in doing so, provided a saying that all of Washington would come to embrace.

"I can't remember who the [reporter] was," Motta later recalled, "but [there were] about three or four cameras, and this guy kept shoving the camera in my face," asking, "'After all these years, how does it feel to [be on the verge of playing for a championship]?'" No matter how Motta responded, the reporter repeated the question. "I couldn't get rid of him," Motta remembered.[3]

In his article for the *Washington Post* the next day, Paul Attner recorded what Motta was to have finally said: "It's not over. It's like an opera. It doesn't end until the fat lady starts singing and that hasn't happened . . . yet." Steve Hershey of the *Washington Star* quoted Motta differently—"the opera's never over until the fat lady sings"—but the meaning was the same. Little did Motta know, but he had just voiced what would become the battle cry for Bullets fans that spring, and, like the team to which it was linked, helped heal a distressed city.[4]

The saying, which almost instantly took the folksier form, "the opera ain't over till the fat lady sings," immediately became part of DC vernacular. Yet when Motta was asked about the line, he was always quick to point out that it had not come from him but rather from a sports journalist in San Antonio named Dan Cook. Funny and plainspoken, Cook wrote for the *San Antonio Express-News* and anchored the sports desk for the paper's TV station, KENS. Cook later claimed that he had included the line in a draft of a column years earlier, but it had been edited out.[5]

Motta's introduction to the line most likely came on Monday, April 17, 1978, a day after the Bullets lost to the San Antonio Spurs in the opening game of the Eastern Conference semifinals. Motta was in his hotel room, watching TV, the knob flipped to channel 5, KENS. "Some television announcer, a guy by the name of Cook, I think, said something about how the series between the Spurs and us was like an opera," Motta told Paul Attner in June 1978. "It wouldn't be over until the fat lady sang."[6]

But if the saying made an impression on him, Motta kept mum about it, at least early on. After Washington won games 2 and 3, he never said the line. Only after the Bullets took the next game did he repeat it—a warning to overzealous Bullets fans not to look past a good San Antonio team.[7]

Curiously, however, the line slipped past a usually astute Washington press corps. In the coverage of game 4, nothing about an opera or a fat lady appeared in the local press. Maybe Motta said the line in passing. Maybe it was poorly articulated. Whatever the case, the historical record is silent. But what is known is that Motta, by his own admission, first uttered the line after the Bullets beat the Spurs in game 4. Two weeks later, he said it again, and within days the nation's capital was all agog with an opera and a fat lady. In the weeks that followed, the excitement would grow. And at the heart of it all lay a determined Bullets team that captured the imagination of a city.

Tradition was no friend of the 1977–78 Bullets. Ever since the 1920s, when professional basketball first appeared in Washington, the sport had struggled to gain a foothold. Even on the rare occasion when local teams played well, residents rarely supported them. Consequently, franchises were shuffled in and out of the city almost as regularly as congressmen representing a perpetually dissatisfied district.

Washington's first professional club, the Palace Five, exemplified such woes. Founded as an independent team in 1923, the Palace Five, alternately dubbed the Laundrymen (the team's owner, George Preston Marshall, also owned the local Palace Laundry chain), became one of the original franchises of the American Basketball League (ABL) in 1925. The Laundrymen had some good years, and for a while attracted large crowds. But unlike Marshall's future team, the football Redskins, they never won a championship. With support waning, the entire roster was dealt to a club in Brooklyn in 1928.[8]

Ten years passed before another squad called DC home. The Washington Brewers took their name from their sponsor: the famous Heurich Brewery in Foggy Bottom. Unfortunately, the Brewers did not fare much better than the Palace Five, and after four seasons they were disbanded.[9]

And on it went. There was, for instance, the Washington Bears, an independent all-black squad whose roster included several holdovers from the celebrated New York Rens. Unlike previous DC clubs, the Bears, who were formed in 1941 and bankrolled by local theater mogul A. E. Lichtman, were an excellent squad. Unbeaten during their first two seasons, the Bears captured the World Professional Basketball Tournament in 1943. Success, though, could not keep them together. By the fall of 1944, most of the best players had left.[10]

That same year, the Washington Capitols started playing in the American Professional Basketball League (APBL). The Capitols won just two of their first ten games before being shipped off to New Jersey. The team was reconstituted in 1946 as an entrant in the newly organized Basketball Association of America (BAA). Coached by future Hall-of-Famer Arnold "Red" Auerbach, the newer Caps finished the year 49-11, but lost to the Chicago Stags in the first round of the playoffs. After having failed to qualify for the postseason in 1948, the Capitols muscled their way to the finals in 1949, only to fall to the Minneapolis Lakers. For each of the Caps' three seasons, fan support was mediocre at best.[11]

Matters worsened. In August 1949, BAA clubs combined with a handful of teams from the National Basketball League (NBL) to create the NBA. Gone was Auerbach, who, following a contract dispute with Capitols owner Michael Uline, became coach of the Tri-Cities Blackhawks. The Caps squeaked into the playoffs, but were swiftly dispatched by the New York Knicks. Halfway through the next season, they disbanded, some $36,000 in arrears. (Earl Lloyd, an African American from Alexandria, Virginia, broke the NBA's color line when he played in the Caps' first game of the 1950–51 season.)[12]

Throughout the 1950's, multiple attempts were made to resurrect professional basketball in the District. None worked. But that did not stop a group of investors, led by Harlem Globetrotters owner Abe Saperstein, from including Washington in a new league it founded in 1961. The league, also called the ABL, had eight teams. DC's was named the Tapers.[13]

Like most of the city's previous squads, the Tapers lacked star power. But Tapers owner Harry Lynn, who also owned the Washington Coliseum (formerly Uline Arena), believed that a spiffed-up coliseum with expanded parking would draw crowds. He was mistaken. In November, after the visiting Pittsburgh Rens beat Washington, 95–84, a local sportswriter wrote that the "Rens scored almost as many points as there were persons in the house." With support like that, it was only a matter of time before Lynn's team was through. Sure enough, on New Year's Eve, 1961, the Tapers were moved to New York.[14]

One last flirtation with a renegade league was in store for Washington. The American Basketball Association (ABA) was established in 1967 with primarily one goal: an ABA-NBA merger. The idea was not so farfetched. A year earlier, the American Football League (AFL) had done much the same thing with the National Football League (NFL).[15]

By the late 1960s, an ABA-NBA deal appeared imminent. Aware of a possible merger, Earl Foreman, a local attorney who moonlighted as a sports entrepreneur, saw an opportunity for profit. In the summer of 1969, he purchased the ABA's Oakland Oaks for $2.6 million and moved the team to Washington. Shrewd and business savvy, Foreman knew he could use his new team, now named—what else?—the Capitols, as leverage if the two leagues ever merged since there was no way the NBA's Baltimore Bullets were going to let another team be located practically right on their doorstep.[16]

But first Foreman had to prove that his was a viable franchise. He had much to live up to. The previous year, the Oaks had gone 60-18 and won the ABA title. Unfortunately, the Caps were not as good. Still, they finished 44-40. In the playoffs, Washington played well, but lost to the Denver Rockets. There were bigger concerns: few people had attended Caps games. More worrisome, the Capitols owed $500,000.[17]

The Caps had survived, but that was all Foreman was really hoping for. As part of a merger agreement reached by NBA and ABA officials in the spring of 1970, he was offered a sweetheart deal: vacate the Washington-Baltimore area—an area that the Baltimore Bullets claimed was theirs, partly because Bullets owner Abe Pollin was eyeing Washington as the new home for his team—and the NBA's $1.25 million admittance fee would be forgiven *and* he would recoup the small fortune he had lost with the Capitols. Foreman happily agreed. In June 1970, the Caps were moved to Virginia and became the Squires.[18]

But it would be another six years before the NBA and ABA merged. Legal wrangles postponed the deal. Meanwhile, the Squires muddled along in the ABA, the fear of bankruptcy hanging over them like a Sword of Damocles. To stave off insolvency, Foreman was forced to sell off the club's stars, including Julius Erving. Finally, in 1974, Foreman relinquished ownership. Two years later, the Squires folded—nine weeks before the NBA admitted four of the six surviving ABA franchises.[19]

Almost from the moment Washington Bullets owner Abe Pollin finished interviewing Dick Motta for the Bullets' vacant coaching position in May 1976, he knew the search was over. As Pollin later remembered: "I had interviewed [Motta] for four hours at my home in Bethesda to see what kind of human being he was. I told him I would get back to him in a couple days. I never waited. In two hours I called his brother's house in Alexandria and told Dick, 'You're my man. You have the job if you want it.'"[20]

Born in Utah in 1931, Motta was the product of an unlikely pair: an Italian émigré father and a mother who was a devout Mormon. Both instilled in him a strong sense of discipline and responsibility. That he was raised on a small vegetable farm during the Depression only reinforced those values. He and his younger brother often helped their parents with the chores of running a family farm. His days were long and tiring, but he gained an appreciation for hard work. It was to be a lesson he never forgot.[21]

After graduating from Utah State Agricultural College (later Utah State University) in 1953, Motta taught junior high and high school and coached basketball. Soon, he was coaching in college. No matter where he was, his teams won. In 1968, after leading Weber State College to a berth in that year's NCAA tournament, he was hired by the NBA's Chicago Bulls. In eight seasons with the Bulls, he went 356-300, and reached the playoffs six times. Accolades followed. In 1971, after Chicago posted a record of 51-31, he was named NBA Coach of the Year. The March 1974 cover of *Sport* showed Motta, sandwiched between Bill Russell and Wilt Chamberlain. Each stood behind a player from their respective teams (Russell was coaching the Seattle SuperSonics, Chamberlain the ABA's San Diego Conquistadores). "Guess Which Coach Is A Winner*," a blurb on the cover asked. "*Hint: He's Under Five-Foot-Eight."[22]

By the 1975–76 season, however, such acclaim was less forthcoming. Souring opinions were several tiffs Motta had gotten into over the years with a number of players. Never mind that most of the squabbles were tied to Motta's other role as director of team personnel. The negative press was hard to live down. The swipes attached themselves to his reputation like barnacles to a ship—unseen whenever there was smooth sailing, but in rough waters they inevitably became exposed.[23]

And during the 1975–76 season, there were plenty of choppy seas for Motta to navigate. The Bulls had their worst season under his leadership, winning just twenty-four games. Not helping matters was the fact that his autobiography, *Stuff It! The Story of Dick Motta, Toughest Little Coach in the NBA*, was published in 1975. During the Bulls' winning years, Motta's no-nonsense approach described in the book attracted little criticism. But in 1975–76 as the Bulls' losses piled up, his martinet style—sportswriter Bob Logan characterized Motta as "a tough, often ruthless, competitor"— increasingly came under attack. Modern athletes, his detractors complained, should not be treated like grunts slogging their way through boot camp.[24]

Motta was also known for haranguing referees. In his autobiography, he recounts the time he was ejected from a game, but then returned to watch from the stands. Spotted by officials, he was reprimanded and fined. In another game, he received *three* technical fouls (the maximum was two, but because he had been so abusive, he was whistled for a third). An altercation with officials after a game in 1974 netted him the then-largest fine in NBA history—$2,000—and a suspension. Never before had an NBA coach been suspended. "Controversy and Motta," Bob Logan wrote, "go together like [songsters] Rodgers and Hart."[25]

But to Pollin and Bullets GM Bob Ferry, Motta represented what their team sorely lacked: discipline, emotion, intensity. More important, they knew he had no problem enforcing rules—something they believed the Bullets' previous coach, K. C. Jones, had avoided doing. "Motta is a strongly disciplined coach," Pollin was quoted as saying partway through Motta's first season in Washington, "and that's a strength that is needed on this team. He's somebody who lives and breathes basketball. He works hard. . . . With the players he has here, I think he will be very successful."[26]

Others were not so sure. On May 29, 1976, a day after Motta's hiring was made official, the *Washington Star*, referencing the dismal season

Motta had just completed in Chicago, headlined: "The Bullets' New Coach is Dick (24-58) Motta." Four days earlier, Steve Hershey of the *Star* wrote: "It seems highly unlikely that the Bullets would hire Motta after all the player problems he's created in Chicago. The fact that he . . . is involved in contract negotiations obviously led to his feuds with [Bulls players], but the records still show that he took a team that won the Midwest Division . . . and in one season disintegrated it into what he called 'the worst team in basketball.' That's not much of a recommendation."[27]

Matters of race loomed large, since Motta, a white man, was taking over from an African American. Resolute, unflappable, and fair-minded, K. C. Jones was well liked in Washington, particularly by his players. A former guard who captured eight consecutive NBA championships with the Boston Celtics, as well as an Olympic gold medal and a pair of NCAA titles before he turned professional, Jones knew what it took to win. He had been hired in June 1973, entrusted with coaching the Bullets during their inaugural season in the nation's capital. Pollin, a Washington construction magnate who became exclusive owner of the Bullets after he bought out the club's two other owners—one of whom was Earl Foreman—in 1968, moved the team from Baltimore in 1973 because support there had been lacking.[28]

Jones's arrival in DC coincided with an important development for black Washingtonians: the Home Rule Act. Established in late 1973, the act ushered in a system that, for the first time in more than a century, delegated authority to locally elected officials, the majority of whom were black. The new government more closely resembled the racial makeup of the city— which in 1971 was 71.1 percent African American. Having a black man coach a predominantly black team in a city with a large black population governed by black officeholders—before Jones, all major teams in the city had been coached by white men—was not only fitting but long overdue. Two months after Jones was hired, Bernie Bickerstaff, a twenty-nine-year-old African American coach from San Diego State University, was named assistant. The addition of Bickerstaff gave the Bullets one of the first all-black coaching staffs in NBA history.[29]

After a modestly successful first season with Jones as coach, the Bullets hit their stride in 1974–75, finishing a franchise-best 60-22 and advancing to the finals, where they met the underdog Golden State Warriors. But in what *Sports Illustrated* later termed as "one of the NBA's great fold-up acts," the Bullets were thoroughly embarrassed, losing four games to none. Even though the series was highly disappointing, and even though the Bullets wound up losing more games the next year, Jones remained popular in Washington. Many fans—and Bullets players, too—were upset after he was dismissed in May 1976.[30]

Three weeks later, Motta became coach. Whether Washingtonians were ready for "Little Big Man"—the moniker sportswriter Frank Deford had used in the title of a 1971 *Sports Illustrated* article about Motta—no one could say for sure. But Motta and the rest of the Bullets were about to find out.[31]

Washington in 1976 was a city starved for a championship. The last time a local team had won a major title was 1942, when the Redskins captured the NFL championship by beating the Chicago Bears. That day, more than 36,000 fans crammed into DC's Griffith Stadium. After the Redskins won, many scampered onto the field and tore down the goalposts.[32]

For more than three decades, DC's sporting hopes languished. Between 1946 and 1970, for example, the Redskins produced only three winning seasons. After losing the World Series in 1933, the Senators never again appeared in the postseason. So awful was their experience, they left the city twice—first the original franchise in 1960, then the expansion team eleven years later. Hockey's Washington Capitals may have been the most hapless of all. In 1974–75, the Caps' inaugural season, they went 8-67-5. The next year, they finished 11-59-10. A 1976 *Washington Star* headline summed it up: "The Caps: A Hockey Team That Knew How to Lose."[33]

The Redskins of the 1970s looked as if they might buck the trend. Each season between 1971 and 1974, DC's most beloved franchise reached the playoffs. Fans could hardly contain their joy. So happy were some that they redefined what winning a championship meant. On New Year's Day, 1973, a day after the Redskins won the National Football Conference title game, a width-of-the-page, above-the-fold headline in the *Post* screamed: "Happy 1973! We're a Winner at Last." As fate would have it, the Redskins lost the Super Bowl, 14–7.[34]

Failure in sports symbolized Washington's other problems: lawlessness, violence, urban decay. Campaigning for the presidency in 1968, Richard Nixon spoke for many when he called DC "one of the crime capitals of the nation." The random attack on Mississippi senator John Stennis in 1973—he was shot in his North Cleveland Park home—reminded Washingtonians that wealthier neighborhoods were not immune from nefarious acts. In poorer sections of the city, areas devastated by the 1968 riot lay rotting with garbage and scorched remains of buildings.[35]

Further tarnishing Washington's image was politically motivated violence carried out in the city. Between 1970 and 1975, the Weather Underground, a radical leftist group, detonated several bombs in government buildings. The Mayday Protests of 1971 spawned clashes between demonstrators and police. In 1976, an erstwhile Chilean diplomat and his aide were killed by a car bomb in Dupont Circle. The 1977 assault on the District Building, the Washington Islamic Center, and the downtown offices of B'nai B'rith by a group of radical Hanafi Muslims shocked Americans.[36]

National crises also cast the city in a poor light. Watergate and Vietnam, the Energy Crisis of 1973–74, elevated unemployment and the ensuing recession—all undermined DC's reputation. In his first State of the Union Address in 1975, President Gerald Ford admitted, "The state of the union is not good." To many, Ford's lament described the federal capital too.[37]

As the start of the 1976–77 season neared, fans doubted if the Bullets had what it took to win a title. Among the skeptics was *Black Sports*. "The Washington Bullets have a new coach, the same Dick Motta of the kamikaze tactics," the magazine noted. "The Bullets are not inclined to surrender their bodies and personal health diving for loose balls. Nor are they, from all reasonable reports, inclined to adjust, without incident, to the Motta school of basketball thought. . . . It may be a rocky time in D.C."[38]

Players were introduced to "the Motta school of basketball thought" on the first day of practice. The Bullets were running a basic passing drill when, suddenly, Motta strode onto the court and, with a loud stomp, halted the action. Inside the Fort Meade gym it sounded like a firecracker had gone off. Irked, Motta huffed: "Three things are important. Be on time, give your best, and don't con me." Intensity dominated the rest of practice.[39]

The Bullets began the season poorly. Players had a hard time adjusting to Motta, and Motta had difficulties figuring out his new team. By the end of November, the Bullets were an uninspiring 7-12. The *Post*'s David DuPree wrote: "The struggling Washington Bullets . . . are like a time bomb ready to self-destruct." Contributing to the erratic play was the likelihood of a trade. Motta wanted to replace veteran point guard Dave Bing. Rumors circulated that other players might also be traded.[40]

Soon, though, Motta's club started to win. Starting in late December, Washington took five straight games, lost, won, lost again, and finished the rest of January unbeaten. "Bullets Reversal Arouses Smiles, Talk of NBA Flag," headlined the *Post* in February.[41]

One reason for the turnabout was because a trade had finally been made. In January, Washington dealt forward Leonard "Truck" Robinson to Atlanta for Tom Henderson, a 6'3" point guard known for his heady play. Henderson initially backed up Larry Wright, a swift-footed rookie from Grambling, but eventually took over lead playmaking responsibilities.[42]

The other reason was the play of forward Elvin Hayes, aka The Big E (playing up the nickname, his autobiography, which came out in 1978, was entitled, *They Call Me "The Big E"*). After a shaky beginning to the season, mostly due to his belief that he might be traded, Hayes found his rhythm, and began playing like the All-Star that he was. Hayes got plenty of help from his teammates. Guard Phil Chenier provided firepower from the perimeter, while Wes Unseld, a 6'7", 250-pound center described by one journalist as having a "boiler-size chest and oil drum legs," was an exceptional rebounder. Reserve center Mitch Kupchak, a rookie from North Carolina, hustled and added points off the bench. By March 3, Washington was 37-24. No other team in the Eastern Conference had more wins.[43]

But the Bullets could not sustain the torrid pace. Still, they won eleven of their last twenty-one games and ended up 48-34, the same record they had had in 1975–76. In the playoffs, Washington beat Cleveland in the first round, but then fell to Houston, four games to two.

The defeat stung. For years, Pollin had been trying to win a title. Given Washington's talent, he believed that 1977 might be the year. But the Bullets had never really gelled, and in the playoffs the Big E had underperformed. Trade rumors resurfaced. Such talk hurt the sensitive star. Interviewed on WTOP radio, he admitted, "For myself and for my nerves . . . another place [would] be better." Days later, Pollin, hoping to reassure Hayes, told the All-Star forward that no trades were in the works.[44]

But the rumors persisted. On June 7 and 8, *Washington Star* sports columnist David Israel, whose dislike of Hayes was no secret, reported that the Bullets were close to making a swap: Hayes would be sent to the Buffalo Braves, and Washington would get Adrian Dantley, a twenty-one-year-old forward who had starred at nearby DeMatha High and who had recently been named NBA Rookie of the Year. The trade, though, never happened. Some believed Israel's reporting might have caused Pollin to call it off.[45]

There were other issues—namely, Dave Bing and his lack of court time. A graduate of DC's Spingarn High and a seven-time NBA All-Star, Bing had been acquired from Detroit in 1975. But after the Bullets traded for Tom Henderson, he was relegated to the bench. Bing begrudged the move, and after the season let Motta know about it. "Everyone is getting on the players," the former Syracuse University star was quoted as saying in May 1977, "but we're no worse than we were last year when K. C. (Jones) got all the blame. . . . Dick made just as many mistakes as K. C. did, but he's not getting any heat for it." Interviewed on WTOP radio, Bing said: "I don't think Motta has tried to relate with players, black or white. . . . I personally think he has a lot of the press and a lot of the public fooled."[46]

For Motta, it had been a trying season. He hinted at the strain, tell-ing David DuPree after Washington had been eliminated, "Heck, I doubled my wins [from 1975 to 1976] in a year. You can't beat that." The remark revealed his less-than-harmonious relationship with players (in March of 1977, *Washingtonian* magazine published an article entitled, "Dick Motta at War With the Bullets"). But for Motta and his players, things would soon get a whole lot better.[47]

For several years, Milwaukee Bucks forward Bobby Dandridge had caught the eye of Bullets GM Bob Ferry. Ferry wanted him in a Washington uni-form. The Bullets were weak at the small forward position, and Dandridge, with his talent and experience, seemed to be the ideal choice. Ferry, though, had never been able to arrange a trade. Fortunately for the Bullets GM, the advent of free agency in 1976 offered a different route. In August 1977, after Dandridge's contract with Milwaukee expired, the Bullets inked the twenty-nine-year-old Norfolk State graduate to a two-year contract worth $500,000.[48]

Motta was thrilled. As coach of the Bulls, he had faced Dandridge numerous times and had come to admire the 6'6" forward. Pairing the do-it-all Dandridge with Hayes, he believed, would give the Bullets a dev-astating offensive duo. Fast, smart, tough, and competitive, Bobby D was perfect for the up-tempo style Motta was planning on using.[49]

Still, no one expected much from the Bullets. Though impressed by the new lineup—Bing was released in September, for which "Motta . . . received an ample supply of vocal cuffing," *Baltimore Afro-American* sportswriter Sam Lacy later wrote—most pundits believed that the Bullets would not win the title. Motta disagreed. In an interview published a day before the start of the season, he told Paul Attner, "I think there are a number of teams capable of winning an NBA championship and the Washington Bullets are one of them." He added: "Our goal is to win the divisional championship, get as many home-court games as you can in the playoffs . . . and then hope . . . you are clicking. And then you have to get a little lucky. You can't hope for anything else."[50]

The Bullets opened the season at home against Detroit. The Pistons kept the game close, but faded in the third quarter, and Washington won, thrilling the 13,276 who attended. After the game, Motta exclaimed, "From a coaching standpoint, I really couldn't find anything wrong. . . . We're a better team than we were last year."[51]

But things were not as rosy as Motta was letting on. Phil Chenier, the Bullets' top guard, was battling a back injury, and Hayes was having difficulties playing alongside Dandridge. On November 5, Hayes played possibly the worst game of his career, tallying a measly 3 points. Frustrated, the All-Star forward believed that management, again, was prepared to trade him. "I've never been in this situation before. If they want to trade me, let them, but I can't play like this," he declared.[52]

Incensed over the remarks, Motta scolded Hayes. The tongue-lashing prompted Hayes to tell his teammates he was sorry, which momentarily cleared the air. The next game, the Big E tallied 21 points and gathered 20 rebounds. But against Milwaukee four days later, he authored yet another dismal performance, including committing two crucial fouls in the waning seconds, which sealed the win for the Bucks. At 3-5, the Bullets were dead last in the Central Division.[53]

If Motta had been hard on Hayes, the press now was downright nasty. In his column for the *Washington Star*, David Israel, who was more than happy to restart his Hayes-should-be-traded campaign, chortled that the Big E stood for "either (a) the Big Enigma, (b) the Big Excuse, or (c) the Big Expendable." Ken Denlinger of the *Post* wrote: "The Big E is afflicted with the Big I—insecurity—and this is the season he and the Bullets either come to terms with one another or part company."[54]

The reality was, Pollin did not want to trade Hayes. To be sure, Hayes had his drawbacks. He could be sullen, and, on occasion, tactless. In 1972, *Basketball Weekly* published an article about Hayes entitled, "The Misunderstood Star." But there were few players who could score and rebound like Hayes. And he was durable. Since coming into the league as a rookie in 1968, he had missed only four games. Fortunately for the Bullets, Hayes began playing up to his capabilities, and the trade rumors vanished. By mid-January, Washington was 24-15.[55]

The winning did not last. During a four-game road trip in January, several players suffered injuries, and the Bullets ended up losing every game. For one game, only seven players were in uniform (Chenier was back home, having reinjured his back ten days earlier; he would miss the rest of the season). Another road trip—a torturous, sixteen-day peregrination—proved equally disastrous. By February 23, the Bullets were 29-28. In less than six weeks, they had gone from leading the Central Division to being six games out of first place.[56]

Frustration, which had been simmering for weeks, boiled over. Forty-four seconds into the opening quarter of a game against Golden State in late February, Motta was tossed for arguing with the officials—the earliest he had ever been ejected in his career. The Bullets nevertheless won, 121–110. Hayes was brilliant, netting 37 points. Kevin Grevey, a 6'5" sharpshooter who had replaced Chenier in January, added 25.[57]

After weeks of battling injuries, the Bullets were finally on the mend, and as players regained their health, they began performing better. Yet inconsistency continued to dog the club. "When our backs are to the wall, we usually win, but then we ease up, lose and it's another crisis," Dandridge told Paul Attner in early April. "Things just don't seem to be jelling like they should." Others were franker. After Dandridge and his teammates lost at home to New York on April 2, the *Star* headlined: "Bullets Finishing the Season as Blanks." On April 5, Motta was quoted in the *Post* telling fans "not to give up on this team too soon." However, later that night against Los Angeles, more than 4,200 Capital Centre seats were vacant. Even the last game of the season against Philadelphia—a game that was played on Sunday and had playoff implications—failed to sell out. The Bullets nonetheless triumphed, 123–113.[58]

The win over Philadelphia bumped Washington's record to 44-38, four fewer wins than the previous year, but good enough to claim third place in the Eastern Conference. Importantly, the victory gave Washington home-court advantage in the opening round of the playoffs. Needless to say, the Bullets were pleased. Their record at home was 29-12. But perhaps the best news of all was that for the first time in a long while, they were injury free.

Since Motta's arrival in Washington in 1976, DC sports teams had been unable to break the city's championship jinx. The Redskins had made the playoffs only once, but then lost in the first round. The firing of George Allen, the team's admired coach, in January 1978, added to the frustration. In hockey, the Capitals remained the NHL's schlemiel. The prospect of bringing baseball back seemed as dim as ever.[59]

Few Washingtonians that April figured Motta's club would be any different. Why should they have? The Bullets had not exactly dominated the league, and their sloppy play of late inspired little confidence. The NBA also had several excellent teams—all with much better records than Washington's. Motta was singled out as the cause for diminished expectations. "With Dick Motta coaching," mused one sportswriter four days before Washington was to begin play in the first round, "the Bullets' post-season presence is academic. They will not advance beyond the second round of the playoffs."[60]

Up first were the Atlanta Hawks, a rugged, defensive-oriented team. Using some muscle of their own, the Bullets were able to negate the Hawks' physicality, and went on to capture the series, two games to none. But Washington had paid a price. Dandridge, who had missed the second game against the Hawks because of an injured neck, looked as if he might have to sit out the first game against the Bullets' next foe, the San Antonio Spurs.

Owners of the third-best record in the league, the Spurs were fast and tall. They also had the league's top scorer, George Gervin, aka the Iceman.

Game 1 was played on Sunday afternoon, April 16, before a nearly sold-out HemisFair Arena in San Antonio. Dandridge was back in Washington, nursing his sore neck. The first half was tight, but in the third quarter the Spurs began to pull away and took the game, 114–103. Motta was disappointed. But he had learned one thing: with a full roster, the Bullets could beat the Spurs. The next day, while relaxing in his hotel room, Motta saw Dan Cook on KENS.[61]

Fortunately for the Bullets, Dandridge was healthy enough to play in game 2. His inclusion in the lineup changed the nature of the series. Before, San Antonio had been the faster-paced squad. But now, Washington was. The Bullets dashed out to an 11-point advantage, and never looked back, defeating the Spurs, 121–117. Washington captured the next two games as well. Speaking to reporters after game 4, Motta likened the series to an opera, but the line went unnoticed. Two days later, on Tuesday, April 25, the Spurs won game 5. Game 6 was scheduled to take place Friday, April 28, in the Capital Centre.[62]

That Friday, something happened that had not occurred all season: the Capital Centre sold out. The large crowd signaled that Washingtonians were ready to back the Bullets. After a tumultuous season, which had been marred by trade rumors and gloomy predictions, Washington was peaking at the right moment. Spurred on by the enthusiastic crowd, the Bullets snuck past San Antonio, 103–100, advancing them to the conference finals.[63]

There was no time to celebrate, however. Less than forty-eight hours later, the Bullets were in the City of Brotherly Love, playing the 76ers. Philadelphia's roster bulged with talent. There were two all-NBA forwards: Julius Erving and George McGinnis. Guard Doug Collins was another top player. More, the 76ers led the league in scoring, and their home record of 39-4 was also a league best. Having swept New York in the other conference semifinal, Philadelphia oozed confidence. No one expected much from Washington.

The Bullets believed otherwise. In the opening game of the series, Washington came out energized, stunning the crowd of 13,708. But the 76ers were too talented a club to be embarrassed on their home court. They trimmed the deficit and eventually forced overtime. But that would be as close as they got. Washington controlled the extra period and prevailed, 122–117.[64]

Unseld was not in the lineup for game 2. He had injured his ankle in game 1, and it still ached too much to play on. Washington could have used him, as the 76ers outmuscled the Bullets, 110–104. Unseld also sat out game 3, but this time Washington was victorious. Tallying 30 points, Dandridge held Erving to just 12. Unseld missed the next game too. Fortunately, his teammates picked up the slack, and routed Philadelphia, 121–105. Like a boxer who has just absorbed a vicious body blow, the 76ers were reeling. But Motta, always the cagey coach, downplayed his team's advantage. Responding to a pesky reporter's questions after game 4, the Bullets coach compared the series to an opera. This time, the line stuck.[65]

Thus began Washington's love affair with the Bullets. In the ensuing weeks, multiple articles about the team appeared daily in the local press. Thousands of T-shirts featuring the famous saying and a cartoonish rendering of an operatic fat lady, modeled after Brunnhilde, the Valkyrie warrior queen, were sold. "Bullets Fever," a catchy ditty written and sung by local rock-and-roller Nils Lofgren, was played over radio stations. Bullets tickets became prized commodities. Mused longtime DC sportswriter Morris Siegel in mid-May, "The Bullets have exploded on Washington liked [sic] no other happening since stand up drinking was legalized." The city pulsed with excitement.[66]

But as excited as Washingtonians were, the fat lady line contained an undeniable truth: the series was not over. In game 5, the 76ers validated Motta's warning, crushing the Bullets, 107–94. But the evening was not a total loss: Unseld had played. If the Bullets were to advance, they would need the leadership from their team captain.[67]

On the evening of May 12, more than 19,000 fans streamed into the Capital Centre. Many waved cards printed with an enormous E. One banner read: "Hark, I hear the fat lady singing." From the start, the game was hard fought. Neither team could break away. Then, with twelve seconds to play and the score tied, 99–99, Unseld powered in a layup. On the ensuing play, 76ers' guard Lloyd Free was whistled for an offensive foul, and Washington ran out the clock for a 101–99 victory.[68]

Immediately the Capital Centre was engulfed in wild rejoicing. Jubilant fans spilled onto the court. At one end of the floor, a basket was knocked over. Inside the Bullets' locker room, players were doused with beer. Pollin gushed, "This is the biggest night in the history of the franchise." The next day, newspapers gave broad coverage to the victory. "'Fat Lady' Sings for Bullets, 101–99," read one headline. "IT'S OVER!" screamed another.[69]

But, of course, it was not. The finals had yet to be played. Many believed that Washington would face the Seattle SuperSonics, who held a three-games-to-one advantage over the Denver Nuggets in the Western Conference finals. Like the Bullets, Seattle had had a tough start to the season. But in late November, Lenny Wilkens, who was then working in the Sonics' front office, was named coach. Under Wilkens, Seattle went 42-18. But even then, few thought the Sonics would do much in the playoffs. Instead, they beat Los Angeles, then Portland (the defending NBA champions), and now were a game shy of eliminating Denver. After losing on May 14, Seattle clinched the series three days later. Two improbable finalists would play for the NBA title.

For Washingtonians, there were reasons to be optimistic. Of the four games played between the Bullets and SuperSonics that season, Washington had won three, including a 106–100 victory in early February—the last time Seattle had lost at home. Still, doubts lingered. Days before the series was to start, Hayes tried to dispel them. "We will win it this year," he announced. "I guarantee it."[70]

The Bullets practiced at Bowie State College on May 19 and departed for Seattle later that evening. Motta was in good spirits. Earlier in the week, Paul Attner noticed Motta's uncharacteristic cheerfulness. "Motta has yelled little in workout[s] this week, a sign that he is pleased," Attner wrote. After arriving in Seattle, the Bullets checked into their hotel and got some much-needed sleep.[71]

Usually in the finals, the team with the better record, which in 1978 was Seattle, hosted games 1 and 2, and, if necessary, 5 and 7. But since the Seattle Coliseum had already been booked to host an RV show—the event could not be moved, prompting one wag to dub it, "the immobile mobile home show"—the normal pattern had to be adjusted. As agreed upon by league officials, games 1, 4, 5, and 7 would be played in Seattle, while games 2, 3, and 6 would be held in Washington.[72]

On Sunday morning, May 21, more than 14,000 rowdy Seattleites filed into the Seattle Coliseum, eager to find their seats before game 1's noontime start. CBS, which owned the rights to the series, did not want the Sunday game interfering with the network's primetime programming on the East Coast. (The NBA was still years away from achieving the kind of popularity that warranted evening coverage. Game 3 of the 1978 finals, for instance, a Sunday afternoon game and the least watched of the series, had a Nielsen rating of 6.4; by comparison, *Snoopy's Musical on Ice* later that evening had 14.9.) Bullets fans watching the game back home were thrilled when their team surged in front by 19 points. But the Sonics got hot, overtook the Bullets, and held on to win, 106–102.[73]

Because game 2 would not be played for another four days, sportswriters had ample time to conduct a thorough postmortem of game 1. Much was made of the Bullets' past failures in final series (in addition to the 1975 fiasco, the Baltimore Bullets were swept in 1971). What was left unsaid was something no one in DC wanted to consider: Were the Bullets destined to lose? Frustration surfaced after Dandridge and Hayes told the *Star*'s Steve Hershey that Unseld should play less, and the offensively capable Mitch Kupchak more. The Seattle press smelled blood. Previewing the second contest, the *Seattle Times* headlined, "Game 2: Bickering Bullets vs. Lovely Sonics."[74]

Several times during the season, the Bullets had proven skeptics wrong. In game 2 they did so again. Energized by the raucous home crowd, Washington withstood a late charge by Seattle, and won, 106–98. Dandridge and Hayes had done the most damage, combining for 59 points. In the postgame press conference, Motta voiced relief. "I'm very glad we finally won one in this round," he confessed, adding, "I don't want to live with past ghosts. It's not fair to my young players and to myself. We weren't around before."[75]

The victory invigorated the Bullets. But Motta knew that the next matchup was more significant. If the Bullets fell behind two games to one, chances were good that the Sonics would capture the title, since games 4 and 5 would be played in Seattle.

At precisely 1:30 on Sunday afternoon, game 3 tipped off. The Capital Centre was jammed with fans. The noise was earsplitting. But if the Sonics were fazed, they did not show it. From the very beginning, their stingy defense rattled the home team. Late in the game, Seattle was ahead by 9. The Bullets rallied, but with time running out, Dandridge missed a jumper that would have won the game, and Seattle prevailed by a single point. "Fat lady isn't singing yet, but Sonics chirp," a *Seattle Times* headline gloated.[76]

Back in October, before the start of the season, Motta had told Paul Attner that success in the playoffs depends on luck. And so it was with the Bullets now. The RV show at the Seattle Coliseum was scheduled to conclude June 1, well past the date for game 4. So officials decided to play the game at the Seattle Kingdome, an indoor stadium that the Sonics planned to use as their home arena for 1978–79. With as many as 40,000 people cheering for Seattle, commentators predicted, Washington stood no chance.[77]

But lost in all the predictions was this: unlike the Seattle Coliseum, whose cramped confines created a hostile environment for visiting teams, the Kingdome was so commodious that it deadened the atmosphere visiting teams found to be so unnerving. One Seattle journalist described the Kingdome as "a vast cave that sucks the sound up to the roof and turns it into mush." In some ways, the Dome resembled a neutral court, not only because the crowd wielded less influence but also because Seattle, like Washington, had never played a game there.[78]

Such thoughts were not on the minds of the 39,457 spectators inside the Kingdome May 30. A banner reading "THE FAT LADY IS DONE SINGIN'" hung from the upper deck. Fans had plenty reason to cheer, too, the Sonics building an early lead and then stretching it to 15 points near the end of the third quarter. Shouts of "We're No. 1!" could be heard coming from the crowd. Bullets fans in attendance must have wondered if the chants were not true. Never before in the history of the finals had a team overcome a three-games-to-one deficit.[79]

The Bullets desperately needed a hero, and now they got one. Charlie Johnson was a twenty-nine-year-old reserve guard whom Washington had claimed off waivers in January. A member of Golden State's 1975 championship squad, Johnson had struggled in the first three games against Seattle, shooting a combined 8-25. Now, in the Dome, CJ found the range, lobbing in high, arcing shots. Invigorated by Johnson's clutch shooting, the Bullets clawed their way back and won in OT. Two days later, at the Seattle Coliseum, the Sonics took game 5. With the Sonics holding a three-games-to-two edge, the series would resume Sunday afternoon, June 4, in Landover, Maryland.[80]

That Sunday, the *Star* headlined: "Today Is the Most Important Day in Bullets' History." Most in attendance agreed, and they did what they could to ensure that the Bullets won. Hand-scrawled signs dotted the arena. One man, garbed in home-fashioned Brunnhilde apparel (wig, dress, Viking helmet, two hubcaps as breast armor) sauntered around as the Fat Lady. Fans twirled white towels. The next day, Steve Hershey wrote: "If you remember Woodstock, the Beatles at Dodger Stadium or Bangladesh at Madison Square Garden, you'll know what it was like yesterday at Capital Centre."[81]

Thrust into that kind of atmosphere, the Sonics were doomed. But for much of the first half, they battled hard. Then, in the final minutes of the second quarter, they sputtered—badly. The rout was on. By the time it was over, Washington had annihilated Seattle, 117–82. No team had ever lost a final-series game by so much.[82]

The Bullets left for Seattle from Dulles airport on Monday afternoon. Their spirits were as high as the jetliner's cruising altitude. Their aching bodies, though, told a different story. Including exhibitions, the Bullets had played a total of 111 games. Number 112—the all-critical game 7—was scheduled for Wednesday, June 7. The flight taking the Bullets to the West Coast was their third in seventeen days. The 1978 finals could have been dubbed the Jet Lag Series.

Seattle was listed as a 4½-point favorite. The thinking was that since game 7 would be played in the Coliseum, where the Sonics had not lost

Dick Motta directing the Bullets during game 4 of the 1978 Eastern Conference finals. Reprinted with permission of the DC Public Library, Star Collection, © Washington Post.

in twenty-two games, Seattle held the advantage. History, too, was on the Sonics' side. In the annals of the NBA, only three teams had won the title after being down three games to two—and only one, the 1968–69 Boston Celtics, had done it winning game 7 on the road. Even the advantage the Bullets seemed to have was dismissed as a fluke. As *Post* columnist Dave Kindred put it: "What happened [in game 6], was as misleading as the Fat Lady's hubcaps."[83]

On the evening of June 7, about the time the Bullets took the floor in Seattle to begin warming up, Bullets fans in Washington readied themselves for the final game. Some held "watch" parties. Others went to bars whose televisions were tuned to the game. Still others listened to the pregame show on WTOP radio. For its part, WDCA-TV ran an hour-long program honoring the Bullets before the 9:05 EDT tipoff.[84]

For a championship game, both teams started out surprisingly loose. By the end of the first quarter, the Bullets led, 31–28, and two quarters later, the margin had swelled to 13 points. The Seattle crowd grew anxious. Then, momentum shifted. With 1:45 to play, Seattle guard "Downtown" Freddy Brown swished a jumper from the left baseline, trimming Washington's lead to four.[85]

The decisive moment of the game occurred next. Charlie Johnson launched a shot from the top of the key, but the ball grazed the front of the rim and dropped to the court. Scrambling, Tom Henderson plunged to the floor and tapped the ball to Mitch Kupchak, who was standing near the basket, unguarded. Kupchak grabbed the ball, and, as he dropped it in the hoop, was hit across the arm by Sonics center Marvin Webster. Awarded a free throw, Kupchak drained the shot. The Bullets led by seven.

But the Sonics were not done. With 18 seconds remaining and Washington in front, 101–97, Seattle forward Paul Silas netted a layup. The Bullets inbounded the ball, but before they could get past half court, Wes Unseld was intentionally fouled. Twelve seconds remained. Fouling Unseld was smart. For the game, he was just 5-10 from the foul line and had just missed two straight attempts.

Unseld took the ball from referee Jack Madden, bounced it a few times and shot. The ball arced high, hit the rim, and bounced off. The crowd erupted with thunderous cheers. Unseld tried again, but this time the ball sailed through. His third attempt—since the Bullets were in the "penalty," he was given a bonus shot—was also good. Down by four, Seattle asked for a timeout.

Sitting inside the coliseum was Frank Herzog, WTOP radio's play-by-play man. Excitable and possessed of a silken voice, Herzog was known for his one-sided narration, which did not bother Bullets fans. During the previous six games, many Washingtonians no doubt had watched CBS's coverage with the radio tuned to Herzog.[86]

The timeout over, referee Earl Strom handed the ball to Sonics forward Paul Silas, who stood by the sideline waiting to restart the game. Silas passed the ball to teammate Dennis Johnson. Thus far in the game, Johnson, usually a reliable shooter, had missed all thirteen of his shots. He now launched number fourteen—but it too failed to connect. Unseld snatched the ball and flipped it to a streaking Dandridge, who dunked it with three seconds left. As the Sonics advanced the ball, Herzog screamed, "Warm up for the Fat Lady! Warm up the Fat Lady! The Bullets are gonna win!" Seattle could not get off a shot, and Washington triumphed, 105–99. The Bullets had won the championship.[87]

As soon as the horn sounded, Washington players scurried off the floor, hollering, laughing, gamboling like schoolchildren. Inside the locker room, the merrymaking continued. Players jumped up and down, high-fived, and hugged. A dewy-eyed Motta told Hayes, "I love you." CBS-TV's Rick Barry, who had played for the ABA Capitols and who was a member of Golden State's 1975 championship team, interviewed several players. In another spot of the locker room, Hayes could be heard saying, mantra-like, "I've got the ring, I've got the ring, I've got the ring."[88]

In Washington, riotous celebrating broke out. People emerged from bars and restaurants, yelling and cheering. Strangers embraced. Shouts of "We're No. 1!" and honking of car horns echoed throughout the early morning. In Georgetown, celebrants danced in the streets. Patrons in one Connecticut Avenue taproom clambered atop tables and started singing "America the Beautiful." WGMS radio blared Wagner's "Ride of the Valkyries" and "Return Victorious" from *Aida*. Lofgren's "Bullets Fever" got plenty airtime.[89]

It was an exhausted Bullets team that arrived at Dulles Airport the next afternoon. Most had stayed up late, partying. Some, like Kevin Grevey, got no sleep at all. The celebrating, though, was only starting. Inside Dulles's main hall were 8,000 fans. Coming into the terminal, players happily mixed with the throng. Wearing a boater hat and checkered jacket, Pollin cradled the championship trophy as if he were holding his newborn grandchild.[90]

Elation carried over onto the pages of the city's papers. "NUMBER ONE," shouted a banner headline in the *Star*'s city edition. "Joy reigns supreme in Bulletland," the *Afro-American* declared. The *Post* ran a cover photo of Unseld and Pollin wrapped in a tight hug. Even Baltimoreans got into the act. "The Fat Lady Sings!" a front-page headline of the *Baltimore*

News American boomed. Morris Siegel wrote: "Downtrodden, beaten-up, disunited, frustrated, maligned Washington, the sports capital with a no-win policy, finally has something to cheer about other than the inaugural parade."[91]

Across the city, troubles were momentarily forgotten. In an editorial titled "A Winner for Washington," the *Star* observed, "There is a grand commonality, something approaching a sense of unity, transient thought it may be, in hailing *our* winning team." To the *Post*, "the championship [was] a gift of particular value to a diverse, often divided community with not all that many recent triumphs to celebrate." The paper added: "For the last couple of weeks, [the Bullets] have been giving cab drivers and politicians, bankers and government workers, and suburban and inner-city youths something nice to share. In a sprawling metropolitan area where there is so little sense of connection—Metro is almost the only other tie that binds—that is no small accomplishment."[92]

The biggest celebration happened that Friday afternoon. Dubbed "Victory Day," it embodied the very civic togetherness discussed by local papers. After a brief ceremony at the Capital Centre, Bullets players, coaches, and personnel climbed into more than two dozen cars—many of which were convertibles—and headed to the District Building, some twelve miles away. On Central Avenue in suburban Maryland, groups of smiling supporters greeted the parade of cars. Into Capitol Heights the procession rolled, onto East Capital Street, over the Anacostia River, toward downtown. All the while crowds grew larger.[93]

On Pennsylvania Avenue, the Bullets were met by a swarm. In some spots, the throng was so thick that the convoy appeared to vanish. The mood was joyous, light. A banner outside the Federal Trade Commission read: "FTC HAILS BULLETS MONOPOLY." H. D. Woodson High's marching band played the theme from *Rocky*. Perched high in the back of a convertible Cadillac, Motta and Bickerstaff high-fived fans. Jerry Sachs, president of the Bullets, told the *Post*: "Black, white, old, young, fat, skinny . . . everyone was along that ride. The Bullets are proud and privileged that we can be a unifying force in the community." The *Post* estimated that 100,000 people watched the procession go by.[94]

Politicians were also present. Before a sun-splashed crowd of nearly 10,000 well-wishers, DC mayor Walter E. Washington awarded Pollin "a hand-crafted key to the city—a memento ordinarily given only to visiting foreign dignitaries," a *Post* reporter wrote. Washington, along with DC city council chairman Sterling Tucker, designated June 9 as "Bullets Day."[95]

Next was a stop at the White House, where President Jimmy Carter hosted a brief ceremony in the East Room. With players and team staff standing behind him, Carter playfully began: "Is the fat lady here?" In a southern Georgia accent, he proceeded to praise Motta and his players, reminding attendees that they were not favored to "win the division. . . . But what made [the title] possible . . . is the fact that it was a team effort. And I think that's the basis of a sound, unconquerable spirit that bound them all together." Flashing a wide smile, Carter was given a Fat Lady T-shirt and a basketball autographed by team members. *ABC Evening News* briefly covered the event.[96]

One official ceremony remained: a gathering with lawmakers in front of the Capitol. A day earlier, Congress had passed two resolutions honoring the Bullets. Introducing H. Res. 1228, DC delegate Walter E. Fauntroy praised the Bullets' "unwillingness to resign to failure." S. Res. 476 applauded the team for being "an inspiration to the country, state and community." Now, on the Capitol's eastside steps, the honorifics continued. South Dakota senator George McGovern boasted, "These are the lean men who made the Fat Lady sing." The formalities concluded with a woman named Betty Clark— "The Bullets official Fat Lady"—belting out Queen's smash hit, "We Are the Champions."[97]

A rally next to RFK Stadium was the final event of the day. Thousands of fans had started congregating earlier that afternoon, so by the time the Bullets arrived, anticipation was running high. As the throng cheered—one banner exclaimed, "She has SUNG"—team members mounted the stage, but within minutes, excited onlookers rushed the platform. Police quickly intervened and escorted the Bullets into RFK. They left via a subterranean passageway.[98]

Save for the commotion at RFK, Victory Day had been a big success. Newspapers did their best to capture the scene. "Red Carpet," announced a front-page headline in the *Post*. One journalist called the celebration "a riot of affection, a 15-mile-an-hour love affair." Four days later, Maryland representative Marjorie S. Holt included a short tribute to the Bullets in the *Congressional Record*. "Mr. Speaker," Holt began, "in the past week the suburban area has been unified in spirit by a unique group of individuals— the Washington Bullets."[99]

Under Motta, the Bullets would have one more outstanding season. In 1978–79 they finished with the best record in the league (54-28), and averaged almost 1,900 more fans per game than they did the previous season. They also returned to the finals, but lost to Seattle, four games to one. The next season, Washington compiled a losing record—the first since the club moved from Baltimore—but made the playoffs. The Bullets lost to Philadelphia in the first round.

Age took its toll on the Bullets. By late 1980, Hayes was thirty-five, and Unseld and Dandridge each were thirty-three—senior citizens, in basketball years. Injuries and untold hours of hustling up and down the court were catching up with them. The Bullets' Big Three simply could not produce like they did in 1977–78.

By the start of the 1981–82 season, the Bullets' championship roster had changed dramatically. Unable to reach the playoffs in 1981, the Bullets traded away Hayes and released Dandridge. Unseld retired. All other players —except for Kevin Grevey and reserve forward Greg Ballard—were either traded or cut, or opted for free agency.

Motta, too, was gone by then. In fact, he left in 1980, accepting an offer to coach the newly created Dallas Mavericks. The Mavs had a rough first year, finishing 15-67. Motta must have known that coaching an expansion team would be no joyride. But that did not mean he was prepared to jettison his unorthodox ways. During halftime of one game, he commandeered a tiger—the animal, along with a monkey, was part of the halftime show— and brought the beast into the locker room. With his wide-eyed players looking on, he thundered, "If you don't start rebounding, this tiger is going to eat every one of you." Motta would go on to have several successful seasons in Dallas.[100]

The fat lady line, or at least a variation of it, reemerged during the 1978–79 season. "The Fat Lady will sing again," was a team slogan and popular T-shirt design. (After winning that year's title, Sonics coach Lenny Wilkens was to have proclaimed, "We removed the fat lady's tonsils.") But it was the original version that endured. One of the first times it appeared outside the sports realm was in 1980, when George H. W. Bush referenced it during the campaign for the Republican presidential nominee. Since then, newspaper columnists, political pundits, screenwriters, detective novelists, and TV news correspondents have used it. It even popped up in ABC's coverage of the O. J. Simpson trial.[101]

Since losing to Seattle in 1979, the Bullets have not played for an NBA title. Even a name change in 1997 could not change their luck. Between 1981 and 2004, the Bullets/Wizards reached the playoffs just seven times. From 1983 to 2004, the franchise failed to win a single playoff series. Such futility contrasted with the success of the Bullets in the 1970s. From fall 1973 to spring 1980, no other club had more regular-season wins and played in more final series than did Pollin's team. The Bullets were the only franchise to appear in the playoffs every season during the 1970s.

The 1977–78 Bullets were a resilient team. They inspired Washingtonians, rekindled hope, and helped bind up a fractious city, albeit however briefly.

After the Bullets lost in the 1979 finals, Vic Gold, author and longtime District resident, recalled with pride the championship from the year before. "[I]n the final minutes of the seventh game in Seattle [in 1978]," Gold wrote in an op-ed for the *Post*, "we came together, we Washingtonians—from Chevy Chase to 14th and U to Fairfax—as one. There had never been anything like it here." Indeed.[102]

13

Assuming "Its Place among the Ice Hockey Centers of the Nation"

The Capitals and Hockey in Washington, DC

John Soares

In July 2009, Moscow witnessed an event that would have been unthinkable twenty years earlier. A black American president, visiting the New Economic School, praised "Russia's timeless heritage" and proclaimed that the United States, like other nations, had "been enriched by Russian culture and enhanced by Russian cooperation. And as a resident of Washington, D.C., I continue to benefit from the contributions of Russians, specifically from Alexander Ovechkin."[1] President Barack Obama, of course, was referring to the Washington Capital's Alexander Ovechkin, one of the greatest ice hockey players in the world and arguably the biggest star of the National Hockey League (NHL).

A few short years before Obama's address, many doubted the United States would ever have a black president. During the Cold War, it had been just as difficult to imagine that any prominent school in Moscow would ever be called a "bastion of liberal economics," as a reporter for National Public Radio did in 2009.[2] When European hockey players, including some from communist Czechoslovakia, began to play in the NHL in significant numbers in the 1970s, no Soviets were among them. There seemed to be little chance that the best Russians would ever play in North America.

Moreover, Washington has rarely been considered a hockey hotbed. Although the *Washington Post* in 1939 rated minor league hockey DC's most popular spectator sport after pro football,[3] there was no professional hockey in the city after the Washington Presidents of the Eastern Hockey League played their final season, in 1959–60. When the Capitals joined

231

the NHL in 1974–75, they set league records for futility that still stand. It was not until the Capitals' ninth season that they even made the playoffs. Portions of the Caps' history seem designed to elicit chortles: a head coach who lasted just nineteen games, another who was only twenty-six years old, and still one more who was fired and replaced with his own brother.

Even when the Capitals started making the playoffs regularly, they were bedeviled by early round losses to divisional rivals that were among the greatest teams ever: the New York Islanders of the 1980s and the Pittsburgh Penguins of the early 1990s. In more recent years, the Capitals have become consistent title contenders. But excellent regular-season performances, including a President's Trophy for the league's best record, have often been followed by early playoff exits. The Caps have never won the Stanley Cup. They made the finals just once, but lost in a four-game sweep.

This record of on-ice frustration, however, obscures the Capitals' historic importance. The Caps were part of the NHL's expansion to American cities located outside the traditional hockey belt, helping fuel "an anti-American whirlwind" in Canada during the 1970s that complicated US-Canadian diplomatic relations. The Capitals were also part of a larger pattern of American pro sports leagues' expansion into cities in the South and West. Like many other sports franchises during the 1970s, they played in a new arena in the suburbs, only to move into a downtown arena a generation later. They were pioneers in employing American, black, and Eastern European players. Two of the greatest Eastern Europeans ever to play in the NHL—Ovechkin and Jaromir Jagr—skated for Washington. Their history is inextricably intertwined with the development of professional sports generally, and hockey more specifically. The Capitals are, quite simply, one of the NHL's most significant franchises.[4]

DC Hockey before the Capitals

The Capitals were not the first hockey team to play in DC. During the late 1930s and early 1940s, the Eastern Amateur Hockey League's Washington Eagles played at Riverside Stadium, which was located where the Kennedy Center presently sits. The Eagles boasted such stars as "Lithe Leslie Ramsey, Bill (Stinky) Davies, Leisurely Len Burrage, Game Gordon Gee, Pounding Paul Courtreau and Ross (Rough 'n Ready) Knipfel." They made quite an impression. In just their first year, the Eagles were so successful that hockey, in the words of the *Post*, had "captured this city more completely than any other athletic innovation with the exception of professional football." The opening of the Uline Arena in 1941 gave hockey another home in the

District and created a rivalry between the two buildings. Uline Arena eventually won out and became the home to DC hockey. During the 1940s and
1950s, another hockey team, the Washington Lions, played there. Over the
years, the Lions were members of the American, Eastern Amateur, or Eastern leagues. The Washington Presidents of the Eastern Hockey League came
next, playing in Uline Arena for several seasons in the late 1950s.[5]

Despite the initial enthusiasm for hockey, and what a writer for the *Post*
believed in 1939 was "evidence that time is not long before [the District]
will take its place among the ice hockey centers of the Nation," Washington
had difficulty keeping teams. Minor league hockey franchises preferred
locations farther north, even in smaller cities like New Haven, Connecticut;
Hershey, Pennsylvania; and Johnstown, Pennsylvania. It was rumored in
the early 1970s that Charlie Finley, owner of the NHL's Oakland Seals and
baseball's Oakland A's, might move both teams to DC as part of a package
deal. That never happened. Pro hockey only returned to Washington with
NHL expansion. In June 1972 the league awarded a franchise to DC. The
team was to begin play in 1974–75.[6]

Politics, Expansion, and US-Canadian Relations

Washington's selection fit the pattern of NHL expansion in the 1960s and
1970s. From World War II until 1967, the league consisted of the "original
six" teams: Boston, Chicago, Detroit, Montreal, New York, and Toronto.
Between 1967 and 1974, however, the league added twelve teams. Like
other pro sports, hockey expanded to cities in the southern and western
United States. In addition to Washington, Los Angeles, Oakland, Kansas
City, and Atlanta were cities in the South or West with new NHL teams.

Though typical of expansion in other sports, the NHL's approach was not
without controversy, especially in Canada. Hockey was Canada's national
game, and the NHL was its top pro league. Yet eleven of these twelve expansion teams were placed in American cities—many of which were outside
the traditional hockey belt. Canadian cities with passionate hockey fans
were left out, and, in some cases, were not even considered viable options
when struggling American franchises tried to relocate. In 1969, for example,
the NHL prohibited the underperforming Oakland Seals from moving to
Vancouver. Even though the NHL orchestrated its round of expansion for
1970 to virtually guarantee a franchise in Vancouver, Canadians perceived
that the NHL was sacrificing Canadian interests for the pursuit of American
dollars. During the 1968 Stanley Cup finals, the NHL decided to schedule
a Sunday afternoon game for its American network rather than a Saturday

evening contest for Canadian Broadcasting Corporation's iconic "Hockey Night in Canada." Popular Canadian books, and even the Canadian government, blamed NHL expansion for watering down the league's talent, diminishing the quality of play, and distorting the game to better appeal to Americans who knew nothing about hockey.[7]

Concerns about the NHL catering to American interests fit into larger trends in US-Canadian relations. During the 1970s, books in Canada with such titles as *Close the 49th Parallel* denounced the "Americanization of Canada." Canadian prime minister Pierre Trudeau, aware of, and encouraging, his nation's growing wariness of its neighbor to the south, promoted a foreign policy designed to make Canada more independent of the United States. Surging anti-Americanism in Canada undercut American power abroad, since Washington needed Ottawa's cooperation in addressing issues like national security, trade, and energy. Hockey and its expansion to American cities like Washington contributed to America's diplomatic headaches.[8]

Despite the problems politics and diplomacy caused for official Washington, politics helped the city land an expansion team. Shortly after Washington's selection, a league official, who refused to be named, was quoted as saying, "With the climate as it is for sports now, it doesn't hurt to have a few friends in Washington."[9] League owners simply could not ignore the potential benefits of having a team in the nation's capital. After it passed over Baltimore in its first round of expansion, the NHL had been the subject of a Justice Department antitrust "preliminary inquiry."[10] The league also faced challenges from the upstart World Hockey Association (WHA). In addition, there was the possibility of labor unrest.[11] Given these concerns, it was politically prudent to seek allies in the American capital. Indeed, a rival applicant city complained that "political pressure" had helped Washington win one of the two bids in 1972. Among those who reportedly assisted in bringing hockey to DC was Massachusetts senator Edward M. Kennedy.[12]

While the award of an NHL expansion franchise was a victory for Washington, the triumph was conditional: DC would get the team only if it had an arena ready for the 1974–75 season. When Washington's selection was announced in June 1972, though, no suitable arena existed in the District—or anywhere nearby.

To the Suburbs—and Back

Washington's Uline Arena (renamed the Washington Coliseum in 1960) had been the home of teams in the American Hockey League (AHL)—the top minor league in North America—during the 1940s and 1950s. Some minor league arenas in other cities were large enough for an NHL team. But with only 6,000 seats, the Washington Coliseum was not. Several weeks after the NHL awarded the nation's capital a franchise, *The Hockey News* reported that the new Washington team "plans to play in the arena which is planned in the projected Eisenhower Center if it can be ready for the 1974–75 season." The Dwight D. Eisenhower Bicentennial Center—a two-building complex consisting of a sports arena and convention center—was to be located near Mount Vernon Square. The facility was intended as a memorial to President Eisenhower and as a tool to help DC's "bid for the 1976 Bicentennial Exposition." The Metropolitan Washington Board of Trade, backed by businesses like ITT-Sheraton, encouraged the NHL to place the team downtown.[13]

Despite support for an arena as part of the Eisenhower Center, or at two separate locations nearby, Caps owner Abe Pollin concluded that a downtown arena would never be ready by the start of the 1974–75 season. Pollin needed to have his arena ready by then because of the conditional franchise award. A new arena was already under construction outside Cleveland, and if the DC arena were not ready in time, the NHL could withdraw its award and put the new team in Cleveland instead. Cleveland also had the benefit of being a northern city with a long record of high-level minor league hockey. Many observers, in fact, believed the Ohio city was a better option for the NHL than Washington.[14]

So Pollin proceeded to build an arena in a section of Prince George's County, Maryland, near present-day Landover. The arena, known as the Capital Centre, was located near six major highways and a planned Metro stop. Supporters promised that the venue would be "America's Newest, Most Modern Sports Arena." Pollin and his architectural team did not disappoint. The arena had a unique, saddle-shaped roof. Inside, there were "sky suites," a precursor to luxury boxes, and a "Telscreen" replay board, purportedly "the most revolutionary and unique scoreboard/entertainment system of any indoor arena in the world" at the time. Similar replay boards would grace the inside of almost every arena in the coming years.[15]

By establishing themselves in Landover, the Capitals were part of professional sports' move to the suburbs. The Kansas City Scouts, for instance, the other NHL expansion franchise in 1974–75, played their games in suburban Overland Park. Basketball and hockey teams in Los Angeles and Cleveland moved to suburban arenas as well. The infatuation with the suburbs was even more pronounced in the National Football League, as teams in Boston, Buffalo, Dallas, Detroit, Kansas City, Los Angeles, and New York all moved to suburban areas during the 1970s.[16]

In the 1990s, the Capitals were again part of a trend in pro sports, as teams in Baltimore, San Francisco, Cleveland, Detroit, and later New Jersey moved from suburban venues to downtown arenas. Pollin was one of the first team owners to unveil his plans to do so. In 1995 he announced that his team would move into a new building downtown by 1997. The new arena would be located near Chinatown, in the heart of the District, and it was to be accessible by three different Metro lines. As had been the case with the Capital Centre, Pollin promised that the new arena would be "a state-of-the-art-wonder." Telecommunications company MCI acquired naming rights and became involved in producing "the first of a new generation of sports venues that will marry live entertainment and the latest tools of the information age." The MCI Center, as the facility was initially called, also featured retail shops that were open even when there was no event inside the arena.[17]

The new arena transformed a "once-neglected and dangerous neighborhood" into a "regional nightlife hub," which in turn increased nearby property values. The replacement of local businesses with national chains brought comments that DC's Chinatown had shrunk to "Chinablock" or even "Chinacorner." Not only did the arena alter the neighborhood, its luxury seating came at eye-popping prices. There were "founder's boxes" for $1,000,000, while less extravagant boxes cost $100,000 to $175,000 per year. For $7,500, one could buy a season's worth of "club seats," which promised "extra leg-room," "wait-staff service" and the opportunity to "share a private concourse with the region's other movers and shakers." The high cost of tickets, some worried, would make it difficult for traditional fans to attend games.[18]

But the Capitals by the late 1990s were a championship contender, with the potential to fill an expensive new arena with fans and with "movers and shakers." In the Caps' first year in the new arena, coach Ron Wilson guided them to the Eastern Conference championship. Although they lost in the Stanley Cup finals to the Detroit Red Wings, the Caps had finally arrived. But they had to go through some terribly difficult seasons to get there.

Early Years

There had been grounds for optimism when the Capitals prepared to join the NHL. The team's first general manager was the longtime Bruins front office man, Milt Schmidt. With Boston, Schmidt had shown himself to be a savvy executive. As assistant general manager, he arranged the trade that brought star Phil Esposito and other important players to Boston. He was general manager when the Bruins won the Stanley Cup in 1970 and 1972.

More relevant to the Capitals, Schmidt won with a team that had been one of the league's worst for years.[19]

Despite the optimism generated by Schmidt's resume—and the fact that the expansion Philadelphia Flyers won the Stanley Cup in 1974—the Capitals faced a herculean task in trying to build an NHL contender. The expansion draft permitted teams already in the league to protect so many players that few of any quality were available to Washington and Kansas City. *The Hockey News* started its coverage of the expansion draft by writing grimly, "The widest, whitest smiles in the room belonged to [Kansas City GM] Sid Abel and Milt Schmidt and nobody could figure out why." Given the limited talent available to them, *The Hockey News* saw no reason for grins.[20]

Still, there was some hope that the Capitals might overcome the obstacles expansion teams faced. One NHL scout rated the Capitals good enough to finish third in their five-team division and claim a playoff berth. The team's first head coach, Jimmy Anderson, a former Bruins' "superscout" with a little more than two years of minor league coaching experience, was quoted as saying that except for league MVP Bobby Clarke and fifty-goal scorer Rick MacLeish, the Stanley Cup champion "Flyers aren't much better than the Capitals."[21]

One DC business group, looking back in the summer of 1975, remarked that the Capitals during their first year "experienced only limited success."[22] That was an understatement. Washington managed just eight wins against sixty-seven losses, with five ties. A *Los Angeles Times* sportswriter rated the Capitals that year the worst team in all of American professional sports. Washington went through three different head coaches—in the franchise's first season. Anderson was gone before Valentine's Day. His replacement, head scout Red Sullivan, said, "I hope I can stay behind the bench in Washington for ten years." His declining health drove him from the post in about six weeks. Schmidt stepped in to finish the season.[23]

The difficulties lingered. Schmidt was dismissed as both GM and head coach midway through the team's second year. The Capitals record at the time was a pitiful 3-28-5. The *New York Times* later that season described the Caps as "atrocious." Heading into their third year, a minor league coach judged the Capitals to be an "average hockey team"—by the standards of a farm league club. Despite some reasons for optimism, such as Dennis Maruk's fifty goals in 1980–81, and his whopping sixty goals and 132 points the next season, the Capitals continued to struggle for years.[24]

Compared to successful expansion teams, Washington lagged badly. By their eighth year, for example, the Philadelphia Flyers had already won their second straight Stanley Cup. As an expansion team in 1972–73, the New

York Islanders set many of the records for futility that Washington would break in 1974–75. By their third year, however, the Islanders were a play-off team. And by their eighth year, the Islanders had won the first of four straight Stanley Cups. In contrast, the Capitals, after eight sad years in the league, had yet to make the playoffs.[25]

The initial excitement of hockey in Washington brought predictions that the team might have 26,000 fans interested in season tickets, a figure that far exceeded the capacity of the Capital Centre, or any other NHL arena. In actuality, there were only 6,800 season ticketholders the first year. So bad were the Caps, and so poorly had they drawn fans, that the Metropolitan Washington Board of Trade organized a program called "Operation Support," which was designed to promote season-ticket purchases by local businesses. Despite these efforts, the number of Caps' season ticketholders actually dropped in their second season to 4,200.[26]

In the early 1980s the Capitals finally became more competitive. Schmidt's replacement as general manager, Max McNab, introduced some stability and held the job until 1981. Under GM David Poile (1982–97) and his successor, George McPhee (1997–2014), the Caps began to experience success. In trying to build a contender, several of these officials tapped into unusual—and historically significant—sources to unearth talent.[27]

Capitals and Race in Hockey

Only one black man had ever played in the NHL before the Capitals joined the league. Willie O'Ree, in January 1958, became the first black to play in the NHL. The Fredericton, New Brunswick, native played forty-five games with the Boston Bruins over two seasons, scoring four goals and fourteen points. After Boston traded him in 1961, the NHL had no black players until 1974–75, when black Canadians Mike Marson and Bill Riley skated for Washington.[28]

Unlike Major League Baseball, the National Basketball Association, and the National Football League, the NHL before expansion consisted of almost entirely Canadian players. And even though more Americans and Europeans have been playing in the NHL since the 1970s, the league is still mostly Canadian. People of African descent were (and still are) a tiny percentage of Canada's population—less than a half of 1 percent for much of the twentieth century, and under 2 percent in the 1990s. In the United States, football and basketball programs at historically black colleges and universities, along with the Negro Leagues in baseball, developed many highly skilled African American athletes who had the talent to play at the highest level, if given the chance. The success enjoyed by such integrated teams as baseball's Brooklyn Dodgers and football's Cleveland Browns showed that lily-white sports franchises were a thing of the past.[29]

But few black Canadians played hockey. Scholars who study Canadian sport history have argued that black Canadian athletes historically came from outside the upper- and middle-income groups that generally supplied the talent for hockey. Moreover, these scholars contend, black Canadian athletes have tended to gravitate toward sports like football and basketball, since they "demand little in the way of special equipment and formal training."[30] There were some hockey leagues for black Canadians, though, like the Colored Hockey League in the Maritime Provinces, which existed during the late nineteenth and early twentieth century.[31] But the Colored League was not as durable or respected as baseball's Negro Leagues. Black Canadian hockey players in the 1940s, like Manny McIntyre and Herb and Ossie Carnegie, played with and against white players in overwhelmingly white amateur or minor leagues. Playing in these leagues, they encountered the ugliness of discrimination. Some white Canadians saw hockey as the preserve of the "white, Canadian male."[32] Despite cross-border difference in race relations, "Canada's midcentury . . . segregation policies were not unlike that of the United States."[33]

Despite facing such obstacles, Herb Carnegie was so talented that Toronto Maple Leafs owner Conn Smythe in the 1940s reportedly offered $10,000 to anyone who could make him white. Carnegie played for a Montreal Canadiens farm team, and he was considered by many observers "to be the best player in [training] camp" when the New York Rangers invited him to tryout in 1948.[34] However, he was never offered an NHL roster spot. A decade later it would be O'Ree who integrated the NHL. But he fell short of the kind of stardom that several African American pioneers in baseball and football achieved. O'Ree finished his NHL career playing for a last-place club. While teams in other pro sports hurt themselves by refusing to sign black players, NHL powerhouses and doormats alike remained lily-white.

In 1974, the Capitals made history by signing early-round draft pick Marson and veteran minor-leaguer Riley. The pair became the first black teammates in NHL history. The Capitals took the 5'9", 200-pound Marson with the first pick of the second round in the 1974 draft. He was the nineteenth player taken overall, ahead of such future stars as Brian Trottier, Mark Howe, and Charlie Simmer. Marson, from the Toronto suburb of Scarborough, had starred with junior hockey's Sudbury Wolves in 1973–74. He was the Wolves' top scorer, tallying thirty-five goals and fifty-nine assists. The Capitals valued the eighteen-year-old Marson so much that they claimed him as a special "underage" pick.[35]

There was speculation that Washington, playing in the only black-majority American city at the time, had selected Marson in an attempt to draw African American fans. General manager Schmidt, who had coached O'Ree with the Bruins, "emphatically denied" that race was a factor. Schmidt explained that the Caps were attracted to Marson's skating, his skill as both a scorer and defender, and his physical play. According to the Caps' general manager, "Color did not enter into it [at] all."[36]

Marson's father was pleased when his son signed with Washington. He remembered listening to a radio interview with future Caps' GM Schmidt while Schmidt was coaching the Bruins. At the time, the Bruins roster included O'Ree, and "Schmidt made it clear on that broadcast that O'Ree was a Bruin[,] not a black Bruin." Favorably impressed, Marson was delighted that his son had joined Schmidt's new team.[37]

During his first year in Washington, Marson was joined by Riley, who was a native of Amherst, Nova Scotia. On December 26, 1974, they played together on the same line, marking the first time in league history that two black players skated on the same unit. In subsequent years, Marson and Riley were sometimes paired as wings on a line that was centered by Gerry Meehan, a white player. The line was nicknamed the "Oreo cookie line." Unlike the teenager Marson, Riley had taken a more circuitous route to the NHL. The twenty-five-year-old Riley was toiling in the minor leagues, playing for the Dayton Gems, when the Capitals signed him to a five-game tryout in December 1974. The December 26 contest was Riley's only game with the Capitals that season, but after another year with Dayton, Riley returned to Washington. The 1976–77 season was the first of three straight years in which Riley played with the Capitals, before he was claimed by Winnipeg in the 1979 expansion draft.[38]

There were moments of optimism with Marson and Riley playing for the Caps. Marson tallied a hat trick in the Capitals' first exhibition win and notched a respectable sixteen goals during the Capitals' abysmal first season, finishing third on the team in goals and points. During his years as a Capital, Riley twice tallied thirteen goals, despite never playing a full season. Partway through 1977–78, Riley was at the thirteen-goal mark when his season was ended by a serious injury that shortened his career.[39]

Despite his promise, Marson faced unique pressures—and not only because of his skin color. Greatly inflated by pressure from the upstart WHA, his large salary caused resentment among his teammates and increased expectations for him. In addition, as a history-making minority on an awful team, he received suffocating media attention. As the *New York Times* pointed out in 1976, "On the team's first swing around the league last season . . . Marson was besieged by reporters wanting to know what it was like being a black in a white man's sport. The second time around, he was asked what it was like constantly being asked the previous question."[40]

Marson also had to deal with assorted racial abuse. He received death threats. He was subjected to dirty play and racial slurs from opponents. Even his own teammates sometimes called him "Uncle Ben" or joked about not wanting to sit too close to him on the bench just in case any of the death threats were carried out. Marson had been one of the best players in a top Canadian junior league, and he made his mark there against players who became NHL stars. But, as he put it, his junior rivals who made the NHL "didn't have to deal with the stuff I had to deal with. Those guys had the luxury to just play the game." Riley later observed that the abuse the nineteen-year-old Marson endured "as a kid kind of destroyed him" and "just cut his heart out."[41]

Despite his promise as a player and the Capitals' investment in him, it is unlikely team officials understood what Marson had to endure or ever took meaningful steps to help the Caps' intended star deal with the unique pressures he faced. Riley recalled: "I don't know if management could have done anything to ease the pressure on Mike. But in all honesty, management never had a clue what it must have been like to be a black man in a white man's sport." Riley also remembered: "There wasn't a guy who could skate like [Marson], and pound for pound he might have been the strongest guy in the NHL. . . . He could have played 10, 12 years" in the league. Despite that promise, Marson never overcame the accumulated obstacles. After a solid first season, his offense declined and he never recovered. After four seasons with the Capitals, and increasing time in the minors, Marson was dealt to the Los Angeles Kings in 1978. By the time he was twenty-five, he was done with professional hockey. Riley likewise saw his career shortened by injury just when it looked ready to take off and found opportunities limited when he sought to build a career in coaching or management.[42]

But Riley and Marson were not the last black Capitals. Black players are still rare in the NHL. Most teams have no blacks on their roster, and seldom does a team have more than one. But the league has become more attentive to racial issues, as have players. The league supports programs to promote diversity, and appointed O'Ree in 1998 to direct the NHL/USA Hockey diversity program.[43] The impact of increasing numbers of black players and heightened awareness of racial issues in hockey was demonstrated by the treatment of the Capitals' Joel Ward in the spring of 2012.

Ward scored an overtime goal in game 7 of Washington's first-round series to eliminate the defending Stanley Cup champion Boston Bruins. After the game, some irate Bruins fans posted racial slurs about Ward on social media sites. The response of the league, players, and even Boston fans was immediate and dramatic. Ward's Capitals teammates rallied around him, as did Philadelphia Flyer Wayne Simmonds, another black player and Ward's friend. The league denounced the racist remarks as "ignorant and unacceptable," saying, "The people responsible for these comments have no place associating themselves with our game." The mayor of Boston called the offenders "a very minute group of angry, ignorant people that do not represent our city." Ward's agent pointed out that no racial comments directed at Ward came from Bruins fans who attended game 7. Ward himself said that "there have been a lot of Boston fans who have supported me" over the episode. *USA Today* reported, "Many have gone after those who posted racist remarks. Some who have made racist comments have already closed their accounts. One person apologized." Referring to Boston's particularly unpleasant racial history, a Boston University professor made a universally relevant point about racial issues by observing that the episode was "an ugly reminder that we have so far to go."[44]

Washington players Marson and Riley helped pave the way for future blacks in the NHL. But the Capitals also played an important role in tapping into other pools of hockey talent that were less controversial but still historically rare for the NHL: the United States and Europe.

American and International Players

While black players remain a rarity in the NHL, American players for decades were also uncommon. During some years of the early 1960s, future Capital Tommy Williams was the only American—and the only non-Canadian—in the league. Williams had played on the 1960 United States Olympic hockey team that won the gold medal, and he was the only player from the team who had an NHL career of any consequence.[45] Even after expansion and the emergence of the WHA, which increased the number of Americans playing professional hockey, it would be decades before there were any American superstars among the sport's very best.

During the 1970s and 1980s, despite a long tradition of medaling at the Olympics, American teams were but mere afterthoughts in the most prestigious international competitions. The Canada Cup tournament, for instance, which debuted in 1976, included teams of the best professionals from Canada and the United States, national teams from the Soviet Union and Czechoslovakia, and the best pro and amateur players from Sweden and Finland or West Germany. But Canadian organizers of the first tournament worried that the Americans would feel so overmatched that they might not even play. Assessing the teams during pre-tournament practices, a Canadian hockey writer in 1976 concluded, "Not one member of the 29-man Team USA could make the Team Canada squad." Lee Fogolin, the son of a former NHL player who was born in Chicago but lived almost his entire life in Canada, was able to play for Team USA by virtue of his birth. As he put it, "There's no way I was going to make Team Canada" because Canada was "going to have to sit out 50-goal scorers." The Americans, for their part, were desperate for even borderline NHL talent. Demonstrating how little respect the American team received, one Canadian hockey expert reported that some of the Americans were so bad that they "likely would ride the bench for the Washington Capitals."[46]

This scenario began to change in the 1980s. Some of the players from the celebrated 1980 United States Olympic team that won the gold medal in Lake Placid had solid NHL careers. Of these players, Dave Christian was the most prolific NHL scorer. He played in Washington for more than six seasons, scoring forty-one goals in 1985–86.[47] But it was not the 1980 Olympians who left the biggest mark on the league. Some of the first Americans to achieve true stardom were two Capitals: the high-scoring Bobby Carpenter and defenseman Rod Langway.

Carpenter was the Capitals' first-round draft pick in 1981. The Caps traded up in the draft to obtain the third overall pick so they could select the schoolboy star from St. John's Prep in Danvers, Massachusetts. It was the earliest any American player had ever been taken in the draft. Carpenter had planned to attend Providence College and had even accepted a scholarship offer before the draft, but in the end decided to sign with Washington. In 1981 he became the first American to jump straight from high school to the NHL. He immediately proved that he belonged, tallying thirty-two goals as a rookie and matching that number the following season. He made history again in 1984–85, notching fifty-three goals and becoming the first US-born player ever to clear the vaunted fifty-goal mark.[48]

One of Carpenter's teammates during these years was Rod Langway, another Boston-area product. After playing at the University of New Hampshire, Langway broke into pro hockey with the WHA's Birmingham Bulls before moving to the Montreal Canadiens. Prior to 1982–83, Langway was traded to the Capitals along with Montreal teammates Craig Laughlin, Brian Engblom, and Doug Jarvis. This blockbuster deal boosted the Caps' credibility and helped Washington to its first playoff appearances. Engblom was an excellent defenseman who had won three Stanley Cups with Montreal. Laughlin became a thirty-goal scorer with the Caps. Jarvis was an outstanding defensive forward who played on four Cup champions in Montreal. With Washington, he won the Frank Selke Award as the league's top defensive forward. Langway would go on to become the best defenseman in the NHL.[49]

In 1982–83, Langway became the first American to win the James Norris Trophy, given annually to the league's top defenseman. It was the first time since 1939 that a US player had claimed one of the league's major awards. Langway repeated as Norris Trophy winner the next year. The strong play of Carpenter and Langway, combined with the efforts of players like Mike Gartner, who reached the magical mark of scoring fifty goals in 1984–85, helped transform the Capitals into a perennial playoff team.[50]

Adding to the Capitals' strength were players from another historically unusual source: Czechoslovakia. Hockey was first played there in 1909, even before it became an independent country. When the international federation began hosting European championships before World War I, Bohemia —a section of what would become Czechoslovakia—was one of hockey's major powers, winning the European title in 1911 and 1914, and finishing second in 1913. In the years after World War II, Czechoslovakia established itself as the strongest European hockey nation. It won the world championship in 1947, finished second to Canada in 1948, and became, in 1949, the first continental European nation to win a world tournament in which Canada participated. But a politically inspired purge of the national team in 1950 set Czechoslovak hockey back almost fifteen years. By the late 1960s, Czechoslovakia had reemerged as one of the strongest hockey countries in the world. During these years, the Slavic nation regularly challenged the Soviet Union, which had by then supplanted Canada as the dominant power in Olympic and world tournaments.[51]

For many years during the Cold War, Czechoslovakia and the Soviet Union had different relations with the NHL. Soviet authorities, despite a number of instances in which NHL or WHA teams expressed interest in signing Soviet players, did not allow their countrymen to play in North America before 1989. That year also saw Alexander Mogilny defect to the Buffalo Sabres, the first time a Soviet hockey player had defected to a North American professional team. By contrast, beginning with Jaroslav Jirik in 1969, the Czechoslovak government had permitted players older than thirty to play outside the country, even in North America. Moreover, Czechoslovak officials could not prevent defections as easily as the Soviets. In fact, Czechoslovaks playing outside their native country was so common that in 1986 a Czechoslovak official quipped, "Leaving is part of hockey here."[52]

Part of the Capitals' inclusion of foreign-born players, Sweden's Rolf Edberg (*left*) and Leif Svensson are all smiles after inking a contract with the team in June 1978. Their wives are in the middle. Reprinted with permission of the DC Public Library, Star Collection, © Washington Post.

Several Czechoslovak players who left their native land—"with permission" and "without permission"—played for the Capitals in the 1970s and 1980s. Milan Novy was a thirty-one-year-old veteran of Olympic, world championship, and Canada Cup play when he joined the Capitals for the 1982–83 season. The Washington team bragged that Novy was "[o]ne of the all-time greats" in Europe. He once scored fifty-nine goals in a forty-four-game Czechoslovak league season. He also had been the leading scorer at the 1980 Olympics in Lake Placid. But with his best hockey behind him, Novy was less valuable to Czechoslovak hockey authorities, which meant that they did not object to him playing in North America. Novy stayed with the Caps for only one season.[53]

By contrast, Prague was not happy with Michal Pivonka's departure. When he arrived in Washington in the summer of 1986, the twenty-year-old Pivonka was the seventeenth Czechoslovak player to come to North America. Pivonka was so young that his defection came not long after he last played for the Czechoslovak junior national team. Typical of defections during the Cold War era, it required subterfuge to get him out. Pivonka and his fiancée told communist authorities that they were traveling to Yugoslavia for vacation. Instead, they went to Italy, where they met Capitals officials who helped them through immigration and into the United States. Noting that the Buffalo Sabres had failed to sign one of their top draft picks despite cooperating with Czechoslovak authorities, Capitals general manager David Poile said, "If we had tried to negotiate Pivonka's release, he never would have gotten out."[54]

Pivonka came to the NHL despite his government's disapproval, and for the rest of the millennium he was one of the Capitals' better players. He regularly topped twenty goals and fifty assists per season. His 418 career assists is still a Capitals record, and his 599 points ranks fourth highest in team history.[55]

Pivonka's fellow countryman, Peter Bondra, exemplified another type of player that became even more common in the 1990s and beyond: athletes who were products of top-notch programs in eastern Europe and who were no longer prohibited from playing professionally in North America by official ideology or Cold War politics. Bondra was drafted by the Capitals and joined the team in 1990, after the collapse of Czechoslovakia's communist regime. He scored more goals and points with the Capitals than any other player in team history, and he twice scored fifty-two goals in a season, including in 1997–98, when he led the Capitals to the Stanley Cup finals. He hit the forty-five-goal mark on two other occasions, and topped thirty goals in nine seasons with the Caps. After the breakup of Czechoslovakia, he played for the national and Olympic teams of Slovakia.[56]

Despite these impressive credentials, Bondra was not the most famous of the Eastern European stars to play in Washington. Those honors belong to Czech star Jaromir Jagr and Russian Alexander Ovechkin. Better known for his achievements with the Penguins and still active as of this writing, Jagr was the big offensive dynamo who wore number 68. He selected it to commemorate the events in Czechoslovakia in 1968, when reformist communist leader Alexander Dubcek attempted to develop "socialism with a human face" but was thwarted by a Soviet invasion that August. Jagr is a national hero in the Czech Republic, which he led to an Olympic gold medal in the 1998 Olympics—the first Winter Olympics that saw the NHL suspend play so its best players could represent their countries. Demonstrating the importance of hockey in the Czech Republic, the Olympic victory was celebrated in Prague in the 2004 opera, *Nagano*.[57]

In Pittsburgh, Jagr won five scoring titles and a Hart Trophy as the league's most valuable player. While a Penguin, he often tormented the Capitals. When the Caps acquired him in the summer of 2001, fresh off his fourth consecutive season in which he led the league in scoring, Washingtonians rejoiced. But he spent two and a half mostly disappointing years with the Capitals before being traded to the New York Rangers.[58]

Ovechkin, a Russian and another post–Cold War Eastern European player, remains the Capitals' biggest star and most recognizable name. He is climbing the list of franchise leaders in every offensive category. With Ovechkin, the Caps won four straight division titles and a President's Trophy for the best record in the league. Among the great players who have been his teammates in recent years were Alexander Semin, another Russian product, and Swedish star Nikolas Backstrom. Following in the footsteps of players like Russian Sergei Gonchar, Swede Calle Johanssen, and German Olaf Kolzig, these players have added to the Caps' tradition of combining Canadian talent with players from a number of hockey playing nations that have sent many stars to the NHL in recent decades.

After years of being the laughingstock of the league, the Capitals have become regular contenders. Some of the top coaches in the game—including Bryan Murray; his brother, Terry; Jim Schoenfeld; Ron Wilson; and Bruce Boudreau—have led the Caps to playoff appearances and Stanley Cup contention. However, the Capitals have appeared only once in the Stanley Cup finals and have made only one other appearance in the conference finals—in 1988, when they were swept by Boston.

But playoff frustration and the lack of a Stanley Cup does not alter the fact that the Washington Capitals have been an important contributor to hockey's growth in the United States. The Capitals gave the game a presence in the nation's capital during three decades when DC had no baseball team. The Caps were also a franchise that took historic steps in signing minorities, as well as American and Eastern European players. The Capitals have contributed to, and been a symbol of, hockey's development as a major entertainment enterprise in the United States. While the *Washington Post*'s 1939 assessment proved premature, DC has finally assumed "its place among the ice hockey centers of the Nation." The Washington Capitals have sunk deep roots that should keep Canada's national game flourishing in the American capital for years to come.

14

"The People's Race"

The Marine Corps Marathon and Distance Running in the Nation's Capital

Joseph M. Turrini

Since its inaugural running in 1976, the Marine Corps Marathon (MCM) has been one of the most popular marathons in the country. Online registration for the 2012 race sold out in less than three hours. Hopeful participants snapped up the 30,000 spots in an astonishing two hours and forty-one minutes.[1] The MCM attracts the masses, but unlike other big-city marathons, it does not attract many elite runners. Few Olympians have ever run in the race, and no one expects the winner to break the world record. The men's record of 2:14:01—set by Jeff Scuffins in 1987—and the women's record of 2:37:00—set by Olga Markova in 1990—are pedestrian compared to marks for other high-profile marathons.[2] The MCM does not feature an international elite field because it does not pay appearance fees or prize money. The lack of remuneration makes it unique among big-city marathons and is the primary reason why it is known as "the People's Race."

The MCM, however, did not start out with the intention of becoming "the People's Race." Rather, it was conceived as a public relations tool for the United States Marine Corps (USMC) to bolster its image in the post–Vietnam War era. Few could have imagined the race's eventual success. The MCM's founder, Colonel Jim Fowler, recalled that before the first race in 1976 he was asked: "Suppose we give this marathon and nobody comes?"[3] The USMC was "amazed at the turnout of the first one," Major Chip Olmstead remembered.[4] The race only grew after the inaugural MCM.

The MCM was created at an ideal time, in an ideal location. Benefiting greatly from both local and national trends in athletics, the DC area as early as the 1960s had developed an unusually vibrant participatory running culture—which the MCM tapped into. In addition, by 1976 a national running boom was in the process of transforming how Americans thought about fitness and distance running. The running craze was one aspect of a larger cultural shift toward individual fulfillment through strenuous physical exercise that occurred in the 1970s and 1980s.[5] Local and national factors combined with the USMC's own interest in physical fitness and athletic competition to establish the MCM as unique and one of the most popular distance running events in the country.

Before the Boom: Distance Running in the District of Columbia, pre-1973

Prior to the 1960s, long distance races in the District were rare and unusual events that catered to runners who were mostly viewed as eccentrics.[6] DC was home to three types of distance races before 1960. One type was the occasional high-profile race. These included races of either ten or fifteen miles sponsored by the *Washington Post* in 1909, 1924, and 1925. The 1909 race featured 106 entrants, but only 47 crossed the finish line. The 1924 and 1925 races saw 110 and 98 runners, respectively. Ninety-five completed the course in 1924, and 81 did it the following year. Each race was a major athletic event, and attracted entrants from New York, Philadelphia, and Baltimore. Among the spectators at the 1924 and 1925 races was President Calvin Coolidge, who congratulated the winners.[7] The national marathon championship of the Amateur Athletic Union (AAU) was the second type of long distance race held in the District before 1960. Twice, in 1933 and 1937, the city hosted the championship.

Races held by local athletic clubs were the third type of long distance events in Washington. Both the Aloysius and City clubs, for example, staged a number of races between five and fifteen miles during the 1920s. Local participants comprised most of the fields.[8] Races were also held in conjunction with other celebrations. The most prominent was the Takoma Park Fourth of July race hosted by the Takoma Park Citizens Association. Held annually from 1929 to 1942, and then again from 1950 to 1956, the race usually included between twenty and sixty-five runners, and often served as the DC AAU 10-Mile Championship. Part of Takoma Park's Fourth of July celebration, the race shared top billing with a parade, picnic, and fireworks display.[9]

Early competitive running competitions in the District prohibited African American participation. Two black runners, William Fauntroy and William Anderson, for instance, were barred from competing in an Aloysius Club race held at Georgetown University in February 1925 and in the race sponsored by the *Washington Post* the following month.[10] The exclusion of African Americans from footraces in the first half of the twentieth century conformed to racial practices in DC sporting events and the capital's social scene more generally. African Americans, for example, were prohibited from taking part in an Amateur Athletic Union (AAU) boxing championship in the District in 1945.[11] Although DC avoided the more overt forms of racial intimidation and violence that was found throughout much of the South, racial segregation in the city nevertheless became more prominent during the early decades of the twentieth century. The District's nascent running culture reflected this fact.[12]

The formation of the District of Columbia Road Runners Club (DC RRC) in 1961 altered the character of local distance running. Sport historian Benjamin Rader has argued that in the 1970s and 1980s a "distinctive runners' culture emerged," which "revolved not only around running, but clubs, special diets, in-group understandings and behaviors, running magazines and books, running celebrities, and a flourishing equipment industry."[13] The DC RRC, however, predated this phenomenon. The central figure of the DC RRC was Hugh Jascourt, a former cross-country star at the University of Pennsylvania who helped organize a roadrunner club in Philadelphia in 1956. In 1959 he moved to Detroit to study law at Wayne State University. With the help of Wayne State track coach Frank McBride, Jascourt formed the Michigan Road Runners Club. After graduating from Wayne State, Jascourt moved to the nation's capital and began working as an attorney for the Department of Labor.[14] But he soon discovered that there were few long distance races in the District. To compete, he had to travel to Baltimore, Philadelphia, and New Jersey. DC did not host distance races, he surmised, because few people were interested in participating. He was determined to change that. In July 1961, he organized the DC RRC.[15]

The DC RRC immediately initiated a vigorous schedule of races and events that increased the opportunities for local distance runners. The highlight of the first season in 1961 was the Bunion Derby, a total of eight races between five and ten miles apiece (the name Bunion Derby recalled the famous coast-to-coast footraces in 1928 and 1929 that carried the same moniker). Points were given to runners who finished in the top twenty places for each race. Whichever competitor had the most points at the end of the eight-race series was declared the winner. As many as forty runners competed in the Derby's first year. The last year of the race, sixty-five contestants took part, the most of the series.[16] One distance running publication in 1961 credited Jascourt and the DC RRC with "the return of long distance running to Washington, D.C."[17]

In January 1962, the DC RRC began holding a different running series called Operation Snowball.[18] Like the Bunion Derby, Operation Snowball was a series of eight distance races in which runners earned points based on their finishing places. The series was held during January and February. Running outside in the dead of winter did not seem to bother DC RRC members. Jascourt was noted for saying, "we'll run where polar bears fear to tread." Operation Snowball culminated with a marathon on George Washington's Birthday. The race eventually became known as the George Washington Birthday Marathon (GWBM).[19] The inaugural GWBM in 1962 was the first full-length marathon held in the District since the AAU marathon championship in 1937.[20] Although Jascourt was disappointed that only seventeen runners participated, the GWBM signaled that competitive, long distance running in the District was back.[21]

The DC RRC was the organization most responsible for establishing a running culture in the nation's capital prior to the running boom of the 1970s. The club encouraged novice runners, children, and women to participate in the running craze. It held shorter, less-competitive, "run-for-your-life" races, in addition to more competitive events.[22] The club also hosted speakers who discussed the health benefits of running.[23] Though the DC RRC's efforts to encourage women runners may have been ineffective at times, the club did promote the notion that running had health benefits for all: old and young; men and women; fit, ex-college runners and recent converts who were relatively sedentary.[24] The DC RRC grew steadily, increasing from fifty members in 1962 to 450 a decade later.[25]

Features unique to the District impacted the formation of the local running culture. For example, DC RRC races always had many competitors who were active military personnel.[26] One explanation for such participation was the proximity of the Quantico Marine Base to the nation's capital. Results from DC RRC races in the 1960s reveal the regular appearance of Quantico Marines.[27] Federal employees, too, had a large presence.[28] College athletes were another group represented. Indeed, the character of the DC running culture was shaped by the fact that the Washington area was home to several universities. College athletes ran in many races, and the DC RRC had access to the schools' track facilities. The presence of these groups, along with the fact that African Americans tended to gravitate toward football, basketball, and, to a lesser extent, baseball, helps explain the apparent white and middle-class nature of DC's early running culture. But it is somewhat surprising that the local running community was almost exclusively white, given that there seems to have been no explicit barriers to African American participation, like those evident in the first half of the twentieth century.[29]

The USMC and Athletics

Although the United States military never created the highly structured and singularly purposed athletic programs found in many Eastern European countries during the Cold War, the four branches of the American military promoted competitive athletics among its members in a variety of sports.[30] The USMC, for example, encouraged the development of elite athletes—in track and field particularly—by providing them release time for training and competitions. Depending on individual circumstances, this commitment fluctuated. USMC officials also believed that athletic training was only a secondary concern. According to the USMC, a marine was expected to "fulfill his duties as a Marine first and train in his off-duty hours."[31] Thus time devoted to athletic training and competition varied. Nevertheless, there are numerous examples of highly successful athletes who after joining the marines continued to compete in international competitions: hurdler Josh Culbreath, distance runners Wes Santee and Billy Mills, and long jumper Randy Williams. Although the USMC began holding the Quantico Relays— an elite track and field invitational that included both military and collegiate track athletes—in 1956, the primary focus of USMC athletics has never been to develop world-class athletes. Instead, the main goal has been to "provide an opportunity for active participation of all personnel, regardless of skill or experience."[32]

The USMC has always had an interest in promoting physical fitness through athletic training and competition.[33] The USMC required soldiers to be physically fit and ready in body for combat. Boot camp was to serve this purpose prior to placement in the Corps. Providing both recreational and competitive athletic opportunities for soldiers was important to the promotion of physical fitness and a positive social environment. The purpose of the USMC's sports programs was to "maintain troop fitness and morale and to provide recreation for military dependents." Beginning in 1955, federal money was budgeted to establish sport and recreation activities at various levels in the marines.[34]

The Running Boom

In the early 1970s, distance running in the United States became a popular activity. In addition to the efforts of such clubs as the DC RRC, Frank Shorter's dramatic win in the marathon at the 1972 Munich Olympics—he was only the third American to have won the event—was a boon to running.[35] Because of Shorter, distance runners were no longer seen as eccentrics. He recalled that winning the Olympic marathon helped legitimize the sport. "Suddenly it was okay *to be a runner*, to train 2 and 3 hours a day," he remembered in his autobiography, *Olympic Gold: A Runner's Life and Times*. The "victory took the stamp of eccentricity off me."[36] After Shorter's triumph, an increasing number of Americans began running for fitness and competing in road races. Running clubs became commonplace in cities throughout the country, and distance races occurred almost every weekend in cities like New York, Chicago, and San Francisco. Already consisting of passionate members, the DC running community was well positioned to take advantage of the national running craze.

Because of the early efforts of such running devotees as Hugh Jascourt, DC had one of the most active and vibrant running communities in the country.[37] From 1972 to 1976, DC RRC membership jumped from 450 to more than 1,300. By the mid-1970s, more than a dozen smaller local clubs had joined the DC RRC.[38] One of the more popular races in the city was the Cherry Blossom Classic 10-Mile Race, which was first held in 1973. The brainchild of a local YMCA leader and DC RRC leader, Gar Williams, the Cherry Blossom Classic was sponsored by Acacia Insurance, which provided invaluable resources to promote the event, such as advertisements in running magazines like *Runner's World*.[39] The growth of the race was phenomenal. In 1973, there were 129 finishers. Five years later, the race had more than 2,200 participants.[40]

But shorter races did not grab as much publicity and media interest as the marathon, which took center stage as the running boom became more popular. In the 1970s, more cities started to host marathons, and the number of participants grew.[41] For example, the first year of the New York City Marathon, in 1970, had 127 competitors. In 1975 the race had more than 500. By 1976, the year the New York Road Runners Club moved the course from Central Park into the five boroughs, there were more than 2,000 runners. Two years later, there were 9,875.[42] Similarly, marathons in other cities—most notably Boston—experienced dramatic increases in participation. Marathons became a popular culture phenomenon. Throughout the 1970s, Americans Frank Shorter and Bill Rodgers were two of the sports' most celebrated stars. In fact, they were so admired that they established their own sports apparel lines. The MCM was born just as the marathon became an incredibly popular, mass-participatory event.

The Marine Corps Marathon

Although the running boom increased distance running opportunities and participation in the District by the mid-1970s, no new marathon had emerged in the city. The DC RRC continued to hold the GWBM. But the race was difficult on runners. Held in late February, the GWBM was notorious for its bad weather. It was also run on a mostly deserted and challenging course, which featured several hills. The 1972 race was contested in below-freezing temperatures with winds gusting up to nearly forty miles per hour. One hundred and seventy hearty souls started the race, but 112 registered runners skipped the event.[43] A writer for the *Washington Post* quipped in 1981 that the GWBW was "known as a race for true-blue runners. Lark seekers stay away."[44] Worse, the event was unappealing to spectators. Only those "with a life-or-death interest in one or more of the runners" came to watch the race, noted one journalist.[45]

The primary reason why the MCM was created was to improve the military's image. The race's founder, Colonel Jim Fowler, came up with the idea while he was recovering in the hospital from a leg wound he suffered in Vietnam.[46] Fowler recalled: "After the Vietnam War, popularity of the military services declined in the eyes of many. At the same time, distance running was gaining considerable positive attention."[47] Fowler believed that distance running could provide an excellent public relations opportunity. He also recognized that DC lacked a major marathon and "thought there was an opportunity for the Marine Corps to establish a race before someone else did."[48] Because the military had a long history of emphasizing participatory athletic competition and health and fitness for all service members, the USMC saw the MCM as an event that had "the value of publicity with an emphasis on fitness and good health."[49] Ever since the late 1950s, the marines had held the Quantico Relays at the nearby Quantico marine base. But in 1975, the USMC held its last Quantico Relays and shifted emphasis to the MCM.[50]

The MCM quickly became *the* marathon in the District. In 1976, the first year the MCM was held, 1,175 runners registered for the race. Of those, 1,018 finished, making it the third-largest marathon in the United States that year. Kenny Moore, a world-class distance runner who came in fourteenth and fourth at the 1968 and 1972 Olympic marathons, respectively, won the inaugural race.[51] More than 2,300 runners finished the second MCM.[52] While the press barely covered the first MCM, the *Washington Post* gave the second race a great deal more coverage, comparing it favorably to the Boston and New York City marathons, and bolstering its profile substantially.[53] By 1981, the MCM had 9,300 runners. Only the New York City Marathon had more entrants.[54]

It was during these early years that the MCM became known as "the People's Race." The *Washington Post* suggested in November 1977 that the

MCM "has suddenly become a 'people's race' which many think could blossom swiftly into national prominence."[55] Earlier, the *Post* had also called the Cherry Blossom Classic "a people's race," and a number of other marathons had been described the same way.[56] But with the MCM, the moniker remained. By the early 1980s, the MCM had secured its reputation as "the people's race." Jeff Darman, an executive at *Running Times*, remarked in 1980 that the MCM was "really designed for Joe-average runner."[57] Author and one-time Boston marathon winner Amby Burfoot commented that he "liked the concept of the [MCM]. It's not a star's race. It's a people's race."[58] The next year Bill Squires, a well-known elite distance coach, observed that the MCM makes "the average runner feel like this is his race and really, it is."[59]

The MCM was called the people's race primarily for two reasons. First, from the earliest days of the race, press coverage emphasized that the field was made up of a large percentage of first-time marathoners. More than 66 percent of runners in the second MCM had never run a marathon before. Although the MCM course is altered in minor ways on a regular basis, it is always scenic and flat, perfect for recreational runners and first-time marathoners. It starts at the Iwo Jima Memorial and goes past many of the most popular monuments, such as the Lincoln and Jefferson Memorials, the Capitol Building, and the Reflecting Pool, which many runners find inspiring.[60] Participants often refer to the MCM as "the run through the monuments."[61]

Second, and perhaps most important, the MCM has never paid athletes to compete. Nor has it ever provided prize money. This feature makes the race unique among big-city marathons. Races in Boston, New York, Chicago, and London have gained much publicity from paying the world's top runners. Interestingly, the nonpayment of athletes grew to become the primary philosophy of the MCM, though some in the USMC believed that the race would eventually attract world-class runners, much like the Boston Marathon did.[62] But paying athletes violated military policy—a point the *Post* conveyed to its readers in 1978, noting, "Department of Defense Code of Standards precludes commercial sponsorship or payment of expenses to runners."[63] The USMC created the race as a stand-alone event, which meant that all the money spent on the MCM came from the race itself, not the USMC budget. The money that other marathons would have spent to attract top runners was used by the MCM for race expenditures.[64] In the world of top-tier marathons, it was impossible to attract world-class international runners without appearance fees. MCM organizers, however, were able to turn an administrative limitation into a marketing bonanza by emphasizing the race's uniqueness. In six short years the MCM had created a niche for itself in the athletic world.

Although the MCM would eventually become one of the most efficiently staged marathons in the world, such was not the case in the early years of the race. In retrospect, the MCM's poor management at first was perhaps somewhat to be expected. The rapid growth of the race accentuated problems, and there was little opportunity to address issues, at least in a way that did not appear so glaringly. Also, because the Marine Corps Reserves, and not the USMC, which had access to far more resources, organized the MCM, the race during its initial years operated on a limited budget. Only in 1978, after the USMC took over the MCM, did finances cease to be a big concern. Perhaps most important, the MCM had no real experience in holding this type of event, and had little input from the local running community. Jeff Darman recalled that "[USMC organizers] were kind of doing their own thing."[65] Most other big-city marathons had emerged from local running communities, which usually meant organizers had some experience staging events for nonmilitary personnel. Colonel Jim Fowler, who directed the first two MCMs, remembered that "it was the first race I'd ever organized."[66] He also acknowledged that the marines were "new at" holding such large-scale athletic events. "In the military there's a manual for doing most things."[67] But there was no manual for putting on a marathon with thousands of participants. During the early years of the MCM, race organizers would make their share of mistakes.

The first five MCMs experienced numerous problems. One official described the "somewhat chaotic" inaugural MCM as a "comedy."[68] The race caused terrible traffic jams, which angered many Washingtonians.[69] The winner of the first race, Kenny Moore, ended up getting lost because the course had been poorly marked, and ran more than 26.2 miles. He also encountered several unmarked intersections.[70] Moore recalled that he "had never been more furious during a race. The marshals were very blase [sic]. They sent me to the Jefferson (Memorial) and after about a quarter-of-a-mile they said, 'Hey, you went the wrong way.' I screamed at the guy. At another place I was stopped to let traffic through." Moore began the race with the intention of winning it, but, as he remembered, "in the middle I almost quit. I was living nearby and it was a 10-minute jog to my house."[71] Though the course was changed for the second race, Washingtonians howled even louder over the "hopelessly congested" traffic caused by "an inexcusable lack of foresight."[72]

Management of the third MCM was transferred from the Marine Reserves to the USMC. The race had become too big an event for the Reserves.

Unfortunately, the race continued to have problems. The third MCM lacked water and cups at several aid stations. There were not nearly enough toilets. And medical help was poor. These were serious and dangerous problems. The running community openly criticized organizers for allowing the race to have such a large number of runners, especially after the previous MCMs had gone so poorly. In response, marine planners vowed to make future races better.[73] Nevertheless, a course-management problem marred the fifth MCM: More than 9,000 competitors had strayed from the course in four spots and ran less than 26.2 miles. After a lengthy investigation, race officials determined that the race was .3013 of a mile short. Understandably, runners were irate, particularly those who planned to use their results as qualifying times for the Boston Marathon. Embarrassed, the USMC scrambled to determine the exact length of the course that had been covered by short-changed participants. To obtain their equivalent 26.2-mile time, runners were told to multiply their short-course MCM finishing time by 1.012625.[74]

The sixth race in 1981 was the first MCM not to experience major problems. The winner of the race, Dean Matthews, a top-level marathoner with a personal best of 2:14:48, thought that the race was "one of the best organized races I've ever run in."[75] Running the MCM as his comeback race from a sciatic nerve injury, Matthews set a course record of 2:16:30. The time was not the only reason for celebration. In the words of race coordinator marine captain Rick Godale, the race went "exactly as planned."[76] In its coverage of the race, the press gladly emphasized the unique features of the MCM: that runners received no remuneration; that a large percentage of competitors were first-time marathoners; and that the course winded through the scenic setting of the nation's capital and passed several monuments. Race-winner Matthews commented, "The Marine Corps Marathon is a very unique race. It's the first time I've ever paid my own entry fee."[77] By 1981, the national press had embraced the MCM. Phil Stewart, editor of the Running Times, a national running magazine, called the MCM "a real mass-participation-type race." Organizers "don't pay to bring top runners in." The magazine editor gave the MCM an endorsement of sorts. "There always seems to be a large number of people who are running slow times," he said. "If you're running it in four or five hours, you're not going to be by yourself."[78]

Between 1982 and 2000 the profile of the MCM expanded and the number of runners continued to increase. Consequently, the MCM remained one of the largest marathons in the country. In addition to emphasizing the people's-marathon characteristics of the race, the press began underscoring the MCM's excellent organization. In 1986, Runner's World wrote that

Runners at the start of "the people's race" in 1979. Reprinted with permission of the DC Public Library, Star Collection, © Washington Post.

there was no other marathon in the world that attracted so many runners without having to pay stars. "Superb organization," the magazine noted, "is a hallmark of this race, not a surprise since the Marines treat this as an opportunity to exercise their logistical capabilities and put on a well-organized people's race."[79]

During the 1980s, the race began to experience the emergence of the celebrity-runner phenomenon, which increased the publicity of the race even more. A number of high-profile competitors from the running community regularly participated in the MCM, including longtime New York City marathon director, Fred LeBow, who competed in his first MCM in 1982. Following the race, LeBow had only positive things to say about the MCM. His enthusiasm would wane somewhat after he ran the MCM again, though he would always express great admiration for the beauty of the course.[80] In 1985, Jack Waitz, the husband of Grete Waitz, the most successful female marathoner in the world, ran the MCM. Grete accompanied him for the first few miles.[81] The general manager of the Washington Redskins, Bobby Beathard, ran the MCM a number of times in the 1980s.[82] National media stars Ted Koppel and Charles Gibson participated in 1983. And it only made sense that politicians would begin running the race as well. Among the politicians who competed in the MCM were Senator Steve Symms of Idaho, Vice President Al Gore, Representative Steve Buyer of Indiana, Senator John Edwards of North Carolina, and Representative Ray LaHood of Louisiana.[83] The MCM had become not just a race for the masses, but also one for the famous and powerful.

The race captured its ultimate celebrity participant when television talk show host Oprah Winfrey ran the MCM in 1994. Winfrey, one of the most famous people in America, had competed in a half-marathon the prior year. When MCM race director, Major Rick Nealis, heard Winfrey was planning to compete in the Chicago Marathon to celebrate her fortieth birthday, he contacted the media star and convinced her to run in the MCM instead. Winfrey was impressed with Nealis, the MCM's reputation as "the People's Race," and the ability of the USMC to assist in security. Perhaps most appealing to Winfrey was that almost 50 percent of the 16,000 entrants would be running their first marathon. The talk show host had never run a marathon before. Only Nealis and those close to him knew of Winfrey's plan to take part. A few days before the race, on her nationally broadcasted television show, Winfrey announced her intentions to participate in the MCM. Her presence created a media frenzy. It also created a greater need for security, which presented additional logistical challenges. Even though Winfrey had her own security detail during the race, several marines were assigned to surround and protect her prior to the start.[84] She completed the course without incident in 4:29:20. At the post-race press conference, Winfrey announced that finishing the marathon was "better than [winning] an Emmy." She told the media that the MCM was her "first and last marathon," adding, "Now that I have done a marathon, I feel like I can do anything."[85]

Winfrey's participation in the MCM ushered in a new phase of marathon growth. If Frank Shorter's 1972 Olympic marathon victory began a distance running boom that led to the first wave of marathon growth in the late 1970s and 1980s, Winfrey's efforts started a "second, more populous movement" that "motivated other first-timers to compete despite not having the prototype runner's body," according to journalist Liz Robbins.[86] The number of people competing in marathons increased in the wake of the 1994 MCM. Winfrey's efforts undergirded four basic attitudes about marathons that were taking shape: most anyone could do it; completing a marathon could change your life; running a marathon did not require as much training as was commonly thought; and the amount of time it took to finish did not matter.[87] Training programs for first-time marathoners, often associated with an ever-growing list of charity organizations, were closely associated with the post-Winfrey marathon running boom.[88]

Winfrey's participation highlighted an increased diversity in DC's distance running culture. Although it is difficult to assess, evidence suggests that African American participation in the MCM was higher than it had been in Washington's distances races during the 1960s and 1970s. Darrell General, an African American runner who grew up and lived in suburban DC, followed Winfrey's high-profile participation with wins at the 1995 and 1997 races. General had competed in the MCM four times (1983, 1984, 1985, and in 1987) before winning in 1995 and 1997. His best marathon time of 2:14:08 made him one of the fastest African American marathoners ever. General, who worked at Sear's in Maryland, epitomized the MCM ethos.[89] He was an excellent amateur runner during a time when winners of most big-city marathons were well-paid professionals. In the 1990s, pictures of runners at the MCM, and personal interest stories about African American competitors in newspapers, indicate that the race had become more racially diverse.[90]

The MCM underwent other important changes in the 1980s and 1990s. Perhaps the most important was the assignment of a civilian to coordinate the race. For many years, the position of MCM race coordinator had been assigned to an active-duty marine. Such an arrangement made little sense since each coordinator would move to another post after he gained the requisite experience. Constantly bringing in new race coordinators created instability and made it unlikely that the MCM's top administrator would be involved in the larger running community.

In 1993 Major Rick Nealis was assigned to be the MCM's race coordinator. Nealis had experience as both a runner and race director, having run three MCMs and overseen several shorter races. After Nealis's two-year stint as active-duty coordinator, he retired from the USMC and started a security company. One of his company's tasks was to guard the Olympic flame as it traveled around the country before the 1996 Atlanta Olympic Games. Shortly after the Olympics ended, Nealis was hired as the first civilian to direct the MCM. And he has directed it ever since, providing much-needed stability and leadership. Although the MCM still does not pay athletes to compete, Nealis began the process of acquiring commercial sponsors to help underwrite the race. He has also overseen increases in in-kind services from companies and organizations. In the mid-1990s, the cost of policing the event was almost nothing. The same service now costs as much as $800,000. To help with expenses, Nealis has courted corporate sponsors.[91] Companies that have been involved with the MCM include Chrysler, FILA, PowerBar and PowerGel, and Healthy Choice.[92]

Nealis also streamlined and modernized the management of the MCM. When he became race coordinator, runners were required to register by filling out a four-page bubble form. Not surprisingly, the error rate was high.[93] But under Nealis's leadership, the MCM has become much more efficient. It has adopted such technological innovations as online registration and the ChampionChip—computer chip technology that tracks runners during the race and provides more accurate finishing times.[94] Nealis has also greatly expanded events related to the MCM, such as the Expo, which was transformed from a little-celebrated Marine Corps Association affair into a hugely popular two-day, pre-race event in which runners pick up their race packets and shop for the latest shoes, clothing, and other running accessories.[95] One of the latest MCM innovations allows runners who are unable to compete to transfer their registration to another participant for a small fee.[96]

The MCM has expanded and now actually encompasses a variety of races, including a Turkey Trot 10K, a half marathon, and several shorter races for children. The MCM is more like an independent brand of race activities than a race in itself. It would be difficult to imagine these changes occurring without Nealis directing the race.[97]

The terrorist attacks of September 11, 2001, changed the MCM in a number of ways. The 2001 race was scheduled to occur on October 28. But several days after the attacks, it was still unclear if the race would even take place. Many runners were concerned for their safety. Moreover, it seemed insensitive to have the course wend its way past the still-damaged portion of the Pentagon. The Army 10-Miler, which was to be run earlier in October, had already been canceled. But less than three weeks after the attacks, Nealis announced that the race would be run, arguing that the event would make an important political statement: "We pledge our conviction to show the terrorists around the world that our spirit for freedom has never been stronger."[98] A good deal of additional security was brought in to ensure the safety of the runners.[99] Six separate police departments agreed to provide security, and the race was held with no problems. The character of the race, however, was altered. The portion of the course where participants passed the damaged Pentagon—between miles 4 and 6—provided the most introspective moments. Most runners stopped momentarily or walked.[100] The winner, retired gunnery sergeant Farley Simon, recalled: "[It] was amazing to see the Pentagon in person. As soon as we made that turn and the Pentagon came into view, I couldn't keep my eyes off of it."[101] It was the second time that the forty-six-year-old Simon won the MCM. Originally from Grenada, he won the MCM in 1983, when he sped to a 2:17:46 victory. He is the only active-duty male marine to have won the race.[102]

Patriotism has always undergirded the MCM. Hundreds of volunteer marines dressed in fatigues and cheering on runners encourages a love of country. Moreover, the course takes competitors past monuments that honor the most important political and military figures in American history. The race also includes a large number of participants from the military.[103] Since 1978, the MCM has served as the marathon championship for the Challenge Cup, a friendly team competition between Britain's Royal Marines and the USMC.[104] Trying to win the Cup stirs patriotic impulses.

But the 2001 race, which occurred weeks after the September 11 attacks and with participants running near the damaged Pentagon building, intensified patriotism even more. John Bingham, an Army veteran and writer for *Runner's World* who had planned on running only the first half of the race, completed the entire marathon because he "felt an unmistakable energy and unrelenting purpose surging through every Marine I encountered. This was not merely a race. This was a mission." Runners carried American flags and chanted, "USA, USA." For many participants, the race was therapeutic. Echoing director Nealis's sentiments for holding the 2001 race, army veteran Bingham said, "Our hearts may be broken, but our spirits are not."[105]

This heightened patriotism has become the hallmark of the MCM during the last ten years. Such feelings are reflected and encouraged by the high level of participation from veterans of the Afghanistan and Iraqi wars—particularly the wheelchair and hand-crank competitors who lost limbs in combat.[106] The close proximity of the Bethesda and Walter Reed Hospitals helps explain their participation.[107] While the actual percentage of military participants has declined over the years, their visibility has actually increased. At the 2005 race, for example, twenty-two members of Third Platoon, Charlie Company, Fourth Recon Battalion, Marine Reserve Unit, ran the race together—even though they had been back from serving in Iraq for only two weeks—to honor a battalion member who had been killed as well as two others who had been injured in combat. First Lieutenant Sean Barrett, who finished third at the 2010 MCM commented, "Wearing the Marine Corps Singlet at this race is a great honor. It's not lost on us that there are a lot of Marines deployed right now."[108] Many injured veterans or people running to honor relatives and friends killed in combat take part in the race.[109] In the past ten years, this patriotism has become an additional characteristic of the MCM. In fact, "the People's Race" could just as accurately be called "the Patriotic Race."

There has also been a noticeable increase in safety concerns at the MCM since the 2001 race. In the weeks preceding the 2002 MCM, the DC area was terrorized by a series of random sniper shootings. Nealis never seriously considered canceling the race, but he did increase security. The race director estimated that approximately 1,000 runners did not participate in the 2002 MCM because of safety concerns, even though the snipers were arrested two days before the race.[110] Homeland Security assisted in the security preparations for the 2004 MCM, which was run on Halloween. It was also held two days before the 2004 presidential election. According to Nealis, there were no specific threats prior to the 2004 race, but the event still required "more focus on safety and security—more than [the previous] year, more than [after] 9/11."[111] Nealis's primary concern has switched from "water and safety pins" to "safety, security, and force protection issues."[112] All big-city marathons face increased security concerns, but the location of the MCM makes it a larger target and heightens security issues. The tragic bombing of the Boston Marathon in 2013 illustrates how much marathons have become targets.

The MCM has settled comfortably into its niche in the running community. In 2006, more than 20,000 runners finished the race, making it the fourth-largest marathon in the United States and the seventh largest in the world. It is now universally known as "the People's Race" because it caters to average runners. What first seemed to be a limitation—that is, not paying elite runners—has become a major marketing asset and the primary characteristic of the MCM. Perhaps that is why the race is regularly rated as one of the top marathons. *Marathon and Beyond* in 2007 noted that although there have been "occasional problems, real and perceived, 'The People's Marathon' lives up to its name. The course is one of the most outstanding you will encounter on any continent, the fans are knowledgeable and are everywhere except Hains Point to encourage and cheer your efforts, and the organization is one of the best you will find anywhere."[113] What began as an attempt to alter the public image of the USMC in the post-Vietnam era has grown into a staple on the marathon calendar.

Still, some argue that the race could be much more. The marathons that compete for the top runners in the world attract far more publicity because of their elite fields. Jim Hage, who was the first person to win back-to-back MCMs, in 1988 and 1989, has been a mainstay in the DC running community for decades and one of the most successful local marathoners to call the Washington area home. He has also competed in marathons on five continents. He has said that "the Marine Corps Marathon is easily" his favorite. Even so, he has argued that catering to everyday runners and having a world-class field are not mutually exclusive. "The MCM is famous around the world," he said in 2005, "but it's not a world-class event" because of its policy of not doling out prize money to lure top runners.[114] Unless "race officials deviate from their long-standing policy of keeping the event strictly amateur, the marathon will be viewed nationally more as a curio than competition."[115]

The MCM is still the only big-city marathon that does not pay appearance fees or offer prize money. And critics are correct in stating that top runners will never compete in the MCM until they are compensated. But these critics seem to be missing the point—in the same way that NYC Marathon director Fred LeBow had done in 1989 when he looked at the MCM as a missed opportunity. The MCM has garnered so much attention precisely because of its "uniqueness." Marketing professionals might call it the race's brand. But the brand was not deliberately created. Nor was it developed in some Madison Avenue boardroom. It evolved naturally—based on the ethos of the USMC and grounded in the DC running culture.

15

Georgetown Basketball in Reagan's America

Zack Tupper

"Patrick, you're scaring me to death," *Sports Illustrated* photographer Lane Stewart announced nervously in the White House Map Room. Patrick Ewing, a seven-foot-tall basketball player, glared back. He wore a gray jersey with "Georgetown" emblazoned in blue letters across his chest. Tension filled the room. Soon President Ronald Reagan would arrive to be photographed with Ewing and Georgetown University's coach, John Thompson Jr. *Sports Illustrated* planned to use the picture for the cover of an upcoming issue—the magazine's first featuring a sitting president. But as he made final adjustments to his lights and camera, Stewart wondered if Ewing would even crack a smile as he posed with his coach next to Reagan.[1]

Thompson, Ewing, and the rest of the Georgetown basketball team had met with the president at the White House shortly after they won their first national championship on April 2, 1984. Reagan congratulated the victorious Hoyas at a press conference held on the Rose Garden lawn. He even commended Thompson for helping the majority of his players earn their diplomas.[2] The *Sports Illustrated* photo shoot, however, which occurred six months later, began with a more frigid reception.

On November 12, 1984, Ewing arrived at the White House front gate, only to be denied entrance. The sole piece of ID he had was his jersey. A security guard eventually recognized the college basketball sensation and allowed him and coach Thompson, who had accompanied Ewing, to proceed inside. Perhaps Ewing refused to smile while waiting for Reagan because he felt snubbed. After all, he was the star player of what many considered the best amateur team in the nation. More, he had also won the "Most Outstanding Player" award in that year's NCAA tournament, which was quickly becoming one of the most popular televised sporting events in the country. When Reagan finally did enter the Map Room, he immediately set Ewing at ease by unsuccessfully spinning a basketball on his own finger.[3]

Thompson stood nearby. He was an imposing figure, nearly seven feet tall, and had a deep baritone voice that punctuated his sharp, sometimes profane tongue. Provocative and intimidating, Thompson never shied away from speaking his mind. Leonard Shapiro, a former sports editor for the *Washington Post*, once described Thompson as "a lightning rod for controversy."[4] On the court Thompson's players mirrored this confrontational style, smothering opponents with unrelenting defensive pressure. To the Hoyas' detractors, which included several sportswriters, Thompson and his majority black team were nothing more than a brawling group of thugs.

But Georgetown also had its share of supporters, and not just on the university's campus. African Americans in Thompson's hometown of Washington, DC, and beyond rallied behind the team, proudly wearing clothes with Georgetown's name and logo. For these fans, Thompson and his players were icons of black success and defiance during a period of racial regression. In the 1980s, many African Americans suffered from deplorable inner-city conditions, exacerbated by a devastating crack cocaine epidemic. Reagan's failure to address such urban decline fueled the impression that he cared little for such ongoing challenges faced by black Americans.

Reading stereotypes of his team in newspapers and watching the decline of the very neighborhoods he grew up in, Thompson himself confronted persisting problems stemming from race relations during the Reagan years. And he did so on his own terms, defying his critics—both on and off the court. He was a foil to Reagan's America, under which many of the coach's most loyal fans struggled. Ironically, Thompson embodied a rejection of the very president whom he and Ewing would be flanking on the cover of *Sports Illustrated*.

The seeds of that meeting between President Reagan and the Hoyas were sown almost sixteen years earlier. On April 4, 1968, civil unrest erupted in cities nationwide following the assassination of Dr. Martin Luther King Jr. In the District of Columbia, rioting blacks torched buildings and looted businesses for four straight days. The nation watched in horror as the mayhem came within blocks of the White House. To quell the violence, President Lyndon Johnson placed federal troops in the nation's capital. The destruction would be extensive: twelve dead and $25 million in property damage. It was one of the bloodiest weeks in the history of the city. An indelible psychological and physical scar was left. Georgetown University, too, would never be the same.

Following the 1968 riots, officials at Georgetown looked to bridge longstanding racial divides between their overwhelmingly white campus and the rest of the city's majority black population. University authorities implemented a Community Scholars program to identify and prepare local minority students for entrance to Georgetown. They also looked to attract young black athletes, particularly those steeped in DC's rich legacy of basketball, which dated back to 1907 when a young Harvard-trained physical education teacher named Edwin Bancroft Henderson—later known as the "Grandfather of Black Basketball"—introduced the sport to African Americans in the city. Casually organized but highly competitive games soon became a fixture of playgrounds across the District. Although some of the nation's most talented players grew up on those courts, few, if any, seriously considered playing for Georgetown's struggling basketball program.[5]

During the 1971–72 basketball season, Georgetown lost twenty-three games, including each of the sixteen they played on the road, and won only three contests—the worst record in the history of the school's basketball program, which dated back to 1906. Many at Georgetown blamed coach Jack Magee. At games, several fans waved signs that read, "Magee Must Go."[6]

Accepting the inevitable, Magee submitted his letter of resignation about a month before the final game against Boston College.[7] Georgetown's dean of admissions, Charles Deacon, chaired a committee of professors, students, and alumni tasked with identifying Magee's replacement. As they evaluated potential candidates, the search committee looked for more than just impressive basketball credentials. What they needed was a coach who could demonstrate the university's commitment to blacks in DC. They needed John Thompson Jr.[8]

Born in DC in 1941, Thompson grew up in Anacostia, the city's poor southeastern section, at a time when racial segregation loomed menacingly over the nation. At an early age, Thompson saw how sports could serve as a vehicle for breaking through racial barriers. He rooted for the Cleveland Indians and their outfielder Larry Doby, who, along with Jackie Robinson, crossed the color line in professional baseball. Thompson also had a love for basketball, a sport that would release him from the shackles of Jim Crow and propel him to national fame.

By his thirteenth birthday, Thompson stood over six and a half feet tall and showed early promise as a basketball player in pick-up games on neighborhood courts. In 1957, he accepted a $200 scholarship to play for Archbishop John Carroll, a predominately white, working-class Catholic high school in Northeast DC. There, Thompson helped the Carroll Lions win fifty-five consecutive games and two city championships. After graduating from high school, Thompson secured another scholarship to attend Providence College, where he led the Friars to a National Invitation Tournament (NIT) title. As a senior at Providence, he shot nearly 60 percent from the field and averaged an impressive 26.2 points and 14.5 rebounds per game. By that point, Thompson was considered to be one of the top college prospects for the National Basketball Association (NBA).[9]

The NBA's Boston Celtics signed Thompson shortly after he earned his college diploma in 1964. (A territorial rule gave the Celtics priority over drafting Thompson due to his alma mater's proximity to Boston.) Thompson watched mostly from the bench as the Celtics won two straight titles, continuing a streak of consecutive championships begun in 1959 under legendary coach Red Auerbach. As a backup to Bill Russell, whose arrival in 1956 inaugurated the era of Celtics dominance, Thompson practiced alongside and learned from one of the greatest centers of all time. With his incredible speed, timing, and athleticism, Russell was a prolific shot blocker who revolutionized the center position. And people knew it. Sportswriters often billed a promising center as "the next Bill Russell." During his college days, Thompson even received the label.[10]

After playing just two seasons with the Celtics, Thompson chose to retire rather than be traded to the expansion Chicago Bulls. He and his wife, Gwen, returned to the District with their three-month-old son, John Thompson III. Back in his hometown, Thompson mentored youths, and within a year he was back on the bench, this time as a coach for St. Anthony's High School. In 1972, while Georgetown finished its worst season ever, Thompson was coaching one of the best high school teams in the city. Under his tutelage, St. Anthony's amassed a record of 128 wins and only 22 losses.[11]

Thompson seemed to offer everything Georgetown was looking for in Coach Magee's replacement. From high school and college championships to professional titles in the NBA, Thompson had prevailed at every level of basketball; as coach at St. Anthony's, he had already gained the admiration of local players. Moreover, the black community in DC deeply respected Thompson, a coach with strong local roots. After all, he had sacrificed a professional career to help children from the very neighborhood he grew up in.

On March 13, 1972, Thompson signed a four-year contract with Georgetown. The signing was the university's strongest effort to reach out to blacks in DC since the 1968 riots. At the press conference announcing Thompson's hiring, Georgetown president Father Robert Henle cited Thompson's "proven ability as a coach, manager, inspirer, and leader of young people."[12] The reaction on the Georgetown campus was overwhelmingly favorable. The president of Georgetown's Black Student Alliance later commented, "I think the addition of Mr. Thompson to the University administration will definitely increase good relations with the D.C. community."[13]

Thompson's hiring fit into a larger effort by administrators to transform Georgetown from a small parochial school into a university of both national and international repute. Few, though, could have foretold how dramatically Thompson's presence would increase Georgetown's fortunes. Many believed he would coach the Hoyas to an occasional NIT appearance. Thompson, however, had bigger aspirations: winning the more competitive and prestigious NCAA tournament. At the time of his hiring, a confident Thompson promised, "[A] national championship flag will fly [at Georgetown]."[14]

To fulfill that pledge, Thompson needed top-notch players. He knew exactly where to find them. The first six players he brought to Georgetown all hailed from DC. Together, they added size, speed, and talent. Five were African American, including four who came from St. Anthony's.[15] These initial recruits represented a major change for the program. To be sure, blacks had played for Georgetown before 1972, but never in the numbers that Thompson recruited. With his first recruiting class, Thompson immediately demonstrated his intention to assemble teams made up of skilled African Americans from DC and other inner cities.

Some of the most sought-after high school recruits would sign letters of intent to play for Thompson. Derrick Jackson, a standout athlete from Illinois, came to Georgetown in 1974. In his freshman season, he sank a twenty-foot jump shot in the waning seconds of a game against the University of West Virginia, helping the Hoyas to their first NCAA tournament appearance in more than three decades. John Duren and Craig "Big Sky" Shelton both joined Georgetown in 1976 from Dunbar High, a powerhouse in DC, and helped the Hoyas to several postseason tournaments. Eric "Sleepy" Floyd, one of the most prolific players ever to don a Georgetown jersey, came two years later, and would go on to become the university's all-time leading career scorer with 2,304 points.

Beyond Thompson's blue chip recruits, a key factor in building the team's reputation was its domination in the Big East conference. Founded in 1979, the Big East consisted of Georgetown, Boston College, Providence, Seton Hall, St. John's, Syracuse, and the University of Connecticut. Later,

John Thompson, with his signature towel, walks past the Georgetown
bench in February 1979. Reprinted with permission of the
DC Public Library, Star Collection, © Washington Post.

Villanova and the University of Pittsburgh joined. Fierce competition and
bruising basketball came to define the conference. Its teams were among the
best in the nation.[16]

During the Big East's inaugural season, a storied rivalry was cemented
between Georgetown and Syracuse. On February 13, 1980, the two teams
played the last game Syracuse would host at Manley Field House, where the
Orangemen looked to continue a record fifty-seven-game winning streak.
But the Hoyas spoiled their night, winning 52–50, mostly due to Big Sky
Shelton's game-high 17 points and Sleepy Floyd's two free throws at the end

of the game. "Manley Field House is officially closed," Coach Thompson said afterward, adding insult to injury for Syracuse fans.[17] Georgetown then went on to win both the Big East regular-season title and postseason tournament, thus establishing itself as one of the premier conference's most successful programs.

Such success helped Thompson attract the coveted high school star, Patrick Ewing. On February 2, 1981, before a crowd of more than two hundred people assembled in Boston, Ewing read from a prepared statement: "After considering all the facts, my decision is to attend Georgetown University." Ewing had immigrated to America from Jamaica in 1975. By his senior year at Cambridge Ridge and Latin High School in Boston, he was considered the best high school player in the country. Coaches from outstanding college programs across the country heavily recruited the seven-footer.[18]

"The main reason I chose to go to Georgetown was definitely John Thompson," Ewing later acknowledged.[19] Ewing also cited Thompson's emphasis on education and familiarity with the center position; Georgetown's location in the predominately black city of Washington, DC; and the chance to compete in the rising Big East conference.[20] With Ewing on the team, Georgetown began to draw huge crowds. The university had to move their home games from McDonough Gymnasium—its small on-campus arena— to the Capital Centre in Landover, Maryland, which could accommodate nearly 20,000 spectators. Georgetown was abuzz as the Hoyas stormed into the 1980s with the best college player in the nation on their roster.

At the end of Ewing's freshman season, the Hoyas played in their first NCAA championship game, against the University of North Carolina. The game ended with one of the most memorable moments in the history of college basketball. Georgetown was behind by one point with less than thirty seconds left when Hoya guard Fred Brown, mistaking UNC's James Worthy for a teammate, accidentally passed him the ball. But Worthy, who scored a game-high 28 points, missed both of his free throw attempts after being fouled. With mere seconds showing on the game clock, there was no time for a final play, and Georgetown lost, 63–62. A star freshman named Michael Jordan had made what turned out to be the game-winning shot. Georgetown players were crushed. Like a father embracing his son, Thompson hugged Brown at the end of the game, consoling the player whose errant pass dashed his team's chance of winning its first national title.[21]

Just across Rock Creek Park, Republican president Ronald Reagan was suffering from his own set of recent losses. During the midterm elections the previous November, Democrats had gained twenty-seven seats in the US House, giving them the majority. As if that were not enough, Reagan's job approval rating had sunk to 35 percent. In 1982, national unemployment exceeded 10 percent—the highest level since the Great Depression. Nine million Americans were out of work. Many blamed Reagan. Few believed he could win reelection in 1984.[22]

The midterm congressional elections in 1982 were seen as an immediate referendum on the course Reagan had charted during his first year in office. The country had swept him into the White House largely because of widespread disenchantment with the malaise of Jimmy Carter's presidency. Under Carter, "stagflation" had crippled the nation's economy, and the Iran Hostage Crisis further threatened America's global supremacy following the war in Vietnam. To recover the nation's footing, Reagan advocated for supply-side tax cuts for the wealthy, an end to government programs that he believed were wasteful, and a vast increase in military spending. Not surprisingly, Speaker of the House Tip O'Neil and other Democratic leaders on Capitol Hill eyed Reagan's tax and budget proposals with great skepticism. The newly elected president had yet to convince the other side of the aisle.

In the midst of this political tug of war, tragedy suddenly struck. On March 30, 1981, a mentally disturbed loner named John W. Hinckley waited in the drizzle outside the Washington Hilton Hotel in Dupont Circle, carrying a .22 caliber pistol. As President Reagan exited the building with security and staff, Hinckley aimed his weapon and fired six shots. Hysteria ensued. Police and Secret Service agents tackled the deranged gunman while Reagan was whisked off to the hospital. One of the bullets had ricocheted off the presidential limousine and lodged in Reagan's chest, nearly taking his life.[23]

During his recovery, Reagan's approval rating shot up to 70 percent. His advisors suggested that he seize the opportunity to gain congressional support to pass his economic policies. On April 28, 1981, less than a month after the attempted assassination, Reagan received a standing ovation as he delivered a televised address to Congress. "The answer to a Government that is too big is to stop feeding its growth," the president announced. By the end of the summer, he had signed both his tax and budget bills into law. Marginal tax rates on the wealthy fell from 70 to 50 percent, while the poorest Americans suffered.[24]

The vast majority of the $35.2 billion in budget cuts that Reagan signed fell on social programs for the disadvantaged. His 1981 budget scaled back or stripped Aid to Families with Dependent Children (AFDC) benefits from 687,000 households. More than one million Americans lost food stamps. School lunch prices rose. Extended benefits ended for 1.5 million unemployed. Residents in the District suffered the highest per capita cut of $682.[25] The budget cuts represented a dramatic turnaround from the expansion of social programs following World War II. Coupled with Reagan's tax cuts for the wealthy, the reductions codified conservatives' controversial supply-side—or "trickle-down"—economic theory, which held that wealth would flow downward to the poor, particularly to disadvantaged minorities.

On several occasions, Reagan employed racially divisive stereotypes to make his case for slashing government programs. He told the following anecdote in 1976, during his failed bid for the Republican presidential nomination, and again in 1981 and 1982:

> There's a woman in Chicago. She has 80 names, 30 addresses, 12 Social Security cards and is collecting veterans' benefits on four nonexisting deceased husbands . . . She's got Medicaid, getting food stamps and she is collecting welfare under each of her names. Her tax-free cash income alone is over $150,000.[26]

A woman named Linda Taylor was the forty-seven-year-old welfare recipient behind Reagan's largely embellished story. He never said her name or race—Taylor was African American—but Reagan's critics accused the president of pandering to racist white voters who undoubtedly envisioned the so-called welfare queen as a black woman.[27] After all, a significant reason for Reagan's electoral success was his ability to consolidate support among traditional Democratic white voters in the South—where Republicans sought to capitalize on President Richard Nixon's "southern strategy" of the late 1960s—and among blue-collar white and ethnic voting blocs in the North. Many of these "Reagan Democrats" felt increasingly abandoned by their party in the 1960s and 1970s because of its support for government spending, especially for programs meant to uplift poor minorities. Reagan successfully tapped into such dissatisfaction by perpetuating the stereotype of a fraudulent welfare queen. It was not the first time he had marginalized black America. Nor would it be the last.

Early in his political career, Reagan had opposed the 1964 Civil Rights Act and the Voting Rights Act of 1965—both landmark pieces of civil rights legislation. In 1964 he also supported Proposition 14, which sought to overturn the Rumford Fair Housing Act, an antidiscrimination law in California's public housing sector. During his successful run for California governor against Democrat Edmund "Pat" Brown in 1966, Reagan's critics equated his anti-civil rights positions to racism. When Reagan heard the charge during a primary debate in front of a group of black voters, he angrily replied: "I resent the implication that there is any bigotry in my nature," and then stormed off.[28]

Reagan's antagonism toward the civil rights community continued into his presidency. The most striking example occurred in 1983, when he opposed the effort to create a federal holiday honoring Martin Luther King Jr. Reagan sided with North Carolina senator and former segregationist Jesse Helms, who led the fight against the holiday. Helms charged that Dr. King had communist sympathies and demanded that his sealed FBI files be opened. Mounting congressional pressure to honor MLK proved too great, and Reagan eventually capitulated. But that did not stop him from defending Helms. Weeks before signing the King holiday into law, Reagan told a reporter, referring to Helms's accusations, "We'll know in about 35 years, won't we?"[29]

Even though Reagan praised Dr. King for relieving America from "the burden of racism," he likened efforts to improve racial equality and integration to "reverse discrimination."[30] The nation had been freed from racism, the president argued; events like the 1968 riots were behind us. Using this logic, conservatives attacked antidiscrimination legislation that they believed gave preferential treatment to one group of people over another. But their reasoning belied the reality for much of black America that Dr. King's long march toward civil rights was far from over.

Had Reagan attended several Georgetown basketball games, he would have seen the racism that continued to plague the country. On January 31, 1983, for instance, Georgetown faced a hostile crowd in Philadelphia during a game against Villanova. As the announcer called Patrick Ewing's name during opening introductions, someone flung a banana peel onto the court. Another person wore a shirt that read: "Ewing Kant Read Dis." From the bench, Coach Thompson saw a group holding a sign with the despicable message: "Ewing is an Ape." Five days earlier, during another away game against his alma mater Providence, Thompson had pulled his team off the court until a sign announcing "Ewing Can't Read" was removed.[31]

Such abhorrent displays were meant to distract Ewing from the game at hand. Some observers believed that such attacks stemmed from resentment over Ewing's choosing Georgetown over other universities, particularly those in the Boston area, where Ewing had played high school basketball. Others saw it as sheer bigotry. "It's cheap racist stuff," Georgetown president Father Timothy Healy told the *Washington Post*. Thompson also took issue with the slurs directed at Ewing, warning, "Sooner or later these kinds of things will cause a riot."[32]

Thompson himself had confronted racism on the court throughout his life. In high school, slurs were shouted at him and the other black players at Archbishop Carroll. (So entrenched were racial attitudes that even DC's summer leagues at that time were segregated.) In 1975, at a home game in McDonough Gym, several Georgetown students unfurled a banner that read: "Thompson, the Nigger Flop Must Go." The hateful banner was seen by a group of local African American children Thompson had invited to watch the game. Thompson had hoped to show them a more hopeful glimpse of college life.[33]

The racism directed at Ewing was all the more striking because it occurred so openly in post–civil rights America, at a time when President Reagan was asserting that the country had been freed from such bigotry. Dr. Harry Edwards, an expert on the relationship between race and athletics, said: "[I]n 1983, for people to be throwing bananas on the floor, to be calling out these ugly racial epithets, I think it's unconscionable."[34]

Georgetown also faced opposition from several sportswriters. Thompson, in particular, had a strained relationship with the media, and defied the press by limiting access to his team and denying interviews. Sportswriters like Curry Kirkpatrick—one of the Hoyas' more notorious critics—believed that Georgetown had something to hide, which he derided as "Hoya Paranoia."[35] The press generally found Thompson combative and surly. Many highlighted his imposing figure and frequent use of colorful language, often casting him as a scowling, big angry black man. One reporter even referred to Thompson as "the Idi Amin of Big East Basketball," weaving a dubious analogy between Georgetown's coach and Uganda's infamous genocidal dictator.[36]

Complementing Thompson's confrontational demeanor was the bruising style of basketball he coached. His teams were known for their suffocating defense. To force turnovers, his players harassed opponents all over the court. An opposing player would often find himself "double teamed," desperately scanning for an open teammate through the outstretched arms of two Hoyas. When the ball was loose, Georgetown players scrambled on the floor after it. When an opponent attempted a shot, the Hoyas challenged him—either with a hand in his face or by swatting the ball away from the basket. And when missed shots rattled off the rim, Patrick Ewing and Georgetown's big men "crashed the boards," aggressively snatching rebounds.

Georgetown thus epitomized the brawling basketball that defined the Big East in the 1980s. The conference was known for heated games in which players routinely jabbed one another with elbows while jockeying for position. Punches were thrown on a few occasions. By the end of the decade, the Big East enacted stricter penalties for unsportsmanlike conduct following a bench-clearing fight between the Hoyas and Pittsburgh.[37]

Michael Graham, whom Kirkpatrick called Georgetown's "glowering hatchet man," was at the center of several scuffles.[38] A native of DC, Graham played for Georgetown during the 1983–84 season. Sportswriters portrayed Graham as a hostile individual whose menacing looks and signature shaved head frightened opposing teams. Sometimes it was warranted. In the 1984 Big East championship game, for example, Graham took a violent swipe at Syracuse's Andre Hawkins. That same year, during a regional final game against the University of Dayton in the NCAA tournament, Graham dunked the ball, turned around, and shoved Dayton's Sedric Toney to the floor. After Graham was assessed a foul, the television announcer offered his own observation: "This is where Georgetown gets accused by many of being a bunch of thugs."[39]

The Hoyas intimidated opponents with their hardnosed style of play. "[Georgetown] completely destroys people, and, yeah, they scare the hell out of you," Lou Carnessecca, who coached St. John's, another of Georgetown's Big East rivals during the 1980s, once said. But the media's description of the Hoyas as thuggish—what Kirkpatrick called their "leather-jackets-and-chains-image"—struck many as a racially charged accusation directed at a predominately black team whose players came from the inner city.[40]

What made the racial implications of Kirkpatrick's portrayal of Georgetown all the more glaring was his positive treatment of Chris Mullin, a white player who starred for St. John's from 1981 to 1985. "Mullin is a glorious throwback to the old days before hang time, when Caucasians got by on guile and guts and something known as ball handling," Kirkpatrick wrote. "[Mullin] has worked and worked. And then worked some more. His ICBM (Irish Catholic Basketball Mind) and work ethic are such that he can hardly stop working."[41] According to Kirkpatrick and others, Mullin was successful because of his intelligence and work ethic, while the Hoyas won because they scared opponents with the same rough, undisciplined play that could be found on city playgrounds.

Thompson frequently challenged this double standard. "We play basketball and we play aggressively," he told reporters in 1984. "If Chris Mullin hustles, he's tough. If [Georgetown's] Gene Smith hustles, he's dirty."[42] Four years earlier Thompson offered an even more candid response to the depiction of his team as undisciplined: "that means nigger. They're all big and fast and can leap like kangaroos and eat watermelon in the locker room."[43]

As the Hoyas faced heated criticism in the press, the Georgetown community rallied behind its team. The university's president Father Healy authored perhaps the most impassioned defense, which the *Washington Post* published in late March 1984—a day before the Hoyas defeated the University of Kentucky in the first round of the Final Four. Healy's editorial was titled "Hoya Paranoia," a phrase he took issue with and which the media repeatedly used to disparage Georgetown. "[M]any of the charges thrown at [Thompson] lie along the fault line in American society, its racism. A totally successful black man who succeeds in his own way and on his own terms in this competitive world is hard for many white Americans to swallow."[44]

Three days after Healy's article, Georgetown played the University of Houston in front of a capacity crowd of 38,471 at the Kingdome in Seattle for the national championship. It featured a classic matchup: Ewing and the Hoyas against Akeem Olajuwon, another seven-footer, and the rest of the so-called Phi Slama Jama, Houston's roster of players with incredible dunking ability. The real difference in the game, though, proved to be the depth of Georgetown's bench, which outscored the Cougars' substitutes, 33–13. Georgetown freshman Reggie Williams, a graduate of Dunbar High School in Baltimore, scored 19 points. Michael Graham added 14, including several thunderous dunks. Although Houston guard Alvin Franklin scored a game-high 21 points, the Cougars were unable to keep up, in large part because Olajuwon had picked up some early fouls. As the final buzzer sounded, Thompson embraced Fred Brown, just as he had done at the end of Georgetown's emotional loss to North Carolina in 1982. This time, however, they were celebrating. The Hoyas had won their school's first NCAA tournament, 84–75. Thompson became the first black coach to win a Division I national basketball title. He returned home to DC, having fulfilled a promise he made in 1972: a national championship banner was flying at Georgetown.[45]

The championship touched off celebrations across the District. Georgetown students chanted "Hoyas!" as they took to the streets following the game. The elation was far from limited to the university's predominately white campus. Throughout the city, many blacks also cheered on their hometown team, which included three players from local high schools. At a rally in DC five days later, Mayor Marion Barry cried out, "The Hoyas are number one!" The crowd shouted back: "The District is number one! The fans in the District of Columbia are number one!"[46]

Ronald Reagan was also victorious that year, having won reelection in a landslide on November 6, 1984. He swept forty-nine states, defeating Democrat Walter Mondale, with 525 electoral votes—the most any American presidential candidate had claimed up to that point—and he won 59 percent of the popular vote.[47] Reagan only lost Mondale's home state of Minnesota and the District of Columbia. But among black voters, Reagan's victory was far from overwhelming: nearly nine out of ten had cast their ballots for the Democratic ticket.[48] During the election, the Reagan campaign claimed in one of its more memorable television ads, "It's morning again in America." However, such optimism failed to resonate with the vast majority of black Americans, especially in Coach Thompson's hometown, which continued to struggle during Reagan's second term.

Only blocks from the White House, and not far from the Georgetown campus, DC residents saw their neighborhoods ripped apart by declining social conditions. A chief reason for this was the increasing availability of cheap and highly addictive crack cocaine. Gangs peddled massive quantities of crack on neighborhood street corners. Violent crime soared to record levels. By the time Reagan left office, the city had the highest murder rate in the country, earning DC the infamous sobriquet as the nation's "murder capital."[49] In 1988, 60 percent of the homicides in the District were drug related—a statistic that demographers did not even record for the city at the outset of Reagan's presidency.[50] DC epitomized the urban decay that was wreaking havoc in many American cities during the 1980s.

Reagan signed legislation to combat this growing drug problem after the highly publicized cocaine overdose of University of Maryland standout and NBA-bound Len Bias in 1986. The Anti-Drug Abuse Act was especially punitive for poor blacks. Under its mandatory sentencing guidelines, a defendant in possession of 5 grams of crack could face the same minimum prison term if they had been arrested with 500 grams of more expensive powder cocaine. This resulted in the disproportionate imprisonment of blacks since crack use was particularly rampant in impoverished minority communities. By 1990 more African American men would be in prison than in college. Coupled with First Lady Nancy Reagan's largely ineffectual "Just Say No" campaign, Reagan's drug policies proved disastrous for African Americans.[51]

A ruthless drug kingpin named Rayful Edmond III was at the center of much of the violence in DC. On April 17, 1989, federal agents and local police arrested Edmond and sixteen of his associates. They were charged with committing thirty homicides and distributing cocaine and crack in excess of 200 kilograms per week in the city—roughly equivalent to 20 percent of the city's drug trade.[52] Fearing reprisals from Edmond loyalists, the judge ordered that jurors' names be kept secret—the first anonymous jury in DC's criminal history.[53]

Like many Washingtonians, Edmond was a diehard fan of the Hoyas. He befriended two of Georgetown's starting players: Alonzo Mourning and John Turner. Federal investigators had even spotted him entertaining Mourning and Turner at a local nightclub.[54] After learning of Edmond's association with his players, Thompson "sent word out on the street" that he wanted to speak with Edmond. Thompson reportedly told the drug dealer to stay away from his team and Edmond complied. Although it remains unclear exactly what was said during their conversation, the encounter illustrates the level of respect that Thompson commanded in the District, even among its most hardened criminals. Thompson had stared down perhaps the biggest threat to African Americans in his hometown during the Reagan years.

Against this backdrop of drug abuse and urban decay, younger generations of blacks identified with hip-hop. The brash cultural movement sprouted out of minority communities in New York City in the 1970s, taking hold across the country during the following decade. The arrival of go-go music in DC paralleled its rise, but hip-hop enjoyed more widespread appeal. Adherents of hip-hop expressed a defiant attitude through their music, dress, and aesthetic appetites. They also took aim at Reagan, holding the president responsible for the decline of their neighborhoods.[55]

Carlton Ridenhour was one such critic. As a student at Adelphi University in New York in the early 1980s, Ridenhour caricatured Reagan as the villainous "President Pruneface" in a running comic he drew called "Tales of the Skind." In one installment, superheroes kidnap the president and force him to look at the homeless on America's streets. "Come President Pruneface and view the scenery of a vast economic wasteland," one kidnapper demands. "There, countless individuals down and out, because of your budget errors and unfulfilled promises."[56] By the end of the decade, Ridenhour would become known across the country as the rapper Chuck D, cofounder of the pioneering and Grammy-nominated hip-hop group, Public Enemy.

At the same time that Chuck D criticized Reagan, he and other minority youths also embraced the Hoyas. "Not only was this a team full of black players who would definitely take it to you," Chuck D said of Georgetown's significance. "[Y]ou had a big-ass black man as a coach who wasn't taking no shit. That was big." The Public Enemy front man also drew inspiration from players like Ewing. "Patrick Ewing influenced hip-hop heavily. Just with defiance, it was that swagger for real," he said.[57] The Hoyas' brazen image meshed perfectly with the aggressive attitude of hip-hop.

Blue and gray satin Georgetown jackets made by the Starter Clothing Company were especially trendy among the burgeoning hip-hop culture.

Chuck D even imagined forming the "Georgetown Gangsters," a rap group whose members all wore the coveted Starter jacket.[58] Youths in DC and other cities who wanted to keep up with the latest hip-hop fashion prized apparel bearing the Hoyas' name and logo. Such gear made a strong statement about the person who wore it. Darryl "D.M.C." McDaniels, cofounder of Run-D.M.C., another highly influential hip-hop group, asserted that putting on a Georgetown Starter jacket "meant that you had attitude [and] that you was bad."[59]

But the team's cultural significance stretched far beyond the clothes worn by its fans. Thompson kept a deflated basketball to remind his players that their time on the court would eventually come to an end. He stressed the importance of attaining an education and achieving financial success. By 1990, 98 percent of his players had earned a Georgetown diploma. A few went on to make millions in the NBA. Thompson himself also led a prosperous career, which included several lucrative endorsements from companies like Nike.[60] As a result, the Hoyas became symbols of upward mobility for black youths who continued to face bleak opportunities.

In 1985 a community-based campaign was created to capitalize on the Hoyas' success. Coca-Cola sponsored the "Kids & Cops" initiative, which sought to improve relations between youths in DC and local police. It included 65,000 sets of fourteen trading cards, each featuring a member of the Georgetown basketball team. Thompson's was the first card in the series and had a picture of him coaching from the sidelines. The card described the ground rules for the "Kids & Cops" campaign: Participants were to ask police officers for the cards, and if they collected all fourteen, they received a stamp and two tickets to a Georgetown game. Cards included pictures of Hoya players with a basketball tip and a life lesson. One showed senior guard and DC native Bill Martin performing a layup. The opposite side of the card declared the hook shot the "only unblockable shot in basketball," while admonishing, "Hooking school closes the door to a job. Education is a clean shot to the future."[61]

Thompson, an advocate for minority access to higher education, famously protested threats to college admissions for black athletes. On January 14, 1989, he walked out of a game against Boston College after the NCAA passed Proposition 42. Enacted days earlier, Proposition 42 denied athletic scholarships to students who failed to attain at least a score of 700 on the SAT and a minimum grade point average in high school of 2.0.[62] Of the 600 student-athletes who would ultimately be affected by the new rule, 90 percent were estimated to be black. Thompson found the NCAA regulation "culturally biased."[63] Other coaches applauded his stand, including one

who called Proposition 42 "the most racist decision I've ever seen made."
With pressure mounting, the NCAA announced its intention to reevaluate
Proposition 42. Satisfied with their commitment, Thompson returned to
coaching his team.[64]

Reflecting on the Big East in 1989, one sportswriter wrote, "[T]he delicate
issue of race always hovers over the Georgetown program."[65] One could
also argue that a similar tension hung over the Reagan administration. The
1980s saw the collision of coach Thompson and President Reagan, two
powerful yet opposing forces. Both men were products of the civil rights
era. Thompson emerged out of segregation to become one of the greatest
coaches in the history of college basketball, while Reagan led a conservative
revolution that drew significant energy from a white backlash to the heady
social changes made in the two decades preceding his presidency. Inevitably,
the paths of the two would cross, revealing a country continuing to grapple
with issues of race.

Shortly after the Hoyas won the 1984 championship, Thompson—
along with the rest of the Georgetown basketball team—met with the president. But it was the *Sports Illustrated* photo shoot at the White House—
held six days after the president had handily won reelection—that revealed
the incongruity between Thompson and Reagan. Both men were at the
height of their careers, though the same could not be said for many black
Americans, including those who had cheered on the Hoyas while having to
endure the frustrations of Reagan's years in office. Many viewed the president as unsympathetic and unwelcoming. They no doubt would have well
understood Patrick Ewing's reply to the photographer who said he looked
menacing: "I'll smile when I'm ready."[66]

16

Washington Baseball Fans

Losers No More

James R. Hartley

The pages of history are filled with examples of courage—brave souls who faced certain defeat, but through their skill, their character, or even divine intervention, somehow managed to survive, not once but time after time. In many ways, the word courageous would be an adequate description of a true-blue follower of Washington, DC, baseball.

For several generations, the plight of the DC baseball fan might be best summed up by the Rodney Dangerfield lament, "It's not easy being me." Year after year, Washington baseball teams finished at or near the bottom of the standing, but the baseball fans of the Nationals/Senators kept coming back for more. Between 1946 and 1971, the original Washington baseball club and the expansion Senators of the American League compiled just two winning seasons—a 78-76 mark under Hall of Fame manager Stanley R. "Bucky" Harris in 1952 and the unexpected 86-76 finish under Ted Williams in 1969. The 1953 Nats finished the season with a record of 76-76, but their fortunes deteriorated rapidly from there. Between 1954 and 1960, Washingtonians watched their heroes stumble to a record of 430-648. That works out to a dismal winning percentage of .399. The futility of watching those mid- to late 1950s teams might be best illustrated by former Senators first baseman Julio Becquer, who described the misadventures of left fielder Carlos Paula one afternoon at Boston's Fenway Park: "A ball was hit to left field for a single and it went through [Paula's] legs," said Becquer. "He turned around and the ball bounced off the wall, and went through his legs again." With tears of laughter in his eyes, Becquer continued. "He finally picked up the ball and when he tried to throw it, he dropped the ball. He made three errors on the same play!"[1]

It took character to endure season after season of losing baseball, and many Washingtonians did just that. A change in the team's name from "Nationals" to "Senators" in 1957 had no effect on the tide of losing. An entire generation of Washington baseball fans spent too many mornings reading newspaper summaries of the previous night's loss. They found joy in the occasional victory and in rooting for their favorite players such as Roy Sievers, Eddie Yost, Mickey Vernon, Jim Lemon, and Pete Runnels. In 1957, Sievers led the American League in home runs and runs batted in. Lemon hit 17 homers, but the two sluggers received very little help from the rest of the lineup.

On May 1, 1957, while the Senators were in the middle of a ten-game losing streak, Eddie Barnett, a thirty-three-year-old parking attendant, climbed a 65-foot high scaffold at 101 New York Avenue in Northeast Washington and vowed not to come down until his Senators had won three games in a row. Barnett sat atop his perch for twenty-nine days before his wish was granted. But even that "accomplishment" was tainted. The first win in the streak was the completion of a game against the Baltimore Orioles that had been suspended on April 21. The official scorer ruled that since the game was completed on May 27, it was indeed part of the three-game winning streak.

Bad luck seemed to befall anyone who donned a Washington Senators uniform. Pitcher Chuck Stobbs, famous for surrendering a titanic home run to Mickey Mantle that cleared the left field bleachers at Griffith Stadium in 1953, lost his last five decisions in 1956 and his first eleven in 1957. Many fans who attended the June 27 contest against the Cleveland Indians arrived with some sort of good-luck charm. The first 2,300 people who entered the ballpark that night were given rabbits' feet. Wearing uniform number 13, instead of his usual 16, Stobbs broke his personal sixteen-game losing streak with a 6–3 win over the Indians.

The 1957 Senators started slowly, but managed to poke their heads above eighth place for a few days in August. The dizzying heights of seventh place seemed too much for the Senators, and they lost twelve of their final thirteen games and finished the season in the basement.

The 1958 Senators settled into last place on June 17 and never escaped. They ended their season with thirteen consecutive losses. In the midst of that thirteen-game collapse, they lost four consecutive games by 2–0 scores. The next game saw an offensive outburst, of sorts. The Senators scored two runs but lost the game, 3–2. The following night, they lost again, by a score of—you guessed it—2–0.

In 1959, the team began to shows signs of respectability. After several years of bouncing back and forth between Washington and the minor leagues, Harmon Killebrew arrived for good in 1959. He joined Sievers, Lemon, and Rookie of the Year Bob Allison to form what was called "the Fearsome Foursome," one of the most formidable power-hitting tandems in all of baseball. Killebrew tied Sievers's franchise record of 42 home runs. Lemon hit 33, Allison 30, and Sievers added 21. The rest of the team combined to hit only 37 long balls.

After dropping the second game of a doubleheader to the Athletics on July 19, the 1959 Senators began a fifteen-game road trip, sporting a record of 43-47. They occupied fifth place, a mere eight games behind the American league co-leaders, the Indians and White Sox. The Senators lost all fifteen games of the trip and returned home in last place. The first two games of a home stand resulted in losses to the Indians, but Truman "Tex" Clevenger shut out the Tribe in the second game of an August 5 doubleheader and halted the losing streak at a franchise record-tying eighteen games. After the game, Senators manager Cookie Lavagetto said: "Maybe I can sleep now. This office of mine was beginning to close in on me. I feel now as if I can breathe again and as if the weight of the world is off my shoulders."[2]

Lavagetto may have felt that his office was closing in on him again when the Senators lost six of their next seven games.

In 1960, the Senators began to show some real improvement. Killebrew, Allison, Lemon, catcher Earl Battey, and improved pitching and defense kept the team around the .500 mark for most of the 1960 season. Washington fans returned to Griffith Stadium, and the Senators recorded their highest attendance figure since 1949. The District of Columbia looked forward to an even better season in 1961.

However, club owner Calvin Griffith had other plans. After the death of his uncle, majority owner and team president Clark Griffith, in 1955, Calvin took over the day-to-day operations of the club. One of his first moves was to trade fan favorite Mickey Vernon to the Boston Red Sox. Soon thereafter, Calvin began exploring options for a possible relocation of the franchise. Cities like Los Angeles, Minneapolis, and Dallas were mentioned as possible relocation sites. However, American League owners, fearing possible loss of their antitrust exemption by the United States Congress, strongly suggested that Calvin stay put. Reluctantly, Griffith kept the team in the nation's capital.

After the Brooklyn Dodgers and New York Giants moved to California for the 1958 season, New York attorney William Shea tried to lure an existing National League team to New York. When his efforts failed, he proposed the establishment of a new professional league with teams in New York, Atlanta, and Minneapolis, among others. Sending a message to all major league owners, Shea announced that Branch Rickey would be the commissioner of the new Continental League. Fearing the loss of their antitrust exemption and the possibility of a new league, the major league owners voted to add two teams to the American League for the 1961 season and two new teams (Houston and New York) to the National League in 1962. The new American League teams would begin play in Los Angeles and the Minneapolis area. Calvin Griffith was given permission to move his Senators to Minnesota, and one of the new expansion franchises replaced the original Senators in Washington, DC.

The first expansion draft was held on December 14, 1960, in Boston. The "new" Senators drafted a group of aging veterans that included Dale Long, Gene Woodling, Billy Klaus, and pitcher Dick Donovan. They added career minor leaguers such as pitchers Ed Hobaugh, Joe McClain, and outfielder Chuck Hinton. Many preseason prognosticators predicted that the Senators would not win fifty games.

The "new" Nats proved the pundits wrong by getting off to a 30-30 start in 1961, but were dealt several severe heart-breaking losses during a disastrous four-game weekend series in mid-June at Fenway Park in Boston. After dropping the Friday and Saturday night games, the Senators held a 12–5 lead with two outs and a runner on first in the bottom of the ninth inning in the first game of a Sunday doubleheader. The third out never came. The Red Sox scored eight runs off three Washington pitchers and won the game, 13–12. More than fifty years later, Washingtonians of a certain age still mention that first game collapse as the most disappointing moment in their pothole-laced history as Senators fans. The Senators lost a 13-inning heartbreaker in the second game. Those four losses in Boston were the start of a ten-game losing streak. But the Senators regrouped in early July and crowds at Griffith Stadium averaged nearly 11,000 during the home stand just prior to the All-Star break. Unfortunately, the second half of the season was a disaster. At one point, the Senators lost fourteen games in a row, won a game, and then lost ten more, completing an unbelievably bad stretch of twenty-four losses in twenty-five games. As the losses piled up, so did the number of empty seats at Griffith Stadium. The final game at the old ballpark drew a mere 1,498 patrons. Clearly, Washington fans had found other ways to spend their time and their hard-earned money.

In 1962, the team and its fans were treated to a change of scenery when the new District of Columbia Stadium became the playground for the new Senators. Attendance increased by more than 130,000, but still ranked eighth in the ten-team American League. Over the next three seasons, the Senators dropped 101, 106, and 100 games, and attendance declined.

Frank Howard arrived in Washington in 1965, and the Senators managed to avoid 100 losses for the next seven years, although they came close several times. But aside from watching Howard's 450-foot home runs drop into the far reaches of DC Stadium's upper deck, there was not much to hold the fans' interest. The Senators finished at or near the bottom of the American League standings and attendance mirrored the club's performance. But the worst was yet to come.

In the days following the assassination of Dr. Martin Luther King Jr. on April 4, 1968, rioting broke out in Washington, DC, and other major cities across the country. Many suburban baseball fans felt that Washington was unsafe and Senators attendance suffered. Opening Day, which drew crowds of 40,000 or more in previous years, drew a mere 32,063 to the 45,000-seat DC Stadium. As the 1968 season drew to a close, 546,661 fans had passed through the turnstiles—a decrease of over 220,000 from the previous season. The citizens of Washington and its surrounding suburbs were not even slightly aware that a radical change was on the horizon.

In December 1967, Senators' majority owner and chairman of the board, James M. Johnston died, and a year later, Johnston's shares of the team were sold to Robert Short, a trucking and hotel magnate from Minnesota, and the former treasurer of the Democratic Party. Short had purchased the NBA's Minneapolis Lakers in 1957, moved them to Los Angeles in 1960, and sold them to Jack Kent Cooke for a huge profit in September 1965. Despite Short's assurances that he did not purchase the team to move it, more than a few people were skeptical.

Short lured Hall of Famer Ted Williams out of retirement to become the Senators new manager. Using an exceptional knowledge of hitting, boundless enthusiasm, and determination, Williams guided the sad-sack expansion Senators, who had won only 65 games in 1968, to an 86-76 record in 1969—Washington's first winning baseball team in fifteen years.

However, there were moments that reminded fans that their team had not yet turned the corner. In the eighth inning of a blowout win against the A's, Tim Cullen was inserted into the lineup as a defensive replacement at second base. "I was leading the league in defense, so [Ted Williams] felt pretty safe putting me in," recalled Cullen.

> Jose Tartabull leads off and hits me a ground ball. The ball hit a rock, came up and hit me in the upper forearm, then bounced off my chin. By the time I got back to it, Tartabull was safe. The next hitter was [Bert] Campaneris. He hits another ground ball and it hits the same rock, comes up, hits me on the same forearm and off the chin. Now they've got two runners on. Reggie Jackson comes to the plate, and I figured I'd make up for all of this. If he hits me a ground ball, we'll turn a double play. Sure enough, he hit me a line-drive, and in my haste to turn the double play, I threw it into left field . . . We got out of the inning. In

fact, the last out of the inning, someone hit me a ground ball and it hit the same rock. This time, instead of bouncing off me, it lodged in my armpit and I was able to throw the guy out. As happens most times, I got to lead off the inning. It was the first time I got a standing boo-vation. In my haste to get out of there, I hit one off the end of the bat down to Tito Francona and it went right between his legs. The people actually turned that standing boo-vation into a standing o-vation.[3]

The 1969 Senators set an expansion franchise attendance record of 916,106. To long-suffering Washington baseball fans, it appeared to be the start of a new, winning era, one that Short called "A Whole New Ballgame." But Bob Short had other ideas. After the initial success, Short announced a second increase in ticket prices. He then traded away popular veterans, and the team's fortunes began to fade. By 1971, Short had traded away fan favorites Ken McMullen, Darold Knowles, Mike Epstein, Eddie Brinkman, and Joe Coleman and replaced them with over-the-hill players such as Don Wert, Curt Flood, Denny McLain, and a cast of mostly unknown players. Yet through it all, Frank Howard remained. The team played poorly, posting a 63-96 record in 1971.

Faced with poor play and the highest ticket prices in baseball, Senators fans stayed home. Attendance declined more than 150,000 from its high-water mark in 1969. Former Senators first baseman and Nationals hitting coach Tom McCraw remembered, "The Senators had a lot of good guys, but it was a bad ballclub. They didn't win. You have to give fans a sense of hope."[4]

Citing huge losses and threatening to file for bankruptcy, in the summer of 1971 Short requested permission to move the team to Arlington, Texas. By a vote of 10–2, the owners granted his request. The unthinkable had happened. After seventy-one years, Washington, DC, a charter member of the American League in 1901, was no longer a major league city.

The fans of Washington initially showed their displeasure by staying away from RFK Stadium during the final home stand of the year. A three-game series against the Indians drew a total of 4,512 fans. By the time the final date arrived, some fans were more than just a little angry. A paid crowd of 14,460 and perhaps 4,000 gatecrashers convened at RFK on the night of September 30, 1971, to say goodbye. Local hero Frank Howard thrilled the crowd by hitting a home run that ignited a four-run rally in the sixth inning. The Senators took a 7–5 lead in the eighth inning, but with two outs in the top of the ninth, fans stormed the field. Despite warnings over the PA system that the game would be forfeited, unruly fans remained on the field, pulling up chunks of grass from the infield and outfield, and removing numbers and letters from the scoreboard. The game was called and the Yankees were awarded a 9–0 forfeit victory.

Eventually, many DC baseball fans switched their allegiance forty miles up the Parkway and became fans of the Baltimore Orioles. But there were also many die-hard Washington fans who chose to keep theirs in DC, hoping that Major League Baseball (MLB) would come to its senses and bring a team back to the nation's capital, either through expansion or relocation. In the meantime, local Washington baseball junkies who had chosen not to travel to Baltimore for their baseball fix had to be content with paying regular-season prices to watch exhibition games, such as the Cracker Jack Old Timers games or meaningless preseason exhibition games at RFK Stadium. The football seats remained in place for the first decade of exhibition games, which led to many cheap home runs and high-scoring games. In the 1990s, the football seats were removed and the field returned to its original base-ball configuration. However, the exhibitions came to an end when the DC Armory Board that controlled RFK declared that the stadium would remain a football-only facility.

In mid-August of 1994, the Montreal Expos had posted the best record in all of baseball, but the players' strike wiped out the remainder of the reg-ular season and the entire postseason. By the time play resumed in 1995, the damage had been done. Star players Larry Walker, Cliff Floyd, and pitcher Ken Hill had been traded. The people of Montreal turned their backs on Major League Baseball and attendance declined rapidly. By 2001, the atten-dance at Olympic Stadium had fallen to just over 642,000 fans.

Soon after the conclusion of the 2001 World Series, baseball commis-sioner Bud Selig announced that MLB had voted to eliminate two teams. Although the identities of the two franchises were never officially announced, most people believed that the Minnesota Twins and the Montreal Expos had been designated for extinction. No one from the commissioner's office denied those rumors. MLB, which now owned the Expos, eventually shelved its plans for contraction and began entertaining bids from cities such as Las Vegas, Charlotte, and Washington, DC. The process dragged on.

The citizens of Montreal were further insulted when MLB scheduled twenty-two of the Expos' "home" games in San Juan, Puerto Rico, in 2003 and 2004. In the spring of 2004, Commissioner Selig announced that a deci-sion on relocating the Expos would be made by the All-Star break.

Meanwhile, Baltimore Orioles owner Peter Angelos fought the reloca-tion of the Expos to the nation's capital. Fearing that a team in Washington would severely affect attendance in Baltimore, Angelos declared, "There are no real baseball fans in Washington."[5]

The 2004 All-Star Game passed with no decision on the fate of the Expos. Fans in Washington, Charlotte, and Las Vegas were left to wonder, "Did Mr. Selig mean *this* year's All-Star break?"

At 5:00 p.m. on November 29, 2004, nearly thirty-three years to the day after the Senators had departed for Texas, DC baseball fans were finally rewarded when the struggling Montreal Expos franchise was transferred to the nation's capital. After what seemed like endless years of negotiations, DC mayor Anthony Williams proudly announced, "Baseball is back in Washington!"

However, in keeping with the Washington baseball fans' proud tradition of losing, the DC City Council decided to amend its original agreement with Major League Baseball regarding the financing and construction of a new stadium. MLB commissioner Selig announced that the city council's proposed changes to the stadium agreement were unacceptable and ordered a suspension of the team's operations. It appeared that Washington was going to lose its new team before it even had a chance to play a game. The city council eventually accepted the original terms of the agreement, and Washington was back in the major leagues.

Charlie Slowes, who had provided play-by-play for the NBA's Washington Bullets between 1986 and 1997, was amazed at how the city of Washington had taken to their new baseball team. "I had come up [to Washington from Florida] in mid-March to get settled into a place to live for the season. Just going around the city and seeing the banners and street signs—everywhere you looked, there was something Nationals, and the team had never been here, never played a game," said Slowes. "You saw the kind of stuff around the city as if the team had been here and already won something, so I knew it was going to be big."[6]

Longtime radio and television sports personality Phil Wood recalled, "I never suffered as a Senators fan. [Losing] was all I knew, and simply having a team, regardless of the won-lost record, was never not fun for me. The suffering arrived on October 1, 1971, and departed on Opening Day, 2005."[7]

The baseball-starved fans of the DC area welcomed its new team with open arms. The Nationals opened their season in Philadelphia on April 4, 2005, and several groups of fans chartered buses to Citizens Bank Park for the game. During a seventh-inning rally, Nationals fans chanted, "Let's Go Nats!" much to the amazement of Phillies fans. Nats infielder Jamey Carroll recalled: "When we heard that, it's like, Wow! This is going to be different. This is the way it's supposed to be! Not that you shouldn't be trying to play as hard as you can, but when you have people that care about what you're doing, and pay attention to what you're doing, it makes a tremendous difference."[8]

The Nationals lost that first game by a score of 8–4, but the thrill of finally cheering for a Washington team playing an official game helped ease the fans' disappointment over the loss.

Ten days later at RFK Stadium, fans waited through long lines at security checkpoints to see the first official baseball game in Washington since 1971. President George W. Bush threw out the ceremonial first pitch and former Washington Senators players such as Frank Howard, Jim Lemon, and Chuck Hinton stood at spots around the field and handed the Nationals' fielders their gloves as the new team took their positions. A crowd of more than 45,000 baseball fans, some with tears in their eyes, watched the Nationals defeat the Arizona Diamondbacks, 5–3. After thirty-four years, baseball was truly back in Washington.

Broadcaster Charlie Slowes remembered, "I don't know if you can top the emotions and the excitement of that night; all the fanfare and the old Senators going out on the field with the gloves of the Nationals players."[9]

The Nationals hung around the .500 mark through the first two months of the season but caught fire in June with a ten-game winning streak that carried them into first place in the National League East. By mid-June the new Washington franchise had surpassed the previous baseball attendance record of 1,027,216 that had been set by the original Nats in 1946. RFK Stadium was becoming the place to be during the summer. Some people made vacation or work plans around the Nats' schedule. Others were entertaining the possibility of playoff games at RFK in October.

Unfortunately, the "Dog Days" of August were not kind to the Nationals. A combination of injuries and bad luck derailed Washington's Pennant Express. Picked to finish last in the powerful American League East, the Nationals did just that, but they finished the season with a surprising 81-81 record.

On the final day of the 2005 season, the fans at RFK Stadium showed their appreciation to manager Frank Robinson and his team of overachievers. Phillies fans who had traveled down I-95 to urge their team to a possible playoff berth watched in amazement as Washington fans gave standing ovations to ineffective pitchers who had been replaced. In the ninth inning, Nationals' reliever Gary Majewski walked off the mound after allowing four runs without retiring a batter. As he walked with his head down toward the dugout, Majewski heard the cheers from the crowd. He looked up, and after a few moments, he realized that the crowd was cheering for him. He smiled and waved in appreciation. After the final out of a 9–3 loss was made, the crowd rose to its feet again and gave the Nationals a five-minute standing ovation.

The reaction of the fans did not go unnoticed by the players. Outfielder Marlon Byrd recalled, "For an inaugural season, for the fans to come out and the support they showed, that was something very special. We were throwing things back into the stands for them. It was a great feeling, and it showed how close this team was and how close the city was."[10]

The team drew 2,731,993 fans to musty, outdated RFK Stadium, but the euphoria was short-lived.

While construction began in 2006 on a new ballpark in Southeast Washington, the Nationals that year struggled. The acquisition of Alfonso Soriano from the Texas Rangers gave Washington fans something to maintain their interest, but the team fell short of their 2005 record. As a result, the magical feeling of 2005 began to wane, but there were a few bright moments.

Young third baseman Ryan Zimmerman, the team's first draft pick the previous June, provided a glimpse of what was to come with a two-run, game-winning home run against the Yankees on June 18, 2006. Washington fans high-fived one another and celebrated in the aisles, while Yankees fans watched in stunned disbelief.

On September 16, in an 8–5 win over the Brewers, Soriano stole his fortieth base of the season and became the fourth member of the "40-40 Club." He finished the season with 41 stolen bases and a new franchise record of 46 home runs in a season. After the World Series, Soriano became a free agent and signed a seven-year contract with the Chicago Cubs. Washington fans were left to wonder how their team was going to replace his run production.

Manny Acta replaced Frank Robinson as manager in 2007, and despite dire preseason predictions by the "experts," the Nats finished the season with 73 wins. On September 23, the Nationals and their fans said goodbye to RFK Stadium with a 5–3 win over the Phillies. Unlike the finale at Griffith Stadium, or the Senators' finale in 1971, a crowd of 40,519 came to pay their respects as the first multipurpose stadium in the country hosted its final major league game.

The Nationals started the 2008 season with a dramatic ninth-inning win in the inaugural game at the new Nationals Park before a sellout crowd and a national television audience. Ryan Zimmerman's game-winning home run in the ninth inning sent the crowd into a state of delirium. The Nationals won their next two games on the road, but then lost ten games in a row. They finished the first season in their new ballpark with a record of 59-102. Things were so bad that pitcher Aaron Crow, Washington's first-round pick in the 2008 draft, opted to wait a year and reenter the draft rather than sign with the Nationals.

The 2009 season was even worse. On April 17, Ryan Zimmerman and Adam Dunn played the first three innings wearing jerseys with the team name misspelled. Zimmerman and Dunn changed out of their NATINALS jerseys, but the damage had been done. The error seemed to symbolize the plight of the team. After a 26-60 start, manager Manny Acta was fired and replaced by bench coach Jim Riggleman. The Nats lost their first five games under

Riggleman but finished the season by winning 33 of their last 70 games. The improved finish could not overcome the dreadful start and the Nats finished the season with 103 losses. Attendance dropped below 1.9 million fans for the first time since baseball's return to the District. Some people blamed the smaller crowds on a sluggish economy, but the Nats' poor performance on the field certainly contributed to the drop in attendance.

On March 1, 2010, Nationals' general manager Jim Bowden resigned amid reports that he was a target of a federal investigation of questionable scouting practices in the team's Latin American program. Bowden was replaced by assistant GM Mike Rizzo, who immediately began the process of reorganizing nearly every facet of the Nationals' operation.

The Nationals improved by ten games in 2010, but there was still work to be done. On May 22, the Nationals and Orioles played the second game of a three-game weekend series at Nationals Park. With two outs and a runner on third base, Orioles center fielder Adam Jones lifted a fly ball to deep center field. Washington center fielder Nyjer Morgan raced back to the fence and leaped, but the ball bounced out of his glove and toward left-center field. Morgan, thinking the ball had cleared the fence for a home run, threw his glove to the ground in disgust. While Morgan continued to stomp his feet and curse his apparent bad luck, left fielder Josh Willingham retrieved the ball. By the time Willingham returned the ball to the infield, Jones had circled the bases with an inside-the-park home run and the Orioles had a two-run lead.

The only advantage of being the team that finishes with the worst record in major league baseball is that the team gets the first pick in the annual first-year player draft. Such was the case when the Nationals selected right-handed pitcher Stephen Strasburg of San Diego State University in June 2009. A client of super-agent Scott Boras, Strasburg signed late and did not pitch in the minor leagues in 2009. In the first few months of 2010, Strasburg excelled at both AA Harrisburg and AAA Syracuse in the minor leagues and Nationals fans wondered when Strasburg would be promoted to the major leagues.

On Tuesday night, June 8, 2010, the fans finally got their wish. An overflow crowd of 41,546 gathered at Nationals Park for the highly anticipated debut of the prized pitcher. The young right-hander exceeded most fans' expectations by striking out fourteen Pittsburgh Pirates and the Nationals won, 5–2. Strasburg left the field after the seventh inning to a long, loud standing ovation. After sweeping the three-game series with the Pirates, the Nationals were only one game under .500 and only five games out of first place. Nationals' fans felt they finally had a reason to be optimistic about the future of baseball in the nation's capital. After enduring four straight losing seasons, Washington fans were hoping that the Nationals had finally turned the corner. Unfortunately, the Nats lost thirteen of their next sixteen games and took up residence in the basement of the NL East. Things got worse on August 21 when Strasburg was forced to leave the game with pain in his elbow. An MRI revealed a torn ligament in Strasburg's right elbow, and the fans' hope for the future underwent Tommy John surgery. Attendance increased just over 10,000 for the 2010 season, but most of the increase was directly attributable to Strasburg. When the rookie phenom wasn't pitching, the Nationals were playing to a nearly half-empty ballpark.

The addition of free agent Jayson Werth, the emergence of Michael Morse as an offensive threat, and an improved defense helped the Nationals improve another eleven games in 2011, and attendance at Nationals Park increased by nearly 120,000. Washington fans were starting to believe that their team was turning the corner when manager Jim Riggleman resigned due to a dispute with general manager Mike Rizzo over discussing a contract extension. After bench coach John McLaren managed the team for a three-game series in Chicago, former Orioles, Reds, Dodgers, and Mets manager Davey Johnson took over.

Washington fans weren't breaking down the gates of Nationals Park, but Philadelphia fans certainly were. A three-game series in August drew an average of 41,418 mostly Phillies fans to Nationals Park. Nationals fans were outnumbered and outshouted by raucous Phillies fans. The Phillies fans verbally and visually abused the Nats fans with chants such as "This is our house!" and bearing signs that read, "Welcome to Citizens Bank Park South." Even Rodney Dangerfield got more respect. But the Nats fans had the last laugh. The upstart Nationals took two out of three from the Phillies and sent their suddenly quiet fans home to Philadelphia with a case of the blues.

During the first six seasons, a typical September crowd in Washington usually numbered in the 15,000 to 20,000 range. As September 2011 rolled around, more and more fans were coming to see the Nationals. After the Nats swept a four-game series from the Phillies at Citizens Bank Park, they came home to face the Braves in a three-game series. That final home series of the year drew 100,441 enthusiastic fans to Nationals Park.

The long wait for a competitive team was apparently paying off for Nats fans. With the addition of a healthy Strasburg and 2011's first overall pick Bryce Harper, some Washington fans were predicting a run at the postseason.

Harper, who was also a client of Scott Boras, signed on August 16 and played in the Arizona Fall League. After playing high school and college

The fortunes of Washington baseball took a dramatic turn with the arrival of
Stephen Strasburg in 2010. Photo by James R. Hartley.

baseball as catcher, Harper was asked to change positions and moved to the
outfield. After a slow start, the prized draft pick showed remarkable progress. During spring training, 2012, some people hoped that Harper would
accompany the team north and start on opening day. However, general manager Mike Rizzo and manager Davey Johnson recommended patience in
dealing with the prized rookie. Harper started the season in AA Harrisburg,
but after two weeks he was promoted to AAA Syracuse.

The Nationals started their 2012 season by winning four of six on the
road. They arrived in Washington, tied for first place, and proceeded to win
eight of ten games at Nationals Park. The Nats' second road trip of the season was not nearly as successful. They dropped the last four games of their
western tour, but a ray of hope emerged when Harper was called up to the
major leagues.

Harper made his debut on April 28 at Dodger Stadium. All he did was
smash a double for his first major league hit, drive in the go-ahead run with
a sacrifice fly in the ninth inning and make an unbelievable throw from left
field that would have cut down the tying run at the plate, if not for catcher
Wilson Ramos dropping the ball. Not bad for a nineteen-year-old in his first

game in the major leagues. Unfortunately, the Nats lost the game, 4–3, in ten innings.

The Nationals returned home to face the Arizona Diamondbacks. The home stand featured Harper's Washington debut. The losing streak reached five when the D'backs took the first of a three-game series. The next evening, the Nats trailed Arizona by a score of 4–3 with two outs in the bottom of the ninth inning. With Harper at second after a leadoff double, shortstop Ian Desmond connected with a J. J. Putz fastball and sent it soaring into the visitors' bullpen in left field for a dramatic, game-winning two-run homer. The next evening, Harper's double to left field drove in Desmond with the winning run in the series finale.

During a series against the Phillies on the first weekend in May, Washington fans overwhelmed Philadelphia fans, not only in numbers, but also in enthusiasm. Nats fans were responding to their winning team and proudly displaying what the Nationals' promotions department called "Natitude." The Nationals rewarded their vocal fans by taking two out of three from the dreaded Phillies. During the Sunday night finale of the series, Harper announced his arrival to the entire country. After being intentionally hit by a Cole Hamels pitch in the first inning, Harper advanced to third base on Jayson Werth's single. When Hamels lobbed a throw to check Werth at first base, Harper said something to third-base coach Bo Porter. As Hamels released another lobbed throw to first, Harper took off for home and beat first baseman Laynce Nix's throw to catcher Carlos Ruiz for a steal of home. Nationals Park erupted.

In the third inning of Washington's 8–5 win over the Padres on May 14, Harper gave the Nats a 4–1 lead with his first major league home run. The homer was a low line drive that landed on the grassy hill behind the center field fence and came off San Diego's Tim Stauffer. Harper sprinted around the bases and completed the circuit in eighteen seconds. "I always have [sprinted around the bases] since I can't remember," Harper said after the game. "I don't want to show up the pitcher."[11]

The Nationals regained first place on May 22 and remained in sole possession of the top spot in the National League East for the remainder of the season—a total of 135 consecutive days.

Suddenly, it was becoming fashionable to be a Washington Nationals fan. Washington baseball fans seemed to pop up everywhere. It was not uncommon to enter shops and restaurants and see several patrons of different ages wearing a Nationals caps or shirts. Twenty-somethings would be completely at ease talking baseball with older folks. The fans of Washington and the surrounding suburbs had gone completely gaga over their baseball team. Nationals gear became one of the most popular items of apparel around the country.

The Nationals were playing an exciting brand of baseball and the entire country was beginning to notice. On September 8, the Nats trailed the Marlins by a score of 6–5 and were ready to bat in the bottom of the ninth inning when a violent thunderstorm with tornado-like wind hit Nationals Park. More than two and a half hours later, play resumed. Jayson Werth led off the bottom of the ninth against Marlins' closer Heath Bell. Werth fouled off several two-strike pitches and worked the count to three balls and two strikes. Bell tried to sneak a fastball past Werth, but the Nationals right fielder was ready and crushed the ball into the seats just to the left of straight-away center field for a game-tying home run. One inning later, Corey Brown delivered a game-winning single that gave the Nationals an improbable 7–6 win and sent the remaining 500 die-hards home with smiles on their faces.

Even the *Washington Post* jumped on the Nationals bandwagon. Prior to the 2012 season, the start of training camp for NFL's Redskins pushed the Nationals to the back pages of the paper's sports section. With an exciting first-place baseball team, the *Post* placed Nationals' game summaries on the front page of the sports section and Redskins training camp became a secondary story. At times, the Nationals game recap was actually above the Redskins headline on page one. It appeared that Washington had taken its first steps toward becoming a baseball town.

When the Nationals clinched a postseason berth on September 20, more than a few old Senators fans had tears in their eyes. One Nats fan exclaimed, "This is better than sex!" DC-area native Phil Wood appeared to be holding back tears as he did his postgame radio show from the left field concourse at Nationals Park.[12]

For the first time in many of their lives, fans who had endured mediocrity (or worse) and a thirty-three-year baseball drought were finally going to see a Washington baseball team play a postseason game. Eleven days later, the Nationals clinched their first division title since the team moved to Washington.

Washingtonian and Senators fan Alan Alper exclaimed, "I am no longer Charlie Brown. Lucy can't take the ball away from me anymore."[13]

Despite losing several key players to various injuries, Davey Johnson managed the Nationals to a major league-best 98-64 record. Their opponents for the first round of the National League Division Series were the defending World Series Champions, the St. Louis Cardinals. Due to the addition of another Wild Card team in 2012, the Nats played their first two games on the road.

After splitting the first two games in St. Louis, the Nats returned to Nationals Park and dropped the first home game to the Cardinals by a score of 8–0. The crowd, desperate to cheer, quietly watched Cardinals starter Chris Carpenter shut down their team.

The following afternoon, Jayson Werth delivered perhaps the most dramatic hit in Washington since Earl McNeely's famed "pebble hit" that won the World Series for the original Nats in 1924. On the thirteenth pitch of his lead-off at-bat in the bottom of the ninth inning, Werth drove a fastball from Cardinals reliever Lance Lynn off the back wall of the visitors' bullpen in left field, giving the Nationals a dramatic 2–1 win that evened the series at two games apiece.

Writer Mark Zuckerman, who has covered the Nationals since 2005, wrote, "Years from now, we may look back on Game 4 as the night Washington became a baseball town."[14]

In Friday night's finale, the Nats built a 6–0 lead after three innings. The Cardinals fought back, scored four times in the ninth despite having two outs, and ended Washington's storybook season with a 9–7 win. With the exception of a few St. Louis fans, the crowd filed out of Nationals Park in stunned silence.

For his efforts, manager Davey Johnson was voted National League Manager of the Year by the Baseball Writers Association of America. Several other Nationals received postseason awards. Shortstop Ian Desmond, center fielder Bryce Harper, and first baseman Adam LaRoche received Silver Slugger Awards. LaRoche received a Gold Glove Award and Harper was voted National League's Rookie of the Year. General manager Mike Rizzo was elected as baseball's Executive of the Year.

Broadcaster Phil Wood echoed the sentiments of many Washington fans. "For the 2012 Nationals to win 98 games and a division title while I was still on the planet was akin to winning the lottery, your ship has come in, the sun will shine, you've made the Dean's List, that chronic rash has finally cleared up—all rolled into one. When they clinched a playoff spot, I thought, even if the Mayans got it right"—according to some, the ancient Mayan calendar projected that the world would end on December 21, 2012—"what a way to go out."[15]

Dryw Freed of Northeast Washington, a self-described "unrepentant homer," arrived in Washington in 2005—just in time to experience the Nationals' inaugural season in the District of Columbia. A love affair between Dryw and her baseball team was born. Summing up the 2012 season, she said, "I think I was dizzy the whole season. It was pure joy. It was six-year-old birthday party joy. I would have loved a World Series, but I didn't need it. The absolute beauty of seeing years of believing pay off was worth it."[16]

With Stephen Strasburg available for a full year and Bryce Harper having his rookie season behind him, Washington Nationals fans spent the off-season dreaming of bigger and better things for the 2013 season. Manager Davey Johnson added fuel to their fire by proclaiming that his theme for the 2013 season is, "World Series, Or Bust!"[17]

After so many years of disappointment and frustration, Washington baseball fans finally have a team they can proudly support. Thanks to general manager Mike Rizzo and his staff, the Nationals have a talented minor league system that is the envy of many major league organizations. The Washington Nationals—yes, *those* Washington Nationals—appear ready to provide the nation's capital with many years of exciting baseball.

17

Washington Sports Memories, Personal and Collective

Daniel A. Nathan

Driving south on Connecticut Avenue, just past Chevy Chase Circle, I'm flooded with memories and a sense of the familiar. A long time ago, I tell my kids, who are sitting in the backseat, these were my stomping grounds. "The first home I remember is just around the corner," I say. My wife has heard these musings many times before. "Daddy and memory lane," she says with a smile, but my son, ten, and daughter, eight, seem interested, for a change.

I moved away from DC for good in 1989, and have lived many places since then: Iowa City, Iowa; southwest Ohio; and upstate New York. Yet all these years later, it still feels comfortable here. It's almost as if the passage of time doesn't much matter. The city and I have changed, of course, mostly for the better, I think and hope. Nonetheless, the feeling I'm experiencing driving into town speaks to the enduring power of place and perhaps imprinting. For all kinds of reasons, Washington has a special purchase on my identity and consciousness. This place feels like home.

Many of my earliest, most vivid, and best memories are set in DC. Trying, mostly unsuccessfully but with a great deal of enthusiasm and determination, to fly a kite with my father on the National Mall, near the Washington Monument. Driving through Rock Creek Park during Hurricane Agnes (not the smartest plan, but it was an adventure and we got where we were going). Visiting the pandas at the National Zoo. Seeing the *Washington Post* on our dining room table with the headline that President Nixon had resigned. Going to the Nutcracker at the Kennedy Center. Walking along the Tidal

Basin when the cherry blossoms were in bloom. Spending countless, fun-filled hours in the Smithsonian. Cheering for the Bullets and Redskins and pretending to be Elvin Hayes and Larry Brown on the schoolyard basketball court and playground.[1] Wearing pajamas and watching the Bicentennial fireworks with my brother, from the back of my mother's station wagon. Like all memories, these are selective, I know, a middle-aged man's imaginative reconstructions. Being aware of that doesn't diminish their vibrancy.

At the same time, I'm not nostalgic about the DC of my childhood and young adulthood. I would like to think that my professional training as a historian and cultural critic helps me avoid romantic remembering. I know that my sense of Washington is and always has been incomplete, which is inevitable. Mine is, for example, an overly Northwest DC perspective. (For those unfamiliar with DC geography, the city is divided into four quadrants of unequal size: Northwest, Northeast, Southeast, and Southwest.) Although NW Washington is large—it encompasses more than a third of the town, including most of its best-known sites, such as the White House and the museums and monuments on the Mall—there are significant socio-economic differences in various parts of the city, especially in Southeast DC, which is generally poorer and experiences more crime than other parts of town.

In this respect Washington is typical of almost every American city. It's big, multifaceted, dynamic, a collection of distinct neighborhoods, an amalgam of different cultures and peoples, who don't always get along. Political scientist Charles C. Euchner notes, "Cities are systems of numerous industries with myriad parts."[2] Yes, and cities are complex for other reasons, too. This might be particularly true of Washington, the nation's capital and an unusually cosmopolitan place by American standards, but one that has less autonomy than other cities, since the US Congress maintains authority over it. For over ten years, DC license plates have read "TAXATION WITHOUT REPRESENTATION" to protest the fact that the District has no voting members of Congress.[3]

In this and other ways, Washington is sui generis. Much of it is simply architecturally beautiful, impressive, and undeniably iconic. The US Capitol, for instance, with its massive white dome, is instantly recognizable to most people. It has become "the ur-symbol for 'United States of America,'" writes satirist and Washington resident Christopher Buckley in a moment of seriousness.[4] My hometown, as I was frequently told as a kid, is the most important and powerful city in the world. It seemed plausible then—and now, too. It has also been the site of all kinds of important events, from Abraham Lincoln's assassination to Martin Luther King Jr.'s "I Have a Dream" speech, from Supreme Court decisions to declarations of war, from presidential inaugurations to protest marches. Big things happen here, regularly. This makes DC an especially interesting place.

Not everyone agrees or appreciates the city. Washington is routinely castigated, for its insularity and alleged dysfunction, for being, in the words of President John F. Kennedy, "a city of Southern efficiency and Northern charm," by people running for elected office who live elsewhere and—believe it or not—want to work and live in DC.[5] And there are other criticisms. "To many outsiders and some people who live in the nation's capital," writes George Solomon, the former *Washington Post* sports editor and columnist, "the Washington area lacks the character and soul of cities like Philadelphia or Cleveland, Baltimore or Detroit, Boston or Chicago. They see the town as a bunch of formless federal office buildings, museums, shrines, monuments and suburbs—populated by bureaucrats, lobbyists and lawyers."[6] For some, these apparently loathsome members of the chattering classes largely define DC. That is probably what journalist Joseph Alsop had in mind when he once described himself as a "sad and rootless thing: a Washingtonian."[7] It's true that the city has many transients, of all sorts. They come and go with every change in administration, and diplomats from countries around the globe always seem to be either leaving or entering the city. But DC also has its share of civic chauvinists and lifers, people deeply rooted to this place. Many Washingtonians take great pride in their city and respective neighborhoods. And they express it numerous ways—sport being one of the most important of all.

No team is more popular or important to Washington's civic identity than the Redskins, the three-time Super Bowl champions (1983, 1988, 1992). The dispiriting years of mediocrity since that last championship have not changed the fact that the Redskins are the "most dominant franchise in town."[8] An old friend of mine, a New Yorker who lived in DC for a few years, was never quite able to fathom how so many Washingtonians seemed to feel and act as if the Redskins were a high school team for a metropolitan area of more than 5 million people. All of the burgundy and gold flags flying in his neighborhood was hard for him to understand, and more than he could stomach.

My memories of the Redskins date back to George Allen and the "Over the Hill Gang." The team was good, a consistent winner—Allen never had a losing season in Washington—but could never put it all together to win a NFL championship. Perhaps because I was a kid at the time, quarterbacks Sonny Jurgensen and Billy Kilmer seemed to be worn-out veterans, tough old men. (It's hard for me to believe, but I'm older now than they were then.) They did their best and had their moments, yet Jurgensen was in the twilight of his Hall-of-Fame career and was always hobbled, and many of Kilmer's passes looked like wounded ducks. Joe Theismann, in contrast, was youthful, athletic, confident, maybe even cocky, and, under the tutelage of coach Joe Gibbs, became a first-rate quarterback. In my storehouse of memories, however, the final play of Theismann's career is the most vivid. More than twenty-five years later, it still makes me wince. For pro football fans, it was an iconic moment long before Michael Lewis used it in *The Blind Side* (2006) to emphasize the importance of left tackles like Michael Oher.

It was November 1985. The game was televised on *Monday Night Football*. The Redskins were at home, playing the New York Giants. In the second quarter, Theismann handed off to running back John Riggins, who flipped the ball back to Theismann. But before he could throw downfield, three Giants rushing from different angles—Lawrence Taylor barreled in from the left—converged on and sacked Theismann, breaking his leg, hideously. Taylor immediately sprang to his feet and frantically waved to the Redskins' sideline, calling for help. Theismann, then thirty-six, never played again. Is there a Redskins fan under the age of fifteen who doesn't remember or know this story? I doubt it. The collective trauma endures.

Fortunately, though, most of my Redskins memories, up until Joe Gibbs retired after the 1992 season, are happy ones, sometimes even joyous. Not that the team was invincible during these years—from 1981 through 1992, the Redskins went 124-60 in the regular season, with sixteen wins and five losses in the playoffs—they were just always competitive and played smart, tough, creative football. If there was a single moment during these years that epitomized Redskins football it was probably when John Riggins shed a Miami Dolphins defender and rumbled forty-three yards down the left sideline for a touchdown on fourth and inches during the fourth quarter of the 1983 Super Bowl. Riggins's touchdown put the Redskins ahead for good. It was the team's first championship in forty years. To say that people in DC were excited would be an understatement. "Sing us no sad songs of the economy today," wrote *Washington Post* sportswriter Dave Kindred, "give us no dreary scoop on who's running or not running for president. Paint the White House a nicer color, a burgundy and gold, and get the confetti ready on Pennsylvania Avenue. These Redskins go on parade there Wednesday, the nicest thing that's happened to the nation's capital since we sprung the hostages from Iran."[9]

Of course running backs like Riggins need linemen, and the Redskins had great ones. They were collectively and affectionately known as The

Hogs, a moniker coined by longtime offensive line coach Joe Bugel. Big, sometimes slovenly, and skilled at doing the necessary dirty work, Jeff Bostic, Russ Grimm, Joe Jacoby (who was *massive*), Raleigh McKenzie, Mark May, and the rest were strong, disciplined, and durable. Did any defense ever figure out how to stop the Redskins' version of the Counter Trey? In many ways The Hogs were the heart of the team. The three Super Bowls, after all, were won with different quarterbacks (Theismann, Doug Williams, and Mark Rypien) and featured different running backs (Riggins, Timmy Smith, and Earnest Byner). Then again, wide receivers Art Monk (who was *finally* inducted into the Pro Football Hall of Fame in 2008), Gary Clark, and Ricky Sanders—collectively termed "The Posse"—were hugely important to the Redskins' success, too. They were all sure-handed, but whereas the tall, lithe Monk was quiet, workmanlike, and modest, the relatively diminutive Clark was acrobatic and fiery, and Sanders was a speedster, an ever-present deep threat. In retrospect, I can't figure out how anyone ever stopped those guys.

The Redskins teams that many Washingtonians and I fondly reminiscence about were good on the other side of the ball, too. Led by defensive coordinator Richie Petitbon, linemen Dave Butz (who played for both George Allen and Joe Gibbs, for a total of fourteen years), Dexter Manly, and Charles Mann; linebackers Monte Coleman (who played in 217 games as a Redskin, from the 1970s to the 1990s), Neal Olkewicz, and Wilbur Marshall; and defensive backs Mark Murphy and Darrell Green and others rarely seemed to get the same amount of attention or respect as the offense did. However, they were a solid, hard-hitting, reliable, underrated unit. Green in particular was extraordinary.

Blazing fast and remarkably durable, physically and mentally tough but also gentlemanly, small (5'8") and relentless, Darrell Green played for the Redskins for *twenty* years. He retired when he was 42, and did so with a great deal of approbation and a résumé chock full of awards, honors, and records. Of all his great plays, two stand out. The first was in his rookie season, against the Dallas Cowboys, on *Monday Night Football*, when Green ran all the way across the field, veering from right to left, to tackle running back Tony Dorsett from behind, limiting the All-Pro to a seventy-something-yard gain. "Nobody ever thought anybody could catch Tony," Joe Theismann recalled years later. "Darrell's legacy and reputation sort of asserted itself in that game."[10] The other memorable moment occurred in the playoffs against the Chicago Bears five years later. On a freezing afternoon at Soldier Field, Green fielded a punt near the 50-yard line and took off down the right sideline, *hurdled a tackler*, hurting himself in the process (he tore rib cartilage) but somehow fought through the pain to cut left, and then kept on running to score the tie-breaking touchdown in a game that Washington eventually won. "To me," said NFL Films director Steve Sabol, "a play like that is a blend of so many things, of historical relevance, of romance, of drama. It's a moment you hand down from generation to generation, sort of a precious heirloom."[11] It's a pleasurable, satisfying memory for all Redskins fans—in part because Green, one of the best cornerbacks ever, was and remains so affable and humble. His warmhearted personality helps explain why, when residents of the Washington metro area were recently asked "to name the greatest sports figure in D.C. history," Green tied Joe Theismann for fifth on the list.[12] (And that seems low to me.)

To their credit, those same fans chose Joe Gibbs as "the greatest sports figure in D.C. history." That makes sense and seems right to me, with all due respect to Hall-of-Famer Walter Johnson, the highest-ranked baseball player on the list, and the legendary sportswriter Shirley Povich, who, amazingly, is not on the list at all.[13]

Gibbs, the self-deprecating leader of the Redskins for sixteen years (1981–92, 2004–7), was the most successful coach of any sport in Washington history, and "perhaps the most respected person in team history," asserts sportswriter Thomas Boswell.[14] Such praise was hard earned and well deserved. Disciplined and focused, Gibbs often slept in his office during the season. He was a modest evangelical Christian and an innovative offensive coach. His glasses and soft southern drawl—he was born and raised in North Carolina—helped convey the sense that he was a thoughtful, sensitive person, especially by NFL standards. He frequently stressed team unity (even during the 1987 players' strike), and he and his team always seemed well prepared. TV commentators often explained that the analytical and creative Gibbs was particularly good at making halftime adjustments. He was also stable, cool. The guy never appeared to get rattled or too upset, but it was also clear that he was extremely competitive.

When Gibbs came out of "retirement" in 2004—he had been running Joe Gibbs Racing, a group of successful NASCAR teams—for a second, well-compensated stint with the Redskins, thus electrifying Redskins fans everywhere, a sportswriter called him "one of the league's most skilled game planners and intellects, a brilliant, gifted, marvelously humorous man with a steely resolve and stunning adaptability."[15] Okay, so his postretirement sequel had its ups and downs and was generally disappointing. In terms of our assessment of and appreciation for Gibbs, it really didn't matter. For Redskins fans, Gibbs was tremendously likable and popular; all the winning helped, of course, but Washingtonians also admired his professionalism and decency. They still do.

Considering everything he accomplished, I'm surprised there isn't a Joe Gibbs statue in front of RFK Stadium or FedEx Field. Then again, Gibbs never seemed mythic or Lombardi-esque, a larger-than-life figure, even after being inducted in the Pro Football Hall of Fame. Yet compared to all of his disappointing successors—Richie Petitbon, Norv Turner, Marty Schottenheimer, Steve Spurrier, Jim Zorn, Mike Shanahan, and now Jay Gruden—Gibbs and his championship-winning teams shine even brighter in many memories.

In addition to the Redskins, I rooted passionately for the Washington Bullets when I was a kid.[16] Back in the day, I loved the team's patriotic red, white, and blue uniforms, with the stars and stripes, a color scheme and design that have been recently reintroduced.[17] For some it's a dim memory or ancient history, but in the 1970s the Bullets were consistently successful. They were always in the playoffs, won the NBA championship in 1978, and made it back to the finals the next year, only to lose to the Seattle SuperSonics. Turning off the TV as the Sonics celebrated their victory in DC, with Bullets fans cheering both teams, I have to admit that I got emotional. Not because of the impressive display of sportsmanship, but because I sensed that the Bullets had reached the end of the line. The team's best players were in their thirties (which was older then than it is now), and they had a lot of miles on them.

The Bullets of my youth were anchored by center Wes Unseld and power forward Elvin Hayes. I never got the impression that they were friends. Perhaps Hayes envied some of Unseld's early success and local popularity.[18] Despite the apparent tension between the two men, their games nicely complemented each other.

Unseld was an undersized center, only 6'7" (if that), but he weighed 245 pounds. He was burly and rugged. "I was country-strong," he recently explained. "I didn't lift weights or work on some Nautilus machine. I grew up in Kentucky, carrying block and brick in construction work with my dad."[19] Unseld was never especially interested in or skilled at scoring (he averaged less than eight points per game during the team's championship season). His forte was defense and rebounding, executing quick and crisp outlet passes, and setting solid picks. He was reliable and relentless. As I remember it, Unseld didn't say much, on or off the court, and usually played with a furrowed brow. Now that I think about it, he didn't seem to be having much fun. (He was in much better spirits at his summer basketball camp, which I attended one year, when it was held at Bowie State University.)

Elvin Hayes was bigger (6'9"), more athletic, and more offensive minded than Unseld. Hayes liked to score and was good at it. The Big E's turnaround jumper was almost as unstoppable as Kareem Abdul-Jabbar's

Dan Nathan, posing with Wes Unseld at Unseld's summer basketball camp at
Bowie State University in 1979. Photo from author's collection.

famous skyhook. A recurrent All-Star, Hayes was strong and quick, a pro-lific scorer and rebounder. If he sometimes seemed sensitive and moody, even prickly, Hayes was also incredibly durable, productive, and consis-tent. When he retired in 1984, he had played a record-setting 1,303 games, 50,000 minutes, and only missed nine games over sixteen years.[20] Somehow, though, Hayes didn't always receive his propers (he was widely thought to be a choker when the game mattered most), despite having a Hall-of-Fame career and, like Unseld, eventually being named one of the NBA's fifty great-est players.[21] True basketball aficionados, though, recognize his greatness. As one hoops expert put it, "To acknowledge Michael Jordan is human; to appreciate Elvin Hayes, divine."[22]

There was of course more to the Bullets during the 1970s than Unseld and Hayes. There was the diminutive but lightning quick point guard Kevin Porter, who had the uncanny (and annoying) ability to hog the ball for most of the shot clock and then drive and dish for an assist. He ended up leading the league in assists four times doing that, twice with the Bullets. There was the lanky forward Nick Weatherspoon, who had a great name and mediocre game. Fans would bellow "Spooooon" whenever he made a good play, which wasn't often. And there was Phil Chenier, who was a ter-rific player. A three-time All-Star, he could shoot, pass, rebound, and play tough defense, which is why Bulletsforever.com describes Chenier as "one of the best all around guards during his era."[23] He was Washington's ver-sion of Walt Frazier, without the look-at-me sartorial splendor. I've always wondered what would have happened if the Bullets had a healthy (and a little younger) Phil Chenier in the 1979 NBA Finals to slow down Seattle's dynamic guards Gus Williams and Dennis Johnson.

The 1977–78 team, which won Washington's only NBA championship, was coached by the acerbic and witty Dick Motta, led by Unseld and Hayes, and included stalwarts Kevin Grevey, Mitch Kupchak, Tom Henderson, Larry Wright, Charles Johnson, and rookie Greg Ballard. It was a mature, disciplined team with good chemistry, rather than overwhelming talent, with one exception besides Unseld and Hayes: the perennially underrated 6'6" forward Bobby Dandridge. In spite of being a former All-Star with the Milwaukee Bucks, where he won a NBA championship with Oscar Robertson and Lew Alcindor (later Kareem Abdul-Jabbar), Bobby "D" rarely received his due.

The versatile Dandridge was one of my favorite players. He joined the Bullets in 1977 as a free agent and quickly became the team's catalyst. Sports columnist Bill Simmons writes: "Before expansion diluted the league in the 1990s, many of the NBA's greatest teams were built around two signature stars, then a third (and more underrated) high-caliber player who sacrificed numbers while maintaining a memorable level of clutchness."[24] I wouldn't call the 1977–78 Bullets one of "the NBA's greatest teams," but Dandridge was that team's "third (and more underrated) high-caliber player" who made all the difference. He could do everything: shoot, pass, defend, play different positions. In 1979, sportswriter Curry Kirkpatrick called Dandridge "the best all-round player at his position in professional basketball." Moreover, Dandridge often delivered in pressure situations, all without seeking much limelight.[25] At the time, Dandridge's teammate Mitch Kupchak said, "No fan can appreciate Bobby enough."[26] My friend Sam seemed to prove Kupchak right. One day, while we were playing one-on-one, Sam argued that, since so many people had proclaimed that Dandridge was underrated, he had become overrated. That made no sense to me then—and it still doesn't.

I've participated in hundreds of basketball conversations over the years and I've never heard *anyone* who didn't follow the Bullets in the late 1970s mention Bobby Dandridge when discussing great players. The authors of one basketball compendium, however, know the sad truth: "a player like Bobby Dandridge, with four seasons over 20 points per game, exists only in the footnotes to greatness."[27] They continue, correctly: "If Dandridge had come twenty years earlier, he'd be in the Hall of Fame by default (see: Bill Sharman). Twenty years later, he'd have been paid by the victory parade, like Robert Horry. But Dandridge was lost to the Dark Ages."[28]

To pro basketball-loving Washingtonians, the late 1970s weren't the Dark Ages: it was our one shining moment. The thirty-plus years since then have been awfully frustrating, to say the least, best not dwelled upon.[29] But they haven't been tragic.

Len Bias's death was.

A local hero from Landover, Maryland, Len Bias was an outstanding basketball player at the University of Maryland during the mid-1980s. He was 6'8" and built like a Greek god, had an amazing vertical, could shoot and rebound, was hard working and coachable (if sometimes sensitive and temperamental), and was twice named the Atlantic Coast Conference Player of the Year. Bias often drew comparisons to Michael Jordan. "Lenny was almost the perfect basketball player," said the late North Carolina State coach Jim Valvano, whose teams played against him in the Atlantic Coast Conference. "The body, the quickness, the jumping ability."[30] Charles "Lefty" Driesell, Maryland's folksy, sometimes overbearing former basketball coach, said that by his junior year Bias "was so good nobody could stop him."[31]

At the conclusion of Bias's All-American senior year at Maryland, the Boston Celtics (who had just won the NBA championship) chose him with the second pick in the NBA draft.[32] Celtics president Red Auerbach had been scheming for three years to get Bias and the entire organization was excited about him joining the team. Just after he was drafted, Bias said, "I was really hoping it was Boston, and my dream came true."[33]

Three days later Len Bias, twenty-two, was dead, due to cardio-respiratory arrest induced by a cocaine overdose. He had been partying through the night with friends at the University of Maryland.

Psychologists call it "flashbulb memory," the sensation that you can vividly recall the circumstances in which you experienced something soul-stirring. It was the morning of June 19, 1986. I was driving to work, a summer job at a pharmacy on Massachusetts Avenue. I heard the news on the car radio but didn't believe it. Len Bias—dead? There had to be some kind of mistake. He was probably unconscious. Dead? That made no sense. He was too strong and things were going too well. At the time, I experienced a welter of emotions—"tragedy and disappointment, annoyance and sympathy," as Thomas Boswell aptly put it in the *Washington Post* a few days later.[34] Like many people in Washington and throughout the country, I was shocked: deeply saddened for Bias, for his family's heartbreaking loss, and by his unfulfilled promise. I still am and I'm not alone. Lefty Driesell, who came under intense scrutiny following Bias's death and resigned as Maryland's coach four months later, says: "It's still hard for me to believe the way he left the Earth, but, you know, God must have had a reason for it."[35]

In *Without Bias* (2010), a documentary produced by Kirk Fraser for ESPN's 30 for 30 series, sports broadcaster James Brown shares his shock and disappointment and asserts that Bias's death "left a mark on this city [DC], it is one of the most significant, indelible marks in this city's history."[36] Likewise, local WRC-TV newscaster Jim Vance, a beloved figure in his adopted Washington, notes, the city "was rocked when the word came out about Len Bias," partly because "Everybody loved them some Len Bias."[37] Former *Washington Post* sportswriter Michael Wilbon calls Bias's death the "most important story" of his career, and adds: "My friend Jay Bilas observed a few years ago that those of us of a certain age mark time with Bias's death the way the generation older than us does with the death of John F. Kennedy—and Bilas wasn't exaggerating."[38] Yes.

It's easy to draw morals from Bias's death, to preach about the evils of drugs, or to muse about the fragility of life, or to think of it as a cautionary tale, "a moralistic passion play, an after-school special come to life."[39] I rarely reminisce or think about Bias and how he died in these ways. My memories of Bias are inflected with bittersweet grief: with joy at remembering what he did on the basketball court and deep sadness at the loss, which was and remains collective.[40]

In terms of Washington sports, nothing compares to Len Bias's premature death.

Yet for all of Bias's success and the sadness his death generated, Georgetown played the most consistently interesting and memorable college basketball in DC during these years. Led by coach John Thompson—a towering, intimidating man with high standards and the first African American head coach to win a Division I national championship—Georgetown basketball was special. Almost entirely comprised of African American ballplayers, Georgetown teams played aggressively, intelligently, and cohesively, with a "unique urban style," not-so-subtle code for black physicality and bravura.[41] Cultural critic Todd Boyd is right: "The Hoyas, led by Thompson, were something that America had to this point not seen in an athletic endeavor: a group of strong, aggressive, unapologetic Black men who would just as well knock your ass down as speak to you. For many the Hoyas were America's worst nightmare, packaged as a college basketball team."[42] For many people in DC, however, black *and* white, Georgetown basketball was exciting, invigorating. I loved Georgetown's ferocity and menacing style of play, which was in reality based on sound fundamentals, discipline, and unselfishness—even if it sometimes unnerved me that a predominately white institution (the country's oldest Catholic and Jesuit university) had a mostly black basketball team. It seemed so, well, mercenary and exploitative. At the time, though, all the winning served as a kind of ethical and emotional anesthetic.

When reminiscing about Georgetown basketball, most people, I assume, first think about the Patrick Ewing years (1981–85), and for good reason. In his four seasons at Georgetown, the Hoyas made it to the NCAA finals three times, winning the NCAA national championship in 1984 against the University of Houston, which featured future Hall of Famer Hakeem Olajuwon. Even when he was on the court with super talented teammates (such as David Wingate and Reggie Williams), the seven-foot Ewing was obviously great, a skilled, hard-working, dominant center who excelled on defense and won all kinds of accolades, including the John R. Wooden Award, which honors the nation's best college basketball player.[43]

But my earliest memories of Georgetown basketball predate the Ewing years by a few seasons. Guards John Duren (1976–80) and Eric "Sleepy" Floyd (1978–82) were the ones who most impressed me. Both were All-Americans and tough, well-rounded players. Floyd, in particular, could light it up and ended up becoming the most prolific scorer in Georgetown history. Go back and watch the 1982 NCAA national championship game against the University of North Carolina, the one made famous by Michael Jordan's game-winning jump shot from the left wing and then Fred Brown's *dummkopf* pass to North Carolina forward James Worthy. Ewing was terrific, despite all the goaltending in the first half. Yet it was Sleepy Floyd's scoring that kept Georgetown in the game during the second half, including the shot that put the Hoyas up by one with just less than a minute to go; sadly, it just wasn't enough.

Two years later, Sleepy Floyd was gone (to the NBA), Patrick Ewing had improved, and the team was more talented, deeper, and battle tested. So it was unsurprising when Georgetown beat Houston to win the 1984 national championship. It felt good and many Washingtonians were excited, of course. But I think most assumed that Georgetown was the better team and should win. What was surprising—shocking, really—was that Georgetown failed to defend its title against underdog Villanova in the NCAA finals the next season, Ewing's senior year.

I remember thinking that the championship game shouldn't and wouldn't be close. Georgetown, after all, had already beaten Villanova twice that year. Frankly, although both of the previous games had been close, and both schools were in the Big East, Villanova didn't seem to be in Georgetown's league. At the tournament's outset, Villanova was only seeded eighth and struggled to win its first-round game. With the exception of 6'9" forward Ed Pinckney, Villanova didn't have any exceptional players (with all due respect to Gary McLain and Harold Pressley). Georgetown, on the contrary, was deep, motivated, and accomplished: the Hoyas were ranked No. 1 in the country, 34-2 going into the championship game, and heavily favored.

None of which mattered. The basketball gods smiled on Villanova, which won the game, 66–64. As *Sports Illustrated* reported, "Villanova played an almost perfect game to dethrone supposedly invincible Georgetown for the NCAA title."[44] While watching the game on TV with my friends, I remember thinking, at some point Georgetown will create more separation and Villanova will crumble under the pressure. It never happened. Most Americans love the Cinderella story. They enjoy seeing David beat Goliath (partly because it happens so infrequently). But watching Villanova beat Georgetown in 1985 was a nauseating experience for me. Villanova shot a NCAA tournament-record 79 percent from the field.[45] It seemed like a bad, surreal joke at the time. A backup guard named Harold Jensen went 5-for-5 from the field and scored 14 points? Give me a break. It was obviously a deeply disappointing and memorable loss, for many of us, fans and players alike. "It's still a hard pill to swallow," admits Patrick Ewing. "Whenever I'm watching ESPN Classic and it comes on, I turn the TV off."[46]

After Ewing graduated and was drafted by the New York Knicks, the Hoyas continued to put strong, winning teams on the court. Alonzo Mourning (1988–92), Dikembe Mutombo (1988–91), and Othella Harrington (1992–96) carried on the tradition of hard working, well-coached, intimidating big men, and Allen Iverson's two years at Georgetown (1994–96) were certainly exciting. My dad and I once saw him play at the USAir Arena; despite being the smallest player on the court, Iverson was remarkably fast and aggressive and close to unstoppable, scoring 40 points against Seton Hall.[47] But the tenacity, especially defensively, and the cultural buzz of the Ewing years were well past. By the time Iverson bolted for the NBA, Georgetown's run as an elite team felt like a distant memory. John Thompson retired in 1999, never having made it back to the Final Four. Still, at least in my lifetime and memory, no college team, in any sport, has come close to captivating Washingtonians like Georgetown basketball did in the 1980s. Beyond that, Georgetown basketball became "the public face of the university and, for many, [it] has connected the cloistered institution with the multicultural city in which it resides," writes Liz Clarke of the *Washington Post*.[48] One need not be a Georgetown student or alum to feel that connection, which is palpable for some people, something like a communal touchstone.

I've excluded more than I have included here, for good reasons. First, that's how memory works: it's selective and partial. Second, we all have space constraints. And finally, most of what I haven't mentioned surely is uninteresting to anyone but me. Take, for example, the 1982 old-timers baseball game at RKF I went to with my father, in which the seventy-five-year-old Luke Appling hit a home run off Warren Spahn. Or the time my dad, brother, and I had breakfast at Roberts restaurant (now long gone) on Wisconsin Avenue, in a booth next to Joe Theismann. Or the sweltering summer I worked at the Sovran Bank/DC National Tennis Classic (now the Citi Open) in Rock Creek Park at the William H. G. Fitzgerald Tennis Center. When I wasn't helping park cars I saw some great tennis, once sitting next to Ion Tiriac, the famous Romanian tennis coach with the bushy mustache and stoic mien, who was managing Boris Becker at the time.

All these and scores of other remembrances—some vivid, some fragmentary, some fading—make up my Washington sports memory. Most of it, I realize, is not monumental stuff, but it is unique and, at least to me, precious. Not because these events were experienced during some kind of Golden Age of DC sports. After all, despite winning a NBA title, three Super Bowls, and a NCAA men's basketball championship, the city had no Major League Baseball team during these years and the Washington Capitals (who never interested me) won exactly one division title until 2000. So DC's overall sports record during these years was mixed at best. No, my Washington sports memories matter because they connect me to DC and my family, because they sustain relationships, allegiances, and feelings that enrich my sense of self.

More important, they are emblematic of memories other people have, some of whom, like me, think of and have experienced sports in DC as a way to forge community. "The favored narrative holds that above all else, love of sports in Washington brings people together across party lines," writes Seth Davis of *Sports Illustrated*, who grew up just outside the city. "Don't buy it—at a game in the capital, politics doesn't enter the equation. I can assure you that Washington politicians care about sports more than Washington sports fans care about politics."[49] Perhaps Davis is right, that sports in DC trumps politics. My experience suggests that local sports teams bring many Washingtonians together; conversely, sports can also be remarkably divisive. Indeed, to some, like journalist Howard Bryant, DC is defined by its divisions, "which makes it hard for the city's teams to build a loyal constituency."[50] It's true that DC is not seamlessly integrated, that the city has longstanding, endemic problems that are exacerbated by partisan politics. It's also true that there aren't many cities that have more loyal and passionate pro football fans than Washington's. I suppose it's a paradox. Ultimately, for many (but certainly not all) people inside and outside the Beltway, DC sports—professional, intercollegiate, interscholastic, recreational—have provided a lingua franca and a storehouse of collective memories that binds us to this place, and to one another.

Notes

Introduction

1. Bio of Short in *Washington Post*, November 5, 1968, D1. For immediate reaction to the move to Texas, see ibid., September 22, 1971, A1, D1, and *Washington Evening Star*, September 22, 1971, A1, A6.

2. *Washington Post*, August 24, 1977, E1.

3. Population information in 1970 census. See US Bureau of the Census, *Statistical Abstract of the United States, 1972* (Washington, DC: Government Printing Office, 1972), 19–20.

4. Mundt quoted in *Washington Post*, July 8, 1958, 19A. For more on governmental involvement with baseball in the District, see Frederic J. Frommer, *The Washington Nationals, 1859 to Today: The Story of Baseball in the Nation's Capital* (Lanham, MD: Taylor Trade Publishing, 2006), 111–13; Tom Deveaux, *The Washington Senators, 1901–1971* (Jefferson, NC: McFarland, 2001), 202–3, 207; James R. Hartley, *Washington's Expansion Senators (1961–1971)* (Germantown, MD: Corduroy Press, 1998, 1997), v; and *Washington Post*, September 21, 1971, D1. The Senators played up the fact that they were located in the nation's capital. A 1970 Senators program, for instance, showed a smiling President Nixon, clapping. "Our No. 1 Fan" read a phrase next to the picture. See Frank Ceresi and Mark Rucker, with Carol McMains, *Baseball in Washington, D.C.* (Charleston, SC: Arcadia, 2002), 105.

5. A variety of sources explore the history of the United States during the 1970s. See Bruce J. Schulman, *The Seventies: The Great Shift in American Culture, Society, and Politics* (New York: Free Press, 2001); Edward Berkowitz, *Something Happened: A Political and Cultural Overview of the Seventies* (New York: Columbia University Press, 2006); Peter N. Carroll, *It Seemed Like Nothing Happened: The Tragedy and Promise of America in the 1970s* (New York: Holt, Rinehart and Winston, 1982), and David Frum, *How We Got Here: The 70's, the Decade That Brought You Modern Life (for Better or Worse)* (New York: Basic Books, 2000).

6. See *Los Angeles Times*, September 24, 1989, 5I, and *New York Times*, October 8, 1992, 20A.

7. Black residents went primarily to Prince George's County in Maryland. See Howard Gillette Jr., *Between Justice and Beauty: Race, Planning, and the Failure of Urban Policy in Washington, DC* (Baltimore: Johns Hopkins University Press, 1995), 206.

8. Several excellent books examine the expansion of the United States in the post–WWII era. See William H. Chafe, *The Unfinished Journey: America since WWII* (New York: Oxford University Press, 1986); Eric F. Goldman, *The Crucial Decade—and After: America, 1945–1960* (New York: Random House, 1960; 1956); James T. Patterson, *Grand Expectations: The United States, 1945–1974* (New York: Oxford University Press, 1996); and Stephen A. Ambrose, *Rise to Globalism: American Foreign Policy, 1938–1980*, 2nd rev. ed. (New York: Penguin Books, 1980).

9. Population figures in U.S. Bureau of the Census, *U.S. Census Population: 1960, Selected Area Reports, Standard Metropolitan Statistical Areas, Final Report PC (3)-1D* (Washington, DC: Government Printing Office, 1963), 154, and *Statistical Abstract of the United States, 1982–83* (Washington, DC: Government Printing Office, 1983), 19. David Brinkley, *Washington Goes to War* (New York: A. A. Knopf, 1988), 282–83.

10. Several sources cover the history of segregation in DC. For instance, see Constance McLaughlin Green, *The Secret City: A History of Race Relations in the Nation's Capital* (Princeton, NJ: Princeton University Press, 1967); Elizabeth Clark-Lewis, *Living In, Living Out: African American Domestics in Washington, D.C., 1910–1940* (Washington, DC: Smithsonian Institution Press, 1994); Kathryn Schneider Smith, ed., *Washington at Home: An Illustrated History of Neighborhoods in the Nation's Capital*, 2nd ed. (Baltimore: Johns Hopkins University Press, 2010); James Borchert, *Alley Life in Washington: Family, Community, Religion, and Folklife in the City, 1850–1970* (Urbana: University of Illinois Press, 1980); Keith Melder, *City of Magnificent Intentions: A History of Washington, District of Columbia*, 2nd ed. (Washington, DC: Intac, 1997); and Blair Ruble, *U Street: A Biography* (Baltimore: Johns Hopkins University Press, 2010). The District's African American population increased from 109,966 in 1920 to 187,266 in 1940. Some of the increase can be attributed to natural growth, but much of it came from African Americans migrating from southern states, particularly North and South Carolina. Figures in *Statistical Abstract of the United States, 1952* (Washington, DC: Government Printing Office, 1952), 32. *Segregation in Washington: A Report of the National Committee on Segregation in the Nation's Capital*. Copy located in Washingtoniana Collection, MLK Library, Washington, DC. *Negro Digest*, March 1948, 44.

11. For information on playground and swimming pool segregation, see Martha Verbrugge's chapter in this collection; Constance McLaughlin Green, *The Secret City*, 270–73, 290–93; and "Final Report of Citizens Committee Against Segregation in Recreation," NAACP Papers, Box II: B67, Folder 5, Manuscript Division, Library of Congress, Washington, DC. Boxing and track and field information in *Baltimore Afro-American*, November 1, 1947, and "Final Report of Citizens Committee Against Segregation in Recreation," 12. For more on Sidat-Singh and the game against Maryland, see *Baltimore Afro-American*, October 30, 1937, 1, and Thomas G. Smith, "Outside the Pale: The Exclusion of Blacks from Organized Professional Football, 1934–1946," *Journal of Sport History* 15 (Winter 1988): 262–63. Marbles tournament in *Segregation in Washington*, 83.

12. Henderson quoted in *Norfolk Journal and Guide*, January 31, 1948, 13. For more on Uline Arena, boxing, and the AAU, see David K. Wiggins, "Edwin

Bancroft Henderson: Physical Educator, Civil Rights Activist, and Chronicler of African American Athletes," *Research Quarterly for Exercise and Sport* 70 (June 1999): 99–101.

13. The first black to play for the Senators was Carlos Paula, an outfielder from Cuba. Paula's initial season was 1954. A thoughtful and detailed account of the inclusion of black players on the 1962 Redskins is Thomas G. Smith, *Showdown: JFK and the Integration of the Washington Redskins* (Boston: Beacon Press, 2012). For more on swimming pools and postsegregation Washington, DC, see Jeff Wiltses, *Contested Waters: A Social History of Swimming Pools in America* (Chapel Hill: University of North Carolina Press, 2007), 193–98.

14. *New York Times*, December 21, 1974, 52. Washington's infatuation with the Redskins is also discussed in *Inside Sports*, October 1979, 32–38.

15. *Washington Post Magazine*, September 4, 1994, 20, and *ESPN The Magazine*, October 15, 2012, 42. The latter contained an inset featuring former *Washington Post* sportswriters Michael Wilbon and Tony Kornheiser explaining why they consider Washingtonians to be apathetic fans of local teams. See *ESPN The Magazine*, October 15, 2012, 41.

16. *Washington Post Magazine*, September 4, 1994, 21. *ESPN The Magazine*, October 15, 2012, cover. The issue of *ESPN The Magazine* was devoted almost exclusively to sports in Washington.

17. Much of the work that exists on the history of sport in Washington covers football and baseball. For an excellent discussion of football, the Redskins, racial issues, and governmental involvement in sport, see Smith, *Showdown*, and Thomas G. Smith, "Civil Rights on the Gridiron: The Kennedy Administration and the Desegregation of the Washington Redskins," *Journal of Sport History* 14 (Summer 1987): 189–208. Other books on the Redskins include Michael Richman, *The Redskins Encyclopedia* (Philadelphia: Temple University Press, 2008); Thom Leverro, *Hail Victory: An Oral History of the Washington Redskins* (Hoboken, NJ: John Wiley & Sons, 2006); and Alan Beall, *Braves on the Warpath: The Fifty Greatest Games in the History of the Washington Redskins* (Washington, DC: Kinloch Books, 1988).

For the history of baseball in Washington, see Brad Snyder, *Beyond the Shadow of the Senators: The Untold Story of the Homestead Grays and the Integration of Baseball* (Chicago: Contemporary Books, 2003); Barry Svrluga, *National Pastime: Sports, Politics, and the Return of Baseball to Washington, DC* (New York: Doubleday, 2006); Frank Ceresi and Carol McMains, "The Washington Nationals and the Development of the America's National Pastime," *Washington History* 15 (Spring/Summer 2003): 26–41; Mark Gavreau Judge, *Damn Senators: My Grandfather and the Story of Washington's Only World Series Championship* (San Francisco: Encounter Books, 2003); Hartley, *Washington's Expansion Senators*; Frommer, *The Washington Nationals, 1859 to Today*; Frederick S. Tyler, "Fifty-Five Years of Local Baseball: 1893–1947," *The Columbia Historical Society, Washington, D.C.* 48/49 (1946–47): 264–79; Stephen J. Walker, *A Whole New Ballgame: The 1969 Washington Senators* (Clifton, VA: Pocol Press, 2009); Deveaux, *The Washington Senators, 1901–1971*; Ted Leavengood, *Ted Williams and the 1969 Washington Senators: The Last Winning Season* (Jefferson, NC: McFarland, 2009); and Henry W. Thomas, *Walter Johnson: Baseball's Big Train* (Washington, DC: Phenom Press, 1995).

Brett L. Abrams and Raphael Mazzone, *The Bullets, the Wizards, and Washington, DC, Basketball* (Lanham, MD: Scarecrow Press, 2013), examine the evolution of professional basketball in DC. A good portion of Bob Kuska, *Hot Potato: How Washington and New York Gave Birth to Black Basketball and Changed America's Game Forever* (Charlottesville: University of Virginia Press, 2004), focuses on the early years of African American basketball in Washington. Pick-up basketball in DC is discussed in Paul Wice, "Safe Haven: A Memoir of Playground Basketball and Desegregation," *Washington History* 9 (Fall/Winter 1997/1998): 54–71. Kirk Fraser, dir., *Without Bias*, 2009, ESPN Films/May 3rd Films is a superb documentary on the tragic death of University of Maryland basketball star Len Bias in 1986.

African American sport in Washington is explored in William H. Jones, `
Recreation and Amusement Among Negroes in Washington, D.C.: A Sociological Analysis of the Negro in an Urban Environment (Washington, DC: Howard University Press, 1927); Ted Chambers, *The History of Athletics and Physical Education at Howard University* (New York: Vantage Press, 1986); Earl Telfair, *The Black Athletes of the District of Columbia during the Segregated Years: Remembering* (Washington, DC: Self-Published, 1999); and Wiggins, "Edwin Bancroft Henderson," 91–112.

The city's athletic venues are the subject of Brett L. Abrams, *Capital Sporting Grounds: A History of Stadium and Ballpark Construction in Washington, D.C.* (Jefferson, NC: McFarland, 2009), and Justine Christianson, "The Uline Arena / Washington Coliseum: The Rise and Fall of a Washington Institution," *Washington History* 16 (Spring/Summer 2004): 16–35. Other sources on Washington sport include Shirley Povich, *All These Mornings* (Englewood Cliffs, NJ: Prentice-Hall, 1969); Lynn Povich, Maury Povich, David Povich, and George Solomon, *All Those Mornings . . . at the Post: The Twentieth Century in Sports from Famed Washington Post Columnist Shirley Povich* (New York: Public Affairs, 2005); Sugar Ray Leonard with Michael Arkush, *The Big Fight: My Life in and out of the Ring* (New York: Viking, 2011); Lara Otis, "Washington's Lost Racetracks: Horse Racing from the 1760s to the 1930s," *Washington History* 24 (2012): 136–54; "Playing Around Town," in *Growing Up in Washington, D.C.: An Oral History*, ed. Jill Connors (Charleston, SC: Arcadia, 2001), 96–124; Bernard Mergen, "Children's Playgrounds in the District of Columbia, 1902–1942," *The Columbia Historical Society, Washington, D.C.* 50 (1980): 383–97; and Robert G. Ainsworth, *Sport in the Nation's Capital: A Pictorial History* (Norfolk, VA: Donning, 1978).

Chapter 1: The Extraordinary History of Cycling and Bike Racing

1. *Washington Post*, April 16, 1984, C7.
2. Robert A. Smith, *A Social History of the Bicycle: Its Early Life and Times in America* (New York: American Heritage Press, 1972), 7.
3. *Wheelman (Outing)* 3 (November 1883), 85. This source was written by a committee of the club for the leading bicycle publication—and later, the leading sports publication—in the country. Other sources place the founding date of the club much later, in fact after the publication of this article. The Smithsonian asserts

on its website that the date was 1884. In *A Social History of the Bicycle*, Smith wrote that the club was not created until 1891. That the club was founded much earlier suggests that Washington had a longer history with the bicycle than scholars might have previously assumed. See "The Capital Bicycle Club and Its Camera Club," http://americanhistory.si.edu/1896/ps01.htm, and Smith, *A Social History of the Bicycle*, 118.

4. Smith, *A Social History of the Bicycle*, 7–8.

5. Ibid., 9.

6. *Washington Post*, May 29, 1881, 4.

7. Ibid.

8. *Wheelman (Outing)* 3 (November 1883), 1–4.

9. Ibid., 7, 13; also see Andrew Ritchie, *Major Taylor: The Extraordinary Career of a Champion Bicycle Racer* (Baltimore: Johns Hopkins University Press, 1996), 29–31.

10. *Wheelman (Outing)* 3 (November 1883), 89.

11. Ibid.

12. James E. McWilliams, *American Pests: The Losing War on Insects from Colonial Times to DDT* (New York: Columbia University Press, 2008), 111. Riley assumed his position of director after his predecessor was killed in a bicycle accident.

13. *Wheelman (Outing)* 3 (November 1883), 89.

14. Ibid., 85.

15. DC Community Archives, collection 57, Capital Bicycle Club (hereafter cited as CBC), series III, box 9, Martin Luther King Library, Washingtoniana Division, Washington, DC.

16. Ibid., 90.

17. *Wheelman (Outing)* 3 (January 1884), 300.

18. Ibid., 3 (November 1883), 90, 95.

19. Ibid., 94.

20. *Outing* 17 (October 1890), 77.

21. *Washington Post*, August 2, 1896, 10.

22. CBC, series I, box 1.

23. *Wheelman (Outing)* 3 (November 1883), 92.

24. *Outing* began as a venture of New Englander Albert Pope and early bicycle enthusiast Charles E. Pratt, while S. S. McClure financed it. Originally titled *Wheelman*, it was a monthly publication that ended up becoming the most important sports journal of its era. See Smith, *A Social History of the Bicycle*, 8–9.

25. *Outing* 17 (October 1890), 65.

26. Ibid., 71.

27. Ibid., 70.

28. Ibid., 75.

29. Ibid., 78.

30. *Wheelman (Outing)* 3 (November 1883), 91.

31. Ibid., 88.

32. *Washington Post*, September 17, 1895, 8. Also see ibid., July 21, 1881, 4.

33. Ritchie, *Major Taylor*, 35–37.

34. *Washington Post*, October 13, 1891, 6.

35. Ibid., July 1, 1900, 8.

36. Ibid., September 15, 1895, 5. Information on Lacy in "Report of the Special Committee on Investigation of the Government Hospital for the Insane," *House Reports: 59th Congress, 2nd Session, December 1906–March 4, 1907: United States Congressional Serial Set, Issue 5066, Vol. 1*, Report Number 7644 (Washington, DC: Government Printing Office, 1907), 253–55.

37. *Washington Post*, July 7, 1896, 8.

38. Ibid., August 14, 1896, 4, and September 15, 1895, 5. Initially, the Ideal Cycle Club had decided in July to put on its own parade in response to the way in which LAW had treated black riders seeking to participate in their parade. However, the District League of Colored Wheelmen attempted to create a more overarching organizational structure that would include all African American riding clubs in the city.

39. *Washington Post*, October 29, 1893, 10.

40. Ibid., September 30, 1883, 8.

41. Ibid., May 20, 1883, 8.

42. *Outing* 17 (October 1890), 2.

43. Ibid., 72.

44. *Washington Post*, August 26, 1892, 6.

45. CBC, series III, box 9.

46. *Washington Post*, July 21, 1892, 2.

47. Ibid., May 20, 1894, 6. Even early in the history of the sport in Washington, few cyclists counted themselves as members of LAW. In 1883, the Washington Cycle Club counted itself as the only LAW affiliated club in the city. See the *Wheelman (Outing)* 3 (December 1883), 231.

48. *Outing* 17 (October 1890), 72.

49. Brett L. Abrams, *Capital Sporting Grounds: A History of Stadium and Ballpark Construction in Washington, DC* (Jefferson, NC: McFarland, 2009), 37.

50. *Washington Post*, February 29, 1896, 7.

51. Abrams, *Capital Sporting Grounds*, 46–48.

52. Ibid., 50–53.

53. Ibid., 52–53.

54. The medical community tended to support bicycling as a healthy activity for women. However, some physicians and public health officials argued that the safety bikes were harmful to female riders. As one woman delicately put it, bicycle riding undermined "feminine symmetry and poise, a disturber of internal organs and an irritant of external tissues." See Smith, *A Social History of the Bicycle*, 65.

55. *Christian Advocate*, September 12, 1895, 70, 37.

56. Abrams, *Capital Sporting Grounds*, 53.

57. *Washington Post*, December 6, 1927, E1.

58. Ibid., July 5, 1896, 19. *Outing* 30 (June 1897), 234.

59. *Washington Post*, August 21, 1896, 7.

60. *New York Times*, October 6, 1896, 3.

61. *Washington Post*, October 19, 1886, 8.

62. Smith, *A Social History of the Bicycle*, 134–35.

63. *Washington Post*, December 6, 1927, E3.

64. Abrams, *Capital Sporting Grounds*, 61–63.

65. Ibid., 67–69.

66. *Washington Post*, November 20, 1927, 23.
67. Ibid., August 16, 1927, 15.
68. Ibid., August 17, 1927, 13, 15.
69. *Pittsburgh Press*, August 22, 1927, 4.

Chapter 2: Less Than Monumental

1. Philip J. Lowry, *Green Cathedrals: The Ultimate Celebration of Major League and Negro League Ballparks* (New York: Walker and Company, 2006).
2. *Washington Post,* December 7, 1959.
3. Ibid., September 23, 2007.
4. See Kate Masur, *An Example for All the Land: Emancipation and the Struggle over Equality in Washington, DC* (Chapel Hill: University of North Carolina Press, 2010).
5. Sandra Fitzpatrick and Maria R. Goodwin, *The Guide to Black Washington: Places and Events of Historical and Cultural Significance in the Nation's Capital* (New York: Hippocrene Books, 1990), 17.
6. United States Census Office, *Compendium of the Ninth Census,* 136. Also see Kathleen M. Lesko, Valerie Babb, and Carroll R. Gibbs, *Black Georgetown Remembered: A History of Its Black Community from the Founding of "The Town of George" in 1751 to the Present Day* (Washington, DC: Georgetown University Press, 1991).
7. Borchert, *Alley Life in Washington*, 2–5, 23–24.
8. Pierre L'Enfant to George Washington, September 11, 1789. In Digges-Morgan Papers, Library of Congress. Cited in Donald E. Jackson, "L'Enfant's Washington: An Architect's View," *Records of the Columbia Historical Society, Washington, D.C.* 50 (1980): 398–420.
9. James H. Whyte, *The Uncivil War: Washington During the Reconstruction, 1865–1878* (New York: Twayne Publishers, 1958), 134–35.
10. *Sunday Mercury,* June 6, 1869.
11. *Washington Post,* June 3, 1924.
12. Michael Benson, *Ballparks of North America: A Comprehensive Historical Reference to Baseball Grounds, Yards, Stadiums, 1845–Present* (Jefferson, NC: McFarland, 1989), 406, and *Sunday Herald and Weekly Intelligencer,* June 20, 1873.
13. *Chadwick Scrapbooks,* May 1860.
14. *New York Clipper,* May 5, 1866.
15. Loren Schweniger, *Black Property Owners in the South, 1790–1915* (Urbana: University of Illinois Press, 1990), 200–204.
16. The phenomena of geographically based social remembrance has moved, in the twentieth and twenty-first centuries, from the front yard of the White House to the steps of the Lincoln Memorial. The value of this public space has been validated repeatedly by public demonstrations, such as Martin Luther King Jr.'s "I Have a Dream" speech. Scott A. Sandage explores this phenomenon further in "A Marble House Divided: The Lincoln Memorial, the Civil Rights Movement, and the Politics of Memory, 1939–1963," *Journal of American History* 80 (June 1993): 135–67.

17. *New York Clipper,* May 15, 1869; *Sunday Mercury,* April 25, 1869.

18. *New National Era,* September 28, 1871.

19. *Sunday Herald and Weekly National Intelligencer,* June 30, 1872.

20. Ibid., September 6, 1874.

21. *Washington Post,* November 2, 1880.

22. *New York Times,* May 14, 1895.

23. US Army Corps of Engineers, http://www.usace.army.mil/About/History/HistoricalVignettes/ParksandMonuments/006WhiteHouse (accessed June 1, 2012).

24. *Washington Post,* May 21, 1885.

25. Ibid., July 22, 1901.

26. Ibid., August 14, 1888.

27. Ryan Swanson, "'I Was Never a Champion at Anything': Theodore Roosevelt's Complex and Contradictory Record as America's 'Sports President,'" *Journal of Sport History* 38 (Fall 2011): 425–46.

28. *Washington Post,* April 19, 1904.

29. Ibid., March 7, 1907.

30. Ibid., October 8, 1905.

31. Ibid., July 5, 1910.

32. Lowry, *Green Cathedrals,* 233.

33. Blair Ruble, *Washington's U Street: A Biography* (Baltimore: Johns Hopkins University Press, 2010), 159.

34. Quoted in Constance M. Green, *The Secret City, A History of Race Relations in the Nation's Capital* (Princeton, NJ: Princeton University Press, 1967), 202.

35. Sandra Fitzpatrick and Maria R. Goodwin, *Black Washington: Places and Events of Historical and Cultural Significance in the Nation's Capital* (New York: Hippocrene Books, 1990), 145–47.

36. Leavengood, *Clark Griffith,* 141.

37. Tom Deveaux, *The Washington Senators, 1901–1971* (Jefferson, NC: McFarland, 2001), 49–60, 84.

38. Ted Leavengood, *Clark Griffith: The Old Fox of Washington Baseball* (Jefferson, NC: McFarland, 2011), 140.

39. *Washington Post,* October 10, 1924.

40. Ibid., October 5, 1924.

41. Baseball-reference.com, http://www.baseball-reference.com/teams/MIN/attend.shtml (accessed June 13, 2012).

42. Ruble, *Washington's U Street,* 153.

43. Fitzpatrick and Goodwin, *Black Washington,* 146, and Raymond Schmidt, "Another Football World," *College Football Historical Society Newsletter* 38 (November 2004): 13.

44. *Washington Post,* October 4, 1937.

45. *New York Amsterdam News,* November 16, 1940.

46. *Washington Post,* October 25, 1923.

47. Ibid., September 4, 1913, and April 22, 1916.

48. Ibid., October 31, 1929.

49. Office of the Clerk, "Congressional Baseball Game," http://artandhistory.house.gov/house_history/baseball/history.aspx (accessed June 26, 2012).

50. *Washington Post,* May 29, 1932.

51. Ibid., May 19, 1932.

52. Dick Clark and Larry Lester, *The Negro Leagues Book: A Monumental Work from the Negro Leagues Committee of the Society for American Baseball Research* (Cleveland, OH: SABR Press, 1994). See also Brad Snyder, *Beyond the Shadow of the Senators: The Untold Story of the Homestead Grays and the Integration of Baseball* (New York: McGraw-Hill, 2004; 2003). Some Negro League experts contend that the Grays won eight of nine Colored World Series.

53. For an excellent account of the financial side of the Negro Leagues, see Michael Lomax, *Black Baseball Entrepreneurs, 1860–1901: Operating by Any Means Necessary* (Syracuse, NY: Syracuse University Press, 1996).

54. *Washington Post,* August 1, 1950.

55. *New York Times,* August 10, 1956.

56. *Washington Post,* January 10, 1959.

57. Jim Reisler, *Black Writers/Black Baseball: An Anthology of Articles from Black Sportswriters Who Covered the Negro Leagues* (Jefferson, NC: McFarland, 2007), and Brian Carroll, *When to Stop the Cheering? The Black Press, the Black Community, and the Integration of Professional Baseball* (New York: Routledge, 2007).

58. For an excellent analysis of the DC Stadium-Redskins integration issue, see Thomas G. Smith, *Showdown: JFK and the Integration of the Washington Redskins* (Boston: Beacon Press, 2011).

59. US Congress, 79th Congress, First Session, Subcommittee of the Committee on Appropriations, United States Senate, "First Deficiency Appropriation Bill for 1945," 165.

60. Ibid., 166.

61. *Congressional Record*, US Senate, November 1, 1945, 10253.

62. For a comprehensive history of the politics surrounding stadium construction in DC, see Brett L. Abrams, *Capital Sporting Grounds: A History of Stadium and Ballpark Construction in Washington, DC* (Jefferson, NC: McFarland, 2009).

63. *Washington Post,* June 13, 1956.

64. US Senate, Report of Proceedings, Subcommittee on Fiscal Affairs, of the Committee on the District of Columbia, July 1, 1957.

65. Public Law 85–300, September 7, 1957, *United States Statutes at Large,* Vol. 71, 619.

66. Abrams, *Capital Sporting Grounds,* 228–29.

67. *Washington Post,* July 9, 1960.

68. Ibid., October 2, 1961; John Keim, *Stadium Stories: Washington Redskins* (Guilford, CT: Globe Pequot Press, 2005), 100.

69. *Chicago Daily Tribune,* September 29, 1961.

70. *Washington Post,* April 10, 1962.

71. US General Accounting Office, "Report to the Congress of the United States: Failure to Construct District of Columbia Stadium in Accordance with the Financial Plan Submitted to the Congress," (Washington, DC, 1964), 17.

72. *Washington Post,* July 7, 1962.

73. US General Accounting Office, "Report to the Congress of the United

States: Failure to Construct District of Columbia Stadium in Accordance with the Financial Plan Submitted to the Congress" (Washington, DC, 1964), 2.

74. District of Columbia Armory Board, *1963 Annual Report* (Washington, DC), S-3; District of Columbia Armory Board, *1967 Annual Report* (Washington, DC), A-3.

75. *Washington Post,* July 7, 1962.

76. Ibid., March 25, 1961.

77. See US Senate, Committee on Rules and Administration, "Authorizing an Investigation into the Financial, Business or Other Interests or Activities of Present or Former Members, Officers, or Employees of the Senate (Construction of the DC Stadium and Matters Related Thereto)," February 4, 1965; US Senate, Committee on Rules and Administration, 89th Congress, 1st Session, "Hearing Pursuant to Construction of the District of Columbia Stadium, and Matters Thereto," Parts 1–3, appendix.

78. US General Accounting Office, "Report to the Congress of the United States: Review of the Change Orders and Other Matters Relating to the Construction of District of Columbia Stadium" (Washington, DC, 1966), 3.

79. *Washington Post,* January 23, 1973.

80. US House of Representatives, Subcommittee on Government Operations and Metropolitan Affairs, Committee on the District of Columbia, 97th Congress, 2nd Session, "To Transfer Ownership of RFK Stadium from the U.S. Government to the Government of the District of Columbia," August 12, 1982, 4.

81. Ibid.

82. *Washington Post,* November 25, 2009.

Chapter 3: The Biggest "Classic" of Them All

I would like to thank Chris Elzey, Tom Jable, and Patrick Miller for providing cogent comments and suggestions on an earlier draft of this manuscript. I would also like to thank Pierre Rodgers for sharing copies of the *Philadelphia Tribune* that were secured from the Lincoln University Library.

1. For examples of works that deal with various aspects of sports behind walls of segregation, see Janet Bruce, *The Kansas City Monarchs: Champions of Black Baseball* (Lawrence: University Press of Kansas, 1985); Susan Cahn, *Coming on Strong: Gender and Sexuality in Twentieth-Century Women's Sport* (New York: Free Press, 1994); Nelson George, *Elevating the Game: Black Men and Basketball* (New York: HarperCollins, 1992); Neil Lanctot, *Negro League Baseball: The Rise and Ruin of a Black Institution* (Philadelphia: University of Pennsylvania Press, 2004); Jennifer H. Lansbury, "'The Tuskegee Flash' and 'The Slender Harlem Stroker': Black Women Athletes on the Margin," *Journal of Sport History* 28 (Summer 2001): 233–52; Pete McDaniel, *Uneven Lies: The Heroic Story of African-Americans in Golf* (Greenwich, CT: American Golfers, 2000); Patrick B. Miller, "'To 'Bring the Race Along Rapidly': Sport, Student Culture, and Educational Mission at Historically Black Colleges During the Interwar Years," *History of Education Quarterly* 35 (Summer 1995): 111–23; Troy D. Paino, "Hoosiers in a Different Light: Forces of Change vs. the Power of

Nostalgia," *Journal of Sport History* 26 (Spring 2001): 63–80; Rob Ruck, *Sandlot Seasons: Sport in Black Pittsburgh* (Urbana: University of Illinois Press, 1987); Robert Gregg, "Personal Calvaries: Sports in Philadelphia's African American Communities, 1920–60," *Sport in Society* 6 (October 2003): 88–115.

2. *Chicago Defender*, December 2, 1922; William H. Jones, *Recreation and Amusement Among Negroes in Washington, D.C.: A Sociological Analysis of the Negro in an Urban Environment* (Washington, DC: Howard University Press, 1927).

3. Raymond Schmidt, *Shaping College Football: The Transformation of an American Sport, 1919–1930* (Syracuse, NY: Syracuse University Press, 2007), 13.

4. See Horace Mann Bond, "The Story of Athletics at Lincoln University," unpublished chapter from Horace Mann Bond, *Education for Freedom: A History of Lincoln University, Pennsylvania* (Princeton, NJ: Princeton University Press, 1976), 3–26; "History of Athletics," *The Bison*, 1924, n.p.; *Baltimore Afro-American*, November 28, 1919; *Pittsburgh Courier*, November 19, 1924, and December 1, 1923; *Chicago Defender*, November 23, 1929.

5. *Philadelphia Tribune*, October 18 and November 1, 1919. See also *Washington Post*, November 28, 1919.

6. There are few autobiographical accounts of the games and the accompanying social activities. One exception was U. S. Young, former Lincoln coach, who wrote an account of the 1925 game in the *Baltimore Afro-American*. See *Baltimore Afro-American*, December 12, 1925. Another exception was the account of the 1925 game written by Tad Lancaster, captain of the Lincoln team. See *Baltimore Afro-American*, December 12, 1925.

7. *Philadelphia Tribune*, December 4, 1920; *Chicago Defender*, December 4, 1920; and *Washington Bee*, December 4, 1920.

8. Bond, "The Story of Athletics at Lincoln University," 28–29; *Philadelphia Tribune*, December 4, 1920; *Chicago Defender*, December 4, 1920; and *Baltimore Afro-American*, December 10, 1920. The first ballpark located at the site of Griffith Stadium was called Boundary Field or National Park. Built in 1891, the ballpark was renamed the American League Park in 1901 when the Washington Nationals baseball team joined Ban Johnson's new American League. In 1911, the ballpark was destroyed by fire, but was rebuilt with a seating capacity of more than 27,000 and called American Baseball Park II. In 1920 the ballpark was once again renamed, this time to Griffith Stadium. See the essay by Ryan Swanson in this volume; Michael Benson, *Ballparks of North America: A Comprehensive Historical Reference to Baseball Grounds, Yards, Stadiums, 1845–Present* (Jefferson, NC: McFarland, 1989), and http://www.ballparksofbaseball.com/past/GriffithStadium.htm (accessed July 7, 2014).

9. Bond, "The Story of Athletics at Lincoln University," 29; *Chicago Defender*, November 19, 26, December 3, 1921; *Howard University Record* 16 (December 1921), 125–26; *Washington Post*, November 21, 25, 1921.

10. *Chicago Defender*, December 3, 1921; *Baltimore Afro-American*, November 25, 1921.

11. Bond, "The Story of Athletics at Lincoln University," 30–31; *Chicago Defender*, November 25 and December 2, 9, 1922; *New York Age*, December 9, 1922; *New York Amsterdam News*, December 6, 1922.

12. For descriptions of the game, see *Chicago Defender,* December 1, 1923; *Baltimore Afro-American*, November 16, 17, 30, 1923, and December 7, 14, 1923; *Pittsburgh Courier*, November 17, 1923; *Boston Daily Globe*, November 30, 1923; *Norfolk Journal and Guide*, December 8, 1923; *New York Times*, November 30, 1923. The Lincoln team of 1923 was extraordinary for both its athletic accomplishments and the professional success of its players in their post-college lives. Five players were named to the All-Central Intercollegiate Athletic Association team, six players were selected to either the first, second, or third teams on Fay Young's *Chicago Defender* All-American squad; and following graduation three players took medical degrees, two PhDs, two law degrees, and another four various types of master's degrees. Bond, "The Story of Athletics at Lincoln University," 30–31; *Chicago Defender*, November 17, 24, 1923; *Howard University Record* 18 (January 1924), 199–200, 202; *Philadelphia Tribune*, December 8, 1923.

13. Bond, "The Story of Athletics at Lincoln University," 21–37; *Howard University Record* 19 (January 1925), 114–16; *Pittsburgh Courier*, November 1, 24, 29, and December 6, 20, 1924; *Chicago Defender*, November 22, 29, and December 6, 1924; *Philadelphia Tribune*, November 22, 27, 29, and December 6, 1924; *Washington Post*, November 28, 1924; *Norfolk Journal and Guide*, December 6, 1924; *Crisis* 29 (February 1925), 171–72; *Howard Alumnus* 3 (January 15, 1925), 62.

14. *Baltimore Afro-American*, November 29, 1924; *Chicago Defender*, December 6, 1924.

15. *Chicago Defender*, December 29, 1924; *Pittsburgh Courier*, December 27, 1924. For a nice secondary account of the Miller affair, see Schmidt, *Shaping College Football*, 138–39.

16. Bond, "The Story of Athletics at Lincoln University," 37; *Chicago Defender*, December 5, 1925; *Pittsburgh Courier*, December 5, 1925; *Washington Post*, November 27, 1925.

17. *Pittsburgh Courier*, December 11, 1926. See also *Chicago Defender*, December 18, 1926; *Norfolk Journal and Guide*, December 18, 1926.

18. Bond, "The Story of Athletics at Lincoln University," 37–38; *Crisis* 34 (March 1927): 7; *Chicago Defender*, November 20 and December 4, 1926; *Pittsburgh Courier*, December 4, 18, 20, 1926; *Philadelphia Tribune*, November 20, 27 and December 4, 1926; *Washington Post*, November 14, 26, 1926; *New York Times*, November 26, 1926. The 1920s witnessed the building of many large stadiums at predominantly white universities. Northwestern University and the University of Missouri, for instance, built new stadiums in 1926, with seating capacities of approximately 40,000 to 50,000. See Raymond Schmidt, *Shaping College Football*, esp. chapter 3.

19. *Washington Post*, November 26, 1926.

20. Howard University Archives (hereafter cited as HUA), Department of Athletics, Box 34, "Programs, 1926–1932," 5 of 6.

21. Bond, "The Story of Athletics at Lincoln University," 38; *Philadelphia Tribune*, November 24, 1927; *Crisis* 35 (February 1928): 45; *Chicago Defender*, November 12 and December 3, 1927. For a good analysis of the conflict between education and athletics during both the Durkee and Johnson years at Howard,

see Miller, "To 'Bring the Race Along Rapidly': Sport, Student Culture, and Educational Mission at Historically Black Colleges during the Interwar Years," 111–23.

22. *Philadelphia Tribune*, November 22, 29, 1928; *Chicago Defender*, November 24, 1928; *Washington Post*, November 29, 1928; *New York Times*, November 30, 1928; and *Washington Afro-American*, May 26, 1934. West became the first African American to play quarterback in the Rose Bowl in 1922 when Washington and Jefferson fought to a 0–0 tie in Pasadena against the University of California. He also qualified for the 1924 Olympic track and field team, but could not participate because of an injury. For specific information on West, see E. Lee North, *Battling the Indians, Panthers & Nittany Lions: Washington & Jefferson College's Century of Football, 1890–1990* (Canton, OH: Daring, 1991), and Allyson Gilmore, "Breaking Barriers: W & J Remembers Legendary Athlete Who Changed the Game for African-Americans in Collegiate Sports," from http://www.washieff.edu/breaking-barriers-wj-remembers-legendary-athlete-who-changed-game-African-Americans-collegiate-sports (accessed February 2, 2013).

23. HUA, Department of Athletics, Box 33, "News Items, 1938–1943," 4 of 5.

24. *Chicago Defender*, November 23 and December 7, 1929; *Philadelphia Tribune*, November 28 and December 5, 1929; *Baltimore Afro-American*, December 14, 1929.

25. For nice overviews of the Carnegie Foundation Report, see Raymond Schmidt, *Shaping College Football*, 217–33, and Ronald A. Smith, *Pay for Play: A History of Big-Time College Athletic Reform* (Urbana: University of Illinois Press, 2011), 59–70.

26. *New York Amsterdam News*, November 27, 1929. See also *Baltimore Afro-American*, December 14, 1929. *Chicago Defender*, December 5, 12, 1936.

27. Bond, "The Story of Athletics at Lincoln University," 26–27. Finding financial data on the Howard and Lincoln games is difficult, but an "income and expenditures" statement from Howard in 1929 indicated that the school netted $4,256.83 from the "classic" that year. The total income from their four other away games in 1929 was $4,800. See "Statement of Athletics: Incomes and Expenditures July 1, 1929 to December 31, 1929," Moorland-Spingarn Research Center.

28. The changing nature of sport and the rise of a consumer culture during the 1920s is nicely analyzed in Mark Dyreson, "The Emergence of Consumer Culture and the Transformation of Physical Culture: American Sport in the 1920s," *Journal of Sport History* 16 (Winter 1989): 261–81.

29. Bond, "The Story of Athletics at Lincoln University," 26–27. For background information on Scott, see Maceo Crenshaw Dailey Jr., "Emmett Jay Scott: The Career of a Secondary Black Leader" (PhD diss., Howard University, 1983).

30. See Dailey, "Emmett Jay Scott"; Edgar Allan Toppin, "Emmett Jay Scott," in *African American National Biography,* ed. Henry Louis Gates Jr. and Evelyn Brooks Higginbotham (New York: Oxford University Press, 2008), 105–6; Louis R. Harlan, *Booker T. Washington: The Making of a Black Leader, 1952–1901* (New York: Oxford University Press, 1972); Louis R. Harlan, *Booker T. Washington: The Wizard of Tuskegee* (New York: Oxford University Press, 1983);

J. L. Nichols and William H. Crogman, *Progress of a Race of the Remarkable Advancement of the American Negro* (Naperville, IL: J. L. Nichols & Company, 1929), 429; W. N. Hartshorn, ed., *An Era of Progress and Promise, 1863–1910* (Boston: Priscilla Publishing Co., 1910), 414–15. Information on both Lewis and Alexander is limited. See, however, Bond, "The Story of Athletics at Lincoln University," 26–28.

31. *Chicago Defender*, November 23, 1929.

32. See Schmidt, *Shaping College Football*, 135.

33. *Chicago Defender*, November 24, 1928.

34. *Philadelphia Tribune*, November 22, 1928. For information on Thanksgiving Day games among predominantly white universities in the late nineteenth century, see Michael Oriard, *Reading Football: How the Popular Press Created an American Spectacle* (Chapel Hill: University of North Carolina Press, 1993), esp. 89–101.

35. *Chicago Defender*, November 19, 1921.

36. *Philadelphia Tribune*, November 22, 1928.

37. For information on the characteristics and requisite features of sport rivalries, see David K. Wiggins and R. Pierre Rodgers, eds., *Rivals: Legendary Matchups That Made Sports History* (Fayetteville: University of Arkansas Press, 2010), and Richard O. Davies, *Rivals! The Ten Greatest American Sports Rivalries of the 20th Century* (Malden, MA: John Wiley and Sons, 2010).

38. Bond, *Education for Freedom*; US Office of Education, *Survey of Negro Colleges and Universities*, Bulletin 1928, No. 7 (Washington, DC: Government Printing Office, 1929).

39. Walter Dyson, *Howard University: The Capstone of Negro Education, A History: 1867–1940* (Washington, DC: Howard University Press, 1941); Rayford Logan, *Howard University: The First Hundred Years* (New York: New York University Press, 1969); Paul E. Logan, ed., *A Howard Reader: An Intellectual and Cultural Quilt of the African American Experience* (Boston: Houghton Mifflin, 1997); US Office of Education, *Survey of Negro Colleges and Universities*.

40. *Chicago Defender*, December 2, 1922.

41. *Lincoln News*, n.d.

42. *Howard University Record* 16 (December 1921): 126.

43. HUA, Department of Athletics, Box 34, "Programs, 1926–1932," 5 of 6.

44. Miller, "To 'Bring the Race Along Rapidly,'" 119.

45. Michael Oriard, *King Football: Sport and Spectacle in the Golden Age of Radio and Newspapers, Movies and Magazines, the Weekly and the Daily Press* (Chapel Hill: University of North Carolina Press, 2001), 321, 323.

46. Schmidt, *Shaping College Football*, 135.

47. Willard B. Gatewood, *Aristocrats of Color: The Black Elite* (Bloomington: Indiana University Press, 1990), esp. chapters 2 and 4.

48. Blair A. Ruble, *Washington's U Street: A Biography* (Baltimore: Johns Hopkins University Press, 2010).

49. Gatewood, *Aristocrats of Color*, 96–97; Charles Hardy, "Race and Opportunity: Black Philadelphia During the Era of the Great Migration" (PhD diss., Temple University, 1989), 131, 178, 441, 445.

50. See *New York Amsterdam News*, December 6, 1922; *Philadelphia Tribune*,

December 8, 1923; *Baltimore Afro-American*, December 6, 1924; *Chicago Defender*, December 5, 1925; *New York Amsterdam News*, December 1, 1926.

51. Jones, *Recreation and Amusement Among Negroes,* 73.

52. *Philadelphia Tribune*, November 21, 1929.

53. *Chicago Defender*, November 29, 1924.

54. *Howard University Record* 15 (January 1921): 133.

55. Raymond Wolters, *The New Negro on Campus: Black College Rebellions of the 1920s* (Princeton, NJ: Princeton University Press, 1975), 278–93.

56. *Washington Afro-American*, May 16, 30, 1925; May 8, 1926; Zora Neale Hurston, "The Hue and Cry about Howard University," in *A Howard Reader*, 138–46.

57. See Hardy, *Race and Opportunity,* 19, 22; Gatewood, *Aristocrats of Color,* 332–48.

58. *Philadelphia Tribune*, November 29, 1919.

59. *Chicago Defender*, December 2, 1922.

60. *Lincoln News*, November 1931.

61. *Washington Post*, September 9 and 10, 2011.

62. Ibid., September 10, 2011.

63. Ibid., September 9, 2011.

Chapter 4: Teeing Off against Jim Crow

1. For example, see Herbert Warren Wind, *The Story of American Golf* (New York: Simon and Schuster, 1956); H. B. Martin, *Fifty Years of American Golf* (New York: Argosy-Antiquarian, 1966); Herbert B. Graffis, *The PGA: The Official History of the Professional Golfers' Association of America* (New York: Thomas Y. Crowell Company, 1975); Al Barkow, *Gettin' to the Dance Floor: An Oral History of American Golf* (New York: Atheneum, 1986); Al Barkow, *The Golden Era of Golf* (New York: St. Martin's Press, 2000); Stephen R. Lowe, *Sir Walter and Mr. Jones: Walter Hagen, Bobby Jones, and the Rise of American Golf* (Chelsea, MI: Sleeping Bear Press, 2000); Mark Frost, *The Grand Slam: Bobby Jones, America, and the Story of Golf* (New York: Hyperion, 2004); Francis Ouimet, *A Game of Golf* (Boston: Northeastern University Press, 2004); Ron Rapoport, *The Immortal Bobby: Bobby Jones and the Golden Age of Golf* (Hoboken, NJ: John Wiley & Sons, 2005); and George Kirsch, *Golf in America* (Urbana: University of Illinois Press, 2009).

2. Richard J. Moss, *Golf and the American Country Club* (Urbana: University of Illinois Press, 2001), 93.

3. *Washington Post*, April 16, 1921, 2.

4. Calvin H. Sinnette, *Forbidden Fairways: African Americans and the Game of Golf* (Chelsea, MI: Sleeping Bear Press, 1998), 57.

5. *Washington Afro-American*, July 18, 1925, 6, and Marvin P. Dawkins and Graham C. Kinloch, *African American Golfers During the Jim Crow Era* (Westport, CT: Praeger, 2000), 38.

6. Graffis, *The PGA*, 196–98.

7. Sinnette, *Forbidden Fairways*, 17.

8. Ibid., 20–21.

9. *Pittsburgh Courier*, July 2, 1927, 6.

10. *Afro-American* (national ed.), June 6, 1925, 8.

11. *Washington Afro-American*, October 17, 1924, 14.

12. Marvin P. Dawkins and A. C. Tellison Jr., "Golf," in *African Americans and Popular Culture, Volume: 2 Sports*, ed. Todd Boyd (Westport, CT: Praeger, 2008), 54. For more on Shippen and Shady Rest, see Larry Londino, dir., *A Place for Us: The Story of Shady Rest and America's First Golf Professional*, a 1994 documentary film.

13. *Washington Afro-American*, October 17, 1924, 14.

14. Sinnette, *Forbidden Fairways*, 13–14.

15. *Washington Afro-American*, June 8, 1925, 8.

16. Ibid.

17. Sinnette, *Forbidden Fairways*, 55.

18. According to Moss, the Morris County Golf Club included an "associate" membership category, which was limited to two hundred men. See Moss, *Golf and the American Country Club*, 71–72. For further discussion of the formation of the Wake Robin Golf Club, see Sinnette, *Forbidden Fairways*, 99–100; Dawkins and Kinloch, *African American Golfers*, 32–33, and M. Mikell Johnson, *The African American Woman Golfer: Her Legacy* (Westport, CT: Praeger, 2008).

19. Sinnette, *Forbidden Fairways*, 99.

20. Dawkins and Kinloch, *African American Golfers*, 32–33.

21. Sinnette, *Forbidden Fairways*, 114.

22. *Washington Afro-American*, September 9, 1967, 13.

23. Dawkins and Kinloch, *African American Golfers*, 32–33.

24. Ibid., 29.

25. Pete McDaniel, *Uneven Lies: The Heroic Story of African Americans in Golf* (Greenwich, CT: American Golfer, 2000), 66. For more on the Langston course, see "Langston Golf Course and Driving Range, African American Heritage Trail," *Cultural Tourism DC*, http://www.culturaltourismdc.org/things-do-see/langston-golf-course-and-driving-range-african-american-heritage-trail (accessed on August 29, 2012).

26. *Washington Afro-American*, June 10, 1939, 22.

27. Ibid.

28. Ibid., June 17, 1939, 22.

29. Ibid., June 24, 1939, 22.

30. Ibid., July 19, 1941, 19.

31. Sinnette, *Forbidden Fairways*, 39–40.

32. *Washington Afro-American*, August 24, 1940, 23.

33. Dawkins and Kinloch, *African American Golfers*, 33.

34. *Washington Afro-American*, July 29, 1939, 23.

35. *Philadelphia Tribune*, July 24, 1941, 10.

36. *Washington Afro-American*, July 5, 1941, 13.

37. Ibid.

38. See *Washington Post*, June 30, 1941, 15; *New York Amsterdam Star-News*, July 5, 1941, 19; *Atlanta Daily World*, July 7, 1941, 5; *Chicago Defender* (national ed.), July 5, 1941, 3; and *Philadelphia Tribune*, July 10, 1941, 3.

39. Ickes quoted in Dawkins and Kinloch, *African Americans Golfers*, 30.

40. PBS Historical Figures series, http://www.pbs.org/nationalparks/people/historical/#ickes (accessed September 4, 2012).

41. Teaching Eleanor Roosevelt Glossary (Harold LeClaire Ickes, 1874–1952), http://www.gwu.edu/~erpapers/teachinger/glossary/ickes-harold.cfm (accessed September 4, 2012).

42. Harold L. Ickes, *The Secret Diary of Harold Ickes: The Lowering Clouds, 1939–1941, Volume III* (New York: Simon and Schuster, 1954), 579.

43. Dawkins and Kinloch, *African American Golfers*, 125–26.

44. *Washington Post*, July 14, 1941, 13.

45. *Washington Afro-American*, July 19, 1941, 19.

46. Sinnette, *Forbidden Fairways*, 124.

47. *Washington Afro-American*, August 1, 1942, 24.

48. *Los Angeles Sentinel*, January 1, 1951, 6B.

49. *Washington Afro-American*, August 28, 1954, 16.

50. For a discussion of the impact of the *Brown* decision on the golf course discrimination case in Atlanta and other cities, see George Kirsch, "Municipal Golf and Civil Rights in the United States, 1910–1965," *Journal of African American History* 92 (2007): 371–91.

51. Dawkins and Kinloch, *African American Golfers*, 156.

52. For a detailed account of legal challenges and other direct action by black golfers, see ibid., 137–52.

53. *Washington Afro-American*, August 29, 1959, 14.

54. Ibid., August 31, 1963, 9.

55. For example, see *Washington Afro-American*, April 5, 1958, 19, and August 27, 1960, 16; *Philadelphia Tribune*, September 10, 1963, 12; *Washington Afro-American*, June 12, 1965, 10, and July 20, 1968, 18.

56. For more on Elder, see John H. Kennedy, *A Course of Their Own: A History of African American Golfers* (Kansas City, KS: Andrews McMeel Publishing, 2000), 221–40.

57. *Washington Afro-American*, August 7, 1979, 10, and September 8, 1979, 10.

58. Vartan Kupelian, *Stalking the Tiger: A Writer's Diary* (Chelsea, MI: Sleeping Bear Press, 1997), 60–61.

Chapter 5: Shirley Povich and the Tee Shot

1. William Carlos Williams, "The Red Wheelbarrow," in *The American Tradition in Literature*, 11th edition, ed. George Perkins and Barbara Perkins (Boston: McGraw Hill, 2001), 1052.

2. Shirley Povich, *All These Mornings* (Englewood Cliffs, NJ: Prentice-Hall, 1969), 9.

3. Ibid., 7.

4. Quoted in Jerome Holtzman, ed., *No Cheering in the Press Box* (New York: Henry Holt, 1995), 119.

5. Povich, *All These Mornings*, 12.

6. Holtzman, *No Cheering in the Press Box*, 122–23.

7. See Michael Emery and Edward Emery, *The Press and America: An Interpretive History of the Mass Media*, 7th ed. (Englewood Cliffs, NJ: Prentice Hall, 1992), 535–40.

8. Povich, *All These Mornings*, 22–23.

9. In addition to Povich's autobiography, a good source for details of his life and career in journalism is Daniel Nathan, "Last Century, with Shirley Povich: The Sportswriter as Chronicler, Critic, and Historian," *Aethlon: the Journal of Sport Literature* 26 (Fall 2008/Winter 2009): 113–31.

10. Quoted in *Washington Post*, June 5, 1998, A41.

11. Quoted in the Foreword to Povich, *All These Mornings*, x.

12. See Stanley Walker, *City Editor* (Baltimore: Johns Hopkins University Press, 1999; 1934), 123–24.

13. Povich, *All These Mornings*, 16.

14. Ibid., 38.

15. Povich, quoted in Holtzman, *No Cheering in the Press Box*, 125.

16. Povich, *All These Mornings*, 15–16.

17. Chalmer M. Roberts, *In the Shadow of Power: The Story of the* Washington Post (Cabin John, MD: Seven Locks, 1989), 183.

18. *Washington Post*, August 3, 1927, 1.

19. Ibid.

20. Povich, *All These Mornings*, 35.

21. Ibid., 81.

22. *Washington Post*, December 9, 1940, 17.

23. Ibid.

24. Ibid., December 10, 1940, 25.

25. Ibid., December 11, 1940, 27.

26. Ibid., December 9, 1940, 17.

27. Povich, *All These Mornings*, 86.

28. Ibid., 88.

29. Ibid., 90.

30. Ibid., 95.

31. Ibid., 88–89.

32. *Baltimore Afro-American*, December 26, 1959, 14.

33. Ibid., November 13, 1937, page number unavailable. Carter's work is collected in the Art Carter Papers, Moorland-Spingarn Research Center, Howard University.

34. *Washington Post*, December 15, 1961, D1.

35. Ibid.

36. See David K. Wiggins, "Edwin Bancroft Henderson: Physical Educator, Civil Rights Activist, and Chronicler of African-American Athletes," *Research Quarterly for Exercise and Sport* 70 (June 1999): 100.

37. Quoted in ibid.

38. See ibid., 101.

39. Liza Cozzens, "Moving Towards Desegregation," retrieved at www.watson. org/~lisa/blackhistory/school~integration/washdc.

40. *Washington Post*, November 20, 1962, A20.

41. Ibid., November 23, 1962, A1.

42. Ibid., D1.

43. Ibid., D2.

44. *Baltimore Afro-American*, December 1, 1962, 12.

45. Ibid., November 27, 1962, 13.

46. The best source on Ashe's days in Richmond is John McPhee, *Levels of the Game* (New York: Farrar Straus Giroux, 1969).

47. *Washington Post*, July 10, 1987, A22.

48. Ibid., September 28, 1933, 17.

49. Nathan, "Last Century, with Shirley Povich," 125.

50. Roberts, *In the Shadow of Power,* 467.

51. Ibid., 429.

52. Thomas Boswell, "For Timeless Player, It Was Time," reprinted in *The Best American Sports Writing: 1999*, ed. Richard Ford and Glenn Stout (New York: Houghton Mifflin, 1999), 69. Povich's "Recent Baseball Feats Require Footnotes" was also included in the collection.

53. *Washington Post*, January 24, 1992, E4.

54. Ibid., December 24, 1991, D4.

55. Ibid., January 24, 1992, E4.

56. Ibid., January 19, D16.

57. Roberts, *In the Shadow of Power*, 476.

58. Ibid., 482.

59. Ibid., 483.

60. "Dave Fay, 1940–2007," retrieved at http://dumpchase.worldpress.com/2007/07/18.

61. Ibid.

62. Dan Jenkins's seminal article on Paterno, "The Idea Is To Have Some Fun— And Who Needs To Be No. 1?" appeared in *Sports Illustrated*, November 11, 1968, 19–21.

63. *Washington Post*, January 14, 2012, D1.

64. Ibid., July 12, 2012, retrieved at www.washingtonpost.com/sports/colleges/joe-paterno-at-the-end.

65. Povich, quoted in Holtzman, *No Cheering in the Press Box*, 124–25.

Chapter 6: Between the Lines

The authors are grateful to the editors for their patience in acquiring the manuscript, and to Chris Elzey for his assistance in obtaining some of the newspaper articles fromthe 1920s.

1. Patricia A. Vertinsky, *The Eternally Wounded Woman: Women, Doctors, and Exercise in the Late Nineteenth Century* (Urbana: University of Illinois Press, 1989), 39, 20; Patricia Campbell Warner, *When the Girls Came Out to Play: The Birth of American Sportswear* (Boston: University of Massachusetts Press, 2006), 7; and Susan E. Cayleff, *Babe: The Life and Legend of Babe Didrikson Zaharias* (Urbana: University of Illinois Press, 1995), 19.

2. *Washington Bee*, September 9, 1905, 3.

3. *Washington Post*, August 5, 1905, 9; *Washington Bee,* November 25, 1899, 8; *Washington Times Magazine*, July 20, 1902, www.chronicling america.loc.gov (image 27); for example, see *Washington Post*, July 5, 1918, 4, and June 25, 1911, M7; and *Washington Herald Magazine of Features and Fiction*, May 29, 1921, www.chroniclingamerical.loc.gov (image 38).

4. State Historic Preservation Office, DC Office of Planning, "District

of Columbia Inventory of Historic Sites," September 30, 2009, http://plan-ning.dc.gov/DC/Planning/Historic+Preservation/Maps+and+Information/
Landmarks+and+Districts/Inventory+of+Historic+Sites/Alphabetical+Edition;
Washington Bee, June 17, 1911, 1, and October 28, 1911, 8.

5. *Washington Evening Star*, July 9, 1925, 31, and July 28, 1925, 24.

6. Ibid., July 9, 1925, 31; August 16, 1925, 38; and July 28, 1925, 24.

7. See following issues of *Washington Post*, July 25, 1926, M23; February 8, 1925, SP1; July 12, 1925, 20; and September 8, 1927, 16.

8. Information contained in ibid., March 27, 1938, S6.

9. In *Washington Times*, November 26, 1926, 24; December 13, 1926, 16; May 24, 1927, 19; and May 12, 1927, 18.

10. *Washington Evening Star*, April 19, 1925, 3, and *Washington Times*, December 4, 1921, www.chroniclingamerica.loc.gov (image 27).

11. *Washington Evening Star*, September 1, 1926, 8; *Washington Herald Magazine*, February 5, 1922, www.chroniclingamerica.loc.gov (image 38); *Washington Times*, December 11, 1921, www.chroniclingamerica.loc.gov (image 56); and *Washington Times*, April 20, 1922, 14.

12. See *Washington Times*, November 22, 1926, 13, and December 13, 1926, 16.

13. *Washington Herald*, August 9, 1929, 13.

14. *Washington Times*, November 26, 1926, 24. Tad also drew a cartoon called "Outdoor Sports." See *Washington Times*, November 29, 1926, 19.

15. See, for instance, two issues of *Washington Herald*, December 21, 1921, 6, and August 19, 1926, 14. Information also in *Washington Times*, December 11, 1921, www.chroniclingamerica.loc.gov (image 46) and *Washington Times*, December 4, 1921, www.chroniclingamerica.loc.gov (image 46).

16. *Washington Post*, January 27, 1924, 4S, and February 17, 1924, sec. 2, 14; Robert Pruter, *The Rise of American High School Sports and the Search for Control, 1880–1930* (Syracuse, NY: Syracuse University Press, 2013), 123–24; and two issues of *Washington Post*, October 31, 1922, 18, and January 12, 1924, S2. For other photographs, see following issues of Washington Post, November 7, 1922, 18; December 21, 1924, S3; and November 10, 1925, 22.

17. *Washington Herald*, August 26, 1929, 14, and September 1, 1926, 10.

18. *Washington Time*, November 26, 1926, 22. For results, see following issues of *Washington Herald*, August 26, 1926, 14; June 30, 1927, 10; August 1, 1929, 15; August 2, 1929, 13; and August 3, 1929, 13. Also see *Washington Times*, January 17, 1922, www.chroniclingamerica.loc.gov (image 18); February 8, 1928, 19; and March 11, 1929, 10.

19. *Washington Evening Star*, July 29, 1925, 26; August 7, 1926, 6; and December 17, 1925, 6. *Washington Daily News*, July 9, 1928, 20. Tennis and golf tournaments in *Washington Post*, August 2, 1929, 13, and August 4, 1929, M14. See also *Washington Daily News*, May 1, 1929, 1.

20. See following issues of *Washington Post*, November 9, 1927, 6; June 25, 1933, 49; and November 23, 1958. Mary Jo Festle, *Playing Nice: Politics and Apologies in Women's Sports* (New York: Columbia University Press, 1996).

21. Linda Jean Carpenter and R. Vivian Acosta, *Title IX* (Champaign, IL: Human Kinetics, 2005), and *Washington Post,* April 22, 1979, P12.

22. In 1982, the NCAA decided that governing women's athletics could be prof-itable financially and in terms of power. The NCAA offered women's teams money

and status, both of which the AIAW lacked. Not surprisingly, the AIAW folded, along with the tradition of women's control of women's athletics, setting the stage for the reliance of women's professional basketball on the existing men's league. *Washington Post,* October 18, 1975, B1, and June 14, 1977, D1.

23. Quotes in following issues of *Washington Post,* September 8, 1978, W34; May 15, 1974, A1; and May 9, 1979, E7. *Chicago Metro News,* February 3, 1979, and Karen L. Stevenson, "Woman's Work," The Rhodes Project, http://www.rhodesproject.com/docs/articles/KarenStevensenWomensWork.pdf.

24. For example, see articles in following issues of *Washington Post,* March 16, 1980, D1; July 27, 1980, E11; August 5, 1984, C7; February 4, 1987, C8; and November 12, 1984, D14.

25. See these issues of *Washington Post,* April 3, 1989, D5; February 5, 1989, C1; October 8, 1989, O18; July 5, 1981, D4; and March 16, 1982, D1.

26. *Chicago Defender* (national ed.), February 15, 1941, and *Washington Post,* April 26, 1984, DC3, and July 12, 1988, E3.

27. *Washington Post,* April 8, 1979, E1.

28. *New York Amsterdam News*, October 16, 1993, 50.

29. Susan Ware, *Title IX: A Brief History with Documents* (Boston: Bedford/St. Martin, 2007), 20 and Jay Coakley, *Sports in Society: Issues and Controversies, 9th Edition* (New York: McGraw-Hill, 2007), 429.

30. See "History of the WNBA," WNBA.com, http://www.wnba.com/about_us/historyof_wnba.html; Joe Dorish, "WNBA Teams with the Best Overall Attendance Records," Yahoo! Sports, June 6, 2011, http://sports.yahoo.com/wnba/news?slug=ycn-8596889; Andy Bernstein, "Will the Third Time be the Charm for the WNBA?" *Sports Business Journal,* June 7, 1999, http://www.sportsbusiness-daily.com/Journal/Issues/1999/06/19990607/No-Topic-Name/Will-The-Third-Time-Be-The-Charm-For-WNBA.aspx; John Lombardo, "Luring Back 'Neglected' Fans to the Mystics," *Sports Business Journal,* May 15, 2006, http://www.sportsbusinessdaily.com/Journal/Issues/2006/05/20060515/This-Weeks-News/Luring-Back-Neglected-Fans-To-The-Mystics.aspx; "Lincoln Holdings Purchases Mystics," WNBA.com, May 24, 2006, http://www.wnba.com/mystics/news/mystics_sold_052405.html; "Johnson a Partner in Lincoln Holdings," *Associated Press,* May 24, 2005, http://sports.espn.go.com/wnba/news/story?id=2067522; and Richard Lapchick, "The 2011 National Women's Basketball Association Racial and Gender Report Card," *The Institute for Diversity and Ethics in Sport,* 14, http://www.tidesport.org.

31. "WPS Archive: magicJack," http://equalizersoccer.com/category/wps/magic-jack; and Matt Bonesteel, "Jim Gabarra Resigns as the Washington Freedom's Head Coach After 10 Years with Women's Club," *Washington Post,* September 28, 2010, http://voices.washingtonpost.com/soccerinsider/2010/09/jim_gabarra_resigns_as_washing.html.

Chapter 7: Exercising Civil Rights

1. Memo from Julius A. Krug, Secretary of the Interior, to Mr. Howard Braucher, President, National Recreation Association, October 9, 1947, 3, in Box 8, File of Letters, 7/1/47–12/31/47, Papers of Julius A. Krug (hereafter cited

as Krug Papers), Coll. MSS 28993, Manuscript Division, Library of Congress, Washington, DC.

2. Local newspapers gave extensive coverage. For example, see *Washington Evening Star*, June 26, 1949, A21, and June 30, 1949, A1, A3.

3. See Bernard Semple Fortner, "A History of the Municipal Recreation Department of the District of Columbia, 1790–1954" (PhD diss., University of Maryland, 1956); Cornelius W. Heine, *A History of National Capital Parks* (Washington, DC: US Department of Interior, National Park Service, National Capital Parks, 1953), available online at http://www.nps.gov/history/history/online_books/nace/adhi.htm; and Bernard Mergen, "Children's Playgrounds in the District of Columbia, 1902–1942," *Records of the Columbia Historical Society, Washington, D.C.* 50 (1980): 383–97.

4. William H. Jones, *Recreation and Amusement Among Negroes in Washington, D.C.: A Sociological Analysis of the Negro in an Urban Environment* (Washington, DC: Howard University Press, 1927; repr. ed., Westport, CT: Negro Universities Press, 1972), 100.

5. African Americans used the Banneker and Francis pools, while whites swam at Takoma, East Potomac, McKinley, and Anacostia. All six pools opened between the late 1920s and late 1930s.

6. See James Borchert, *Alley Life in Washington: Family, Community, Religion, and Folklife in the City, 1850–1970* (Urbana: University of Illinois Press, 1980); Steven Mintz, "A Historical Ethnography of Black Washington, D.C.," *Records of the Columbia Historical Society, Washington, D.C.* 52 (1989): 235–53; and Jacqueline M. Moore, *Leading the Race: The Transformation of the Black Elite in the Nation's Capital, 1880–1920* (Charlottesville: University Press of Virginia, 1999).

7. See Jones, *Recreation and Amusement Among Negroes*, 100–101; Andrew W. Kahrl, *The Land Was Ours: African American Beaches from Jim Crow to the Sunbelt South* (Cambridge, MA: Harvard University Press, 2012), 89–114, 230–31; Marya Annette McQuirter, "Claiming the City: African Americans, Urbanization, and Leisure in Washington, D.C., 1902–1957" (PhD diss., University of Michigan, 2000), 132–77; and Victoria W. Wolcott, *Race, Riots, and Roller Coasters: The Struggle over Segregated Recreation in America* (Philadelphia: University of Pennsylvania Press, 2012), 181–83, 205–6.

8. General histories include Constance McLaughlin Green, *The Secret City: A History of Race Relations in the Nation's Capital* (Princeton, NJ: Princeton University Press, 1967); Constance McLaughlin Green, *Washington: Capital City, 1879–1950* (Princeton, NJ: Princeton University Press, 1963); McQuirter, "Claiming the City"; and Wendell E. Pritchett, "A National Issue: Segregation in the District of Columbia and the Civil Rights Movement at Mid-Century," *Georgetown Law Journal* 93 (April 2005): 1321–33.

9. The District's color line was not absolutely rigid. People from disparate backgrounds frequently encountered each other around the city, especially in public areas. Various cultural performances, some sports events, and a handful of commercial establishments were open to everyone, as were many public sites including major museums, main public library, Library of Congress, national zoo, and Botanic Garden. See McQuirter, "Claiming the City."

10. George Lipsitz, *How Racism Takes Place* (Philadelphia: Temple University

Press, 2011), 28. On Washington, DC, see Margaret E. Farrar, "Health and Beauty in the Body Politic: Subjectivity and Urban Space," *Polity* 33 (Fall 2000): 1–23; and Howard Gillette Jr., *Between Justice and Beauty: Race, Planning, and the Failure of Urban Policy in Washington, D.C.* (Baltimore: Johns Hopkins University Press, 2000).

11. Dominick Cavallo, *Muscles and Morals: Organized Playgrounds and Urban Reform, 1880–1920* (Philadelphia: University of Pennsylvania Press, 1981); Joe L. Frost, *A History of Children's Play and Play Environments* (New York: Routledge, 2010), 62–172; and Richard F. Knapp and Charles E. Hartsoe, *Play for America: The National Recreation Association, 1906–1965* (Arlington, VA: National Recreation and Park Association, 1979), 1–126.

12. Real estate firms and other private businesses were also keenly interested in land development. But that topic lies outside the scope of this chapter. See Ocean Howell, "Play Pays: Urban Land Politics and Playgrounds in the United States, 1900–1930," *Journal of Urban History* 34 (September 2008): 961–94.

13. The overview is based primarily on Michael Bednar, *L'Enfant's Legacy: Public Open Spaces in Washington, D.C.* (Baltimore: Johns Hopkins University Press, 2006), 7–32; Fortner, "History of the Municipal Recreation Department"; Green, *The Secret City*; Green, *Washington*, especially II: 132–46; Frederick Gutheim and Antoinette J. Lee, *Worthy of the Nation: Washington, D.C., from L'Enfant to the National Capital Planning Commission*, 2nd ed. (Baltimore: Johns Hopkins University Press, 2006), 118–233; Heine, *National Capital Parks: A History*; Jones, *Recreation and Amusement Among Negroes*; and Mergen, "Children's Playgrounds."

14. On the L'Enfant and McMillan plans, see Bednar, *L'Enfant's Legacy*, 7–32, 49–57; Green, *Washington*, II: 20–21, 134–36, 147; Gutheim and Lee, *Worthy of the Nation*, 8–35, 118–43; and Sue A. Kohler and Pamela Scott, *Designing the Nation's Capital: The 1901 Plan for Washington, D.C.* (Washington, DC: US Commission of Fine Arts, 2006).

15. Green, *Washington*, II, 187–89.

16. *Washington Post*, September 25, 1927, M24; Fortner, "History of Municipal Recreation Department," 43; and Mergen, "Children's Playgrounds," 388–91.

17. A cofounder of the Playground Association of America, along with Luther Gulick, Joseph Lee, and Jane Addams, Curtis exemplified the country's burgeoning playground movement being spearheaded by urban reformers and recreation professionals. Curtis promptly acquired recreational land for the District, developed municipal and schoolyard playgrounds, and hired a staff to handle program development and site supervision. See Knapp and Hartsoe, *Play for America*, 26, 28–31; and Mergen, "Children's Playgrounds," 392 (quotation).

18. On the WPA and DP, see Fortner, "History of Municipal Recreation Department," 53–57; and Mergen, "Children's Playgrounds," 393.

19. Fortner, "History of Municipal Recreation Department," 117; Gutheim and Lee, *Worthy of the Nation*, 178–79; and *Washington Post*, June 10, 1925, 22.

20. Fortner, "History of Municipal Recreation Department," 116–17, 125; and Gutheim and Lee, *Worthy of the Nation*, 180 (quotations), 193–94.

21. On the plans, see Fortner, "History of Municipal Recreation Department," 129–33, 139. A typical editorial can be found in *Washington Post*, June 4, 1925, 6.

22. Fortner, "History of Municipal Recreation Department," 135–36; Green, *Washington*, II: 289–92; and Gutheim and Lee, *Worthy of the Nation*, 214–15.

23. Fortner, "History of Municipal Recreation Department," 56, Table I; Green, *Secret City*, 262; and Mergen, "Children's Playgrounds," 390.

24. Fortner, "History of Municipal Recreation Department," 118–20, 159, 218–19; Jones, *Recreation and Amusement Among Negroes*, 34, 37 (quotation), 38, 40, 41, 55; and US Department of Labor, Children's Bureau, *Facilities for Children's Play in the District of Columbia*, Miscellaneous Series No. 8, Bureau Publication No. 22 (Washington, DC: Government Printing Office, 1917).

25. Jones, *Recreation and Amusement Among Negroes*, 37 (quotation); see also 34, 38, 40, 41, 55. On facilities in 1916, see US Department of Labor, *Facilities for Children's Play*, 7–14, 19–25.

26. US Department of Labor, *Facilities for Children's Play*, 8; subsequent information in same source, 10–14, 15–17, 20, 21, 67–68.

27. The statute forbidding individuals to play, loiter, or congregate on District sidewalks and streets was passed in 1892 and amended in 1898; see ibid., 67–68.

28. For an overview through 1927, see Jones, *Recreation and Amusement Among Negroes*, 37–38.

29. *Washington Post*, May 16, 1918, 9, and April 19, 1922, 8. The bathing beauty contests were canceled in 1923 to improve the "tone of the beach"; see ibid., March 31, 1923, 5.

30. Ibid., July 24, 1921, 41; September 11, 1921, 16; and May 20, 1923, 33.

31. Ibid., July 2, 1921, 2.

32. Ibid., June 5, 1924, 4.

33. Ibid., December 3, 1924, 9; June 5, 1924, 6; February 8, 1925, 1; February 18, 1925, 1; February 18, 1925, 4; February 19, 1925, 1; and February 25, 1925, 1.

34. For example, see editorials in ibid., July 8, 1925, 6, and September 5, 1925, 6.

35. Ibid., December 19, 1924, 13.

36. Ibid., February 18, 1925, 4, and February 27, 1925, 5.

37. Ibid., February 19, 1925, 1.

38. Ibid., 3.

39. Ibid., June 10, 1925, 1, 8.

40. For examples of congressional spats, see ibid., June 14, 1925, 1–2; June 15, 1925, 2; and June 16, 1925, 2.

41. Ibid., June 23, 1925, 2, and July 21, 1925, 18.

42. Ibid., June 11, 1925, 22.

43. Ibid., September 11, 1925, 22; September 18, 1925, 24; January 3, 1926, 2; January 5, 1926, 6 (information in editorial); and July 22, 1928, 2.

44. Ibid., April 23, 1926, 1.

45. Ibid., May 8, 1926, 22. See also ibid., May 12, 1926, 1, 9, and May 16, 1926, M11. By contrast, Superintendent Grant and white civic groups endorsed the location. See ibid., May 12, 1926, 9, and May 13, 1926, 22.

46. Ibid., May 28, 1926, 12.

47. Ibid., July 28, 1926, 1, 9; July 29, 1926, 2; August 25, 1926, 20; and September 16, 1927, 24.

48. Ibid., June 28, 1928, 20. See also ibid., June 27, 1928, 20.

49. I am indebted to Drew Yingling, my research student (Bucknell University, Class of 2015), for this insight.

50. See *Washington Post*, June 28, 1928, 20, and June 27, 1928, 20.

51. Ibid., June 28, 1928, 20, and July 12, 1928, 18.

52. Ibid., September 30, 1928, M10.

53. Gutheim and Lee, *Worthy of the Nation*, 221.

54. Heine, *National Capital Parks*, ch. 3: "Parks of the National Capital, 1933–1951."

55. Fortner, "History of Municipal Recreation Department," 144.

56. Ibid., 144, 181–82; Green, *Washington*, II: 396; and Gutheim and Lee, *Worthy of the Nation*, 222.

57. Green, *Washington*, II: 396; see also Gutheim and Lee, *Worthy of the Nation*, 227.

58. Fortner, "History of Municipal Recreation Department," 144, 172–74; and *Washington Post*, August 3, 1934, 1, 3.

59. Fortner, "History of Municipal Recreation Department," 181, 183, 185, 200.

60. Ibid., 222, tables XI–XII, and 225.

61. Letter from Julius A. Krug, Secretary of the Interior, to President Harry S. Truman, April 4, 1949, 1; copy available online at http://www.trumanlibrary.org/whistlestop/study_collections/trumancivilrights/documents/index.php?pagenumber=1&documentdate=1949-04-04&documentid=8-3.

62. Green, *Secret City*, 262–63.

63. "An Act to create a Recreation Board for the District of Columbia, to define its duties, and for other purposes," Public Law 534 (H.R. 5075), 77th Cong., 2nd sess., *U.S. Statutes at Large*, ch. 265 (April 29, 1942), 261–64.

64. Recreation Board, "By-Laws, Rules, and Regulations," 1942, in Box 4, Folder: Recreation, January–July 1942, Papers of Harry S. Wender (hereafter cited as Wender Papers), Kiplinger Research Library, Historical Society of Washington, DC, Washington, DC (hereafter cited as KRL-HSWDC).

65. *Washington Post*, December 31, 1942, 7.

66. For the CCRR membership list, see *Washington Evening Star*, August 1, 1943, A1. On the NCSNC, see Pritchett, "A National Issue."

67. The records of the CRD/CCR and CCASR are interfiled with the Papers of the DC Branch of the National Association for the Advancement of Colored People (hereafter cited as NAACP-DC Papers), Coll. 78, at Moorland-Spingarn Research Center (hereafter cited as MSRC), Howard University, Washington, DC. See also Papers of Edwin B. Henderson (hereafter cited as Henderson Papers), MSRC; and David K. Wiggins, "Edwin Bancroft Henderson: Physical Educator, Civil Rights Activist, and Chronicler of African American Athletes," *Research Quarterly for Exercise and Sport* 70 (June 1999): 91–112.

68. Fortner, "History of Municipal Recreation Department," 258, n. 32.

69. Judge William H. Hastie, "General Statement Opposing Exclusion from Public Recreational Facilities in the District of Columbia Because of Race," 1, in "Statements or Excerpts of Committee Against Segregation in Recreation before the Board of Education," July 17, 1945, in Box 44-3, Folder 59, Henderson Papers.

70. Chapter 4, section 2.2. of "By-Laws, Rules, and Regulations," Box 3, Folder: Race Relations, 1948, Wender Papers.

71. Box 3, Folder: Race Relations, 1935, and Box 4, Folder: Recreation, 1945, Wender Papers; and Box 78-15, Folders 257–69, NAACP-DC Papers.

72. See note 5.

73. Box 4, Folder: Recreation, January–June 1946, and Folder: Recreation, July–December 1946, Wender Papers.

74. On federal sites, see following dates for *Washington Post*, July 26, 1947, B2; September 27, 1947, 10 (information contained in editorial); and October 5, 1947, B4 (James E. Schwab, letter to editor).

75. This section is based on Kent Boese's research. A professional librarian, Boese serves as an advisory neighborhood commissioner for the Park View area (ANC 1A08). See "Ending Segregation in D.C. Playgrounds: The Experience at Park View Playground" (a paper presented at the 40th Annual DC Historical Studies Conference, November 16, 2013); and National Register of Historic Places application for the Park View Playground and Field House (available online at http://www.anc1a.org/Landmark%20nominations/Park%20View%20 Playground%20nomination.pdf).

76. *Washington Post*, July 14, 1948, B1.

77. Summary based on Mastin G. White, Solicitor, "Use of Park Areas in the District of Columbia for Public Recreation: Opinion, August 2, 1948" (M-34963), in Box 78-74, Folder 1577, NAACP-DC Papers; and letter from Stephen Gill Spottswood, President, NAACP-DC, to Attorney General Tom Clark, November 6, 1948, in Box 78-16, Folder 270, NAACP-DC Papers. Quotations from the former.

78. The same held true for land that the NCPPC tried to assign after 1942. In White's view, the organic act of 1942 had terminated the NCPPC's authority, except as an advisory or planning agency.

79. Documents in Box 4, Folder: Recreation, January–June 1948, and Folder: Recreation, July–December 1948, Wender Papers.

80. *Segregation in Washington: A Report of the National Committee on Segregation in the Nation's Capital, November 1948*, text by Kenesaw M. Landis (Chicago: The Committee, 1948), 88. On recreation, see 82–84.

81. *Washington Post*, February 24, 1949, 1, 4, and March 9, 1949, 1, 19.

82. The playgrounds were Rose Park in Georgetown and the East and West Garfield parks. See ibid., May 11, 1949, 1, 14, and *Washington Evening Star*, June 16, 1949, B2.

83. Fairlawn Citizens Association, Inc., *Fairlawn: From the Flats to the Heights* (Washington, DC: The Author), 4–5; accessed online at http://www.fairlawndc.org/ FairlawnHistoryReport.pdf. I am indebted to Drew Yingling, a Bucknell University history major, for his help in researching and writing this section. See Martha H. Verbrugge and Drew Yingling, "Exercising One's Civil Rights: The Struggle over Racial Segregation and Public Recreation in Washington, D.C., 1945–1950" (paper presented at the 40th Annual DC Historical Studies Conference, November 16, 2013, Washington, DC); Wolcott, *Race, Riots, and Roller Coasters*, 81–85; and "Comment: Racial Violence and Civil Rights Law Enforcement," *University of Chicago Law Review* 18 (Summer 1951): 773–75.

84. *Washington Evening Star*, June 26, 1949, A21.

85. Ibid., June 28, 1949, A1, A6.

86. Ibid., A6.

87. *Washington Post*, June 29, 1949, B2.

88. Ibid. See also *Washington Evening Star*, June 29, 1949, A2.

89. *Washington Evening Star*, June 30, 1949, A1, A3.

90. Ibid., A3.

91. District of Columbia Recreation Board, *Ten Years of Recreation Progress, 1942–1952* (Washington, DC: The Board, 1952), 7 (Article II, Chapter 1, section 2 of By-Laws, Rules, and Regulations).

92. *Washington Post*, July 20, 1949, 3 (quotation); and *Washington Evening Star*, July 20, 1949, A1.

93. "Memorandum of Agreement between the District of Columbia Recreation Board and the National Park Service," August 9, 1949, in Box 4, Folder: Recreation, August–December 1949, Wender Papers (quotations, 3); and *Washington Evening Star*, August 18, 1949, B2.

94. *"James Byrd et al. v. Recreation Board of District of Columbia, Milo Christiansen (Superintendent of Recreation), Board of Commissioners, Board of Education, and Julius Krug (Secretary of Interior),"* Civil Action No. 3808-49, US District Court for the District of Columbia, September 9, 1949; copy in Box 4, Folder: Recreation, August–December 1949, Wender Papers. Little information is available about the suit or its disposition.

95. See Paul Cooke Jr., "Public Accommodations in the Nation's Capital, 1947–1958," in *Civil Rights in the Nation's Capital: A Report on a Decade of Progress*, ed. Ben D. Segal, William Korey, and Charles N. Mason Jr. (Annandale, VA: Turnpike Press, 1959), 44–55.

96. *Washington Post*, July 7, 1951, 1.

97. Ibid., November 15, 1951, B1.

98. Ibid., April 25, 1952, B1 (first quotation), and May 8, 1952, B1 (second quotation).

99. Ibid., July 17, 1951, 10. Information contained in letter to editor by Frank M. Snowden, who chaired the Joint Recreation Committee of the Brookland Civic Association and the Slowe P-TA.

100. Ibid., May 8, 1952, B1.

101. Ibid., April 25, 1952, B1.

102. Phineas Indritz, "Racial Ramparts in the Nation's Capital," *Georgetown Law Journal* 41 (March 1953): 309, 325 n. 93; Robert B. McKay, "Segregation and Public Recreation," *Virginia Law Review* 40 (October 1954): 710 n. 65; and *Camp et al. v. Recreation Board for District of Columbia et al.*, Civil Action No. 3582-51, US District Court for the District of Columbia, April 10, 1952.

103. Wolcott, *Race, Riots, and Roller Coasters*, 109–10.

104. *Washington Evening Star*, April 7, 1950, A1, A4; *Washington Post*, September 17, 1951, B11; and Wolcott, *Race, Riots, and Roller Coasters*, 83.

105. The District of Columbia Recreation Board, *10 Years of Recreation Progress, 1942–1952* (Washington, DC: The Author, 1952), 7.

106. Quoted in Fortner, "History of Municipal Recreation Department," 387.

107. *Washington Post*, May 20, 1954, 10.

108. For example, *Central Amusement Company, Inc., v. District of Columbia*, No. 1753, Municipal Court of Appeals for the District of Columbia, decided April 3, 1956. The case dealt with racial discrimination at a local bowling alley.

109. Risa L. Goluboff, *The Lost Promise of Civil Rights* (Cambridge, MA: Harvard University Press, 2007); Gilbert Jonas, *Freedom's Sword: The NAACP and the Struggle Against Racism in America, 1909–1969* (New York: Routledge, 2007); Manning Marable, *Race, Reform, and Rebellion: The Second*

Reconstruction and Beyond in Black America, 1945–2006, 3rd ed. (Jackson: University Press of Mississippi, 2007); Harvard Sitkoff, *The Struggle for Black Equality, 1954–1992*, rev. ed. (New York: Hill and Wang, Noonday Press, 1993); and Thomas J. Sugrue, *Sweet Land of Liberty: The Forgotten Struggle for Civil Rights in the North* (New York: Random House, 2008).

110. Book-length studies include Marvin P. Dawkins and Graham C. Kinloch, *African American Golfers During the Jim Crow Era* (Westport, CT: Praeger, 2000): Jeff Wiltse, *Contested Waters: A Social History of Swimming Pools in America* (Chapel Hill: University of North Carolina Press, 2007), 121–80; and Wolcott, *Race, Riots, and Roller Coasters*. Case studies of specific communities or sports are now available as well.

Chapter 8: "The Greatest High School Basketball Game Ever Played"

1. Phil Pepe, *Stand Tall: The Lew Alcindor Story* (New York: Grosset & Dunlap Publishing, 1970), 53. Donohue later said, "[The] game had a tremendous impact on . . . high school basketball." See *Washington Post*, January 30, 1985, D1.

2. "Kareem Abdul-Jabbar," Basketball-Reference.com, http://www.basket-ball-reference.com/players/a/abdulka01.html (accessed August 7, 2012).

3. Ibid.; Jerry Wizig, "It's been twenty years since they've played The Game of the Century," *Houston Chronicle*, January 20, 1988, http://www.chron.com/CDA/archives/archive.mpl?id=1988_517381 (accessed August 7, 2012).

4. Kareem Abdul-Jabbar and Peter Knobler, *Giant Steps* (New York: Bantam Books, 1983), 38, 100–101.

5. *Baltimore Sun*, January 30, 1965, 16. Since no national championship tournament existed at the time, crowning a team "national champions" was largely subjective.

6. Morgan Wootten and Bill Gilbert, *From Orphans to Champions: The Story of DeMatha's Morgan Wootten* (New York: Atheneum, 1979), 37–39; Morgan Wootten, phone interview with author, January 26, 2012 (hereafter, Wooten interview).

7. *Chicago Daily Defender*, April 9, 1963, 22.

8. *New York Herald-Tribune*, January 22, 1964, 25; *Philadelphia Tribune*, January 25, 1964, 13; *Baltimore Afro-American*, February 20, 1965, 10; Pepe, *Stand Tall*, 54.

9. Mickey Wiles, phone interview with author, January 17, 2012.

10. *New York Herald-Tribune*, February 2, 1964, sec. 4, 4, and *Baltimore Sun*, February 2, 1964, 11.

11. Estimates of the crowd size at the 1964 and 1965 Power-DeMatha games ranged between 12,000 and 13,500. Most estimates fell somewhere in the middle, at 12,500.

12. J. Samuel Walker, *ACC Basketball: The Story of the Rivalries, Traditions, and Scandals of the First Two Decades of the Atlantic Coast Conference* (Chapel Hill: University of North Carolina Press, 2011), 41; Wootten interview.

13. *Converse Basketball Year Book* (Malden, MA: Converse Rubber Company, 1964), 42; Bob Petrini, phone interview with author, January 18, 2012 (hereafter, Petrini interview).

14. Abdul-Jabbar, *Giant Steps*, 69–95, 102.

15. Sid Catlett, phone interview with author, January 20, 2012 (hereafter, Catlett interview); Wiles interview; Sid Catlett, e-mail to author, August 13, 2012; Red Auerbach and John Feinstein, *Let Me Tell You a Story: A Lifetime in Basketball* (New York: Little, Brown and Company, 2004), 127.

16. Petrini interview; Wooten interview.

17. Ned Merchant, phone interview with author, January 18, 2012 (hereafter, Merchant interview); Petrini interview.

18. Howard Gillette Jr., *Between Justice and Beauty: Race, Planning, and the Failure of Urban Policy in Washington, D.C.* (Baltimore: Johns Hopkins University Press, 1995), 42. For more information on the history of Washington DC, especially pertaining to race and neighborhoods, see Gillette (cited above), and Kathryn Schneider Smith, ed., *Washington at Home: An Illustrated History of Neighborhoods in the Nation's Capital*, 2nd ed. (Baltimore: Johns Hopkins University Press, 2010). For more on Wilson's policy of federal segregation, see Kathleen L. Wolgemuth, "Woodrow Wilson and Federal Segregation," *Journal of Negro History* 44 (April 1959): 158.

19. Campbell Gibson and Kay Jung, "Historical Census Statistics On Population Totals by Race, 1790 to 1990, and by Hispanic Origin, 1970 to 1990, for Large Cities and Other Urban Places in the United States," *The U.S. Census Bureau*, February 2005, http://www.census.gov/population/www/documentation/twps0076/twps0076.html (accessed December 13, 2012).

20. For more on Thurgood Marshall, see Geoffrey M. Horn, *Thurgood Marshall* (Milwaukee, WI: World Almanac Library, 2004).

21. David K. Wiggins, "Edwin Bancroft Henderson: Physical Educator, Civil Rights Activist, and Chronicler of African American Athletes," *Research Quarterly for Exercise and Sport* 70 (June 1999): 91–112. For more on Jackie Robinson, see Jules Tygiel, *Baseball's Great Experiment: Jackie Robinson and His Legacy* (New York: Oxford University Press, 1999).

22. Ron Thomas, *They Cleared the Lane: The NBA's Black Pioneers* (Lincoln: University of Nebraska Press, 2002), 71–85, 109–31.

23. Walker, *ACC Basketball*, 241.

24. "State High School Champions," *Converse Basketball*, 42; "State High School Champions," *Converse Basketball Year Book* (Malden, MA: Converse Rubber Company, 1965), 42.

25. *Washington Post*, February 3, 1964, A19; Wooten interview.

26. Petrini interview.

27. *New York Herald-Tribune*, January 22, 1964, 25, and *Washington Daily News*, January 30, 1965, 17.

28. Wiles played at both Georgia and Maryland; Austin at Syracuse; Petrini at Pittsburgh; Williams at LaSalle; and Catlett and Whitmore at Notre Dame.

29. *Washington Daily News*, January 30, 1965, 17.

30. *Philadelphia Tribune*, January 25, 1964, 13; *Pittsburgh Courier*, March 6, 1965, 23; *Washington Daily News*, January 26, 1965, 36; and *Chicago Tribune*, April 14, 1965, C3.

31. *Washington Daily News*, January 30, 1965, 17.

32. *Look*, February 9, 1965, 86–90.

33. *New York Herald-Tribune*, January 30, 1964, 1.

34. This claim is based on research of black newspapers, including the *New York Amsterdam News*, the *Chicago Defender*, the *Philadelphia Tribune*, the *Baltimore Afro-American*, the *Washington Afro-American*, the *Norfolk Journal and Guide*, and the *Atlanta Daily World*.

35. Wootten, *From Orphans*, 36–37; *Washington Post*, January 31, 1965, C3.

36. Wiles interview.

37. Chad Carlson, "A Tale of Two Tournaments: The Red Cross Games and the NCAA-NIT Relationship," *Journal of Intercollegiate Sport* 5 (December 2012): 260–80.

38. Danny Stooksbury, *National Title: The Unlikely Tale of the NAIB Tournament* (Bradenton Beach, FL: Higher Level Publishing, 2010), 7–9.

39. Carlson, "A Tale"; *New York Herald-Tribune*, January 20, 1964, 21.

40. *Washington Post*, January 30, 1985, D1.

41. Wootten interview.

42. Petrini interview; Auerbach, *Let Me Tell You*, 124.

43. Catlett interview.

44. Ibid.

45. Wiles interview; Catlett interview; Wootten, *From Orphans*, 45, 47; *New York Times*, January 31, 1965, S1.

46. *Baltimore Sun*, January 31, 1965, A1, and *Washington Daily News*, February 1, 1965, 28.

47. *New York Herald Tribune*, January 31, 1965, sec. 4, 3.

48. *Washington Star*, January 31, 1965, F1, and *New York Herald-Tribune*, January 31, 1965, sec. 4, 3. Information for following paragraph from same sources.

49. *New York Post*, January 31, 1965, 66.

50. *Washington Daily News*, February 1, 1965, 28.

51. *Washington Post*, February 1, 1965, A19, and Merchant interview. For Donohue's visit to the locker room, see *Washington Post*, January 31, 1965, C3.

52. Headlines in *Washington Daily News*, February 1, 1965, 28; *Washington Post*, January 31, 1965, C1 (article located in microfilm at MLK Library, Washingtoniana Room, Washington, DC); and *Washington Sunday Star*, January 31, 1965, F1. Pictures in *Washington Sunday Star*, January 31, 1965, F1, F2. *Washington Daily News*, February 1, 1965, 28.

53. *Baltimore Sun*, February 1, 1965, 17.

54. Merchant interview; Wiles interview.

55. Merchant interview; *Washington Post*, January 30, 1985, D1; Wootten interview.

56. Wootten interview; *Washington Post*, January 26, 1978, MD1; Petrini interview.

57. Wootten interview.

58. Morgan Wootten and Bill Gilbert, *A Coach for all Seasons* (Indianapolis: Masters Press, 1997), 4.

Chapter 9: Whips, Darts, and Dips

1. *New York Times*, July 15, 1968, 37.

2. David Wangerin, *Soccer in a Football World: The Story of America's*

Forgotten Game (Philadelphia: Temple University Press, 2006), 31. Sadly, Wangerin passed away during the writing of this article. He has provided the most in-depth analysis on soccer in the United States. Other names ascribed to the league include "Professional Association Football League," *Washington Post,* August 5, 1894, 15; "American League of Professional Football Clubs," in Andrei S. Markovits and Steven L. Hellerman, *Offside: Soccer and American Exceptionalism* (Princeton, NJ: Princeton University Press, 2001), 105; and "Professional League of Association Football Players," *Washington Post*, March 2, 1894, 6.

3. Ibid., January 18, 1913, 8.

4. Elliott J. Gorn and Warren Goldstein, *A Brief History of American Sports* (Urbana: University of Illinois Press, 2004).

5. Constance M. Green, *Washington: Village and Capital, 1800–1878* (Princeton, NJ: Princeton University Press, 1962). See also Alan Lessoff, *The Nation and Its City: Politics, "Corruption," and Progress in Washington, D.C., 1861–1902* (Baltimore: Johns Hopkins University Press, 1994).

6. Constance M. Green, *Washington: Capital City, 1879–1950* (Princeton, NJ: Princeton University Press, 1963). See also Francine C. Carey, ed., *Urban Odyssey: A Multicultural History of Washington, D.C.* (Washington, DC: Smithsonian Institution Press, 1995).

7. *Washington Post*, August 1, 1907, 2.

8. Ibid., December 6, 1912, 8. In 1915, there were 1,500 youths playing baseball and 1,243 participating in "general athletics." See ibid., December 5, 1915, SP1.

9. David L. Andrews, "Contextualizing Suburban Soccer: Consumer Culture, Lifestyle Differentiation and Suburban America," in *Football Culture: Local Contests, Global Visions*, ed. G. P. T Finn and R. Giulianotti (London: Frank Cass, 2000), 31–53.

10. See following issues in *Washington Post*, January 12, 1964, C3; January 26, 1964, C2; December 6, 1965, D5.

11. Ibid., October 8, 1967, C10.

12. In 1967, the NHL doubled in size. The following year, the American Basketball Association (ABA) was established to rival the NBA.

13. *Washington Post*, April 15, 1967, E1.

14. Ibid., March 9, 1967, E1.

15. Ibid.

16. Ibid., May 22, 1967, D6, and May 24, 1967, D1.

17. Ibid., May 24, 1967, D1.

18. Expenses included $95,000 for the transportation, wages, food, and lodging of the Aberdeen players; approximately $150,000 for stadium items; and another $250,000 for local and league administrative costs. See *Washington Post*, April 6, 1967, H5.

19. Ibid., April 12, 1967, D3.

20. Ibid., June 8, 1967, E4, and May 27, 1967, E1.

21. Ibid., April 6, 1967, H5.

22. *New York Times*, July 16, 1967, 152.

23. *Washington Post*, July 2, 1967, E2, and *Washington Evening Star*, June 12, 1968, D5.

24. *Washington Post*, January 22, 1968, D4.

25. Ibid., February 18, 1968, C2. See also *Washington Evening Star*, June 11, 1968, A20.

26. Ibid., June 11, 1968, A20.

27. *Washington Post*, April 17, 1968, D4.

28. Ibid., June 5, 1968, D4.

29. Ibid., June 10, 1968, D7.

30. Ibid., June 12, 1968, D1.

31. Ibid., June, 30, 1968, D4.

32. Ibid., July 15, 1968, D1.

33. *Washington Evening Star*, July 15, 1968, A13.

34. *Washington Post*, September 7, 1968, C1.

35. Ibid., April 12, 1968, D4.

36. Ibid., March 27, 1970, D4.

37. Ibid., February 27, 1970, D4.

38. In 1965, Casa lost his arm in a shooting accident in Argentina. See *Washington Post*, April 10, 1970, D8.

39. Olivia Cadaval notes that many of the District's first Latino immigrants hailed from Cuba, Dominican Republic, and Puerto Rico—nationalities with a strong affinity for baseball. It was not until the 1980s that a sizable immigrant group that appreciated soccer—Salvadorians—began settling in the DC region. See Olivia Cadaval, "The Latino Community: Creating an Identity in the Nation's Capital," in *Urban Odyssey: A Multicultural History of Washington D.C.*, ed. Francine C. Cary (Washington, DC: Smithsonian Institution Press, 1995), 231–49.

40. Following NASL's inaugural 1968 season, five teams played an abbreviated schedule in 1969. In 1970, the league featured six teams, enough to create two divisions of three teams.

41. *Washington Post*, September 5, 1970, C3.

42. Ibid., September 19, 1970, E1.

43. Ibid., May 3, 1971, C5.

44. Ibid., August 17, 1971, C3, and August 19, 1971, C3.

45. Ibid., August 17, 1971, C3.

46. Ibid., August 29, 1971, C4.

47. Players included Kurt Kuykendall from American University, George Taratsides from the University of Maryland, Mori Diane from Howard University, and Bill Bedenbaugh from Frostburg State University.

48. *Washington Post*, April 5, 1974, D3.

49. Ibid.

50. Ibid., February 19, 1974, D2.

51. Ibid., April 17, 1974, C1.

52. Ibid., April 21, 1974, 240.

53. Ibid., May 1, 1974, D1.

54. Ibid., May 5, 1974, 1D.

55. Ibid., June 19, 1974, 7D.

56. Others included basketball stars Tom McMillen and Kevin Porter, and local boxer Johnny Gant. Ibid., June 23, 1974, D1.

57. Ibid., July 14, 1974, D1.

58. Ibid., August 12, 1974, D6.

59. Ibid., February 2, 1975, 43.
60. Ibid., April 24, 1975, E4.
61. Ibid., May 17, 1975, C1.
62. Ibid., May 18, 1975, 50. See also *Washington Post*, June 1, 1975, 50.
63. Ibid., June 21, 1975, D1.
64. Ibid., August 11, 1975, D5.
65. Author's interview with Paul Cannell, August 1, 2012.
66. *Washington Star*, July 14, 1976, E2.
67. *Washington Post*, July 16, 1976, D1.
68. *Washington Star*, July 12, 1976, D1.
69. *Washington Post*, March 10, 1977, D2.
70. Ibid., December 25, 1975, E11.
71. Ibid., December 26, 1976, D13, and August 5, 1977, D1.
72. Ibid., June 30, 1977, 82.
73. Ibid., July 29, 1978, C1.
74. Ibid., February 26, 1980, D1.
75. Ibid., March 9, 1980, D4.
76. Ibid., June 2, 1980, A1.
77. Ibid., June 24, 1980, D1.
78. Ibid., December 9, 1980, D1.

Chapter 10: Uniting a Divided City

1. James R. Hartley, *Washington's Expansion Senators, 1961–1971* (Germantown, MD: Corduroy Press, 1998; 1997), 79–80.
2. Lacy's quote is referenced at http://parkviewdc.wordpress.com/2011/05/05/baseballs-lenny-green.
3. *Washington Post*, October 4, 2012, D1.
4. http://espn.go.com/mlb/attendance.
5. *Washington Post*, February 13, 1969, C1.
6. Ibid., February 8, 1969, D1.
7. Ibid.
8. Ibid.
9. Washington Senators Baseball Club. Press-Radio-Television Guide, 1969.
10. All statistics cited in this chapter are from www.retrosheet.org.
11. Author's interview with Jim Hartley, November 28, 2007 (hereafter, Hartley interview).
12. *Washington Post*, February 16, 1969, 41.
13. Ibid., March 4, 1969, D1.
14. Ibid., February 22, 1969, E1.
15. Author's interview with Hank Allen, November 14, 1998 (hereafter, Allen interview).
16. Ron Briley, *Class at Bat, Gender on Deck and Race in the Hole: A Line-Up of Essays on Twentieth-Century Culture and America's Game* (Jefferson, NC: McFarland, 2003), 206.
17. Author's interview with Ron Menchine, February 2005 (hereafter, Menchine interview).

18. Author's interview with Brant Alyea, May 2007.

19. This quote and previous one from Allen interview.

20. Quote taken from a teammate of Allen's who asked to remain anonymous.

21. Author's interview with Bob Humphreys, June 6, 2007.

22. *Washington Post*, June 30, 1968, D4. Quotes and references in following two paragraphs also taken from same source.

23. Author's interview with Del Unser, March 18, 2008 (hereafter, Unser interview).

24. Allen interview.

25. Ibid.

26. Ibid.

27. Menchine interview.

28. Allen interview.

29. Michael Seidel, *Ted Williams: A Baseball Life* (Lincoln: University of Nebraska Press, 2000).

30. Author's interview with Frank Howard, February 9, 1999.

31. Allen interview.

32. *Washington Post*, April 8, 1969, D1, D2.

33. Allen interview.

34. Ibid.

35. Author's interview with Lee Maye, November 18, 1998.

36. *Washington Post*, July 7, 1969, C1.

37. Ibid.

38. Unser interview.

39. *Washington Post*, July 23, 1969, D1, D2.

40. Ted Leavengood, "Do You Believe in Magic? Baseball Returns to D.C.," *Elysian Fields Quarterly: The Baseball Review* 22 (Summer 2005): 9–19.

41. Author's interview with Darold Knowles, January 15, 2007.

42. Hartley interview.

43. Hochberg made these remarks at the 1969 Senators reunion breakfast on November 9, 1998.

44. Hartley interview.

45. Author's interview with Jeff Flippo, November 8, 1998.

46. Author's interview with Jerry Bush, November 8, 1998.

47. Author's interview with Charlie Gray, November 9, 1998.

48. Remarks by Phil Wood at 1969 Senators reunion breakfast, November 9, 1998.

49. Ibid.

50. Remarks by Ron Menchine at 1969 Senators reunion breakfast, November 9, 1998.

51. Remarks by Ted Williams at 1969 Senators reunion breakfast, November 9, 1998.

Chapter 11: George Allen, Richard Nixon, and the Washington Redskins

1. James S. Olson and Randy Roberts, *Where the Domino Fell: America and Vietnam, 1945–1995* (New York: St. Martin's Press, 1996), 136.

2. *Washington Post*, January 6, 1972.

3. *Chicago Tribune*, January 5, 1972; *Washington Post*, January 6, 1972.

4. *Washington Post*, December 3, 1972.

5. Jennifer Allen, *Fifth Quarter: The Scrimmage of a Football Coach's Daughter* (New York: Random House, 2000), 100, 149–50; *Washington Post*, January 2, 1973.

6. Stephen H. Norwood, "Corporate Cowboys and Blue-Collar Bureaucrats: The Dallas-Washington Football Rivalry," in *Rivals: Legendary Matchups That Made Sports History*, ed. David K. Wiggins and R. Pierre Rodgers (Fayetteville: University of Arkansas Press, 2010), 270; William Gildea and Kenneth Turan, *The Future Is Now: George Allen, Pro Football's Most Controversial Coach* (Boston: Houghton Mifflin, 1972), 1–2; *Washington Post*, October 8, 1978.

7. *Sports Illustrated*, July 2, 1979, 69, 74, 77, 80.

8. *Washington Post*, May 30, 1977.

9. *Los Angeles Times*, November 14, 1971. For the guest list, see *Washington Post*, November 3, 1971.

10. Allen, *Fifth Quarter*, 110.

11. Gildea and Turan, *The Future Is Now*, 218.

12. *New York Times*, January 15, 1984.

13. *Washington Post*, September 9, 1985.

14. Ibid., October 4 and 25, 1971; Gildea and Turan, *The Future Is Now*, 224, 226.

15. *Wall Street Journal*, January 28, 1983; George Solomon, *The Team Nobody Wanted: The Washington Redskins* (Chicago: Henry Regnery, 1973), 13.

16. Ibid., November 17, 1969; *New York Times*, November 17, 1969. George Marshall, owner of the Washington Redskins from 1937 until his death in 1969, had, after the end of World War II, tried to persuade President Harry Truman to attend pro football games. In 1946 he and NFL commissioner Bert Bell presented Truman, a Redskins fan, with a gold-plated pass that provided free admission to any NFL game. Truman never used it because he feared "too many" people would complain about his attending a sports contest on Sunday. *New York Times*, September 26, 1946, and *Washington Post*, July 21, 1948. NFL commissioner Pete Rozelle made the same offer to President Kennedy in 1961. *Washington Post*, August 26, 1961. President Johnson attended an NFL exhibition game in 1966. *New York Times*, October 10, 1968.

17. David Maraniss, *When Pride Still Mattered: A Life of Vince Lombardi* (New York: Simon & Schuster, 1999), 446.

18. Michael MacCambridge, *America's Game: The Epic Story of How Pro Football Captured a Nation* (New York: Random House, 2004), 271.

19. Michael Oriard, *King Football: Sport & Spectacle in the Golden Age of Radio & Newsreels, Movies & Magazines, the Weekly & the Daily Press* (Chapel Hill: University of North Carolina Press, 2001), 220, 222.

20. *Washington Post*, November 27, 1970.

21. Stephen H. Norwood, *Strikebreaking and Intimidation: Mercenaries and Masculinity in Twentieth-Century America* (Chapel Hill: University of North Carolina Press, 2002), 226–30.

22. Jefferson Cowie, *Stayin' Alive: The 1970s and the Last Days of the Working Class* (New York: New Press, 2010), 44.

23. Duane Thomas and Paul Zimmerman, *Duane Thomas and the Fall of America's Team* (New York: Warner Books, 1988), 58–59.

24. *Dallas Morning News*, November 23, 1990.

25. Bill Libby, *Life in the Pit: The Deacon Jones Story* (Garden City, NY: Doubleday, 1970).

26. *New York Times*, November 4, 1917.

27. Ibid., May 20, 1918.

28. *Washington Post*, August 11, 1918. The *Post*'s article was entitled "Tackles and Ends Stop the Germans."

29. *New York Times Sunday Magazine*, September 16, 1973. For characterizations of linebackers by two of the premier offensive players in the NFL during the 1970s, Bert Jones and Greg Pruitt, see Stephen H. Norwood, *Real Football: Conversations on America's Game* (Jackson: University Press of Mississippi, 2004), 77, 412. Jones comments: "Of all the positions, linebacking is the most animalistic. It takes a little bit different kind of guy to want to go around hitting people with a full running head start as often as you can."

30. Olson and Roberts, *Where the Domino Fell*, 217.

31. Norwood, *Real Football*, 6.

32. Libby, *Life in the Pit*, 11.

33. John Klawitter and Deacon Jones, *Headslap: The Life and Times of Deacon Jones* (Amsterdam, NY: Prometheus Books, 1996), 446; Marv Levy, *Where Else Would You Rather Be?* (Champaign, IL: Sports Publishing, 2004), 140; Norwood, *Real Football*, 367.

34. *Washington Post*, January 10 and 30, 1966, and February 7 and 19, 1970. Huff was accompanied to Vietnam by Baltimore Colts quarterback Johnny Unitas, Green Bay Packers defensive end Willie Davis, and former New York Giants halfback Frank Gifford, at that time a broadcaster.

35. *Washington Post Magazine*, October 28, 1973.

36. *Washington Post*, January 12 and February 25, 1971.

37. Ibid., November 8, 1969; Maraniss, *When Pride Still Mattered*, 477–78. The *Post* headlined its article "Redskins to Give Flag Equal Time." Sports teams' sponsorship of patriotic displays in their stadiums dated to World War I. During opening day ceremonies at the Polo Grounds a few days after the United States entered the war, the New York Yankees marched onto the field "in full battle array," carrying their bats on their shoulders like rifles. The Yankees made "a fine showing as soldiers," going "through all the maneuvers of military formation." *New York Times*, April 12, 1917.

38. Maraniss, *When Pride Still Mattered*, 477; *New York Times*, December 6, 1969. As general manager of the Green Bay Packers in 1968, Lombardi had sponsored a patriotic halftime display similar to "The Flag Story." The ceremony was intended to be "a flag-waving answer to young antiwar demonstrators and draft card burners." The Packers passed out more than 50,000 miniature American flags to fans, Boy Scouts recited the Pledge of Allegiance, and the St. Norbert's College choir sang "This Is My Country" and "God Bless America." The NFL office congratulated Lombardi by sending him a one-word telegram at halftime that read "Wonderful." Maraniss, *When Pride Still Mattered*, 452.

39. Michael Rosenberg, *War As They Knew It: Woody Hayes, Bo Schembechler, and America in a Time of Unrest* (New York: Grand Central, 2008), 43. Hayes had

visited troops in Vietnam, where he "insisted on boarding choppers to dangerous areas, against the advice of military personnel." Rosenberg, *War As They Knew It*, 5.

40. *New York Times*, May 10, 1970.

41. *Washington Post*, October 24, 1969.

42. Ibid., November 6, 1969, and July 31, 1971.

43. Ibid., December 10, 1969.

44. Allen, *Fifth Quarter*, 125; *New York Times Sunday Magazine*, September 16, 1973, 93. Nixon was a member of the Whittier football team from his sophomore through his senior years, but sat on the bench and did not appear in games. He did, however, participate in practice scrimmages.

45. *Chicago Tribune*, October 16, 1968.

46. Allen remarked that Nixon "follows all football very closely, not only tactics but personnel, and you can converse with him [about the sport] intelligently." *New York Times Sunday Magazine*, September 16, 1973, 93–94.

47. Conversation No. 35-8, Richard Nixon and George Allen, December 26, 1972, Richard M. Nixon Presidential Library, Yorba Linda, CA. Allen told Nixon that it was no accident that the Pro Bowl, the annual postseason All-Star Game, was being held in Dallas. Reflecting a paranoia Allen shared with the president, who had compiled an "enemies list" in the White House, Allen referred darkly to an "arrangement" between Cowboys owner Tex Schramm and NFL commissioner Pete Rozelle. He implied that Rozelle was unfairly favoring Dallas in making it the host city for the financially lucrative game.

48. Conversation No. 35-40, Richard Nixon and Charles W. Colson, Richard M. Nixon Presidential Library.

49. Obituary of Charles W. Colson, *New York Times*, April 21, 2012.

50. *Washington Post*, May 4, 1973.

51. Allen, *Fifth Quarter*, 93.

52. Tony Peters, defensive back with the Cleveland Browns, 1975–77, and Washington Redskins, 1978–85, commented on Allen's paranoia in Norwood, *Real Football*, 322.

53. Allen, *Fifth Quarter*, 93.

54. *Los Angeles Times*, November 8, 1962.

55. David Greenberg, *In Nixon's Shadow: The History of an Image* (New York: W. W. Norton, 2003), 144–45, 152, 154.

56. Allen, *Fifth Quarter*, 117–18.

57. Ibid., 118–19.

58. *Sports Illustrated*, October 25, 1971, 72; Allen, *Fifth Quarter*, 93.

59. On differences between the caliber of play in the NFL and in college, see Norwood, *Real Football*, passim.

60. Gildea and Turan, *The Future Is Now*, 1, 14; Levy, *Where Else Would You Rather Be?* 144.

61. Gildea and Turan, *The Future Is Now*, 19–20, 22, 26; Levy, *Where Else Would You Rather Be?* 150–52.

62. Gildea and Turan, *The Future Is Now*, 25; *Sports Illustrated*, October 25, 1971, 74; Levy, *Where Else Would You Rather Be?* 152–53.

63. Levy, *Where Else Would You Rather Be?* 133, 165.

64. Jerry Kramer, *Instant Replay: The Green Bay Diary of Jerry Kramer*, ed.

Dick Schaap (New York: Signet Books, 1968), 23. NFL players used military terminology when discussing special teams play. For example, Joe Washington, who played in the NFL from 1976 to 1985 and was one its premier kickoff returners, compared that assignment to "being a kamikaze pilot." Norwood, *Real Football*, 192. Marv Levy called the Redskins kickoff coverage teams his "swarming horde." Levy, *Where Else Would You Rather Be?* 165.

65. David Hackett Fischer, *Growing Old in America* (New York: Oxford University Press, 1977), 132.

66. Dave Meggyesy, *Out of Their League* (Berkeley, CA: Ramparts Press, 1970), 222.

67. Kramer, *Instant Replay*, 48, 50.

68. *Washington Post Magazine*, September 6, 1981; Gildea and Turan, *The Future Is Now*, 16.

69. *Washington Post*, September 1, 1991.

70. Ibid., December 9, 1966.

71. *Los Angeles Times*, October 24, 1967.

72. *Washington Post*, July 24, 1983.

73. *Los Angeles Times*, October 23, 1967.

74. Norwood, *Real Football*, 107–8; *Los Angeles Times*, October 20, 1967.

75. *Washington Post Magazine*, September 15, 1974. *Washington Post*, September 25, 1973.

76. See comparisons of drive blocking and pass blocking by Joe Washington and Ken Mendenhall in Norwood, *Real Football*, 192, 355, 357. Hubbard quoted in *New York Times*, October 26, 1947.

77. *Washington Post Magazine*, September 15, 1974.

78. *Washington Post*, September 5, 1973.

79. Allen, *Fifth Quarter*, 159; *Washington Post*, January 30, 1983.

80. *Washington Post*, January 30, 1983.

81. *Wall Street Journal*, January 28, 1994.

82. Kramer, *Instant Replay*, 64–65.

83. *New York Times*, April 26, 1974.

84. MacCambridge, *America's Game*, 300.

85. *New York Times Sunday Magazine*, September 16, 1973.

86. *Chicago Tribune*, December 19, 1982.

87. Levy, *Where Else Would You Rather Be?* 174.

88. Solomon, *The Team Nobody Wanted*, 77–78.

89. *New York Times*, January 15, 1973; Allen, *Fifth Quarter*, 159.

90. Solomon, *The Team Nobody Wanted*, 143.

91. Allen, *Fifth Quarter*, 14.

92. *Los Angeles Times*, January 14, 1973.

93. Allen, *Fifth Quarter*, 9.

94. Ibid., 217. When Nixon resigned, George Allen, along with John Wayne, wrote to him offering encouragement. Allen told him: "This too will pass." *Los Angeles Times*, December 1, 1986.

95. *Newsweek*, July 19, 1976, 35.

96. *Sports Illustrated*, July 8, 1974, 17–18.

97. *Washington Post*, September 27, 1974.

98. Maurice Isserman and Michael Kazin note that conservatives began building a mass movement before the New Left and "kept expanding their numbers for years after the young radicals had splintered in various directions." Isserman and Kazin, *America Divided: The Civil War of the 1960s* (New York: Oxford University Press, 2000), 206.

99. James William Gibson, *Warrior Dreams: Violence and Manhood in Post-Vietnam America* (New York: Hill & Wang, 1994), 5, 9–12; Olson and Roberts, *Where the Domino Fell*, 272.

100. Klawitter and Jones, *Headslap*, 493.

101. Allen, *Fifth Quarter*, 202–3, 205–6.

Chapter 12: A Little Big Man, a Fat Lady, and the Bullets' Remarkable Season

1. Author's telephone interview with Dick Motta (hereafter cited as Motta interview), November 30, 2012. Paul Attner and Richard Darcey, *The Fat Lady Sings for the Bullets*, August 1978.

2. Dick Motta with Jerry Jenkins, *Stuff It! The Story of Dick Motta, the Toughest Little Coach in the NBA* (Radnor, PA: Chilton Books, 1975), 137–38. *Washington Post*, May 8, 1978, D4.

3. Motta interview.

4. Quoted in *Washington Post*, May 8, 1978, D4, and *Washington Star*, May 8, 1978, C1.

5. *San Antonio Express-News*, November 6, 1992, 8A. The origins of the saying are difficult to trace. The line has been attributed to Yogi Berra, the Marx Brothers, W. C. Fields, Kate Smith, a sports information director from Texas Tech University, Casey Stengel, and southern linguistic culture. See Fred Shapiro, ed., *Yale Book of Quotations* (New Haven, CT: Yale University Press, 2006), 133; Ralph Keyes, *Nice Guys Finish Seventh* (New York: HarperCollins, 1992), 41–42; John Simpson, comp. with Jennifer Speake, *The Concise Oxford Dictionary of Proverbs*, 2nd ed. (New York: Oxford University Press, 1992; 1982), 193–94; and *San Antonio Express-News*, November 6, 1992, 8A. For more on Cook, see *The Best of Dan Cook: Collected Columns from 1956 to 1990* (San Antonio: Corona Publishing Company, 2001).

6. Quoted in *Washington Post*, June 11, 1978, D6. According to Gary DeLaune, a former KENS-TV newsman and Spurs broadcaster, Cook worked the sports desk on weeknights only. Since the first game of the Bullets-Spurs series occurred on Sunday, April 16, it is reasonable to assume that Motta first heard the line on April 17. Author's telephone interview with Gary DeLaune, November 14, 2012.

7. Motta told *Washington Post* columnist Ken Denlinger that he first said the line in the San Antonio series. See *Washington Post*, May 28, 1978, D6.

8. The history of the original ABL is covered in Robert W. Peterson, *Cages to Jump Shots: Pro Basketball's Early Years* (Lincoln: University of Nebraska Press, 2002; 1990), 84–94. For more on the history of professional basketball in Washington, see Brett L. Abrams and Raphael Mazzone, *The Bullets, the Wizards, and Washington, DC, Basketball* (Lanham, MD: Scarecrow Press, 2013).

9. The history of the Heurich brewery is discussed in Garrett Peck, *Capital Beer: A Heady History of Brewing in Washington, D.C.* (Charleston, SC: American Palate, 2014), 69–74, 78–84, 121–26.

10. The Washington Bruins, another all-black team, preceded the Bears. Organized in 1940, the Bruins consisted of several players who later starred for the Bears. The Bruins' owners included two prominent African American sports journalists, Art Carter and Sam Lacy. Information on both the Bruins and Bears in Art Carter Papers, Box 170-24, Folders 18, 20, 21, 22, 23, Moorland-Spingarn Center, Howard University. See also Bob Kuska, *Hot Potato: How Washington and New York Gave Birth to Black Basketball and Changed America's Game Forever* (Charlottesville: University of Virginia Press, 2004), 182–83.

11. Information on the 1946–47 Caps in Charley Rosen, *The First Tip-Off: The Incredible Story of the Birth of the NBA* (New York: McGraw Hill, 2009), 195–210.

12. The early NBA is discussed in Leonard Koppett, *24 Seconds to Shoot: An Informal History of the National Basketball Association* (New York: Macmillan, 1968), 1–54. For more on Earl Lloyd and the Capitols, see Earl Lloyd and Sean Kirst, *Moonfixer: The Basketball Journey of Earl Lloyd* (Syracuse, NY: Syracuse University Press, 2010), 59–67, and Ron Thomas, *They Cleared the Lane: The NBA's Black Pioneers* (Lincoln: University of Nebraska Press, 2002), 2, 36, 76–81.

13. For more on the ABL, see Murry R. Nelson, *Abe Saperstein and the American Basketball League, 1960–1963: The Upstarts Who Shot for Three and Lost to the NBA* (Jefferson, NC: McFarland, 2013); Roger Meyer, "American Basketball League, 1961–62, 1962–63," in *Total Basketball: The Ultimate Basketball Encyclopedia*, ed. Ken Shouler et al. (Wilmington, DE: Sport Classic Books, 2003), 429–32; and Paul Ladewski, "The Forgotten League: The ABL (1961–1963)," in *The Official NBA Encyclopedia,* 3rd edition, ed. Jan Hubbard (New York: Doubleday, 2000), 71.

14. *Washington Post*, November 12, 1961, C5.

15. For more on AFL, see Larry Felser, *The Birth of the New NFL: How the 1966 NFL/AFL Merger Transformed Pro Football* (Guildford, CT: Lyons Press, 2008) and Ken Rappoport, *The Little League That Could: A History of the American Football League* (Lanham, MD: Taylor Trade, 2010).

16. *Washington Star*, August 21, 1969, C1, and *Washington Post*, August 21, 1969, B1, B5.

17. The Caps' attendance was 104,722. Only the Los Angeles Stars and Pittsburgh Condors had worse attendance. See *Converse Basketball Yearbook 1971*, 52.

18. *Potomac*, November 22, 1970, 11, 37, 39, 42. *Potomac* was a Sunday magazine insert of the *Washington Post*. See also *Washington Star*, March 10, 1974, H6, and *Washington Post*, August 5, 1973, D8.

19. Purchase of Squires in *Washington Post*, February 9, 1974, C2.

20. Quoted in *Washington Star*, June 8, 1978, D5.

21. Motta and Jenkins, *Stuff It!*, 24–25.

22. *Sport*, March 1974, cover.

23. For run-ins with players, see *Baltimore Sun*, November 10, 1974, B10, and January 11, 1976, B7; *Sports Illustrated*, May 29, 1978, 100; and Chet Walker

with Chris Messenger, *Long Time Coming: A Black Athlete's Coming-of-Age in America* (New York: Grove Press, 1995), 239–43.

24. Logan quoted in *Washington Post*, June 1, 1976, 1D.

25. Motta, *Stuff It!*, 133, 135–36, 179. The fine and suspension received wide coverage. See *Washington Star*, January 16, 1974, 2C; *Boston Globe*, January 16, 1974, 58; and *New York Times*, January 16, 1974, 47. Logan quoted in *Washington Post*, June 1, 1976, 1D.

26. Quoted in *Washingtonian*, March 1977, 56.

27. *Washington Star*, May 29, 25 1976, B2, D3.

28. Since arriving from Chicago in 1963, the Bullets ranked well below the league's average attendance. See Ken Shouler et al., *Total Basketball*, 324; NBA attendance in Robert Bradley, *Compendium of Professional Basketball* (Tempe, AZ: Xaler Press, 1999), 471.

29. For 1970 census data, see US Census Bureau, *Statistical Abstract of the United States, 1982–83* (Washington, DC: Government Printing Office, 1982), 24. The 1972–73 Detroit Pistons had the first all-black coaching staff (excluding Bill Russell with the Celtics in the late 1960s). Earl Lloyd and assistant Ray Scott coached the team. There were two other teams with all-black coaching staffs in 1973–74: the Detroit Pistons, with Ray Scott and player/assistant Jim Davis, and the Seattle SuperSonics, with Bill Russell and assistant Emmette Bryant.

30. *Sports Illustrated*, December 7, 1977, 26.

31. Ibid., October 25, 1971, 46. "Little Big Man" was a reference to the 1970 movie with the same name. It starred Dustin Hoffman and Faye Dunaway.

32. The game is recounted in *Washington Post*, December 14, 1942, 1, 11, 12, 13; *Washington Star*, December 14, 1942, 13; Michael Richman, *The Redskins Encyclopedia* (Philadelphia: Temple University Press, 2008), 24–26; and Alan Beall, *Braves on the Warpath: The Fifty Greatest Games in the History of the Washington Redskins* (Washington, DC: Kinloch Books, 1988), 13–17.

33. *Washington Star*, March 21, 1976, C4.

34. *Washington Post*, January 1, 1973, A1.

35. Nixon quoted in *Los Angeles Times*, June 23, 1968, 2A. For DC and crime, see Harry S. Jaffe and Tom Sherwood, *Dream City: Race, Power, and the Decline of Washington, D.C.* (New York: Simon and Schuster, 1994), 26, 88–89; David L. Lewis, *District of Columbia: A Bicentennial History* (New York: W. W. Norton, 1976), 122–24, 183–85; and *Harper's Magazine*, January 1975, 68.

36. The buildings were the US Capitol, the Pentagon, and the State Department. Mayday Protests in Lucy G. Barber, *Marching on Washington: The Forging of an American Political Tradition* (Berkeley: University of California Press, 2002), 204–18. During the Hanafi attack, DC councilmember Marion Barry was shot as he exited an elevator in the District Building. For more on the Hanafi attack, see Jonathan I. Z. Agronsky, *Marion Barry: The Politics of Race* (Latham, NY: British American Publishing, 1991), 181–82; Marion Barry Jr. and Omar Tyree, *Mayor for Life: The Incredible Story of Marion Barry, Jr.* (Largo, MD: Strebor Books, 2014), 96–98; and Jaffe and Sherwood, *Dream City*, 109–12. *Washington in the '70s*, a video produced by WETA and released in 2010, discusses the social history of DC during the decade. A good overview of DC history is Keith Melder, *City of Magnificent Intentions: A History of Washington, District of Columbia*, 2nd ed. (Washington, DC: Intac, 1997).

37. Unemployment rate in US Census Bureau, *Statistical Abstract of the United States, 1982–1983* (Washington, DC: Government Printing Office, 1982), 375. Ford quoted in *Washington Star-News*, January 15, 1975, A1. America's struggles during the 1970s are the subject of several books. See Bruce J. Schulman, *The Seventies: The Great Shift in American Culture, Society, and Politics* (New York: Free Press, 2001); Edward Berkowitz, *Something Happened: A Political and Cultural Overview of the Seventies* (New York: Columbia University Press, 2006); Peter N. Carroll, *It Seemed Like Nothing Happened: The Tragedy and Promise of America in the 1970s* (New York: Holt, Rinehart and Winston, 1982); and David Frum, *How We Got Here: The 70's, the Decade That Brought You Modern Life (for Better or Worse)* (New York: Basic Books, 2000).

38. *Black Sports*, October 1976, 22, 27.

39. Motta quoted in *Washington Post*, September 25, 1976, C1. David DuPree attended the practice and wrote about it for the *Post*.

40. Ibid., December 2, 1976, E1.

41. Ibid., February 22, 1977, D1.

42. *Washington Star,* January 21, 1977, F1, and *Washington Post*, January 21, 1977, D1.

43. Elvin Hayes and Bill Gilbert, *They Call Me "The Big E"* (Englewood Cliffs, NJ: Prentice-Hall, 1978). *Christian Science Monitor,* May 8, 1975, 24. Philadelphia had a slightly higher winning percentage, but Washington had more wins. League standings in *Boston Globe*, March 3, 1977, 32.

44. Hayes quoted in *Washington Star*, May 12, 1977, C1. *Washington Star*, May 24, 1977, C1.

45. Pollin quoted in *Washington Post*, May 5, 1977, 114. Israel's stories in *Washington Star*, June 7, 8, 1977, D1, E1. For Israel and the proposed trade, see *Washingtonian*, February 1978, 74.

46. Bing quoted in *Washington Post*, May 13, 1977, C1, and *Washington Star*, May 12, 1977, C1.

47. Motta quoted in *Washington Post*, May 3, 1977, D1. *Washingtonian*, March 1977, 55.

48. *Washington Post*, August 17, 1977, D1.

49. Dandridge won an NBA title in 1971 with the Milwaukee Bucks, where he played with Lew Alcindor (later Kareem Abdul-Jabbar) and Oscar Robertson. In 1977, Steve Hershey called him "one of the league's premier running forwards." See *Washington Star*, August 17, 1977, C5.

50. *Baltimore Afro-American*, June 17, 1978, 9. Motta quoted in *Washington Post*, October 20, 1977, G1.

51. Motta quoted in *Washington Star*, October 22, 1977, B1.

52. Hayes quoted in ibid., November 6, 1977, D1.

53. *Washington Post*, November 7, 11, 1977, D1, E1.

54. *Washington Star*, November 11, 1977, C1, and *Washington Post*, November 11, 12, 1977, E1, D1.

55. *Basketball Weekly*, November 21, 1972, 8. The games Hayes missed were regular-season matchups. League standings in *Boston Globe*, January 14, 1978, 20.

56. Bullets' injury woes in *Washington Star*, January 21, 1978, B1. League standings in *Boston Globe*, February 23, 1978, 46.

57. *Washington Post*, February 27, 1978, D1.

58. Dandridge quoted in ibid., April 2, 1978, D1, and *Washington Star*, April 3, 1978, C1. Motta quoted in *Washington Post*, April 5, 1978, F1.

59. MLB commissioner Bowie Kuhn, local columnists, and some politicians advocated for baseball's return to DC. See *Washington Post*, August 5, 1976, D1, December 8, 1976, D1, March 24, 1977, B1, and March 20, 1977, A21; *Washington Star*, March 8, 1977, C1; and *Congressional Record*, 124th Congress, 10060–61.

60. *Basketball Digest*, June 1978, 31, and *Washington Afro-American* (Blue Star ed.), April 8, 1978, 18.

61. *Washington Post*, April 17, 1978, D1, D4, and *Washington Star*, April 17, 1978, D1, D6.

62. *Washington Post*, April 19, 1978, E1, E7, and *Washington Star*, April 19, 1978, E1.

63. *Washington Post*, April 29, 1978, D1, D4, and *Washington Star*, April 29, 1978, B1, B5.

64. *Philadelphia Inquirer*, May 1, 1978, C1, C5.

65. *Washington Post*, May 1, 4, 6, 8 1978, D1, and *Philadelphia Inquirer*, May 1, 6, 1978, C1.

66. For an image of the T-shirt, see *Washington Post*, May 29, 1978, D3. Siegel in *Washington Star*, May 16, 1978, D1.

67. *Washington Post*, May 11, 1978, D1.

68. *Philadelphia Inquirer*, May 13, 1978, C1. Banner in *Washington Post*, May 13, 1978, D1, D4. *Washington Star*, May 13, 1978, C1, C4.

69. Pollin quoted in *Washington Post*, May 13, 1978, D1. More information on game in ibid., May 13, 1978, A1, and *Washington Star*, May 13, 1978, A1.

70. Hayes quoted in ibid., May 19, 1978, C1.

71. *Washington Post*, May 19, 1978, E4.

72. For more on the RV show, see *Washington Star*, May 15, 1978, D1.

73. *The Weekly*, May 24–30, 1978, 20–21. *Nielsen National TV Ratings, 2nd May 1978 Report*, A33, A34.

74. *Seattle Times*, May 25, 1978, E1.

75. Motta quoted in *Washington Post*, May 26, 1978, E1.

76. *Seattle Times*, May 29, 1978, B4.

77. The decision to play the Sonics' 1978–79 season in the Kingdome was made in July 1977. See *Seattle Times*, July 30, 1977, D2. For more on the Sonics and the Kingdome, see *Sonics Magazine*, October–November 1977, 41–42, and September–November 1978, 49.

78. *The Weekly*, June 21–27, 1978, 2.

79. Sign in *Sonics Magazine*, September–November 1978, 53. Shout in *Washington Star*, May 31, 1978, D1. *The Weekly*, June 7–13, 1978, 17.

80. *Washington Star*, May 31, 1978, D1, D4, and *Washington Post*, May 31, 1978, D1, D4.

81. *Washington Star*, June 4, 5, 1978, C1, C1.

82. *Washington Post*, June 5, 1978, D1, D4, and *Washington Star*, June 5, 1978, C1, C5.

83. *Washington Post*, June 6, 1978, D1.

84. *Washington Star*, June 8, 1978, A1, A7. WDCA broadcast in *Washington Post*, June 7, 1978, B10.

85. Ibid., June 8, 1978, D1, D4, and *Washington Star*, June 8, 1978, D1, D6. Following three paragraphs from aforementioned sources.

86. For more on Herzog, see *Washington Post*, May 21, 1978, D5.

87. *The Weekly*, June 7–13, 1978, 16. Herzog quoted in *Drugfair Presents: The Fat Lady Sings for the Washington Bullets*. Recording in Music and Sound Division, Library of Congress, Washington, DC.

88. Motta and Hayes quoted in *Washington Post*, June 8, 1978, D1.

89. For celebration, see ibid., June 8, 1978, A1, A11, and *Washington Star*, June 8, 1978, A7.

90. Author's interview with Kevin Grevey, December 6, 2012. For descriptions of scene at Dulles, see *Washington Post*, June 9, 1978, A1, A14, and *Washington Star*, June 9, 1978, D1, D5.

91. Ibid., June 8, 1978, A1; *Washington Afro-American* (Blue Star ed.), June 10, 1978, 1; *Washington Post*, June 8, 1978, A1; *Baltimore News American*, June 8, 1978, 1; and *Washington Star*, June 8, 1978, D4.

92. *Washington Star*, June 9, 1978, A10, and *Washington Post*, June 9, 1978, A18.

93. Victory Day in *Washington Post*, June 10, 1978, A1, A6; D1, D3; *Washington Star*, B1, B5; *Washington Afro-American* (Blue Star ed.), June 17, 1978, 21; and *Sports Illustrated*, June 19, 1978, 70, 73. FTC banner in Attner and Darcey, *The Fat Lady Sings for the Bullets*. The following five paragraphs are based on the aforementioned sources, unless otherwise noted.

94. Picture of Motta and Bickerstaff in Bullets 1978–79 press guide. Guide in Michael J. O'Brien Historical Resource Center, Naismith Memorial Basketball Hall of Fame, National Basketball Association Press Release, Box 1, Folder: Media Guide, 1978–79. Sachs quoted in *Washington Post*, June 10, 1978, A8.

95. *Washington Post*, June 10, 1978, A8.

96. Jimmy Carter, "Washington Bullets Basketball Team Remarks at a White House Reception," June 9, 1978. Online by Gerhard Peters and John T. Wooley, *The American Presidency Project*. http://www.presidency.ucsb.edu/ws/?pid=30927 (accessed November 11, 2012). *ABC Evening News,* June 9, 1978, Vanderbilt Television News Archives.

97. Fauntroy quoted in *Congressional Record*, June 8, 1978, 16790. S. Res. 476 and H. Res. in ibid., 16861, 16789. McGovern and Clark in *Washington Post*, June 10, 1978, A6.

98. Sign in ibid., June 10, 1978, A1. Motta interview.

99. *Washington Post*, June 10, 1978, A1, D3. Holt quoted in *Congressional Record*, June 8, 1978, 17728.

100. Tiger story and Motta quote in Bryan Burwell, *At the Buzzer: The Greatest Moments in NBA History* (New York: Doubleday, 2001), 169.

101. Wilkens quoted in *Los Angeles Times*, June 3, 1979, C13. Bush quoted in *Los Angeles Times*, March 15, 1980, A12, and *New York Times*, April 15, 1980, B15. Art Buchwald included the line in a column. See *Washington Post*, September 30, 1993, B1. The saying also appeared in the TV series *Dallas*. See Keyes, *Nice Guys Finish Seventh*, 41. Author Dale L. Gilbert used the line in *Black Star Murders*. See Simpson with Speake, *The Concise Oxford Dictionary of Proverbs,*

194. Reference in O. J. Simpson trial located in transcript of *ABC Breaking News*, January 24, 1995. Also see transcripts of CNN's *The World Today*, October 21, 1998; White House Bulletin, August 29, 1996; and *ABC News*, October 12, 1996. All transcripts in LexisNexis–Library Express.

102. *Washington Post*, June 4, 1979, A27.

Chapter 13: Assuming "Its Place among the Ice Hockey Centers of the Nation"

1. "Remarks at a Graduation Ceremony at the New Economic School in Moscow, Russia," July 7, 2009, *Compilation of Presidential Documents*, from gpo.gov website, http://www.gpo.gov/fdsys/search/home.action (accessed June 19, 2012).

2. Anne Garrels, "US, Russia Relations Face Challenges," NPR, July 8, 2009. Transcript online at http://www.npr.org/templates/story/story.php?storyId=106376617 (accessed August 27, 2012).

3. Justine Christianson, "Uline Arena/Washington Coliseum: The Rise and Fall of a Washington Institution," *Washington History* 16 (Spring/Summer 2004): 23.

4. "Anti-American Whirlwind," in John Herd Thompson and Stephen J. Randall, *Canada and the United States: Ambivalent Allies* (Athens: University of Georgia Press, 2002), 247. The purpose of this article is to explain the Capitals' place in political, economic, and social history. Readers more interested in the on-ice developments of the franchise should consult the team's latest media guide, which is available at the official team website (http://capitals.nhl.com), or see "Washington Capitals," in Dan Diamond, ed., *Total Hockey: The Official Encyclopedia of the National Hockey League*, 2nd ed. (Kingston, NY: Total Sports Publishing, 2000), 280–82.

5. *Washington Post*, December 24, 1939, 15; Christianson, "Uline Arena/Washington Coliseum," 21–23, 28; Diamond, *Total Hockey,* 419–22.

6. *Washington Post*, December 24, 1939, 15, and May 11, 1972, E2.

7. *New York Times*, February 19, 1969, 54. The league's expansion plan specified that Vancouver would get a franchise for 1970 "[i]f an acceptable applicant for a franchise in the Vancouver territory complie[d]" with the plan's requirements by December 1, 1969. "NHL Plan of Expansion 1970–71," September 15, 1969, attached to National Hockey League to David Willoughby, September 25, 1969, Greater Washington Board of Trade Records, MS 2029, Box 239, folder 29, Gelman Library, George Washington University, Washington, DC (hereafter cited as GWBTR). For scheduling during the 1968 finals, see Bruce Kidd and John Macfarlane, *The Death of Hockey* (Toronto: New Press, 1972), 31. For official government concern, see *Report of the Task Force on Sports for Canadians* (Ottawa: Queen's Printer, 1969). For a historical critique of US influence on Canadian hockey, see Bruce Kidd, *The Struggle for Canadian Sport* (Toronto: University of Toronto Press, 1996), esp., 184–231, 262–70.

8. Ian Lumsden, ed., *Close the 49th Parallel Etc.: The Americanization of Canada* (Toronto: University of Toronto Press, 1975); Norman Hillmer and J. L. Granatstein, *Empire to Umpire* (Toronto: Irwin Publishing, 2000), 300–303; Robert Bothwell, *Alliance and Illusion: Canada and the World, 1945–1984* (Vancouver: University of British Columbia Press, 2007), 343–50.

9. Quoted in *Chicago Tribune*, June 9, 1972, C1.

10. For more on this, see *Washington Post*, February 17, 1966, G5, and March 13, 1966, C3. For insight into the diplomatic headaches brought on by the Justice Department's need to interview Canadian citizens living in Canadian cities as part of the investigation, see Telegram 11220, Department of State to AmEmbassy Ottawa, April 20, 1966; Telegram 1442, Ottawa to SecState, April 26, 1966; Telegram 1509, Ottawa to SecState, May 6, 1966; Telegram 1547, Ottawa to SecState, May 17, 1966; Telegram 1579, Ottawa to SecState, May 20, 1966; Airgram No., CA-12256, Department of State to AmEmbassy, Ottawa, June 16, 1966; all in Record Group 59 General Records of the State Department, Central Foreign Policy Files 1964–66, Culture and Information, box 336, file: CUL-15, Private Cooperation Program, 1/1/64, National Archives II, College Park, Maryland.

11. Although the NHL was largely unaffected, the 1960s and 1970s saw the emergence of effective players' unions and subsequent labor disputes in baseball and football.

12. *Washington Post*, June 8, 1972, D1.

13. Christianson, "The Uline Arena/Washington Coliseum," 27, 30; *Hockey News* 25 (July 1972), 2; *Washington Post*, November 19, 1969, E5. For business support for an NHL team downtown, see John W. Stadtler to William W. Wirtz, May 23, 1972, and Robert C. Durbin to William W. Wirtz, May 19, 1972, both in GWBTR, box 239, folder 30.

14. The summary in this paragraph is based on a reading of *Washington Post* coverage from May through August 1972.

15. "Capital Centre: Quick Reference Fact Sheet," in GWBTR, box 245, folder 15; "The Capital Centre—America's Newest, Most Modern Sports Arena," Press Release for November 21, 1972, GWBTR, box 245, folder 15, 1, 4; *Washington Post*, February 4, 1974, B1, and March 5, 1974, D1; and *Washington Capitals 1974–1975 Yearbook and Press Guide*, 5.

16. For a contemporary view, see *Washington Post*, July 27, 1972, D1, D6.

17. Ibid., June 8, 1995, A1, and July 21, 1995, D1, D5.

18. Ibid., July 11, 2011, A1; June 3, 1995, C1, C2; and October 30, 1995, A1.

19. After the Bruins won Stanley Cups—with Schmidt as a star player—in 1939 and 1941, they did not win the Cup again until 1970. In eight straight seasons from 1959–60 through 1966–67, the Bruins finished in last or next-to-last place and missed the playoffs. The Caps were able to hire Schmidt in the spring of 1973, despite his success in Boston, because changes in the Bruins organization had altered Schmidt's position and reduced his responsibilities. See Diamond, *Total Hockey*, 206, and *Boston Globe*, February 10, 1973, 22. Disclosure: The author, at age six, knew Milt Schmidt's son. Connie Schmidt captained the 1970–71 Brown University hockey team, which was coached by the author's father, J. Allan Soares.

20. *Hockey News* 27 (July 1974), 3. Like the Capitals, the Kansas City Scouts also struggled. The franchise lasted just two years in Kansas City before moving to Denver, and later to New Jersey. They missed the playoffs in twelve of their first thirteen years. Diamond, *Total Hockey*, 247.

21. *Washington Post*, October 8, 1974, D1, and May 31, 1974, D1. Anderson quoted in *Hockey News* 28, (October 25, 1974), 6.

22. Clarence Arata to G. Dewey Arnold, August 13, 1975, GWBTR, box 245, folder 16.

23. *Washington Post*, February 12, 1975, D1; *Los Angeles Times*, February 14, 1975, F10; *Washington Post*, March 23, 1975, 41, March 23, 1975, B2; *2011–2012 Washington Capitals Official Guide*, 171.

24. *Washington Post*, December 30, 1975, D1; *New York Times*, March 21, 1976, 191; *Washington Post*, September 26, 1976, 43; Diamond, *Total Hockey*, 1385.

25. Diamond, *Total Hockey*, 251, 260, 282.

26. *Washington Post*, June 18, 1972, D6, and December 30, 1975, D1. For "Operation Support," see Clarence A. Arata to G. Dewey Arnold, August 13, 1975.

27. *2011–2012 Washington Capitals Official Guide*, 171.

28. Willie O'Ree with Michael McKinley, *The Autobiography of Willie O'Ree: Hockey's Black Pioneer* (New York: Somerville House, 2000), 58–59, 65, 77–80; Diamond, *Total Hockey*, 781; and *New York Times*, January 19, 1998, C9.

29. Canadian census data found in "Table I: Percentage Distribution of the Population by Racial Origin, for Canada, 1881 and 1901–1941," in *Report of the Eighth Census of Canada, 1941, vol. 1: Review and Summary Tables* (Ottawa: Edmond Cloutier, 1950), 222; M. C. Urquhart, ed., *Historical Statistics of Canada* (Cambridge and Toronto: Cambridge University Press and Macmillan Company of Canada, 1965), 18; and Paul Robert Magosci, ed., *Encyclopedia of Canada's Peoples* (Toronto: University of Toronto Press, 1999), 148, 1336–39.

30. Joseph Mensah, *Black Canadians: History, Experience, Social Conditions*, 2nd ed. (Halifax: Fernwood Publishing, 2010), 191. Also see Carl E. James, "Race and the Social/Cultural Worlds of Student Athletes," in *The Politics of Race in Canada,* ed. Maria Wallis and Augie Fleras (Don Mills, Ont.: Oxford University Press, 2009), 181–94.

31. For more on this league, and the innovations in hockey for which its players deserve credit but have been overlooked, see George Fosty and Darril Fosty, *Black Ice: The Lost History of the Colored Hockey League of the Maritimes, 1895–1925* (New York: Stryker-Indigo, 2004).

32. James, "Race and the Social/Cultural Worlds of Student Athletes," 189.

33. Neil Longley, Todd Crosset, and Steve Jefferson, "The Migration of African-Americans to the Canadian Football League During the 1950s: An Escape from Racism?" *International Journal of the History of Sport* 25 (2008): 1379.

34. Peter James Hudson, "Honkey Night in Canada," *Transition* 96 (2006): 80; Colin D. Howell, "Two Outs: Or, Yogi Berra, Sport and Maritime Historiography," *Acadiensis* 29, no. 1 (1999): 120; Cecil Harris, *Breaking the Ice: The Black Experience in Professional Ice Hockey* (Toronto: Insomniac Press, 2003), 35–51.

35. *Washington Post*, July 25, 1974, D6; Diamond, *Total Hockey*, 315, 1381.

36. *Washington Post*, May 30, 1974, E1. The club presumably was "aware that his success could contribute substantially to increasing interest in the area's black community." Ibid., July 25, 1974, D6.

37. *Hockey News* 28, no. 3 (October 25, 1974), 6.

38. Hudson, "Honkey Night in Canada," 80; Harris, *Breaking the Ice*, 165; Diamond, *Total Hockey*, 1564–65.

39. *Boston Globe*, October 4, 1974, 33; *2011–2012 Washington Capitals Official Guide*, 170; Diamond, *Total Hockey*, 1564; and Harris, *Breaking the Ice*, 167.

40. Ibid., 64; Witteman, *New York Times*, 191.

41. Harris, *Breaking the Ice*, 59–73. Riley quotes on 62, 67.

42. Riley quoted in *New York Times*, February 25, 1990, S9; Harris, *Breaking the Ice*, 168–70; and Diamond, *Total Hockey*, 1381.

43. O'Ree, *The Autobiography of Willie O'Ree*, 101–4; *New York Times*, January 19, 1998, C9, and December 22, 2007, D1.

44. Kevin Allen, "Caps' Ward: Racist Tweets Didn't Ruin My Day," *USA Today*, April 26, 2012, found online at http://www.usatoday.com/sports/hockey/nhl/story/2012-04-26/joel-ward-interview/54557232/1 (accessed August 9, 2012); includes quotes from league and Ward. Wood's agent's comments summarized and Boston University professor quoted in Abby Goodnough, "Hockey Loss Sets Off Slurs, and Boston Asks, 'Again?'" *New York Times*, April 26, 2012, found online at http://www.nytimes.com/2012/04/27/us/joel-ward-slurs-embarrass-boston.html (accessed August 9, 2012).

45. *Boston Globe*, January 28, 1962, C56, and July 14, 1981, 45. In thirteen NHL seasons between 1961–62 and 1975–76, Williams played 663 games with the Boston Bruins, Minnesota North Stars, California Golden Seals, and Washington. He also played two seasons with the WHA's New England Whalers. See Diamond, *Total Hockey*, 1757.

46. For Canadian concerns that the United States might refuse to play, see Douglas Fisher to Allan MacEachen, June 2, 1975; No. FAI-1074, Under-Secretary of State for External Affairs to the Canadian Embassies, Moscow, Prague, Helsinki, Stockholm, Washington, March 1, 1976; both in Record Group [RG] 25, External Affairs, vol. 10920, file: 55-26-HOCKEY-1-CDACUP-1976, part 1, file title: Cultural affairs—Sports competition—Hockey—Between Canada and other countries—Canada Cup Hockey—1976, Library and Archives Canada, Ottawa, Ontario. For Canadian assessments of the American team, see *Globe and Mail* (Toronto), August 13, 1976, 26, and August 14, 1976, 37.

47. Diamond, *Total Hockey*, 971.

48. *Globe and Mail* (Toronto), March 22, 1985 (Lexis-Nexis).

49. *Washington Capitals 1992–93 Yearbook* (no publication data), 49; Diamond, *Total Hockey*, 1059, 1222, 1309; *2011–2012 Washington Capitals Official Guide*, 239.

50. Bill Beacon, untitled, United Press International, June 8, 1983 (Lexis-Nexis); *Washington Capitals 1992–93 Yearbook*, 49; and Diamond, *Total Hockey*, 1299–1300.

51. "IIHF European Championships," IIHF website, http://www.iihf.com/iihf-home/history/all-medallists/men.html (accessed July 13, 2012); Jan Velinger and Katrin Bock, "Czechs in History: A Brief History of Czech Ice Hockey," April 28, 2004, Radio Prague accessible online at www.radio.cz/en/article/53259 (accessed August 29, 2012).

52. *Chicago Tribune*, September 12, 1969, C4; Diamond, *Total Hockey*, 1226; and *Washington Post*, July 27, 1986, C1, C5, and July 26, 1986, B6. In the 1970s the Minnesota North Stars and the Toronto Maple Leafs both offered the Soviet government $1 million for the chance to sign Valerii Kharlamov. The Boston Bruins tried to involve the United States government in arranging a cultural

exchange that would allow the Bruins to obtain Aleksandr Yakushev. The WHA's Toronto Toros tried to convince the Soviets to permit Aleksandr Firsov to join them as a player-assistant coach. The Montreal Canadiens later drafted Vladislav Tretiak in hopes that Soviet authorities would permit him to spend at least one year at the end of his career in Montreal.

53. *The 1982–83 Official Yearbook of the Washington Capitals* (no publication data), 52; Diamond, *Total Hockey*, 1480–81; *Final Report, XIII Olympic Winter Games: vol. 2, Official Results* (no publication data), 107.

54. *The 1986–87 Washington Capitals Yearbook* (Alexandria, VA, n.d.), 52, and *Washington Post*, July 27, 1986, C1, includes Poile quote.

55. *2011–2012 Washington Capitals Official Guide*, 191; and *2011–2012 Washington Capitals Playoff Guide* (Arlington, VA, n.d.), 124.

56. *2011–2012 Washington Capitals Official Guide*, 133, 147, 174; *2011–2012 Washington Capitals Playoff Guide*, 124; and Diamond, *Total Hockey*, 907.

57. *Pittsburgh Post-Gazette*, February 23, 1998, D1, and Karel Janicek, "Olympic Hockey Victory Turned Into Opera By Czech National Theatre," Associated Press Worldstream, March 18, 2003 (Lexis-Nexis).

58. Jagr led the league in scoring in 1995, 1998, 1999, 2000, and 2001; he was MVP in 1999. *Sports Illustrated 2008 Almanac* (New York: Sports Illustrated Books, 2007), 389–90.

Chapter 14: "The People's Race"

1. "Spots in the 37th Annual Marine Corps Marathon Sell Out in Record Time," *Washington Post* (online edition), March 7, 2012, http://www.washington post.com/sports/2012/03/07/gIQAi5qpxR_story.html (accessed August 22, 2012); Sylvia Carignan, "Marine Corps Marathon Registration Begins Today," *Washington Post* (online edition), March 7, 2012, http://www.washingtonpost. com/blogs/the-buzz/post/marine-corps-marathon-registration-begins-today/2012/ 03/07/gIQAAVznwR_blog.html (accessed August 22, 2012).

2. As of this writing, the men's course records are: Boston, 2:03:02; New York, 2:06:05; Chicago, 2:05:37; London, 2:04:40; Berlin, 2:03:38. The women's course records are: Boston, 2:20:43; New York, 2:22:31; Chicago, 2:17:18; London, 2:15:25; Berlin, 2:19:12.

3. *Washington Post*, November 3, 1984.

4. Ibid., November 4, 1989.

5. This included not just long distance running, but also an expansion in other forms of physical exercise, such as aerobics and weightlifting. See Benjamin G. Rader, "The Quest for Self-Sufficiency and the New Strenuosity: Reflections on the Strenuous Life of the 1970s and the 1980s," *Journal of Sport History* 18 (Summer 1991): 255–66.

6. The development of the running community occurred within a larger District-area that included northern Virginian and suburban Maryland counties.

7. See following issues of *Washington Post*, May 27, 1909; May 29, 1909; May 30, 1909; February 17, 1924; February 21, 1924; February 23, 1924; February 8, 1925; February 13, 1925; February 26, 1925; March 2, 1925; March 3, 1925; March 4, 1925; and March 4, 1925.

8. Ibid., January 20, 1921; February 9, 1921; January 31, 1925; February 5, 1925; February 9, 1925; February 11, 1925; February 15, 1925; February 23, 1926; May 23, 1928; May 26, 1928; May 27, 1928; and May 21, 1929.

9. On races as complementary events to larger celebrations, see Ted Vincent, *The Rise of American Sport: Mudville's Revenge* (Lincoln: University of Nebraska Press, 1981), 54–59, 66.

10. *Afro-American* (Baltimore ed.), March 14, 1925, 9.

11. *Afro-American*, January 26, 1946, 22; *Farrall et al. v. District of Columbia Amateur Athletic Union et al.*, United States Court of Appeals, District of Columbia, February 25, 1946.

12. Constance McLaughlin Green, *Washington: Capital City, 1879–1950* (Princeton, NJ: Princeton University Press, 1963), 207, 216–17.

13. Rader, "The Quest for Self-Sufficiency and the New Strenuosity," 260.

14. *Washington Post*, February 25, 1962, and July 30, 2005. *Long Distance Log* (hereafter, *LDL*) vol. 4 (April 1959), 13; RRCA "History of the Road Runners Club of America," 2, http://www.rrca.org/downloads/about/RRCA_Detailed_History_from_Handbook.pdf (accessed on August 14, 2012); and *LDL*, vol. 4 (August 1960), 9.

15. *LDL*, vol. 6 (February 1961), 62, 9, 20–21, 22; *LDL*, vol. 6 (March 1961), 11, 13; *LDL*, vol. 6 (April 1961), 11, 22; *LDL*, vol. 6 (May 1961), 9, 19, 21; *LDL*, vol. 6 (August 1961), 2.

16. See these issues of *Washington Post*, June 18, 1961; September 3, 1961; and September 4, 1961. For more on the Bunion Derbies of 1928 and 1929, see Charles B. Kastner, *Bunion Derby: The 1928 Footrace across America* (Albuquerque: University of New Mexico Press, 2007), and Charles B. Kastner, *The Bunion Derby: Johnny Salo and the Great Footrace Across America* (Syracuse, NY: Syracuse University Press, 2014).

17. *LDL*, vol. 6 (August 1961), 2.

18. The DC RRC continues to hold both the Bunion Derby Series and the Operation Snowball Series in much the same way it did during the 1960s. Operation Snowball is now called the Snowball Series. See the DC RRC website for the most recent editions: DC RRC, "2011–2012 Snowball Series Rules," http://www.dcroadrunners.org/races/race-rules/427-snowball-series.html; DC RRC, "2012 Bunion Derby Series" http://www.dcroadrunners.org/races/race-rules/1739-2012-bunion-derby.html (both accessed on August 30, 2012).

19. *Washington Post*, January 7, 1962; *LDL*, vol. 7 (March 1962), 21.

20. *LDL*, vol. 7 (April 1962), 10–11; *Washington Post*, February 22, 1962, and February 23, 1962.

21. The George Washington Birthday Marathon has been held every year since 1961, except 2003 and 2010. The race was planned for those years but canceled because of excessive snowfall. In 1979 the race was held, but the weather conditions were so bad that the race director encouraged people not to compete. *Washington Post*, February 19, 1979.

22. The DC RRC introduced "run-for-your-life" races in 1964. The club included a shorter, less-competitive race that complemented almost every other race. The idea spread to other RRCA clubs. RRCA, "History of the Road Runners Club of America," 5; *LDL*, vol. 9 (August 1964), 18–19; Jeff Darman, author's phone interview, August 3, 2012 (hereafter, Darman interview).

23. *Washington Post*, February 16, 1962; *LDL*, vol. 7 (April 1962), 10–11; and *Washington Post*, November 11, 1964.

24. For examples of early support of women runners, see *LDL*, vol. 4 (October 1959), 23–24; *LDL*, vol. 8 (April 1963), 2; *LDL*, vol. 10 (November 1965), 18–19. RRCA, "History of the Road Runners Club of America," 4–5.

25. *Washington Post*, February 15, 1971.

26. Darman interview.

27. Quantico is about thirty-five miles from DC. For examples of Quantico-based marines competing in DC distance races, see results in following issues of *LDL*, vol. 7 (December 1962) 15–16; vol. 8 (February 1963), 12; vol. 8 (November 1963), 19; vol. 9 (February 1964), 13; vol. 10 (March 1965), 15.

28. *LDL*, vol. 7 (March 1962), 21; *Washington Post*, January 15, 1962.

29. Darman interview.

30. *The Final Report of the President's Commission on Olympic Sports*, vol. 1 (Washington, DC: January 1977), 103.

31. "The Marine Corps," draft report for President's Commission on Olympic Sports, 6–7, Military Sports Folder, President's Commission on Olympic Sports Collection (hereafter, PCOS), Gerald R. Ford Presidential Library, Ann Arbor, MI. For examples of how time was provided and expectations of military responsibilities, see *Leatherneck*, May 2010, 41–45.

32. The formal name of the Quantico Relays was the Marine Corps Relays. But it was more commonly known as the Quantico Relays. See Rawson, *Leatherneck*, May 2010, 41–45, and "The Marine Corps," PCOS Records, 2.

33. For information on the military and athletic competitions from the late 1800s to World War II, see Wanda Ellen Wakefield, *Playing to Win: Sports and the American Military, 1898–1945* (New York: State University of New York Press, 1997).

34. *The Final Report of the President's Commission on Olympic Sports*, vol. II (Washington, DC: January 1977), 315.

35. Liz Robbins, *A Race Like No Other: 26.2 Miles Through the Streets of New York* (New York: Harper Publishers, 2008), 3; Ron Rubin, *Anything for a T-Shirt: Fred Lebow and the New York City Marathon, the World's Greatest Footrace* (Syracuse, NY: Syracuse University Press, 2004), 27; John Bryant, *The London Marathon: The Greatest Race on Earth* (London: Hutchinson, 2005), 9. Although Shorter's win is a convenient marker, there were other factors, including the activities of running clubs like DC RRC. The Road Runners Club of America, founded in 1958, encouraged running for fitness and competition and had grown significantly prior to 1972. Moreover, in 1967 University of Oregon track coach and cofounder of Nike, Bill Bowerman, published *Jogging*, an influential guide to fitness running. William Bowerman and W. E. Harris, *Jogging: A Physical Fitness Program for All Ages* (New York: Gosset and Dunlap, 1967).

36. Frank Shorter, with Marc Bloom, *Olympic Gold: A Runner's Life and Times* (Boston: Houghton Mifflin, 1984), 91–92.

37. On the running boom in DC, see Darman interview, and three issues of *Washington Post*, October 25, 1975; April 3, 1977; and July 16, 1980.

38. *Washington Post*, January 8, 1978.

39. Darman interview.

40. *Washington Post*, April 3, 1977.

41. Ibid., April 16, 1978.

42. Robbins, *A Race Like No Other*, 3; Peter Gambaccini, *The New York City Marathon: Twenty-Five Years* (New York: Rizzoli International Publishers, 1994), 168–69.

43. *Washington Post*, February 21, 1972.

44. Ibid., February 16, 1981.

45. Ibid., November 4, 1977.

46. Ibid., November 3, 1984.

47. Quoted in Marine Corps Marathon, "MCM History" Marine Corps Marathon website, http://www.marinemarathon.com/MCM_Vault/MCM_History. htm (accessed August 23, 2012).

48. Quoted in George Banker, *The Marine Corps Marathon: A Running Tradition* (Oxford: Meyer and Meyer Sport Ltd., 2008) 15.

49. *Leatherneck*, May 2010, 45.

50. Ibid. Major Rick Nealis, author's phone interview, August 2, 2012 (hereafter, Nealis interview); Lieutenant Colonel Charles A. Fleming, Captain Robin L. Austin, and Captain Charles A. Braley, *Quantico: Crossroads of the Marine Corps* (History and Museums Division Headquarters, US Marine Corps, Washington, DC: 1978), 99, http://www.scribd.com/doc/48232689/Quantico-Crossroads-of-the-Marine-Corps (accessed August 12, 2012.)

51. *Washington Post*, March 27, 1977; Banker, *The Marine Corps Marathon*, 69–71.

52. *Washington Post,* November 7, 1977; Banker, *The Marine Corps Marathon*, 75. By comparison, the GWBM drew fewer than five hundred in 1977, which was much more than the GWBD Marathon usually had. *Washington Post*, February 21, 1977.

53. See following issues of *Washington Post*, November 4, 1977; November 5, 1977; and November 6, 1977.

54. New York was the largest with more than 14,000 starters. Gambaccini, *The New York City Marathon*, 168, and *Washington Post*, November 2, 1981.

55. *Washington Post*, November 6, 1977.

56. Ibid., April 7, 1977; Souza, *The Chicago Marathon*, 20, 22, 72, 93; Bryant, *The London Marathon*, 100, 188.

57. *Washington Post*, October 30, 1980.

58. Ibid., November 1, 1980.

59. Ibid., October 31, 1981.

60. Nealis interview.

61. *Washington Post*, November 4, 1978.

62. Ibid., November 6, 1977.

63. Ibid., November 4, 1978, and October 30, 1980.

64. The USMC provided substantial in-kind support, particularly USMC manpower in the earlier races. Nealis interview.

65. Darman interview.

66. *Washington Post*, November 3, 1984.

67. Ibid., November 1, 1984.

68. Ibid., November 6, 1977.

69. Ibid., November 4, 1977.

70. Ibid., November 6, 1977, and November 1, 1984.

71. Ibid., November 4, 1989.

72. Ibid., November 12, 1977. See "Letters to the Editors."

73. Ibid., November 3, 1979.

74. Banker, *The Marine Corps Marathon*, 83.

75. *Washington Post*, November 2, 1981.

76. Ibid.

77. Ibid., October 28, 1981.

78. Ibid., October 31, 1981.

79. Ibid., October 27, 1986.

80. Ibid., November 1, 1989.

81. Ibid., November 3, 1985.

82. *New York Times*, August 29, 1984.

83. Al Gore's race in 1997 garnered the most attention. See *Runner's World*, February 1998, 52–55, and the following issues of *Washington Post*, October 27, 1997; June 24, 1998; and October 31, 1981.

84. Nealis interview.

85. *Washington Post*, October 24, 1994.

86. Robbins, *A Race Like No Other*, 3.

87. For example, see Suozzo, *The Chicago Marathon*, 153–56. On this phenomenon and how it benefited the MCM, see *New York Times*, November 1, 1999.

88. On the growth of charity running and the reserve registration, see Nealis interview, and *Washington Post*, June 18, 2006. For more on the phenomenon at the Chicago Marathon, see Suozo, *The Chicago Marathon*, 125–40.

89. For more on Darrell General, see Banker, *The Marine Corps Marathon*, 192–93, and *Washington Post*, April 26, 1990, B6.

90. The increased diversity should not be overstated since distance running and marathon participation continue to be disproportionately white. For recent discussions on the relatively low African American participation in long distance running, see Nick Patowksi, *Runner's World*, January 4, 2008, and November 15, 2011. For a story highlighting an African American runner in the MCM, see *Washington Post*, January 31, 1994, D5.

91. Nealis interview.

92. *Leatherneck*, January 1998, 45.

93. Nealis interview.

94. *New York Times*, November 1, 2001.

95. Nealis interview, and *Washington Post*, October 30, 2010.

96. Ibid., June 7, 2011.

97. In 2010, Road Race Management honored Rick Nealis as the Race Director of the Year. Road Race Management press release, "Rick Nealis Named 2010 MarathonFoto/Road Race Management Race Director of the Year" http://www.rrm.com/rdm/10rdypressrelease.htm (accessed August 25, 2012).

98. *New York Times*, September 19, 2001.

99. *Leatherneck*, January 2002, 35; Nealis interview.

100. Nealis interview.

101. *Leatherneck*, January 2002, 34.

102. The only active-duty marine to win the women's division was marine lieutenant Joanna Yundt Martin in 1979. *Washington Post*, November 5, 1979.

103. In some of the first races, more than 30 percent of the participants were military. This percentage slowly decreased as the race grew and, according to Nealis, as more military personnel were sent to Afghanistan and Iraq.

104. The MCM has also been the Armed Forces Marathon Championships since 1998. Banker, *The Marine Corps Marathon*, 60–68, 198–200; *Washington Post*, November 4, 1991, and October 24, 1992.

105. *Runner's World*, March 2002, 102.

106. For one of the many examples of injured returned veterans competing in the wheelchair division, see *Washington Post*, October 31, 2005, and *Spikes and Spokes*, January 2008, 34.

107. Nealis interview.

108. *Washington Post*, November 1, 2010.

109. Nealis interview.

110. *Washington Post*, October 27, 2002.

111. Ibid., October 24, 2004.

112. Nealis quoted in *Runner's World,* October 18, 2005, www.runnersworld.com/print/25576 (accessed December 18, 2012).

113. *Marathon and Beyond*, March/April 2007, 184.

114. *Washington Post*, September 10, 2006.

115. Ibid., October 23, 2005.

Chapter 15: Georgetown Basketball in Reagan's America

1. Account in *Sports Illustrated*, November 26, 1984, 4.

2. Leonard Shapiro, *Big Man on Campus: John Thompson and the Georgetown Hoyas* (New York: Henry Holt and Company, 1991), 226.

3. As described in *Sports Illustrated*, November 26, 1984, 4.

4. Shapiro, *Big Man on Campus*, 10.

5. Ibid., 82–83. For discussion of Edwin Bancroft Henderson, see David K. Wiggins, "Edwin Bancroft Henderson: Physical Educator, Civil Rights Activist, and Chronicler of African American Athletes," *Research Quarterly for Exercise and Sport* 70 (June 1999): 91–112, and Bob Kuska, *Hot Potato: How Washington and New York Gave Birth to Black Basketball and Changed America's Game Forever* (Charlottesville: University of Virginia Press, 2004).

6. Leonard Shapiro, *Big Man on Campus*, 80–81. Photograph of students with "Magee Must Go" signs in Special Collections Archive (hereafter SCA), Lauinger Library, Georgetown University.

7. *The Hoya*, February 11, 1972, 16.

8. Leonard Shapiro, *Big Man on Campus*, 83–87.

9. For description of Thompson's early years through college, see Leonard Shapiro, *Big Man on Campus*, 19–49. Thompson's college stats in Mike Douchant, *Encyclopedia of College Basketball* (Detroit, MI: Gale Research, 1995), 115.

10. Thompson's professional career in Shapiro, *Big Man on Campus*, 49–63.

11. For Thompson's high school coaching career, see ibid., 66–77.

12. *Washington Post*, March 14, 1972, D1.

13. *The Hoya*, March 17, 1972, 3.

14. Jordan Kranis, prod., *Perfect Upset: The 1985 Villanova vs. Georgetown NCAA Championship* (HBO Sports Documentaries, 2005), DVD.

15. *The Hoya*, September 3, 1972. See also Shapiro, *Big Man on Campus*, 96–98.

16. For a description of the founding of the Big East, see Shapiro, *Big Man on Campus*, 160–67.

17. *Washington Post*, February 13, 1980, D1.

18. Ibid., February 8, 1981, D1.

19. Spike Lee, dir., *Real Sports: Coach Thompson* (HBO Sports, 1995), DVD.

20. *Washington Post*, February 3, 1981, D6. See also *Perfect Upset: The 1985 Villanova vs. Georgetown NCAA Championship*.

21. *Washington Post*, March 30, 1982, D4. See also Shapiro, *Big Man on Campus*, 201–3.

22. Sean Wilentz, *The Age of Reagan: A History, 1974–2008* (New York: HarperCollins Publishers, 2008), 147–50.

23. A good source on the assassination attempt is Del Quentin Wilber, *Rawhide Down: The Near Assassination of Ronald Reagan* (New York: Henry Holt, 2011).

24. Sean Wilentz, *The Age of Reagan*, 142–44. See also "President Reagan's Address on Economy," *Congressional Quarterly Almanac 1981*, vol. 37 (1982): 20-E.

25. "Health/Education/Welfare," *Congressional Quarterly Almanac 1981*, vol. 37 (1982): 461; US Congress, House of Representatives Committee on the District of Columbia, *Changing the Course: Federal Grants-In-Aid Funding, 1964–83: The Effects of the Reagan Administration Budget Cuts on the District of Columbia and Other Urban Centers*, 99th Cong., 2nd sess., 1986, H. Rep., serial S-5, 81, 88–89, 91.

26. *New York Times*, February 15, 1976, 51. Also see Lou Cannon, *President Reagan: The Role of a Lifetime* (New York: Simon & Schuster, 1991), 518.

27. As discussed in *New York Times*, February 1976, 51, and Cannon, *President Reagan*, 518.

28. Matthew Dallek, *The Right Moment: Ronald Reagan's First Victory and the Decisive Turning Point in American Politics* (New York: Oxford University Press, 2000), 200–201.

29. Wilentz, *The Age of Reagan*, 182–83.

30. Ibid., 181.

31. *Washington Post*, February 9, 1983, D1.

32. Ibid.

33. Shapiro, *Big Man on Campus*, 30, 113.

34. *Washington Post*, February 9, 1983, D6.

35. *Sports Illustrated*, March 19, 1984, 22.

36. *Washington City Paper* (hereafter cited as *WCP*), March 8, 2013, http://www.washingtoncitypaper.com/articles/43995/hoya-euphoria-georgetown-basketball-the-big-east-syracuse-john-thompson (accessed April 19, 2013).

37. *The Hoya*, February 26, 1988, 1.

38. *Sports Illustrated*, March 19, 1984, 24.

39. Recording of the Georgetown versus Dayton game from March 24, 1984, in SCA.

40. *Sports Illustrated*, March 19, 1984, 23.

41. Ibid., November 26, 1984, 49–50.

42. *Washington Post*, March 20, 1984, D1.

43. *Sports Illustrated*, December 1, 1980, 94.

44. *Washington Post*, March 30, 1984, A19.

45. *New York Times*, April 3, 1984, B7. See also Shapiro, *Big Man on Campus*, 221–22.

46. *Washington Post*, April 8, 1984, A1.

47. Cannon, *President Reagan*, 493.

48. "The Demographics/ USA Results," in *The 84 Vote*, ed. Carolyn Smith (New York: ABC News), 42. See table 1-3.

49. *Crime in the United States*, Uniform Crime Reports 1984, Federal Bureau of Investigation, 71; ibid., 1985, Federal Bureau of Investigation, 71; ibid., Uniform Crime Reports 1986, 71; "Crime Rates, by Type—Selected Large Cities: 1988," in *Statistical Abstract of the United States 1990*, US Census Bureau (Washington, DC: Government Printing Office), 172.

50. Cannon, *President Reagan*, 25.

51. *Washington Post*, June 20, 1986, A1; "Congress Clears Massive Anti-Drug Measure," *1986 Congressional Quarterly Almanac* 42 (1987): 92, 98; Troy Duster, "Pattern, Purpose, and Race in the Drug War: The Crisis of Credibility in Criminal Justice," in *Crack in America: Demon Drugs and Social Justice*, ed. Craig Reinarman and Harry G. Levine (Berkeley: University of California Press, 1997), 264–66; Cannon, *President Reagan*, 25, 813.

52. *Washington Post*, April 17, 1989, A1, A4.

53. Ibid., September 10, 1989, B1, B8.

54. Ibid., April 28, 1989, A1. Also see Alonzo Mourning, *Resilience: Faith Focus, Triumph* (New York: Ballantine Books, 2008), 59.

55. For a comprehensive history of hip-hop, see Jeff Chang, *Can't Stop Won't Stop: A History of the Hip-Hop Generation* (New York: Picador Books, 2005).

56. *The Delphian*, November 10, 1982, 17. Access to the comic was provided courtesy of the Adelphi University Archives and Special Collections, Adelphi University, Garden City, New York. Also see Chang, *Can't Stop Won't Stop*, 237–38.

57. Chuck D quoted in *WCP*.

58. Ibid.

59. *Perfect Upset: The 1985 Villanova vs. Georgetown NCAA Championship*.

60. Shapiro, *Big Man on Campus*, 9.

61. *The Hoya*, February 22, 1985, 14. Kids & Cops trading card in SCA.

62. For all provisions of Proposition 48, see *Washington Post*, January 15, 1989, A27.

63. *The Hoya*, January 17, 1989, 1–2.

64. Ibid., January 27, 1989, 1.

65. Bill Reynolds, *Big Hoops: A Season in the Big East Conference* (New York: New American Library Books, 1989), 17.

66. *Sports Illustrated*, November 26, 1984, 4.

Chapter 16: Washington Baseball Fans

1. Julio Becquer, speaking at Washington Senators Reunion, Bethesda, Maryland, March 22, 2003.

2. *Washington Post*, August 6, 1959, D2.

3. Tim Cullen, phone interview, May 2, 1997.

4. *Tampa Tribune*, May 31, 2005, 4S.

5. Quoted in *Washington Post*, March 15, 2005, B1.

6. Charlie Slowes, interview, November 17, 2005 (hereafter, Slowes interview).

7. Phil Wood, e-mail interview, December 27, 2012 (hereafter, Wood interview).

8. Jamey Carroll, interview, October 18, 2005.

9. Slowes interview.

10. Marlon Byrd, interview, November 17, 2005.

11. *Washington Post*, May 15, 2012, D5.

12. Quote from Nats fan Alan Alper. Author's recollection of Phil Wood's "Nats Talk Live," which aired after the game.

13. Alan Alper, telephone interview, December 21, 2012.

14. *Nats Insider*, December 30, 2012.

15. Wood interview.

16. Dryw Freed, e-mail interview, December 27, 2012.

17. *Nationals Journal*, December 4, 2012.

Chapter 17: Washington Sports Memories, Personal and Collective

Many thanks to Chris Elzey, Irvin Nathan, and Greg Pfitzer for their careful reading and constructive criticism of this chapter.

1. By this time, the second iteration of the Senators was already in Texas. So, like many of my family members and friends, I was and remain a devoted Orioles fan.

2. Charles C. Euchner, *Playing the Field: Why Sports Teams Move and Cities Fight to Keep Them* (Baltimore: Johns Hopkins University Press, 1993), 61.

3. See http://www.dcvote.org/media/release.cfm?releaseID=226 (accessed November 1, 2012).

4. Christopher Buckley, *Washington Schlepped Here: Walking in the Nation's Capital* (New York: Crown Journeys, 2003), 27.

5. Kennedy quoted in Henry Allen, "True Grit and Imitation Grandeur," in *Katharine Graham's Washington*, ed. Katharine Graham (New York: Alfred A. Knopf, 2002), 64.

6. George Solomon, "One Team, One Town," in *Redskins: A History of Washington's Team*, ed. Noel Epstein (Washington, DC: Washington Post Books, 1997), v.

7. Quoted in Buckley, *Washington Schlepped Here*, 10.

8. Howard Bryant, "The long national nightmare is over," *ESPN The Magazine*, October 15, 2012, http://espn.go.com/nfl/story/_/id/8448606/can-washington-redskins-qb-robert-griffin-iii-make-dc-sports-town-again-espn-magazine (accessed November 1, 2012).

9. *Washington Post*, January 31, 1983, A1.

10. Quoted in Mike Diegnan, "MNF's Greatest Games: Dallas-Washington 1983," December 4, 2002, http://espn.go.com/abcsports/mnf/s/greatestgames/dallaswashington1983.html (accessed September 30, 2012).

11. Quoted in Michael Richman, *The Redskins Encyclopedia* (Philadelphia: Temple University Press, 2007), 154.

12. Joe Theismann was good but he was no Darrell Green. On my list, Green

would rank third, behind only Joe Gibbs and Walter Johnson. See "Washington Post Poll," November 1, 2011, http:// www.washingtonpost.com/wp-srv/sports/ postpoll_DC sportspoll_1011.html (accessed September 30, 2012).

· 13. This is what *Washington Post* blogger Dan Steinberg says about the subject: "Assuming 'sports figure' means 'coaches, owners and/or athletes,' a few names jump out to me. Joe Gibbs, because he made the Redskins a national power to the extent no other team from this city has ever been. Jack Kent Cooke, for the same reason. John Riggins, for authoring the single greatest play in team history. Sammy Baugh and Walter Johnson, because old people say so. Wes Unseld, for being a league most valuable player and world champion. John Thompson Jr., for being one of the most important figures in college basketball history." Dan Steinberg, "The greatest sports figure in D.C. history," *Washington Post*, November 2, 2011, http://www. washingtonpost.com/blogs/dc-sports-bog/post/the-greatest-sports-figure-in-dc-history/2011/ 11/02/gIQAqsC1fM_blog.html (accessed October 19, 2012).

14. Thomas Boswell, "Working Through Their Emotion," *Washington Post*, December 3, 2007, http://www.washingtonpost.com/wp-dyn/content/article/2007/ 12/02/AR2007120201964.html (accessed November 10, 2012).

15. *Sporting News*, January 19, 2004, 30.

16. Like many, I've always been uncomfortable calling the team the Wizards, its name since 1997.

17. Michael Lee, "Washington Wizards' new uniforms and logo became a reality more quickly than for most NBA teams," *Washington Post*, May 10, 2011, http://www.washingtonpost.com/ sports/wizards/wizards-went-from-plan-to-new-uniform-and-logo-quicker-than-most-nba-teams/2011/05/10/AF0e7XkG_story. html (accessed October 19, 2012).

18. When they were rookies, Unseld not only won the NBA's Rookie of the Year award, but the MVP award, too, despite the fact that Hayes, who was then with the San Diego Rockets, had a much better scoring average and nearly as many rebounds per game.

19. Quoted in *Baltimore Sun*, March 24, 2009, http://apps.baltimoresun.com/ top-athletes/top-10-athletes.php (accessed October 29, 2012).

20. See http://www.basketball-reference.com/players/h/hayesel01.html (accessed November 1, 2012).

21. See http://www.nba.com/history/50greatest.html (accessed November 1, 2012).

22. FreeDarko, *The Undisputed Guide to Pro Basketball History* (New York: Bloomsbury, 2010), 99.

23. See http://www.bulletsforever.com/2008/8/16/595153/bf-5-phil-chenier (accessed November 1, 2012).

24. Bill Simmons, "The Harden Disaster," October 30, 2012, http://www. grantland.com/story/_/idid/8573213/the-harden-disaster (accessed November 1, 2012).

25. *Sports Illustrated*, January 15, 1979, 22.

26. Quoted in ibid., 25.

27. FreeDarko, *The Undisputed Guide to Pro Basketball History*, 101.

28. Ibid.

29. "The Wizards," notes sportswriter Howard Bryant, "formerly the Bullets, haven't won 50 games since they went to the Finals back when Jimmy Carter was turning down the thermostat in the White House." Looking back over the past thirty-plus years of Bullets/Wizards history, I see at least three dozen remarkably talented players (ranging from Moses Malone to Bernard King to Muggsy Bogues to Chris Webber to Rod Strickland to Michael Jordan to Antawn Jamison to Gilbert Arenas, and many others) who either blossomed elsewhere or were past their prime while in DC. None of them was able to get the team very far in the playoffs or sustain their limited success. During many of those years, the team just flat-out stunk. Bryant, "The long national nightmare is over."

30. Quoted in *Sports Illustrated*, June 30, 1986, 27.

31. Quoted in Kirk Fraser, prod., *Without Bias* (ESPN Home Entertainment, 2010), DVD.

32. The first pick in the 1986 NBA draft was University of North Carolina center Brad Daugherty, who was selected by the Cleveland Cavaliers. The Celtics had the second pick due to an earlier trade: in 1984, Boston sent guard Gerald Henderson to the Seattle SuperSonics in exchange for Seattle's first-round pick in 1986, which ended up being the second pick in the draft.

33. Quoted in Fraser, *Without Bias*.

34. *Washington Post*, June 21, 1986, C4.

35. Quoted in Fraser, *Without Bias*.

36. Ibid.

37. Ibid.

38. Michael Wilbon, "For Michael Wilbon, a fond farewell to The Post," *Washington Post*, December 7, 2010, http://www.washingtonpost.com/wp-dyn/content/article/2010/12/06/ AR2010120606607.html (accessed November 1, 2012).

39. Michael Weinreb, "The Day the Innocence Died," June 17, 2011, http://sports.espn.go.com/ espn/eticket/story?page=bias (accessed September 15, 2011).

40. For more on Bias and his premature death, see Lewis Cole, *Never Too Young to Die: The Death of Len Bias* (New York: Pantheon Books, 1989); C. Fraser Smith, *Lenny, Lefty, and the Chancellor: The Len Bias Tragedy and the Search for Reform in Big-time College Basketball* (Baltimore: Bancroft Press, 1992); Amy Goldstein and Susan Kinzie, "Bias Death Still Ripples Through Athletes' Academic Lives," *Washington Post*, June 19, 2006, http://www.washingtonpost.com/wp-dyn/content/article/ 2006/06/18/AR2006061801051.html (accessed March 22, 2010); Jack McCallum, "Twenty-five years later, Bias' death remains a seminal sports moment," June 17, 2011, http://sportsillustrated.cnn.com/2011/writers/jack_mccallum/06/17/len. bias/index.html (accessed November 1, 2012); and Jeff Barker, "After 25 years, Len Bias' legacy lives on," *Baltimore Sun*, June 18, 2011, www.baltimoresun.com/sports/terps/bs-sp-len-bias-legacy-0619-20110618,0, 6230397.story (accessed November 1, 2012).

41. Todd Boyd, *Young, Black, Rich and Famous: The Rise of the NBA, the Hip-Hop Invasion, and the Transformation of American Culture* (New York: Doubleday, 2003), 77.

42. Ibid., 76.

43. See http://espn.go.com/nba/player/bio/_/id/237/patrick-ewing (accessed February 27, 2013).

44. *Sports Illustrated,* April 8, 1985, 32.

45. *Washington Post,* April 2, 1985, D1.

46. See http://espn.go.com/classic/s/add_villanova_georgetown.html (accessed February 27, 2013).

47. *Washington Post,* December 4, 1994, B1.

48. Liz Clarke, "Georgetown takes lead in preserving basketball tradition of 'Catholic 7,'" *Washington Post,* February 21, 2013, http://www.washingtonpost.com/sports/colleges/ georgetown-takes-lead-in-preserving-basketball-tradition-of-catholic-7/2013/02/21/40193304-7c2d-11e2-82e8-61a46c2cde3d_story.html (accessed February 27, 2013).

49. *Sports Illustrated,* October 1, 2012, 51.

50. Bryant is specific: "By the forces of gentrification that have pushed Chocolate City into surrounding counties and diluted the traditional soul of the city. By Marion Barry and the history of rising black political power. By the tensions between police and the residents of predominantly black Prince George's County. By the pride for its most popular team and its incorrect name and dreadful racial history. And, of course, by the steel-cage paradigm that is Republicans vs. Democrats, which turns this town over every two years." Bryant, "The long national nightmare is over."

Contributors

Chris Elzey teaches in the History/Art History Department at George Mason University. He also oversees the Sport and American Culture Minor and codirects the Center for the Study of Sport and Leisure in Society at George Mason. He has written on the Olympics, and basketball.

David K. Wiggins is professor and codirector of the Center for the Study of Sport and Leisure in Society at George Mason University. His primary research interest is issues of race and sport. He has published numerous essays and written or edited several books, including *Glory Bound: Black Athletes in a White America* and *Rivals: Legendary Matchups That Made Sport History*. He is the former editor of *Quest* and the *Journal of Sport History*.

John Bloom is an Associate Professor in the Department of History and Philosophy at Shippensburg University. He is the author of several articles and books on sports and culture in the United States, including *There You Have It: The Life, Legacy, and Legend of Howard Cosell* and *To Show What an Indian Can Do: Sports at Indian Boarding Schools*. He is currently working on a history of bicycle messengers and the culture of cycling in Washington, DC.

Jomills Henry Braddock II is a Professor in the Department of Sociology at the University of Miami. His research interests focus on issues of social justice in education and employment and the role of sport as a social institution. His current project examines African American male's experiences of discrimination.

Chad Carlson is an Assistant Professor of Kinesiology and an assistant men's basketball coach at Hope College. His research interests include the sociocultural aspects of sport and physical activity. Carlson has written on the metaphysics of play and games, sport ethics, race and sport, and the history of basketball. His work has been published in a variety of journals and edited collections. He is currently working on a book about the history of the NCAA and NIT basketball tournaments.

Marvin P. Dawkins is Professor in the Department of Sociology at the University of Miami. His research interests focus on issues of race and social equity in such areas as education, career aspirations and mobility, substance abuse prevention, and sports. He is the coauthor of *African American Golfers during the Jim Crow Era*. He is currently completing a study of the media treatment of black golfers from the Jim Crow era to the present.

Sarah K. Fields is an Associate Professor in the Department of Communication at the University of Colorado, Denver. She has published numerous articles in scholarly journals. She is the author of *Female Gladiators: Gender, Law, and Contact Sport in America* and coeditor of *Sport and the Law: Historical and Cultural Intersections*, which was recently published by the University of Arkansas Press.

Dennis Gildea is a Professor of Communications at Springfield College (the birthplace of basketball) where he teaches journalism and American literature. He regularly teaches a course on sport media history. A former sportswriter, he is the author of *Hoop Crazy: The Lives of Clair Bee and Chip Hilton*.

James R. Hartley was born in Washington, DC, and is a lifelong baseball fan. He has written three books on Washington baseball and is the editor of *Nats News*, a quarterly newsletter published by the Washington Baseball Historical Society. He resides in Silver Spring, Maryland, with his wife, Lisa.

Daniel A. Nathan is an Associate Professor of American Studies at Skidmore College. He is the author of the award-winning *Saying It's So: A Cultural History of the Black Sox Scandal* and editor of *Rooting for the Home Team: Sport, Community and Identity*. He is also the President of the North American Society for Sport History and serves on the *Journal of Sport History* editorial review board.

John Nauright is Professor of Sport and Leisure Cultures at the University of Brighton in Eastbourne, England, and Director of the Centre for Sport, Tourism and Leisure Studies at Brighton. He is the author of *Long Run to Freedom: Sport, Cultures and Identities in South Africa* and the coeditor of several books, including *Beyond CLR James: Shifting Boundaries of Race and Ethnicity in Sport* and *The Routledge Companion to Sports History*. He is also the editor of *SportsWorld: The Journal of Global Sports*.

Stephen H. Norwood is Professor of History at the University of Oklahoma. He is the author of five books on American history, most recently *Antisemitism and the American Far Left*. His book *The Third Reich in the Ivory Tower* was a finalist for the National Jewish Book Award for Holocaust Studies. Norwood coedited the prize-winning two-volume *Encyclopedia of American Jewish History*. He is the winner of the Herbert G. Gutman Award in American Social History and cowinner of the Macmillan/SABR Award in Baseball History. His most recent sports history publications include articles in *Rivals: Legendary Matchups That Made Sport History* and *Modern Judaism*, as well as the book *Real Football*.

Charles Parrish is an Assistant Professor at Western Carolina University in Cullowhee, North Carolina. He served as coeditor and a contributing author for *Sports Around the World: History, Culture, and Practice*, as well as *Soccer Around the World: History, Culture, and Practice*. He has published in several notable journals and contributed to anthologies. His primary research interests include sport-based fandom and stadiums as events venues.

John Soares teaches history at the University of Notre Dame. In autumn 2010 he was Fulbright Visiting Research Chair in North American Studies at Carleton University in Ottawa. Among his recent publications are contributions to Cold War International History Project Working Papers 68 and 69, a chapter in *Diplomatic Games*, and a Routledge Prize–winning article in the August 2013 edition of the *International Journal of the History of Sport*.

Ryan A. Swanson is an Assistant Professor in the Honors College and Director of the Lobo Scholars Program at the University of New Mexico. He is the author of *When Baseball Went White: Reconstruction, Reconciliation, and Dreams of a "National Pastime."*

Zack Tupper studied history at Georgetown University. He wrote his senior honors thesis about Georgetown University's basketball team and President Ronald Reagan's administration. He lives in his hometown of Seattle, Washington.

Joseph M. Turrini is an Assistant Professor and Coordinator of the Archival Administration Program in the School of Library and Information Science at Wayne State University. His research has focused on labor history, sport history, and archival administration. He is the author of *The End of Amateurism in American Track and Field*. He has published articles in a variety of journals, including *Michigan History*, *American Archivist*, and the *Journal of Sport History*.

Martha H. Verbrugge is Presidential Professor in the History Department at Bucknell University, where she teaches the history of science and medicine. She is the author of *Active Bodies: A History of Women's Physical Education in Twentieth-Century America*, which examines sports and physical education in the public school system in Washington, DC, before 1954, as well as the women's program at Howard University.

Stephen J. Walker is a longtime DC sports fan. He is the author of *A Whole New Ballgame: The 1969 Washington Senators* and numerous articles on the Washington Nationals and Washington baseball history. He lives in Ellicott City, Maryland, with his wife and three sons.

Claire M. Williams is an Assistant Professor in the Department of Kinesiology at St. Mary's College of California. She teaches classes in sport and recreation management, sport law, sport marketing, and women in sport. Her research interests include women in sport, Title IX, the discrimination and harassment of GLBT athletes, and the marketing of female athletes.

Index

A

Aaron, Hank, 172, 176
Abbott, Robert, 50
ABC Evening News, 227
Abdul-Jabbar, Kareem. *See* Lew Alcindor
Acta, Manny, 294
Adams, Adelaide, 64
Adams, George, 61, 63
"African American Festival Style," (article), 48
African Americans: as bicyclists, 8–10; baseball and the White Lot, 22–24; baseball and Griffith Stadium, 25–30; and Howard University-Lincoln University Thanksgiving Day football games, 27–28, 37–56; and rituals and cultural styles, 46–48; as golfers, 57–72; and segregation and public recreation, 105–28; on the Washington Senators, 172; and the Washington Bullets, 211; and dearth of distance runners, 252; and increased participation in the Marine Corps Marathon, 261; as avid supporters of Georgetown basketball, 268; and drug abuse and urban decay in the District of Columbia, 280–81
Agnew, Spiro, 187; as admirer of George Allen and football, 195–97
Akron Pros, 39
Alcindor, Lew, 309–11; and college and professional career, 129–30; performance in 1964 game against DeMatha, 132–33; and admiration for Wilt Chamberlain, 133; being shielded from the press, 138; performance in 1965 game against DeMatha, 141–44
Alda, Alan, 138
Alexander, W. G., 44
Allen, Etty, 202–3
Allen, George, 185, 217, 305, 307; befriended by Richard Nixon, 186; and popularity in Washington, DC, 188; and forging relationships between football and American presidency, 194–95; and contempt for the press, 196–97; and personnel changes on Redskins, 198–99; and

treatment of Sonny Jurgensen, 200–201; and obsession with winning, 201–3; and praise from Gerald Ford, 203; and post-Redskin career, 204
Allen, Hank: perceived treatment by the Washington Senators, 169–70; performance with the Washington Senators in 1968, 172; positive relationship with Ted Williams, 172–75
Allen, Jennifer, 197, 202–3
Allen, Richie, 169–70
Allison, Bob, 287
Aloysius Club, 250
Alper, Alan, 299
Alpha Golf Club, 60
Alsop, Joseph, 305
Amateur Athletic Union (AAU), xv, 82, 93; and national championship basketball tournament, 140; and national marathon championship, 250; and discrimination against African American boxers, 251
American Association for Health and Physical Education, 93
American Basketball Association (ABA), 208
American Basketball League (ABL), 103, 207
American College Athletics (report), 43
American Football League (AFL), 199, 208
American Friends Service Committee, 121
American Hockey League (AHL), 234
American League of Professional Foot Ball, 148–49
American League Park, 25, 39, 42, 76
American Professional Basketball League (APBL), 207
American Soccer League (ASL), 149–50, 154
American Tennis Association (ATA), 56
American University, 99–101, 156
Amico, Louis, 131
Anacostia Swimming Pool, 105–6; and fight over segregation, 121–23
Anderson, Donny, 199
Anderson, Jimmy, 237
Anderson, Marian, 66, 116
Angelos, Peter, 291
Appling, Luke, 316
Archbishop John Carroll High School, 136, 140, 270

131–32; and 1965 victory over Power
Memorial High School, 141–44
Denlinger, Ken, 85, 216
Denver Nuggets, 219–20
Department of Playgrounds (DP), 110, 112,
116
Department of Recreation, 106, 117
Department of the Interior, 105, 121
Deportivo Peru, 149
Desmond, Ian, 298, 300
Detroit Express, 162
Detroit Pistons, 214
Detroit Red Wings, 236
Detroit Tigers, 176, 178
Devine, Jack, 144
DeWitt, Bill, 30
Dickey, John Miller, 46
Dimaggio, Joe, 29, 178
Dismond, Henry Binga, 50
distance running: in the District of Columbia
prior to 1973, 250–52; dearth of African
American participants, 252; during
the running boom of the early 1970s,
253–54; and influence of Oprah Winfrey,
260–61
District League of Colored Wheelman, 10
District of Columbia: and social conditions,
212–13; and drug abuse and urban
decay, 280–81
District of Columbia Armory Board, 32–34
District of Columbia Road Runners Club
(DC RRC): and sponsorship of races,
251–52, 255
District of Columbia Stadium Act, 31–32,
288
District of Columbia v. Thompson, 125
Doby, Larry, 29, 269
Dolich, Andy, 161
Donohue, Jack, 129; and preference for
playing DeMatha in Washington, DC,
136; and shielding Lew Alcindor from
the press, 138; praising DeMatha's 1965
victory, 143
Donovan, Dick, 288
Donovan, Eddie, 132
Dorsett, Tony, 307
Driesell, Charles "Lefty," 312–13
Dunbar High School, 136, 141
Dunn, Adam, 294
Dunn, Willie, Jr., 59
Dunphy, Charlotte, 90
Dupree, David, 215
Duren, John, 271, 314
Durkee, Stanley, 42, 53
Dwight D. Eisenhower Bicentennial Center,
235
Dynamo Kiev, 159

E

Eastern Amateur Hockey League, 232
Eastern Golf Association (EGA), 62
Eastern (high school): and 1962 football city
championship, 82–83
East Potomac Park Golf Course, 57, 65,
68–69
Eastern Hockey League, 231, 233
East-West All-Star Game, 28, 45, 56
Eaton, Matt, 1
Edberg, Rolf, 245
Ederle, Gertrude, 92–94, 96, 98
Edgewood Playground, 124
Edmond, Rayful, III: as fan of Georgetown
basketball, 280–81
Edwards, Harry, 277
Edwards, John, 260
Eintracht Frankfurt, 151
Elder, Lee, 70–72
Elmer Ferguson Memorial Award, 86
Emekli, Hacabi "Turk," 154
Engblom, Brian, 243–44
Epstein, Mike, 180, 290
Erving, Julius, 209, 218
ESPN Classic, 315
ESPN Magazine, xvii–xviii
Esposito, Phil, 236
Euchner, Charles C., 304
Ewing, Patrick, 314–15; and meeting with
Ronald Reagan at the White House,
267–68, 283; and choosing Georgetown,
273; and influence on hip-hop culture,
281

F

Fachet, Robert, 86
Fairlawn Golf Course, 68–69
Fairlawn Park, 121
Fairleigh Dickinson University, 137
Fairview Golf Club, 61
Farrugia, Charley, 132
Fauntroy, Walter E., 227
Fauntroy, William, 250
Fay, Dave: and coverage of Washington
Capitals, 86–87
Federation of Citizens Associations, 117–18
Federation of Civic Associations, 118
Federation of Parent-Teacher Associations, 117
FedEx Field, 104
Feinstein, John, 85
Feller, Bob, 77
femininity: and access to sport, 90–91, 94;
and stigmatization of women athletes, 100
feminism: and rise in popularity of profes-
sional football, 189–90
Fenway Park, 285

Matthews, Ralph, 42–43
Mauro, Roberto, 153
May, Mark, 307
Maye, Arthur Lee: and feelings toward Ted
    Williams, 176
Mays, Bill, 70
McClain, Joe, 288
McClane, Charles P., 40
McDole, Ron, 198
McDonough Gymnasium, 273, 277
McGeehan, W. O., 75
McGinnis, George, 218
MCI Center, 35
McIntyre, Manny, 239
McKenzie, Raleigh, 307
McKinley Technical High School, 92, 96
McKnight, Dorothy, 99
McLain, Denny, 290
McLain, Gary, 315
McLaren, John, 296
McLean, Edward B.: and meeting with
    Shirley Povich, 73–74, 76
McMillan, James, 109
McMullen, Ken, 290
McNab, Max, 238
McNichol, Tom, xvii
McParlend, Peter, 150
McPhee, George, 238
Meador, Ed, 200
Meggyesy, Dave, 199
Menchine, Ron, 170, 181, 183
Merchant, Ned, 143–44
Meridian Hill, 49
Miami Gatos, 156
Michigan Road Runners Club, 251
Mikan, George, 167
Miles, Leo, 102
Miller, Kelly, 53
Miller, Patrick, 48
Miller, Robert, 40
Mills, Billy, 253
Milwaukee Bucks, 215–16, 311
Minneapolis Lakers, 207
Minnesota Twins, 30, 291
Minor, Davage: and integration of the NBA,
    135
Minot, George, Jr.: comments on Paul
    Casanova, 171
Mitchell, Bobby, xvi, 31, 81, 166
Mogilny, Alexander, 244
Mondale, Walter, 279
Monday Night Football, 306–7
Monk, Art, 307
Montreal Canadians, 239, 243–44
Montreal Expos, xiii, 35; and team's move
    to Washington, DC, 292
Moore, Kenny, 255; and frustration with the
    Marine Corps Marathon, 257

Morehouse College, 55
Morgan, Major Thomas P., 4–5
Morgan, Nyjer, 295
Morris County Golf Club, 62
Morris, William, 68
Morse, Michael, 296
Moss, Richard, 57
Motta, Dick: and interview following the
    1978 Eastern Conference finals, 205–6;
    and hiring by Abe Pollin, 209; birth and
    early years in Utah, 209; and relationship
    with players and referees, 210–11; and
    contentious relationship with players,
    213–15; and criticism of Elvin Hayes,
    216
Mourning, Alonzo, 280, 315
M Street School, 49, 91, 94
Mul-Key, Herb, 157
Mullin, Chris: and portrayal by Curry
    Kirkpatrick, 278
Mundt, Karl, xiv
Municipal Stadium, 42
Murphy, Mark, 307
Murray, Bryan, 247
Murray, Terry, 247
Musial, Stan, 29
Mutombo, Dikembe, 315
My Life with the Redskins (book), 79

N

Nagy, André, 152–54
Naismith, James, 139–40
NASCAR, 308
Nathan, Daniel A.: and personal recollec-
    tions of Washington, DC, sports, 303–17
National Amateur US Cup, 149
National Association for the Advancement
    of Colored People (NAACP): and the DC
    branch's Committee on Recreation, 118
National Association of Intercollegiate
    Athletics (NAIA): and national champi-
    onship basketball tournament, 140
National Baseball Park, 39
National Basketball Association (NBA), xiii–
    xiv, 103, 167, 205, 207, 238, 270, 282,
    311–12, 316; and Kareem Abdul Jabbar,
    129–30; and integration, 135; and 1978
    finals between the Washington Bullets
    and Seattle Supersonics, 220–25, 309
National Basketball League (NBL), 207
National Capital Park and Planning
    Commission (NCPPC), 110, 113–18,
    120–21
National Capital Park Commission (NCPC),
    110, 113
National Capital Parks (NCP), 69, 105–6,
    115–17